同等学力人员申请硕士学位全国统一考试辅导丛书

—— 全国同等学力统考命题研究组　组编 ——

英 语

新大纲新题型备考全攻略

（最新版考试大纲配套用书）

北京理工大学出版社
BEIJING INSTITUTE OF TECHNOLOGY PRESS

版权专有　侵权必究

图书在版编目(CIP)数据

英语新大纲新题型备考全攻略 / 全国同等学力统考命题研究组组编. —北京：北京理工大学出版社，2018.9(2019.8 重印)

(同等学力人员申请硕士学位全国统一考试辅导丛书)

ISBN 978-7-5682-6334-4

Ⅰ.①英… Ⅱ.①全… Ⅲ.①英语-硕士-水平考试-自学参考资料 Ⅳ.①H310.421

中国版本图书馆 CIP 数据核字(2018)第 210724 号

出版发行 / 北京理工大学出版社有限责任公司	
社　　址 / 北京市海淀区中关村南大街 5 号	
邮　　编 / 100081	
电　　话 / (010)68914775(总编室)	
(010)82562903(教材售后服务热线)	
(010)68948351(其他图书服务热线)	
网　　址 / http://www.bitpress.com.cn	
经　　销 / 全国各地新华书店	
印　　刷 / 三河市鑫鑫科达彩色印刷包装有限公司	
开　　本 / 787 毫米×1092 毫米　1/16	
印　　张 / 18.5	责任编辑 / 梁铜华
字　　数 / 461 千字	文案编辑 / 梁铜华
版　　次 / 2018 年 9 月第 1 版　2019 年 8 月第 2 次印刷	责任校对 / 周瑞红
定　　价 / 45.80 元	责任印刷 / 边心超

图书出现印装质量问题，请拨打售后服务热线，本社负责调换

百分百系列编委会成员（按姓氏拼音排序）

陈能军：中国人民大学经济学博士，深圳大学理论经济学博士后，广东省金融创新研究会副秘书长，广东省国际服务贸易学会理事，安徽大学创新管理研究中心研究员，中合博士后智库科研研究院研究员。主要从事文化金融、国际经济的研究。

褚建航：北京理工大学管理学硕士，学苑教育青年辅导教师。独立出版《实用面试技巧》《新富滚钱术》等数本经济、管理类著作，具备咨询工程师、基金和证券从业资格。拥有多年工商管理同等学力申硕考试辅导经验，熟悉各学科知识框架与重点、难点。

黄卫平：中国人民大学教授，博士生导师，中国世界经济学会理事，中国-欧盟研究会理事，中美经济学教育交流委员会执行主任。国际经济关系、国际经济学、发展经济学为其主要研究领域。

李自杰：对外经济贸易大学国际工商管理学院副教授，经济学博士，对外经济贸易大学海尔商学院执行副院长。企业理论、产权理论、管理经济学和管理理论为其主要研究领域。

刘　刚：中国人民大学商学院副教授，商学院院长助理，MBA项目中心主任，管理学博士，中国企业管理研究会常务理事。企业战略与文化、市场营销、供应链管理与物流、危机管理、产业竞争、艺术市场为其主要研究领域。

吕随启：北京大学经济学院金融学系副主任，中国金融研究中心副主任，经济学博士，副教授。金融学为其主要研究领域。

舒燕飞：中央民族大学经济学院副教授，经济学博士，中国宏观经济管理教育学会理事。经济增长、宏观调控和西方经济制度为其主要研究领域。对同等学力考试分析独特，具有丰富的教学经验。

宋　华：中国人民大学教授，经济学博士，日本京都大学博士后，中国物流学会理事，南开大学现代物流研究中心兼职研究员。物流与供应链管理、企业战略管理为其主要研究领域。

宋莉莉：北京大学应用心理学硕士，学苑教育青年辅导教师，北京大学人格与社会心理学研究中心理事。曾参加多项国家自然科学基金项目的研究，成功参与并完成国家863计划项目子课题，现从事973计划项目课题研究，所在科研团队获得2016年度北京市科技进步一等奖。在学苑教育多年的教学中，积累了丰富的辅导经验，能精准把握考点，深谙答题技巧，学员通过率高，口碑极佳。

孙　杰：北京外国语大学英语语言文学硕士，学苑教育英语研究小组核心成员。擅长在职人员英语考试语法、完形、翻译等题型，参与编辑同等学力申请英语应试教材。

孙茂竹：中国人民大学教授，全国高校财务理论研究会理事。著有《管理会计》《企业会计学》《公司理财学》《审计学》等。财务管理、管理会计为其主要研究领域。

王　蕙：中国青年政治学院杰出的青年教师，英语语言学硕士，京城著名在职英语"王牌组合"的"二王"之一。著有多部在职英语教科书及辅导用书。

王利平：中国人民大学商学院教授，管理学博士。先后出版《管理学原理》《经济管理基础》《商业企业经营学》《现代企业管理基础》等专著和教材。管理理论、企业理论、企业战略管理、连锁经营管理为其主要研究领域。

闫相国：中国人民大学管理学硕士，北京大学心理学硕士，《广州日报·求学指南》专家顾问团成员，学苑教育教学研究中心主任。企业战略管理和公司财务管理为其主要研究方向。

前　言

2012年6月国务院学位委员会办公室颁布了《同等学力人员申请硕士学位英语水平全国统一考试大纲》(第六版)(简称第六版《大纲》)。从2013年起同等学力人员申请硕士学位英语水平全国统一考试将按照第六版《大纲》命题。与第五版《大纲》相比，新版《大纲》在总分要求、题型设置等方面有了较大的变化。对于考生而言，只有了解这些变化，才能制定科学合理的学习计划和实现有针对性的复习训练。

第六版《大纲》取消了试卷二必须达到18分的要求、汉译英的题型，这些变化在一定程度上降低了考试的难度，减轻了考生的负担，但是新版《大纲》在口语交际、阅读理解两部分题型上的变化以及新增加的短文完成则是广大考生十分陌生的，也是其他同类考试所没有的，这无疑给考生的备考增加了一定的难度。

为了帮助考生深入了解新题型的命题特点，我们根据多年同等学力英语考试的辅导经验，紧密结合新版《大纲》，精心编写了本书，以帮助考生轻松备考，更好地应对新题型的挑战。本书具有以下特色：

1. **精辟分析新题型的命题特点及备考要点**

本书通过分析第六版《大纲》提供的三套样题，全面详尽地分析了新版《大纲》口语交际、阅读理解及短文完成三种新题型的出题思路，为考生总结了各个题型的考试要点。

2. **全面提供新题型所需的核心知识储备**

本书提供了口语交际所需的交际场景核心词汇、常用表达以及口语习语，阅读理解所需的话题词汇及阅读技巧，短文完成所需的常用词组、语法和语篇知识等。此外，本书还对知识点进行了分类归纳整理，便于考生学习和记忆。

3. **紧密结合《大纲》新题型的命题特点**

由于考生很难在同类考试中找到相同题型的练习，本书特别提供了大量模拟题：口语交际和短文完成各10套，阅读理解15套。模拟题在选材、出题等方面严格按照新版《大纲》的出题思路，为考生提供了宝贵的练习材料，这是本书的一大亮点。

4. **详尽解析解题思路和做题技巧**

本书对《大纲》的三套样题以及每个新题型中的模拟题进行了细致的讲解，不仅给出了题目的详尽译文，更清晰地阐述了做题思路和有效的做题技巧，这是本书的另一大亮点。

当然，由于编者时间有限，书中难免有疏漏之处，希望广大考生和专家批评指正，以帮助我们不断地改进和提高。

编　者

学苑教育简介

学苑教育自1997年建立以来,作为全国最早的在职研究生考试辅导培训机构,以其优异的师资团队和完善的教学服务,20余年来帮助数万名考生通过了在职研究生考试,顺利获得硕士、博士学位。教研中心拥有自己的专职教师队伍、专业教学研发团队和自行研发出版的学员用书,同时与数百位国内外管理专家以及多家国内外知名的管理培训机构建立了紧密的合作关系,共同推出了各个系列的培训课程及图书教材,并在此基础上打造了学苑教育(www.xycentre.com)、学苑教育在线(www.xycentre.org)等多个服务性培训网络平台。学员和社会的认可,愈发证明学苑已成为在职培训领域中的领跑者。

我们将始终以"智力服务于中国,提高企业与个人整体竞争力"为目标,用我们恒久不变的真诚与努力,与您共同"启迪广袤思维,追求卓越表现,迈向成功之路"。

目 录

第一章　口语交际 ……………………………………………………………（ 1 ）

    第一节　大纲要求简介 ………………………………………………………（ 1 ）

    第二节　大纲样题精讲 ………………………………………………………（ 1 ）

    第三节　考试要点归纳 ………………………………………………………（ 11 ）

    第四节　核心知识储备 ………………………………………………………（ 12 ）

    第五节　模拟试题精练 ………………………………………………………（ 26 ）

    第六节　答案及解析 …………………………………………………………（ 48 ）

第二章　阅读理解 ……………………………………………………………（ 65 ）

    第一节　大纲要求简介 ………………………………………………………（ 65 ）

    第二节　大纲样题精讲 ………………………………………………………（ 65 ）

    第三节　考试要点归纳 ………………………………………………………（ 74 ）

    第四节　核心知识储备 ………………………………………………………（ 75 ）

    第五节　模拟试题精练 ………………………………………………………（156）

    第六节　答案及解析 …………………………………………………………（178）

第三章　短文完成 ……………………………………………………………（205）

    第一节　大纲要求简介 ………………………………………………………（205）

    第二节　大纲样题精讲 ………………………………………………………（205）

    第三节　考试要点归纳 ………………………………………………………（215）

    第四节　核心知识储备 ………………………………………………………（216）

    第五节　模拟试题精练 ………………………………………………………（256）

    第六节　答案及解析 …………………………………………………………（269）

第一章

口 语 交 际

第一节 大纲要求简介

第六版《大纲》对口语交际部分的评价目标是"能用英语进行日常口语交流。对于生活、学习和工作中的常见英语交流，能理解交流情境、说话人的意图和会话的含义，并能运用相应的知识和判断进行恰当的交流。能正确理解英语口语中常见的习惯用法。"对于口语交际部分在题型、题量、分值方面的规定是：

本部分共设10题，每题1分，考试时间为15分钟。本部分包括A、B两节，A节为完成对话，B节为完成访谈或问答等。在每段对话、访谈或问答等口语转写材料中设置3~4个空白，并在材料前给出同等数量的出现材料本身的备选答案。要求考生从备选答案中为每个空白选出一个最佳答案，使转写材料完整。

第二节 大纲样题精讲

尽管第六版《大纲》和第五版对口语交际部分的评价目标是相同的，但是在题型方面是完全不同的。由于这种新题型在同等学力人员申请硕士学位英语水平全国统一考试中从未出现过，而且在全国性质的其他英语统考中也极为少见，所以很多考生对此不太熟悉，因此下面我们就第六版《大纲》提供的三套样题进行具体的分析，帮助考生分析出题思路，明确备考要点。

样卷一

Part One Oral Communication (15 minutes, 10 points)

Section A

Directions: *In this section there are two incomplete dialogues and each dialogue has three blanks and three choices A, B and C, taken from the dialogue. Fill in each of the blanks with one of the choices to complete the dialogue and mark your answer on the* **Answer Sheet**.

Dialogue One

A. when it comes to the exam

B. you need to go over it yourself

C. then I can go through it again next time

Student: I mean I want to do some of these problems.

Teacher: Yeah.

Student: But it's taking time to do them.

Teacher: When we cover something in the lesson, (1) _____. Work out the exercises in it. Erm, when you get a little bit stuck, sort it out yourself, and then think.

Student: Yeah.

Teacher: I know I see how you do it. And maybe if you're totally stuck, (2) _____.

Student: Yeah.

Teacher: It's really the more you do, Mm, on your own. Because (3) _____, you're gonna be on your own. Keep working on it and you'll be okay.

答案 1. B   2. C   3. A

详解

这是师生之间关于该如何学习的一段对话。首先，应该明确三个答案选项的语法功能和语义。A选项是状语从句，语义是：说到考试；其中when it comes to（当提到）是习惯用语。B选项是完整句，意思是：你需要自己复习它；其中go over（复习）是常用的动词词组。C选项是完整句，意思是：那时我会在下次课上把它过一遍；其中go through（经过，仔细检查）是常用的动词词组。

其次，认真阅读对话，特别是仔细体会空白处的上下文的语义。根据语法判断，第1题用在时间状语从句后，应该是主句；根据上下文的语义判断，正确答案应该是B。完成后句子完整的语义是：当我们在课堂上涉及某些内容的时候，你需要自己复习它，和下文中谈到自己做相关练习，语义是连贯的。第2题用在条件状语从句后，应该是主句；根据上下文的语义判断，正确答案应该是C。完成后句子完整的语义是：如果你彻底卡住了，那时我会在下次课上把它过一遍。第3题用在主句前，因此正确答案是A。完成后句子完整的语义是：就考试而言，你必须依靠自己。

Dialogue Two

A. It's been paining me all night.

B. Let's have a look and see what they've done to you.

C. Do I take these Sofradex that they're prescribed here, Doctor?

Doctor: Well, what can we do for you today?

Patient: Oh, I've an infection in my gum, Doctor.

Doctor: In your gum?

Patient: Up here. I've some tablets and, er, I don't know.

Doctor: (4) _____ Aye, the Sofradex is not doing very much for that, is it?

Patient: I've never taken them. I've just, I stopped taking them.

Doctor: Aye, I don't think they're doing very much to you.

Patient: (5) _____ Doctor.

Doctor: Aye.

Patient: I'm just wondering if it's my teeth or that it's just my blood that's doing it.

Doctor: I think it might be the teeth. It'd be worth getting the dentist to have a look at your place.

Patient: (6) _____

Doctor: Yes, yes. Keep on with those just now.

Patient: Yes, Aye, two four, one or two four times a day.

Doctor: Yes, one four times a day.

Patient: Fine, yeah.

答案 4. B　5. A　6. C

详解

这是一段医生和病人之间关于牙龈疼痛和某种药物的药效的谈话。首先，应该明确三个答案选项的语法功能和语义。A 选项是完整句，语义是：我疼了整整一晚上。B 选项是祈使句，意思是：让我们来看一下它们对你有什么作用。C 选项是一般疑问句，意思是：医生，我应该用这儿开的 Sofradex 药吗？

其次，认真阅读对话，特别是仔细体会空白处的上下文的语义。根据语法判断，第 4 题是独立的完整句；根据语义判断，正确答案是 B。第 4 题之前，病人说：大夫，您看，我吃的这些药。第 4 题之后，医生接着说：Sofradex 这药好像没起什么作用。而且，只有这句话可能是医生说的。第 5 题最简单直接的判断线索是其后出现的 Doctor，在这应该不会重复说 Doctor，所以正确答案是 A。第 6 题正确答案是 C。第 6 题之前，医生建议病人再找个牙医看一下，之后，建议他目前可以接着吃这些药，第 6 题在这两句话中间，应该是问药的问题。做此题时应该特别注意 Keep on with those just now 中 those 的指代作用。

Section B

Directions: *In this section there is one incomplete interview which has four blanks and four choices A, B, C and D, taken from the interview. Fill in each of the blanks with one of the choices to complete the interview and mark your answer on the **Answer Sheet**.*

A. Well, about costumes

B. But you know me with fashion

C. I kind of feel that it is more about music itself

D. So you have to change just enough

Interviewer: Does the show have a concept?

Interviewee: Well, it's going to be much more— (7) _____. Not that we didn't do that before. It's putting more emphasis on big orchestra, music, musicians, singers, songs. We want to do music at the purest as possible, like the old days I guess. So if it's a concept—

Interviewer: How about costume—

Interviewee: I think it is.

Interviewer: How about costume-costume changes?

Interviewee: (8) _____—yes, I think people like to see artists change in different outfits. Again, it's a—you have to be careful with that. People want you to change. They want to see outfits. And if you change too much, they say it's too much. And if you change too little, they say it's not enough.

(9) _____. You can't please everybody. But I have a wonderful stylist, Annie Horth, that I'm going to be working with again and who will make sure that we can please as many people as possible. (10) _____. I enjoy that very, very much. So I will try to change, not too little, not too much.

答案 7. C 8. A 9. D 10. B

详解

这段采访主要是关于艺人在开演唱会时的服装问题。首先，应该明确四个答案选项的语法功能和语义。A选项是介词词组，语义是：啊，关于服装。B选项是主语+谓语，缺少宾语；语义不完整，意思是：但是，你知道关于流行。C选项是主从复合句，意思是：我有点觉得它更是关于音乐本身；其中kind of（有几分，有点）是常见的口语习语。D选项是完整句，意思是：所以你必须换得足够。

其次，认真阅读对话，特别是仔细体会空白处的上下文的语义。做第7题时更多地考虑语义而不是严格的语法规定，因为在口语中很多时候，不需要严格地遵循语法规则。因此，尽管从语法上来看，第7题用在it's going to be much more后面，最合适的是介词词组，可是就下文中的具体阐述来看，这次音乐会的重点更多地放在big orchestra（大乐队），music（音乐），musicians（音乐家），singers（歌手）以及songs（歌曲），所有这些词都是和音乐有关系的，所以正确答案是C。在口语表达中，常常会有语句重复的现象。完成后句子完整的语义是：这次更多的是关于，我有点觉得它更是关于音乐本身。就语法判断，第8题用在完整句前，应该是状语；就语义连贯来看，前文两次提到了costume（服装），后面也提到了outfit，在这应该是"行头"的意思。因此，正确答案应该是A。第9题应该根据语义连贯来做题，前面提到：如果你换得太少了，观众会觉得不够。因此，下面应该紧接着说：所以你必须换得足够，可见正确答案应该是D。第10题正确答案是B。就语法来看，10题之后的I enjoy that very, very much作的是you know的宾语，当然完全合乎语法规定的书面语句还是有出入的；就语义来看，在这谈的是说话人个人的观点。完成后句子完整的语义是：但是，你知道关于流行，我是非常非常喜欢的。

样卷二

Part One Oral Communication (15 minutes, 10 points)

Section A

Directions: *In this section there are two incomplete dialogues and each dialogue has three blanks and three choices A, B and C, taken from the dialogue. Fill in each of the blanks with one of the choices to complete the dialogue and mark your answer on the **Answer Sheet**.*

Dialogue One

A. By the way, how much is it?

B. What is your destination?

C. I'd like to catch a return flight on the twenty-ninth.

Travel Agent: Freedom Travel. How may I help you?

Caller: Yes, I'd like to make a flight reservation for the twenty-third of this month.

Travel Agent: Okay. (1) _____

Caller: Well, I'm flying to Helsinki, Finland.

Travel Agent: Okay. Let me check what flights are available. And when will you be returning?

Caller: Uh, well, (2) _____ Oh, and I'd like the cheapest flight available.

Travel Agent: Okay. Let me see. Um, hmm...

Caller: Yeah?

Travel Agent: Well, the price for the flight is almost double the price you would pay if you leave the day before.

Caller: Whoo. Let's go with the cheaper flight. (3) _____

Travel Agent: It's only $980.

Caller: All right. Well, let's go with that.

Travel Agent: Okay. That's flight 1070 from Salt Lake City to New York, Kennedy Airport, transferring to flight 90 from Kennedy to Helsinki.

答案 1. B   2. C   3. A

详解

这是一段电话对话，是顾客给旅行社打电话来预订机票。首先，应该明确三个答案选项的语法功能和语义。A 选项是特殊疑问句，询问价格，意思是：顺便问一下，多少钱？其中 By the way（顺便）是常用词组。B 选项是特殊疑问句，问目的地；意思是：你的目的地是哪？C 选项是完整句，意思是：我打算坐 29 日的飞机回来。

其次，可以判断说话人的身份。A 和 C 选项应该是 Caller（打电话的人）所说；而 B 则是 Travel Agent 所说。由此可见，最好填的是第 1 题，说话人是 Travel Agent（旅行代理人），因此正确答案是 B，而且与下面的顾客回答的地点刚好相符。针对第 2 题前的问题 when will you be returning?（你什么时候回来？）这道题的正确答案是C。根据第3题后面 Travel Agent 给出的 It's only $980（只要980美元）的答案来看，问题应该是A。

Dialogue Two

A. Please open your bag.
B. I'll be staying in a room at a hotel downtown for the entire week.
C. What is the purpose of your visit?

Customer officer：Next. Uh, your passport please.
Woman：Okay.
Customer officer：Uh, (4) _____
Woman：I'm here to attend a teaching convention for the first part of my trip, and then I plan on touring the capital for a few days.
Customer officer：And where will you be staying?
Woman：(5) _____
Customer officer：And, uh, what do you have in your luggage?
Woman：Uh, well, just my personal belongings, um…clothes, a few books, and a CD player.
Customer officer：Okay. Uh, (6) _____
Woman：Sure.
Customer officer：Okay…Everything's fine. Uh, by the way, is this your first visit to the country?
Woman：Well, yes and no. Actually, I was born here when my parents were working in the capital many years ago, but this is my first trip back since then.
Customer officer：Well, enjoy your trip.
Woman：Thanks.

答案　4. C　5. B　6. A

详解

这是在入境处海关人员和旅客的一段对话。首先，应该明确三个答案选项的语法功能和语义。A选项是祈使句，意思是：请打开你的行李。B选项是完整句，意思是：我一整个星期都会住在市区的一家旅馆里。C选项是特殊疑问句，意思是：你此次旅行的目的是什么？

其次，认真阅读对话，特别是仔细体会空白处的上下文的语义。根据第4题后面女士的回答 I'm here to attend a teaching convention for the first part of my trip（我这次行程的前半段会参加一个教学会议），应该是对旅行目的的回答，因此这道题的正确答案是A。根据第5题前的问题 where will you be staying?（你打算住哪？），因此正确答案应该是B。第6题的正确答案是A，是对旅客的行李进行检查。

Section B

Directions: *In this section there is one incomplete interview which has four blanks and four choices A, B, C and D, taken from the interview. Fill in each of the blanks with one of the choices to complete the interview and mark your answer on the **Answer Sheet**.*

A. And how about website authoring skills?

B. I'm afraid I've never used those CGI things.

C. I think I have ALL the information I need!

D. First of all, tell me about your last job.

Man: Okay, Mr. Taylor, let's go ahead and begin. (7) _____

Mr. Taylor: Well, as stated on my resume, I worked for five years at Hi Tech Computers.

Man: Okay. Hi Tech. And what do you know about computer networks and operating systems including DOS, Windows, Macintosh OS, and UNIX?

Mr. Taylor: Um…well…I did come in contact with computers every night at my last job.

Man: Hum! … (8) _____ We are looking for someone to create and manage our company's website which would include the development, configuration, and use of CGI scripts.

Mr. Taylor: Umm…uh, web page, web page. Huh… I don't think I've read that book, and (9) _____

Man: Huh? And what about experience with Java or JavaScript?

Mr. Taylor: Well, I think I've tried Java at a foreign coffee shop one time, if that's what you mean.

Man: Okay, Mr. Taylor, (10) _____

Mr. Taylor: Oh, and I really like computer games. I play them everyday.

Man: Right, right. Thanks, Mr. Taylor. We'll be in touch.

答案 7. D   8. A   9. B   10. C

详解

这段对话是招聘者面试求职者的一段对话。首先，应该明确四个答案选项的语法功能和语义。A 选项是省略的特殊疑问句，语义是：关于网络写作技巧怎么样？其中，how about（关于……怎么样）是口语中常用表达。B 选项是完整句，意思是：我恐怕从未用过公共网关接口这些东西。C 选项是完整句，意思是：我想我已经获得了我需要的所有信息。D 选项是祈使句，意思是：首先，请谈一下你前一个工作的有关情况。

其次，可以判断说话人的身份。A、C、D 选项应该是 Man（招聘者）说的；B 应该是 Mr. Taylor（求职者）说的。由于 7~10 题中，只有第 9 题是 Mr. Taylor 说的，因此，先可以确定本题的答案是 B。第三，认真阅读对话，特别是仔细体会空白处的上下文的语义。第 7 题是招聘者说的第一句话，因此正确答案是 D，First of all（首先）具有最为明显的提示作用。第 8 题同样是招聘者说的，出现在 we are looking for someone to create and manage our company's website…（我们正在招聘能够创建和管理我们公司网络的人……）之前，因此正确答案应该是 A，招聘者想知道求职者网络方面的能力。第 10 题出现在对话结尾处，因此正确答案应该是 C，招聘者借此来结束本次面试。

样卷三

Part One Oral Communication（15 minutes, 10 points）

Section A

Directions：In this section there are two incomplete dialogues and each dialogue has three blanks and three choices A, B and C, taken from the dialogue. Fill in each of the blanks with one of the choices to complete the dialogue and mark your answer on the **Answer Sheet**.

Dialogue One

A. Um…about 1978. I think, when I was eighteen.
B. What about you?
C. Yeah, I really like that.

Steve：Francesca, what's your favourite piece of music, would you say?
Francesca：I think it's "Pie Jesu" by Andrew Lloyd-Webber.
Steve：Really?
Francesca：(1) _____
Steve：When did you first hear it?
Francesca：Oh, about five years ago my sister was in a choir concert and that was the first time I heard it, and I thought it was really beautiful. (2) _____ What's your favourite?
Steve：Well, it's a big piece. It's Mahler's second symphony.
Francesca：Oh! What, the whole thing?
Steve：Oh, yeah, yeah!
Francesca：When…when did you first hear that?
Steve：(3) _____
Francesca：A long time ago.
Steve：Yeah. But it stays with me and I've seen it performed several times since then.

答　案 1. C　　2. B　　3. A

详解

这段对话是朋友之间讨论彼此最喜欢的音乐。首先，应该明确三个答案选项的语法功能和语义。A 选项是时间状语，应该是回答对方关于时间方面的提问；意思是：大概是 1978 年，我想是我 18 岁时。B 选项是省略的特殊疑问句；意思是：那么，你呢？其中，What about（关于……怎么样）是口语中常用表达，与 how about 语义和用法相同。C 选项是肯定回答，应该是对一般疑问句的回答；意思是：是的，我确实很喜欢它。

其次，认真阅读对话，特别是仔细体会空白处的上下文的语义。第 1 题是对 Steve 说的 "Really?"（真的吗？）的回答，在这 Really? 的功能等同于一般疑问句，因此正确答案应该是 C。后面两道题中好做的是第 3 题，因为它在 when did you first hear that?（你什么时候第一次听到它的？）之后，所以正确答案应该是 A，对时间的回答。第 2 题正确答案是 B，在这里，Francesca 介绍完第一次听自己最喜欢的那首曲子的经历后，开始询问对方喜欢哪一首。其后的 What's your favourite?（你最喜欢什么？）是进一步明确问题是什么。

Dialogue Two

A. I didn't realize you were such a good cook

B. I'll do them myself later

C. Well, you know, if you want to

John：Oh Anne, that was a wonderful dinner. That's the best meal I've had in a long time.

Anne：Oh thank you! Thank you very much.

John：Can I give you a hand with these dishes?

Anne：Uh-uh, don't bother. (4) _____. Hey, would you like me to fix some coffee?

John：Uh, thanks a lot. I'd love some. Uh, would you mind if I smoke?

Anne：Why, not at all. Here, let me get you an ashtray.

John：Aw, thanks very much…Oh Anne, (5) _____.

Anne：Actually, I've only just learned how, you know. It's because I've been taking these courses.

John：Why, I can't cook at all, can't even boil an egg.

Anne：No kidding. (6) _____, you could take a couple of classes over at Sheridan college and learn how to do it too.

John：Aw, thanks a lot.

答案　4. B　5. A　6. C

详解

这是一段在朋友家吃完晚饭后与主人的对话。首先，应该明确三个答案选项的语法功能和语义。A 选项是完整句，意思是：我真没想到你是这么好的厨师。B 选项是完整句，意思是：一会儿我自己刷碗。C 选项是状语从句，意思是：你知道，如果你愿意的话。

其次，认真阅读对话，特别是仔细体会空白处的上下文的语义。第 4 题主要是对

John 说的"Can I give you a hand with these dishes?"（需要我帮你刷碗吗？）的回答，所以正确答案是 B。第 5 题后的 Actually, I've only just learned how, you know.（事实上，你知道我也是刚学的。）应该是对 A 的回答。第 6 题用在主句前，应该是状语，所以正确答案是 C。

Section B

Directions: *In this section there is one incomplete interview which has four blanks and four choices A, B, C and D, taken from the interview. Fill in each of the blanks with one of the choices to complete the interview and mark your answer on the **Answer Sheet**.*

A. That's right, John.

B. Why should we believe you this time?

C. But Mrs. Faulkes, you said that five years ago when you were campaigning for the last general election.

D. How's the campaign going?

Interviewer: In our radio car we have Geraldine Faulkes who is on the campaign trail in the constituency of Liverpool north-east. Good morning, Mrs. Faulkes.

Mrs. Faulkes: Good morning, John.

Interviewer: Now, Mrs. Faulkes. It's only three weeks till the general election. (7) _____

Mrs. Faulkes: I'm fully confident that the Conservative Party will win this general election and that the people of this country will welcome five more years of good Conservative Government.

Interviewer: I see. Now I believe that your party is promising tax cuts if it wins the election.

Mrs. Faulkes: (8) _____ We are the party of low taxation and we believe that our economic policies over the past five years have been the right policies. Our economy is growing stronger and now is the right time for income tax cuts.

Interviewer: (9) _____ You said you would lower taxes five years ago, bud you didn't, did you?

Mrs. Faulkes: Our economic policies over the last five years have given us one of the strongest economies in Europe with some of the lowest interest rates. We said that we were going to lower interest rates at the last election and we have delivered our promise. And what's more we believe that interest rates will remain low if we are elected for another term.

Interviewer: But I don't think low interest rates are the same as lower taxes. You said you would lower taxes and you didn't. (10) _____

Mrs. Faulkes: The economy of the country is now very healthy thanks to good government, and I believe that now is the time for tax cuts.

答案 7. D   8. A   9. C   10. B

详解

这段对话是电台主持人对正在参与利物浦东北选区竞选的候选人的采访。首先，应该明确四个答案选项的语法功能和语义。A 选项是完整句，对对方的观点表示赞同；语义是：是这样的，约翰。B 选项是特殊疑问句，意思是：我们这次为什么要相信你？C 选项是完整句，意思是：但是，福克斯夫人，在五年前您上次竞选的时候，您说过的。D 选项是特殊疑问句，意思是：选举进展情况如何？

其次，可以判断说话人的身份。B、C、D 选项应该都是 Interviewer 说的；A 选项应该是 Mrs. Faulkes 说的。由于 7～10 题中，只有第 8 题是 Mrs. Faulkes 说的，因此，先可以确定本题的答案是 A。第三，认真阅读对话，特别是仔细体会空白处的上下文的语义。第 7 题是采访的开始，根据上下文，特别是 Mrs. Faulkes 的具体回答，正确答案应该是 D。第 9 题是对前面 Mrs. Faulkes 说的 now is the right time for income tax cuts （现在是降低收入税的恰当时机）的反应，而且根据第 9 题后面的 You said you would lower taxes five years ago（你五年前就说要减税），本题的正确答案应该是 C；而 B 的语气放在这太过强烈，所以不合适。第 10 题正确答案是 B，B 在此处表达的是对 Mrs. Faulkes 给出的解释的不满。

此外，这段对话特别值得一提的是涉及了政治方面的话题，这是前些年同等学力的英语考试真题中很少出现的话题。在本段对话里出现的大量的政治经济方面的术语值得考生总结和学习，包括：on the campaign trail（正在参与竞选）；constituency（选区，选民）；the general election（大选）；the Conservative Party（保守党）；Conservative Government（保守党政府）；tax cuts（减税）；income tax（所得税）；interest rates（利率）；deliver our promise（兑现承诺）。

第三节 考试要点归纳

通过对《大纲》三套样题 9 段常用对话的分析，我们可以看出 A 节完成对话部分重点在考查日常生活中不同场景下有关生活、工作、学习等方面的对话。本部分在样题中涉及的交际场景包括：学校、医院、旅行社以及机场海关；涉及的人物关系有教师和学生、医生和病人、职员和顾客、海关关员和旅客以及亲密的朋友。由于 A 节涉及的是日常生活，因此对话的内容是大家较为熟悉的，而且语言难度相对较低。考生在本部分的主要困难在于能否理解不同交际场景中使用的一些典型的词汇和表达法。

B 节完成访谈或问答，包括两种主要形式：求职面试和记者采访。求职面试有明显的对话模式和套路，相对容易准备；而记者采访则由于采访的对象不同、话题不同，难度会有较大的差异。不管是求职面试还是记者采访都是日常交际中较为正式的场合，因此对话中使用的语言也更为正式一点，语言难度要高于 A 节对话，再加上如果采访的话题不是大家熟悉的，例如这两套样题中采访艺人和政客的访谈，其难度就将更大。考生在本部分的主要困难在于理解一些以前在阅读理解方面才能遇到的一些政治、经济、科技、文化、娱乐以及种种社会问题可能会涉及的词汇。

就答案选项而言，主要以句子为主，也包含一定量的词组。总的来说，语言难度适中，并没有出现太多偏难的习语俚语，但也出现了一些习惯用语。

因此，考生在口语交际备考过程中应该着重做好以下几点：第一，进行充分的知识储备。根据对样题的分析，本部分的知识储备主要包括两部分：日常交际场景涉及的核心词汇和常用表达；常见的习惯用语。第二，掌握有效的做题方法。第三，进行有针对性的训练。本章第四节为考生提供了口语交际所需的核心知识；第五节提供了十套样题；第六节样题详解中除了解释做题涉及的知识点，还介绍了做具体每道题目最直接有效的方法。

 第四节 核心知识储备

一、交际场景

（一）学校场景

1. 核心词汇

teacher： 教师：	president 大学校长	dean 系主任	supervisor 导师	advisor 指导老师
	professor 教授	instructor 教师	principal 中小学校长	visiting scholar 访问学者
student： 学生：	undergraduate 大学生	graduate 大学毕业生	postgraduate 研究生	exchange student 交换的留学生
	freshman 大学一年级学生	sophomore 大学二年级学生	junior 大学三年级学生	senior 大学四年级学生
homework： 作业：	assignment 作业	paper 论文	thesis 论文	dissertation （学位）论文
curriculum： 课程：	compulsory/required courses 必修课		optional/elective courses 选修课	
exam： 考试：	quiz 小测验	test/exam 考试	mid-term exam 期中考试	final exam 期末考试
	makeup 补考	credits 学分	pass/fail 及格/不及格	marks/grades/scores 分数
	school record/report 成绩单	scholarship 奖学金	fellowship 奖学金/助学金	
degree： 学位：	Bachelor's degree 学士学位	Master's degree 硕士学位	Doctor's degree 博士学位	
	diploma 文凭	certificate 证书		

library:	borrow/return	renew	due	overdue	fine
图书馆：	借书/还书	续借	到期	超期	罚款
	periodicals	fiction	reference books	magazines	
	期刊	小说	参考书	杂志	
	volume	issue	reading room	shelf	
	卷，册	期	阅览室	书架	
	library card	library catalogue	circulation desk		
	借书卡	目录	借书处		
Other words：	department	major	minor	enroll	
其他词汇：	系	专业	辅修	招生	
	academic year	term/semester	schedule	office hour	
	学年	学期	进度表	办公时间	
	register	admission	quit school	drop a course	
	注册	入学	退学	退选课	
	dinning hall	dorm	language lab		
	食堂	宿舍	语音室		

2. 常用表达

① Every one must receive 9 years of compulsory education. 每人必须接受九年的义务教育。

② Children enter primary school at the age of 7. 孩子们7岁进小学。

③ Some students quit school due to poverty. 一些学生因贫困而辍学。

④ There is fierce competition in the college Entrance Examination. 高考竞争激烈。

⑤ He majors in English. 他主修英语。

⑥ She is working for her double major in English and Law. 她正在修英语和法学双学位。

⑦ I graduated from Harvard University 3 years ago. 三年前，我从哈佛大学毕业。

⑧ Your history paper is due next Friday. 下周五交你的历史课作业。

⑨ I've rearranged my class schedule so I'll have my afternoons free. 我重新调整了我的课程表，以便下午腾出空来。

⑩ This year I'm in a co-ed dorm. 今年我住在男女生合住的宿舍。

⑪ I have a heavy course load this semester, so I don't have the time for any more extra-curricular activities. 这学期我课程负担有些重，所以没有更多的时间从事课外的活动了。

⑫ As a senior, John is writing his thesis. 作为大学四年级学生，约翰正在写毕业论文。

⑬ I think I'll try out for the Drama Club. 我想在戏剧俱乐部（大学社团）试试看。

⑭ What field did you specialize in? 你专攻什么领域？

⑮ Tomorrow is the deadline for choosing classes. 明天是选课的截止日期。

⑯ Have you decided which university you are going to apply to? 你决定申请哪个学校了吗？

⑰ I'm applying for admission to the MIT. 我正在申请麻省理工学院。
⑱ What's the tuition for international students? 留学生的学费是多少？
⑲ I've been granted a full scholarship. 我获得了全奖。
⑳ The teacher threw a pop quiz at us again, and I came top. 老师又给我们来了一次突然测验，我全班第一。

（二）医院场景

1. 核心词汇

doctor	surgeon	physician	patient	
医生	外科医生	内科医生	病人	
flu	cold	have a fever/temperature	pain/ache	cancer
流感	感冒	发烧	疼痛	癌症
broken	have a sore throat	infect	epidemic	
骨折	咽喉疼痛	感染	传染病	
disease	bird flu	mad cow		
疾病	禽流感	疯牛病		
check	diagnose	prescribe	treatment	cure
检查	诊断	开药	治疗	治愈
medicine/drug	injection/shot	pill/tablet	capsule	pain killer	dose
药物	注射	药片	胶囊	止疼片	剂量
prescription	drug store/the chemist's/pharmacy			
处方	药房			
recover	get better/get worse			
好转	好转/恶化			

2. 常用表达

① What's the matter? /What's wrong with you? 你哪不舒服？
② What seems to be the trouble? / What's the trouble with you? 你哪不舒服？
③ How long have you been like this? 你这样有多久了？
④ It hurts me when I breathe. 我喘气的时候，这很疼。
⑤ I'd like to fill the prescription. 我想抓药。
⑥ Take the medicine, and you'll be better. 吃了这些药，你就会好多了。
⑦ I should say you've caught a cold. 我看你感冒了。
⑧ You need an injection. 你需要打针。
⑨ Is it serious? 我的病严重吗？
⑩ Do I need to be hospitalized? 我需要住院吗？
⑪ I don't feel very well. 我觉得不舒服。
⑫ Peter is up and about now. 彼得病后复原了。
⑬ What sort of medicine do you take? 你吃的是什么药？
⑭ The doctor says that I should not eat anything oily. 医生说我不能吃油腻的东西。
⑮ I had a shot of penicillin. 我打了一针青霉素。

⑯ The doctor gave me a chest X-ray and took my blood pressure. 医生给我做了 X 光胸透并量了血压。

⑰ My fever is gone. 我的烧已经退了。

⑱ Take two pills and have a good rest. 吃两片药,好好休息一下。

⑲ She is in good shape. 她的身体状况良好。

⑳ You're running a temperature. 你发烧了。

（三）餐馆场景

1. 核心词汇

customer	waiter/waitress	hostess	manager
顾客	服务员	领座员	经理
reserve/book a table	menu	order	drinks
预定位子	菜单	点菜	饮料
appetizer	main dish	dessert	specialty
饭前开胃品	主菜	甜点	特色菜
tip	pay the bill	go Dutch/split the bill	
小费	付账	AA 制	

2. 常用表达

① Could you show us the menu? 我们能看一下菜单吗?

② Would you like to see the menu? 您要看一下菜单吗?

③ What do you recommend? 你有什么可以推荐的吗?

④ What are your specialties? 哪些是你们的特色菜?

⑤ How would you like that prepared/done? 您要怎么做?

⑥ What would you like to drink, tea or coffee? 您要喝点什么,茶还是咖啡?

⑦ We will go Dutch. /Let's spilt the bill. 我们 AA 制。

⑧ Tonight's on me. /It's my treat tonight. 今晚我请客。

⑨ What would you like to eat? 你想吃点什么?

⑩ Are you ready to order? 您要点菜了吗?

⑪ I'd like some steak and bread. 我要牛排和面包。

⑫ What would you like for dessert? 你要什么甜点?

⑬ Bring me the bill please. 我要买单。

⑭ Can I pay by check or credit card? 我能用支票或信用卡吗?

⑮ Sorry, we only take cash. 对不起,我们只收现金。

⑯ I'd like something light, please. 请给我一点清淡的东西吃。

⑰ Please don't snack; you will ruin your dinner. 请别吃点心了,你会对正餐失去胃口的。

⑱ Do you have a reservation, sir? / Have you made a reservation, sir? 先生,您预约了吗?

⑲ How would you like your steak served, rare, medium, or well-done?
您的牛排要什么样的,生一点,还是熟一点?

⑳ Will that be here or to go? 您是在这吃，还是外带？

（四）旅馆场景

1. 核心词汇

receptionist	reception desk	room service
招待员	前台，接待处	客房服务
book/reserve a room	make a reservation	single/double room
预订房间	预定	单人/双人房间
a vacant room	fully booked	check in/check out
空房间	订满	登记入住/结账离开

2. 常用表达

① Are there rooms available for tomorrow evening? 明天晚上有空房间吗？

② Can I book a double room with a bath for this weekend? 我能预定一间这周末的带有淋浴的双人房间吗？

③ How many people are in your party? 你们聚会上有多少人？

④ Are you with a company? 有人跟您一起住吗？

⑤ There is some discount for company booking. 团体预定后会有一定的折扣。

⑥ What special terms are there for groups? 对于团体，有什么特别条款吗？

⑦ How much is boarding and lodging a day? 膳宿费一天要多少钱？

⑧ There will be an extra charge of 10% for the service. 要额外收取10%的服务费。

⑨ Do you require a deposit to confirm a reservation? 要确认预定需要交押金吗？

⑩ We are fully booked for that weekend. 我们这周末已经客满。

⑪ We're particularly full up until September 10th. 9月10日前我们实际上已经客满。

⑫ Do you have a reservation with us? 您在我们这有预约吗？

⑬ Have you got any identification? 您有身份证件吗？

⑭ You have to register individually. 你们需要分别登记。

⑮ I'll get the porter to take your luggage up. 我会叫行李员帮您把行李搬上去。

⑯ Can you make up my room early? 你能早一点收拾我的房间吗？

⑰ Could you give me a wake-up call at seven tomorrow morning? 你明天早上7点叫醒我好吗？

⑱ I'm glad to tell you with an unexpected cancellation we do have a room for one night. 很高兴告诉您由于有人临时取消预定，所以我们还有一间空房能住一晚上。

⑲ I'm afraid some of you have to double up because there aren't enough rooms. 房间不够了，恐怕你们有几位只能两个人住一间了。

⑳ Just tell the desk, and they'll see to it. 只要告诉服务台就行，他们会处理的。

（五）购物场景

1. 核心词汇

check-out counter	store hours	opening/closing time
收款台	营业时间	开门/关门时间
cheap/bargain/reasonable	expensive/costly/dear	discount/on sale/…% off

第一章　口语交际

便宜的		昂贵的	打折
shop assistant/sales girl/sales man	customer	cashier	refund
售货员	顾客	出纳员	退货
in stock/out of stock	sold out	receipt	style
有货/没货	卖光	发票	款式

2. 常用表达

① May/Can I help you? / What can I do for you? 您想买点什么？

② I'm just looking around. 我随便看看。

③ We have a clearance sale today. 今天我们清仓大甩卖。

④ May I try it on? 我能试试吗？

⑤ Do you have this in stock? 这个还有货吗？

⑥ This is too small for me. Do you have a bigger one? 这个太小了，有大点的吗？

⑦ What's your size? 你穿多大号？

⑧ That's not quite what I'm looking for. 那不是我想要的东西。

⑨ We have some real good buys. 我们有些真正的便宜货。

⑩ I'm afraid we don't have any on hand. 今天恐怕没货了。

⑪ Could you come down a bit? 你能再便宜点吗？

⑫ That is a steal. 那可是便宜货。

⑬ I'll meet you half way. 我让一半。

⑭ You get a chance like this only once in a blue moon. 这可是千载难逢的好机会。

⑮ It's a little overpriced. 这有点太贵了。

⑯ Cash back? 找你现金吗？

⑰ Here's your change. 这是找你的钱。

⑱ I'll take it. 我买了。

⑲ I think I'll keep on looking. 我想我要再逛逛。

⑳ Sorry, things on sale are not allowed to be refunded or exchanged. 抱歉，打折的东西不退不换。

（六）机场场景

1. 核心词汇

air hostess/stewardess	passenger	airplane/ flight/airline	customs
女乘务员	旅客	航班	海关
luggage	passport	boarding pass	departure gate
行李	护照	登机牌	登机口
check in	take off/land	fasten the safety-belt	claim the luggage
办理登机手续	起飞/着陆	系好安全带	认领行李
delay	declare	first class	economy class
延误	申报	头等舱	经济舱
take off	land	contraband	fare
起飞	着陆	违禁品	机票费用

destination	round flight	return flight	reservation
目的地	往返	回程	预定

2. 常用表达

① Is the flight non-stop? 这趟航班是直飞吗？

② Can I break my journey in Hawaii? 我能在夏威夷中途停留吗？

③ How much carry-on luggage is permitted? 规定能带多少手提行李？

④ What's the allowance of luggage? 行李的重量限额是多少？

⑤ Is it valid for two full weeks? 有效期是两周吗？

⑥ Will the flight arrive on schedule? 飞机会准时到达吗？

⑦ There is a two-hour layover in Tokyo. 飞机会中途停东京2小时。

⑧ Seats are only available for first class and business. 只有头等舱和商务舱还有座位。

⑨ AA Flight 104 from New York is overdue owing to engine trouble. 自纽约起飞的美航104班机因为引擎故障而晚点了。

⑩ I'd like to confirm my connecting flight reservation. 我想确认一下我联运班机的预订票。

⑪ I'm sorry we're booked up for the CA Flight 812. 很抱歉，国航812班机已经订满了。

⑫ Hand-baggage is not to be weighed. 手提行李是不用称重的。

⑬ Would you please put your luggage on the scales? 请把行李放到磅秤上好吗？

⑭ The free allowance for luggage is 20 kilos. 免费行李限额是20公斤。

⑮ There is no excess to pay. 不需要付超重费。

⑯ I've to charge you for overweight. 我得收您超重费。

⑰ Can you tell me how to transfer at the JFK airport in New York? 您能告诉我在纽约的肯尼迪机场怎样转机吗？

⑱ My next flight will depart at 3：20 p. m. Will I be able to make my connection? 我的下一趟航班下午3：20起飞，请问我还能赶上吗？

⑲ Put your bags and coat in the overhead luggage compartment. 请把行李和外衣放到头上的行李架上。

⑳ We've only got the duty-free allowances. 我们携带的所有物品都是免税的。

（七）邮局场景

1. 核心词汇

registered mail	air mail	postage	parcel	printed matter
挂号信	航空信	邮资	包裹	印刷品
postcard	zip code	address	envelope	
明信片	邮编	地址	信封	

2. 常用表达

① How long does it take for a letter to get to America from Beijing? 信从北京到美国要多久？

② You've got an express mail. 你有特快专递。

③ To make it fast, you can send a fax. 要想快点的话就发个传真。

④ Would you please tell me how to post a letter abroad? 麻烦能告诉我一下怎么寄封信到国外？

⑤ Do you wish to send it as an ordinary or a registered mail? 您想寄平信还是挂号信？

⑥ What's the postage for an air-mail to Washington? 请问寄封航空信到华盛顿邮费是多少？

⑦ It's overweight, so you have to pay extra. 超重了，所以你需要另付超重费。

⑧ Please send this parcel off special delivery. 请用邮政快递邮寄这个包裹。

⑨ What's the surcharge for this express mail? 这个快递包裹的额外收费是多少？

⑩ I'd like to pick up my package, and this is the notice. 我来取包裹，这是包裹单。

⑪ If I want wire some money off, what is the upper limit? 我想电汇一些钱，请问上限是多少？

⑫ What do I have to do to send a money order? 请问怎样寄汇款单？

⑬ If your cable is urgent, the rate will be doubled. 如果电报是加急的，费用将加倍。

⑭ When will the post be dispatched? 这批邮件什么时候发出？

⑮ Is it possible for me to catch the last mail today? 我还能赶上寄今天的末班邮件吗？

（八）银行场景

1. 核心词汇

cash the check	open an account	withdraw/draw	deposit
支票兑现	开户	取钱	存钱
interest rate	savings account	principal	loan
利率	储蓄户头	本金	贷款
exchange	cash ratio	bank note	credit transfer
兑换	外汇汇率	纸币，钞票	银行转账
green bucks	denomination	bankbook	bank statement
美元	面值	存折	银行结单

2. 常用表达

① We'd like to open a joint checking account. 我想开个联名的支票账户。

② What's the procedure for opening a checking-savings account? 开个支票储蓄户头，需要什么手续？

③ Do you charge for checks? 你们收支票手续费吗？

④ Will $50 be enough for a minimum deposit? 50美元够最低起存金额吗？

⑤ What if overdraw? 如果透支了怎么办？

⑥ Can I renew the certificate on maturity? 到期我可以续存吗？

⑦ Is there any minimum for the first deposit? 第一次储蓄有最低限额吗？

⑧ With a checking-savings account, you will have a bank book and a check book. 如果开个支票储蓄户头，你会有一个存折和一个支票本。

⑨ What's the monthly service charge? 每月的服务费是多少？

⑩ My fixed deposit certificate fell due yesterday. 我的定期存折昨天到期了。

⑪ Your deposit is exhausted. 你的存款取完了。

⑫ Do you want large or small bills? 你需要多少面值的现金？

⑬ Give me some small notes please. 请给我一些小面值的钞票。

⑭ What's your buying rate for American dollars in remittance? 你们今天美元现汇的买入价是多少？

⑮ Could you find out the exchange rate between American dollars and RMB for me? 你能帮我查一下今天美元和人民币的兑换率是多少吗？

⑯ I suggest you remit the money by telegraphic transfer. 我建议你用电子汇款。

⑰ Traveler's checks are not valid until they are countersigned. 旅行支票只有在背面签字后才有效。

⑱ I take it you can supply references. 我想你可以提供证明人吧。

⑲ Checks issued must be made payable to a specified person only. 签发的支票必须由指定的人支取。

⑳ We honored the check as the overdraft was only for $500. 我们承兑这张支票的透支额是 500 美元。

（九）打电话场景

1. 核心词汇

switchboard	extension	operator	phone booth
总机	分机	接线员	电话亭
in-coming calls	out-going calls	collect call	leave/take a message
来电	去电	对方付费电话	留言
dial	put sb. through	get through	
拨号	接通	打通	
the line is busy/engaged	hold the line/hold on		
占线	别挂断		

2. 常用表达

① —Hello. May I speak to Mr. Green? 你好，我找格林先生。
　—Speaking. /Yes, speaking. /His speaking. 是的，我就是。

② Hi, my hands are tied. I'll get back to you in a minute. 嗨，我现在正忙，稍等一下。

③ Can I call back? Something has come up. 我一会打回来好吗？突然有点事。

④ I'm afraid you've got the wrong number. 不好意思，你打错电话了。

⑤ Hang on a second/a moment. 等一会儿。

⑥ Would you like to hold? 等一会儿。

⑦ Hold the line, please. 等一会儿。

⑧ He's not available now. Can I take a message? 他不在，我能替他捎个口信吗？

⑨ I want to make a long distance call. 我想打个长途电话。

⑩ Would you tell Mr. Green that I called? 你能告诉格林先生我给他打了个电话吗？

⑪ I must have dialed a wrong number. 我一定拨错号了。

⑫ I couldn't get through. 我打不通。

⑬ I have to hang up now. 我得挂电话了。

⑭ Would you call back tomorrow? 你能明天回个电话吗?

⑮ There's something wrong with the phone. 电话出了点儿毛病。

⑯ I tried to call you, but the line was busy. 我试着给你打电话,但老占线。

⑰ Could you get me extension 7835? 能给我转一下分机 7835 吗?

⑱ Operator, we've been cut off; could you connect us? 接线员,我们的电话线断了,能帮我们接上吗?

⑲ Please have her return my call. 请让她给我回电话。

⑳ You pick up the receiver and wait for the signal. They are long beeps. 你拿起话筒,等一下信号,那是长的嘟嘟声。

(十) 租房场景

1. 核心词汇

rent	lease	tenant/lodger	landlady/landlord
出租/租金	出租合同	房客	房东
deposit	central heating	apartment/flat	
押金	中央供暖	公寓	

2. 常用表达

① This house is for rent. It has central heating. 此房出租。房子里有供暖设备。

② It's really a bargain. 租金很便宜。

③ I want to rent a furnished house. 我想要租有家具的房子。

④ I want an apartment with two bedrooms and a kitchen. 我想要一套有两间卧室和一个厨房的公寓。

⑤ The houses downtown are very expensive. 市区的房子很贵。

⑥ How much is the rent for a month? 每月租金多少?

⑦ I feel at home living here. The landlady is very kind to me. 我觉得住在这里像在家里一样。房东太太对我很好。

⑧ We have a few kitchen things and a dining room set. 我们有一些厨房用具和一套餐厅设备。

⑨ There's no gas range in the kitchen, but you can use the electric stove. 厨房里没有煤气灶,但你可以用电炉。

⑩ There is a shower in the bathroom. 浴室里有淋浴器。

⑪ The room has a big closet. You can put your baggage in it. 房间里有一个很大的壁橱,你可以把你的行李放进去。

⑫ Are you looking for a one-bedroom or a two-bedroom apartment? 你要租一居室还是两居室?

⑬ Will you live here alone or with others? 你自己住还是和别人一起?

⑭ If everything is agreeable, you have to sign the lease. 如果一切没问题的话,你需要签一下这个合同。

⑮ I'm looking for a two-bedroom apartment with a full kitchen. 我想租一套两居室带全套厨房设备的公寓。

（十一）求职场景

1. 核心词汇

job advertisement	letter of application	applicant	job interview
招聘广告	申请信	申请人	面试
resume	curriculum vitae（CV）	employment	working experience
简历	简历	雇佣	工作经历
reference	salary expectation	acceptance	refusal
证明推荐人	工资预期	接受	拒绝
post（position）	job vacancies	promotion	educational qualifications
职位	招聘广告	升职	学历
job hunting			
找工作			

2. 常用表达

① Do you have any plan for your career? 你对未来有什么计划吗？

② I hope that I can get a decent job with a good salary. 我希望有一份既体面，收入又高的工作。

③ I worked as an intern in that firm last summer. 去年夏天我在那家商行实习。

④ I found an excellent position through an employment agency. 我通过职业介绍所找到了一份很棒的工作。

⑤ It's the kind of work I've always wanted to do. 这是我一直想做的工作。

⑥ I have a lot of responsibility in my job. 我的工作责任重大。

⑦ My schedule is very flexible, and I am given a lot of freedom. 我的工作表很灵活，使我十分自由。

⑧ I'm looking for a part-time job to help put me through school. 为了能够从学校毕业，我正在找兼职工作。

⑨ I want to work for a while before returning to college. 我希望返回学校之前先工作一段时间。

⑩ I won the university scholarship for four years on end. 我大学连续四年获得奖学金。

⑪ I wonder whether you have any position open. 我想知道你们是否有空缺的职位。

⑫ Do you have a good command of English? 你英语水平高吗？

⑬ Could you tell me something about your time with that company? 你能告诉我一些你在那家公司工作的情况吗？

⑭ I hope to find a job which offers me an opportunity for advancement. 我希望找一份有上升空间的工作。

⑮ What do you think you could bring to the job? 你觉得你能为这份工作带来什么呢？

⑯ Why do you want to quit your present job? 你为什么要辞去现在的工作？

⑰ Can you tell us what made you apply for this post? 你能告诉我你为什么要申请这个

职位吗?

⑱ Do you mind working on the night shift? 你介意上夜班吗?

⑲ I'll take you on one month's probation. 我得让你先试用一个月。

⑳ What's your educational background? 你的学历是什么?

(十二) 旅行场景

1. 核心词汇

destination	traveling expense	high season	out season
目的地	旅行费用	旅游旺季	旅游淡季
tourist party	conducted tour	package tour	optional tour
旅行团	有导游的团体旅行	包办旅行	自助游
admission ticket	summer resort	tourist spots	sightseeing tour
景点门票	避暑胜地	旅游景点	观光游
group travel	tourist attraction	admission fee	admission free
团体旅游	旅游胜地	景点门票费	门票免费

2. 常用表达

① Do you like to take a local train or an express? 你想坐普通火车还是特快?

② I have bought a ticket for a sleeper. 我买了张卧铺票。

③ Have you reserved your ticket? 你订票了吗?

④ I'd like to see all places of renown in Beijing. 我想看一下北京的所有著名景点。

⑤ If you go on a package tour, you don't have to worry about accommodation, or meals during the day. 如果你参加这种包办旅游,你就不用担心旅行中住宿或者用餐的问题。

⑥ What a treat to get into the peace and quiet of the country! 能够体验乡村的宁静是多好的享受啊!

⑦ Do you have an open ticket? 有能够改签的票吗?

⑧ Surely I'll quote you the price from here to Seattle. 当然我会给你报一下从这儿到西雅图的价格。

⑨ It is advisable to make a reservation now since the flights are pretty crowded at this time of the year. 你最好现在就预定,因为每年这个时候机票都挺紧张的。

⑩ Have you decided which airline you want to fly with? 你决定了要选择哪家航空公司了吗?

⑪ What kind of transportation is available from the airport into town? 从机场到市里有什么样的交通方式?

⑫ It's full board, that is, everything from meals to local transport is included. 这是全包的,也就是说,一切费用都在里面,包括三餐和市内交通。

⑬ What else do you include in the price apart from the air tickets. 除了机票以外,这个价钱还包括什么?

⑭ We'd like to go on a guided tour around Beijing. 我们想跟一个有导游的团游览北京。

⑮ The outward flight from Beijing is 10∶30 in the morning and the return is 7∶15 early evening local time. 从北京出发的航班时间是早上10∶30，返程航班的时间是当地时间晚上7∶15。

二、习惯用语及短语

after all 到底	anything but 绝对不	at one's service 随时帮助某人	back up 支持
be sick/tired of 厌倦	be through with 完成	be up to 胜任	between you and me 对外保密
beyond the reach of sb. 超出某人能力之外	bite off more than one can chew 贪多嚼不烂	break down 出毛病	brush up 复习
by all means 无论如何	care for 喜欢	carry out 执行	clear up 雨过天晴
come along 出现，进行	come around 恢复	come down with 生病	come up with 提出，想出
cool off 冷静	count in 包括在内	count out 排除在外	cut down on 减少
drop off 让下车	drop out of 退学	easier said than done 说得容易	end up 结果
fall back on 依赖	feel free to 随意	few and far between 稀少	figure out 解决，领会到
for nothing/for free 免费	get along 进展，生活	get going 出发，使开动	get nowhere 毫无进展
get on sb.'s nerves 激怒	give sb. a ride 让某人搭车	give sb. a hand 帮助某人	go ahead 去吧，前进
go round 流传	good bargain/buy 便宜货	have a way with words 会说话	have things in one's own way 以自己的方式行事
hand out 分发	head and shoulder above 胜过	hold off 拖延	hold up 阻挡
in ages 很久	in shape 处于良好状态	in good/bad shape 身体健康/健康不佳	in next to no time 很快
in the event that 在……情况下	in the red 负债	in a mess 零乱	keep an eye on 留意
keep from 避免	lay off 解雇	learn the ropes 学会窍门	leave sth. up to 由……决定

let go	look up to	make ends meet	make the most/best of
放开，释放	尊敬	收支平衡	充分利用
make up	meet each other half way	no way	not a bit/not in the least
弥补	妥协	决不	一点也不
not yet	off /on campus	on a diet	on the tip of one's tongue
还未	校内/校外	节食	一时想不起
one in a million	once in a while	out of business	out of place
很少见	偶尔	停业	不合适
out of the world	put up with	put sb. up	raise the roof
绝妙的	容忍	提供住宿	勃然大怒
reach the bottom of the barrel	run out of	rush hour	see to
弹尽粮绝	用光	高峰	照顾
show up	slip one's mind	stand up for	stay up
出现	一时想不起	支持	熬夜
take it easy	take one's time	talk sb. into sth.	talk sb. out of sth.
放松	不着急	劝某人做某事	劝某人不做某事
tell apart	the other day	the sooner, the better	there's no rush
分辨	前几天	越快越好	别着急
think much/highly of	think little of	too good to be true	turn down
喜欢	不喜欢	不现实	降低，拒绝
turn one's back on	turn out	up in the air	work out
拒绝	结果	悬而未决	解决
fill one's shoes/fill in for	have one's hands full with	make it	from top to bottom
代替	忙于	达到目的	彻底
one step at a time	touch on	tire up	ring a bell
逐渐	涉及	忙于	耳熟
go all out	in one ear and out the other	under the weather	tear oneself away from
全力以赴	耳旁风	身体不适	使离开
up to one's eyes/neck	push around	pull one's leg	keep one's shirt on
忙于	欺骗	愚弄，取笑	保持冷静，忍耐

cool it	joy ride	red-letter day	go up in smoke
冷静一点	兜风	大日子	成为泡影
hit the road	shape up	scare the shit out of someone	pull strings
上路	表现良好	吓死某人了	运用关系，暗中操纵
all Greek to sb.	be hard up	in hot water	break the ice
某人完全不懂	缺钱	陷入困境	打破僵局
knock it off	on the house	get the sack	in the soup
停止，别这样	免费的	被开除了	在困境中
That's it.	There you go again.	What's new?	What do you say?
不错，就是这样	啊呀！你又来了！	有什么新闻吗？	你觉得怎么样？
So what?	What's up?	come clean	pill the beans
那又怎么样？	有什么事情吗？	全盘托出，招供	说漏了嘴
jump the gun	take a shine to	third wheel	rock the boat
草率行事	有好感	累赘，电灯泡	捣乱
blow it	in hot water	drop a line	go with the flow
搞砸了，弄坏了	有麻烦	写信	随从大家的意见
act up	hit it off	have it good	in the dumps
胡闹，出毛病	投缘，一见如故	享受得很	垂头丧气
horse around	go whole hog	get the ball rolling	get on the ball
嬉闹	全力以赴	开始	用心做
have a passion for	pep talk	way back	hung over
钟爱	打气，鼓励的话	好久以前	宿醉未醒
has-been	take a rain check		
过时的人或物	改天再说		

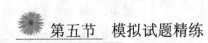

第五节 模拟试题精练

Model Test One

Part One Oral Communication (15 minutes, 10 points)

Section A

Directions: In this section there are two incomplete dialogues and each dialogue has three blanks and three choices A, B and C, taken from the dialogue. Fill in each of the blanks with one of the choices to complete the dialogue and mark your answer on the **Answer Sheet**.

Dialogue One

A. By the way, what about salary?

B. What else are they asking for?

C. You might be interested.

Susan: Oh, I'm fed up with my job.

Mike: Hey, there's a perfect job for you in the paper today. (1) _____

Susan: Oh, what is it? What do they want?

Mike: Wait a minute. Uh, here it is. The European Space Agency is recruiting translators.

Susan: The European Space Agency?

Mike: Well, that's what it says. They need an English translator to work from French or German.

Susan: So they need a degree in French or German, I suppose. Well, I've got that. What's more, I have plenty of experience. (2) _____

Mike: Just that. A university degree and three or four years of experience as a translator in a professional environment. They also say the person should have a lively and inquiring mind, effective communication skills and the ability to work individually or as a part of the team.

Susan: Well, if I stay at my present job much longer, I won't have any mind or skills left. (3) _____ I just hope it isn't lower than what I get now.

Mike: It's said to be negotiable. It depends on the applicant's education and experience. In addition to basic salary, there's a list of extra benefits. Have a look yourself.

Susan: Hm, travel and social security plus relocation expenses are paid. Hey, this isn't bad. I really want the job.

Dialogue Two

A. You would?

B. And how did you meet?

C. You're kidding?

Sue: Who's your best friend, Tom?

Tom: Well, I guess Harry. We've been going to baseball games together for ten years.

Sue: Oh? (4) _____

Tom: Well, it was really funny. See, Harry's a police officer. And one day I was late getting to a baseball game, and, well, I was in a real hurry. And he pulled over and stopped me for speeding. I explained why I was in such a hurry, and I found out he was a big baseball fan, too.

Sue: (5) _____

Tom: No, no…so we arranged to go to a game together the next weekend. But I still had to pay for the speeding ticket.

Sue: Well, what's Harry like?

Tom: Well, you know, he's a…he's a really interesting guy. You know, he's got this great sense of humor and he loves meeting people. He's very sociable. What about you? Who's your best friend?

Sue: Oh, my best friend is Ann. We met in France one summer about five years ago…

Tom: What's Ann like?

Sue: What's she like? Well, she's a good companion, a really creative person. She writes short stories.

Tom: Huh! You know, I'd like to meet her sometime.

Sue: (6) _____ Well, I'm planning to see her next Saturday. Maybe you could bring your friend Harry and we could go on a double date. How about that?

Tom: Yeah, it sounds great!

Section B

Directions: *In this section there is one incomplete interview which has four blanks and four choices A, B, C and D, taken from the interview. Fill in each of the blanks with one of the choices to complete the interview and mark your answer on the **Answer Sheet**.*

A. And who would I report to?

B. That's good to hear.

C. Do you have any questions?

D. Do you have any other questions?

Interviewer: Please have a seat, Mr. Thunders. I received your resume last week, and I was very impressed.

Interviewee: Thank you!

Interviewer: We are a small financial company trading mostly stocks and bonds. May I ask why you are interested in working for us?

Interviewee: Your company has an impressive reputation and I always want to work for a smaller company.

Interviewer: (7) _____ Would you mind telling me a little bit about your present job?

Interviewee: I'm currently working in a large international company in charge of a team of 8 brokers, we buy and sell stocks for major clients worldwide.

Interviewer: Why do you think you are the right candidate for this position?

Interviewee: As a head broker, I have a lot of experience in the stock market, I deal with the clients on the daily bases, and I enjoy working with people.

Interviewer: Well, you might just be the person we've been looking for. (8) _____

Interviewee: Uh-hum, if I were hired, how many accounts would I be handling?

Interviewer: You will be working with two other head brokers, in other words, you will be handling about a third of our clients.

Interviewee: (9) _____

Interviewer: Directly to me.

Interviewee: I see. What kind of benefits package do you offer?

Interviewer: Two weeks of paid vacation in your first year employment, you are also entitled to medical and dental insurance, but this is something you should discuss with our Personnel Department. (10) _____

Interviewee: No, not at the moment.

Interviewer: Well, I have to discuss your application with my colleagues and we'll get back to you early next week.

Interviewee: OK, thanks, it's very nice meeting you!

Model Test Two

Part One Oral Communication (15 minutes, 10 points)

Section A

Directions: *In this section there are two incomplete dialogues and each dialogue has three blanks and three choices A, B and C, taken from the dialogue. Fill in each of the blanks with one of the choices to complete the dialogue and mark your answer on the **Answer Sheet**.*

Dialogue One

A. Oh, you told me about her.

B. Everyone should have a close friend.

C. I believe you can be good sister of hers.

Tim: Did you stay at home last night?

Balvir: No, I went out with my friend. Well, actually, she's my best friend. Have you ever met her?

Tim: Er, I don't think so.

Balvir: Lisa?

Tim: (1) _____

Balvir: I did. She's a Greek girl.

Tim: I remember that you mentioned her last summer.

Balvir: She's really pretty…and she's got long dark hair. Um, yeah, we had a good time. We met… gosh… we've known each other now…for 15 years. Can you believe that?

Tim: Oh, wow.

Balvir: Yeah, we met…I was working for her dad. I tell you those were wild days but, er, we met working there together and um, she has a sister, an elder sister, and she doesn't get along with her very well, sometimes quarrels. So I always like to say that I'm like her sister. I'm like the sister she never had.

Tim: (2) _____

Balvir: Sure. But we don't have a lot in common. She's a housewife, a full time mother. She's got a little boy.

Tim: How old is he now? In kindergarten?

Balvir: No, he's about …he's about 11 now…difficult age. But we still get together about once or twice a month, and it's always good to see her.

Tim: (3) _____

Balvir: I think so.

Dialogue Two

A. I suppose so—but he knows it.

B. Ok, that's rude, but he's broke.

C. Well, he was unfriendly.

Rose: What do you think of Jake?

Meg: He's all right.

Rose: You don't like him, do you?

Meg: (4) _____

Rose: Oh, he's just shy, that's all.

Meg: Shy? You must be joking—five minutes after meeting me he asked me to buy him a drink! That's not what I call shy!

Rose: (5) _____

Meg: Huh, I'm poor myself and I'm trying to save up for my holiday.

Rose: All right, all right, I'll pay you back. He's good-looking, though, isn't he?

Meg: (6) _____ I think he's really big-headed.

Rose: You're just jealous.

Meg: No, I'm not. I don't want him. He's mean, big-headed and stupid too.

Rose: What do you mean stupid? You're stupid too.

Meg: Shut up!

Rose: No, you shut up!

Section B

Directions: *In this section there is one incomplete interview which has four blanks and four choices A, B, C and D, taken from the interview. Fill in each of the blanks with one of the choices to complete the interview and mark your answer on the **Answer Sheet**.*

A. And I hope I'll never find out.

B. Oh, you are really resourceful.

C. I suppose I might write another one.

D. And I've been writing ever since.

Interviewer: Hi, Miss Rowling, how old were you when you started to write? And what was your first book?

Miss Rowling: I wrote my first Finnish story when I was about six. It was about a small animal, a rabbit, I mean. (7) _____

Interviewer: Why did you choose to be an author?

Miss Rowling: If someone asked me how to achieve happiness. Step One would be finding out what you love doing most. Step two would be finding someone to pay you to do this. I consider myself very lucky indeed to be able to support myself by writing.

Interviewer: Do you have any plans to write books for adults?

Miss Rowling: My first two novels were for adults. (8) _____ But I never really imagine a target audience when I'm writing. The ideas come first. So it really depends on the ideas that grasp me next.

Interviewer: Where did the ideas for the "Harry Potter" books come from?

Miss Rowling: I've no ideas where the ideas came from. (9) _____ It would spoil my excitement if it turned out I just have a funny wrinkle on the surface of my brain, which makes me think about the invisible train platform.

Interviewer: How did you come up with the names of your characters?

Miss Rowling: I invented some of them. But I also collected strange names. I've got one from ancient saints, maps, dictionaries, plants, war memoirs and people I met.

Interviewer: (10) _____

Model Test Three

Part One Oral Communication (15 minutes, 10 points)

Section A

Directions: *In this section there are two incomplete dialogues and each dialogue has three blanks and three choices A, B and C, taken from the dialogue. Fill in each of the blanks with one of the choices to complete the dialogue and mark your answer on the **Answer Sheet**.*

Dialogue One

A. Have you ever wished you were older or younger than you are?

B. Is that a good age to be?

C. Oh, and which do you prefer?

Teacher: How old are you, Freddie?

Freddie: Twelve.

Teacher: (1) _____

Freddie: Yeah…you've grown up enough to be semi-independent but still young. At school I've just gone from being one of the oldest in my old school to being one of the youngest in secondary school.

Teacher: (2) _____

Freddie: Well, it was good being the oldest because I could boss people around but it's quite good being the youngest too because we're let out early for lunch and we can go home at two o'clock on Wednesday afternoon. Also having an older brother in the same school helps.

Teacher: How old is your brother?

Freddie: Sixteen.

Teacher: What differences are there between being 12 and being 16?

Freddie: He smells and I don't. Hah. Also, he's got exams and I haven't.

Teacher: (3) _____

Freddie: Yeah. I'd like to be old enough not to tidy my room.

Teacher: Hah. But you have to tidy your room whatever age you are.

Freddie: Yeah, but if I was old enough to leave home and have my own place, I wouldn't always have to keep my room neat and tidy.

Dialogue Two

A. I think I have just the place for you.

B. you could move in this weekend.

C. I think I can afford it.

Lynn: Mr. Wang, I'm Lynn Olsen, and I heard that you have an apartment for rent.

Charles: Actually, there are several. Are you looking for a one-bedroom or a two-bedroom apartment?

Lynn: I'm looking for a two-bedroom apartment with a full kitchen, a dining room, and a living room.

Charles: (4) _____ In fact, it has an excellent view of the river and it's pretty quiet. Will you live here alone or with others?

Lynn: Alone, but sometimes my brother comes out to visit, so I need a second room.

Charles: Ok. However, the rent is $400 a month. Is that all right with you?

Lynn: Yes. I work part-time and have a fixed income. (5) _____

Charles: That's good. I'll have you fill out a few papers, and if everything is agreeable, (6) _____

Lynn: Thank you so much.

Section B

Directions: *In this section there is one incomplete interview which has four blanks and four choices A, B, C and D, taken from the interview. Fill in each of the blanks with one of the choices to complete the interview and mark your answer on the **Answer Sheet**.*

A. I've nothing at all to do with undergraduates.

B. Really, what does that involve?

C. Well, I've been doing the same job.

D. Unfortunately, I'll miss my contact with students.

Interviewer: Sara, you work in the admission's office, don't you?

Sara: Yes, I'm...I've been here for 10 years as an assistant director.

Interviewer: (7) _____

Sara: Well, I'm in charge of all the admissions of postgraduate students in the university.

Interviewer: Only postgraduates?

Sara: Yes, postgraduates only. (8) _____

Interviewer: Do you find that you get a particular..., sort of...different national groups? I mean you get large numbers from Latin America or...

Sara: Yes, well, of all the students enrolled last years, nearly half were from overseas; they were from Africa countries, the Far East, the Middle East and Latin America.

Interviewer: Em. But have you been doing just that for the last 10 years or have you done other things?

Sara: (9) _____ Er, before that, I was Secretary of the Medical School at Birmingham. And further back, I worked in the local government.

Interviewer: Oh, I see.

Sara: So I've done different types of things.

Interviewer: Yes, indeed. How do you imagine your job might develop in the future? Can you imagine shifting into a different kind of responsibility or doing something...?

Sara: Oh, yeah. From October 1, I'll be doing an entirely different job. There's going to be more committee work; I mean more policy work, and less dealing with students. (10) _____

Model Test Four

Part One Oral Communication (15 minutes, 10 points)

Section A

Directions: *In this section there are two incomplete dialogues and each dialogue has three blanks and three choices A, B and C, taken from the dialogue. Fill in each of the blanks with one of the choices to complete the dialogue and mark your answer on the **Answer Sheet**.*

Dialogue One

A. How I envied them!

B. but I think I'll agree with you.

C. I had somebody else in the room with me.

Sharon: Did you have your own room when you were little, Wang Qiang?

Wang: No, for I think the first seventeen years of my life, (1) _____

Sharon: I always wanted my own room, you know, because there were five of us in the family and we always have to share rooms. I had my...my own room with the first time when I was about 15 or something.

Wang: I was very happy when my sister got married because then I could take her room.

Sharon: Oh, really?

Wang: And for the first time in my life I had my own room. I felt very proud and wrote in my diary, "I will treasure this new freedom!"

Sharon: Well, a lot of my friends had their own rooms when they were very young, some even as babies. (2) _____ But there were only three bedrooms in our house for seven people so we really were…

Wang: By the way, what do you think of letting a small baby sleep in a separate room? Many Chinese parents are astonished at this idea.

Sharon: I think it's…I think it's generally good. I think whenever possible because it makes people feel more independent and maybe a…

Wang: Well, I don't know, (3) _____

Dialogue Two

A. That's the table done!

B. You had it last!

C. I've got it!

Mr. Evans: Have you seen the corkscrew anywhere?

Mrs. Evans: (4) _____

Mr. Evans: Don't you remember where I put it?

Mrs. Evans: Try the bottom left-hand corner of the cupboard. If it's not there, have a look in the drawer of the sideboard.

Mr. Evans: It's not there!

Mrs. Evans: If you can't find it, then we'll have to borrow one from next door.

Mr. Evans: (5) _____ It was in the cupboard.

Mrs. Evans: Do you think we'll have enough drink?

Mr. Evans: There should be plenty.

Mrs. Evans: (6) _____ Put the wine glasses on the small table, please. We'll have the wine first. Will you remind me about the beef? The vegetables are nearly done.

Mr. Evans: Mmm. Everything's ready as far as I can see. (The doorbell rings)

Mrs. Evans: That's them already! I was afraid they'd be delayed by the traffic. Let them in, Bill, while I see to the food.

Mr. Evans: Hello, Barbara; hello…

Section B

Directions: *In this section there is one incomplete interview which has four blanks and four choices A, B, C and D, taken from the interview. Fill in each of the blanks with one of the choices to complete the interview and mark your answer on the **Answer Sheet**.*

A. I always cook a meal rather than have a take-away.

B. I generally find out what I do is effective for me.

C. I enjoy a mental challenge.

D. How do you relax in the evening?

Interviewer: So, why exactly does your job have reputation for being stressful?

Interviewee: Stress is generally driven by the feeling of being out of control of a situation and the feeling of a situation controlling you. Trading in financial markets combines both.

Interviewer: (7) _____

Interviewee: I very rarely do anything work-related so it's easy to escape the markets. I generally go to the gym or go for a run, especially if I had a bad day. (8) _____ To do something my brain will regard as creative.

Interviewer: Do you think what you do to relax is an effective way to beat stress?

Interviewee: I don't think there is a specific rule about how to beat stress. (9) _____

Interviewer: Would you consider changing your job because of the high stress factor?

Interviewee: I have considered leaving my job due to stress-related factors. However, I do think that an element of stress is a good thing, and if used the right way, can actually be a positive thing.

Interviewer: What do you enjoy about the stressful aspects of your job?

Interviewee: Having said all that, I do actually enjoy an element of uncertainty. (10) _____ Trading generates a wide range of emotions second by second. How you deal with and manage those emotions dictates short, medium and long-term trading performance and success.

Model Test five

Part One Oral Communication (15 minutes, 10 points)

Section A

Directions: *In this section there are two incomplete dialogues and each dialogue has three blanks and three choices A, B and C, taken from the dialogue. Fill in each of the blanks with one of the choices to complete the dialogue and mark your answer on the* **Answer Sheet**.

Dialogue One

A. I can understand that

B. It sounds like we're both busy bees

C. I don't have a green thumb.

Amy: You know, since Peter went off to college, it's easier to take care of the house.

Mary: (1) _____, I remember when my last child moved out. It almost seemed like there was nothing to do. Before the children left, we would all get up in the morning and have a good breakfast, then the kids would go off to school, and Sam would leave for work. I'd have the rest of the day to work around the house.

Amy: That sounds pretty much like my family before Peter left. When I'm not working in the house, I like to go outside and work in my vegetable garden. Most of the vegetables I grow are for my family. But I give a lot to my neighbors, too.

Mary: I admire people who can do that. (2) _____ I do experiment a little now and then, but with no luck. In fact, sometimes I think I can kill plants just by looking at them.

Amy: Oh, really!

Mary: I often think so. Anyway, I'm not good at growing things. But I'm good at needle work. I like to sew, to mend clothes.

Amy: (3) _____, we like to keep ourselves busy. Well, I guess some people are like that.

Dialogue Two

A. Times are different now.
B. Why don't you watch the video and find out?
C. Well, I guess it won't hurt...

Mrs. Cooper: Look what my grandson is doing—are you watching TV again, Paul? Isn't that the same show that was on yesterday?

Paul: It's not just one show, Grandma. They are actually a lot of different show. They are music videos.

Mrs. Cooper: Oh, really.

Paul: Why don't you sit down and watch a couple? They're really good.

Mrs. Cooper: (4) _____ what's that girl holding the stick supposed to be doing?

Paul: She's singing.

Mrs. Cooper: Do you call that singing?

Paul: Sure.

Mrs. Cooper: Humm. Music was very different when I was young. It was...pleasant to the ear. It made you feel happy. It wasn't just a lot of angry noise. And singers certainly wouldn't shake their fists at people in anger, like that.

Paul: Music today isn't just angry noise, Grandma. (5) _____

Mrs. Cooper: I suppose so... Is this another video?

Paul: Yeah. This one's great. I saw it yesterday.

Mrs. Cooper: Who's that guy?

Paul: Which guy?

Mrs. Cooper: The one wearing the funny hat.

Paul: He's the leader of the band. But in this video he's just a normal kid who stands on the corner all day, playing his guitar. Then this big, shiny car comes along...

Mrs. Cooper: And?

Paul: Well. (6) _____

Mrs. Cooper: Humm. In my day, "normal" kids didn't stand around on corners all day, waiting for big, shiny cars to come along.

Section B

Directions: *In this section there is one incomplete interview which has four blanks and four choices A, B, C and D, taken from the interview. Fill in each of the blanks with one of the choices to complete the interview and mark your answer on the **Answer Sheet**.*

A. Oh, and I also love tap-dancing very much.

B. What do you do for a living?

C. Could you tell me a little more about yourself?

D. No, I'm living in Ibiza now.

Interviewer: (7) _____

Nancy: Sure. I was born in London. But I want to tell you that I've got dual nationality because my mother's from Nicaragua.

Interviewer: Do you still live in London?

Nancy: (8) _____

Interviewer: Oh, really? How long have you been there?

Nancy: Not long. I moved from London with my two daughters, Assisi and Amba, about six months ago.

Interviewer: Are you happy there?

Nancy: Yeah, very happy. We love outdoor life. Also my mother's Spanish speaker and I feel more comfortable in a Latin country.

Interviewer: Have you made any friends?

Nancy: Yeah, I've made lots of new friends there. A few English, but my two best friends are Argentinian and Spanish.

Interviewer: (9) _____

Nancy: I'm a painter, but I've recently started a jewelry business with a friend and that takes up most of my time. I also do some modeling when I need the cash.

Interviewer: And what do you do in your free time?

Nancy: Well, with a business and two young children, I don't have much free time, but I love painting and listening to music. (10) _____

Model Test Six

Part One Oral Communication (15 minutes, 10 points)

Section A

Directions: *In this section there are two incomplete dialogues and each dialogue has three blanks and three choices A, B and C, taken from the dialogue. Fill in each of the blanks with* one of the choices to complete the dialogue and mark your answer on the **Answer Sheet**.

Dialogue One

A. Alright, but that's no excuse.

B. I'm quite disappointed as a matter of fact.

C. I'm afraid there is.

Mrs. Sears: Waiter! I'd like to speak to the manager please… immediately if possible.

Waiter: Is anything wrong, Madam?

Mrs. Sears: (1) _____ The service here has been terrible. We had to wait twenty minutes for a glass of mineral water.

Waiter: I see. Well, I'm sorry to hear that. The trouble is we're a bit short of hands at present. Two waitresses are ill.

Mrs. Sears: (2) _____ My husband asked for goose and he was brought chicken instead. It's just unbelievable! And my beans weren't cooked properly. It wasn't a very enjoyable meal at all.

Waiter: This is most regrettable.

Mrs. Sears: Look at this bill. We've been overcharged. We only had one dessert, not two. Can you check the bill again, please?

Waiter: I do apologize, Madam.

Mrs. Sears: I'm afraid I'm not going to pay the service charge, or give a tip as I don't feel satisfied with it. (3) _____

Waiter: I'll pass on your complaints to the manager and check your bill right away.

Mrs. Sears: Thank you.

Dialogue Two

A. I'd like to know what's on.

B. Every night except Sunday.

C. Well, you might get a ticket at a reduced price.

Clerk: Hello, can I help you with something?

Lady: Yes. You see, I'm spending a few days in the city and (4) _____

Clerk: Well, there's a musical, "Elephant Fountain," at Baoli Theater. They all say it's very good.

Lady: When's it on, exactly?

Clerk: (5) _____ Hold on, let me get some specific information… Yes, the show will run until the beginning of July. It begins at 8 o'clock and lasts two and a half hours, finishing at 10:45. There's an afternoon performance Wednesday and Saturday. Performances for the afternoon time start at 2:00 and end at 4:45.

Lady: And how much are the tickets?

Clerk: Tickets are 80 yuan, 100 yuan, and 150 yuan.

Lady: That's a bit expensive.

Clerk: (6) _____ It says here, "some tickets may be sold at half price half an hour before the performance starts."

Lady: Mm. I'll think about that. Oh, by the way, is there an age limit for children?

Clerk: Generally, not under 7. But this musical is a talk about three children and an elephant. So children are welcome except for babies. Besides, food and drinks are not allowed.

Section B

Directions: *In this section there is one incomplete interview which has four blanks and four choices A, B, C and D, taken from the interview. Fill in each of the blanks with one of the choices to complete the interview and mark your answer on the **Answer Sheet**.*

 A. I'd prefer to work in the morning

 B. you are well qualified for the job

 C. You may start next week.

 D. I'm aware of that.

Interviewer: I see from your application that (7) _____, Mrs. Sharp. We would be interested in having you work for us.

Eddie: Well, thank you. I have done this kind of work before. I love children, and of course I did a good job raising my own son.

Interviewer: Are you interested in part-time or full-time employment?

Eddie: Only part time, forty hours in one week is too much for me.

Interviewer: You know that part-time employees don't get any other benefits besides their wages.

Eddie: Yes. (8) _____ May I ask you if I can decide the hours I would work?

Interviewer: I can only give you the choice of working from 7:00 a.m. till noon or from noon till 5:00 p.m. Our part-time work week is 25 hours.

Eddie: (9) _____, because I have a lot of work to do around the house everyday. And besides, I have to prepare dinner for my husband.

Interviewer: Ok. Mrs. Sharp, or should I say Eddie? You're hired. Just sign your name on this sheet of paper. (10) _____ Mrs. Clarkson has got something ready for you—a blackboard, some chalks, crayons and a tape recorder. She'll show you around later.

Model Test Seven

Part One Oral Communication (15 minutes, 10 points)

Section A

Directions: *In this section there are two incomplete dialogues and each dialogue has three blanks and three choices A, B and C, taken from the dialogue. Fill in each of the blanks with one of the choices to complete the dialogue and mark your answer on the **Answer Sheet**.*

Dialogue One

A. Is that all it is?

B. I wish I could, but I can't.

C. That's no big deal.

Eddie: Look at this picture. It's a beautiful boat. The rooms on the boat look comfortable and each has a private bath. I think there's a TV in every room too.

Karen: (1) _____ You could stay home and have the same thing.

Eddie: Come on, Karen. You've been working so hard on your book. You really need a rest.

Karen: Yes, but I'm sure it'll be very expensive.

Eddie: It is expensive, but we really can afford it. We've both been working very hard and we deserve it, don't you think so?

Karen: (2) _____

Eddie: Why not? Your book is almost finished. You haven't gotten behind in your writing, have you?

Karen: No. Look, the problem is that I get seasick. I mean really seasick. Last time when I was on a sea voyage, I nearly got myself killed. I've tried all kinds of medicine. Nothing works. I'm really sorry.

Eddie: (3) _____ Listen, Karen, there's an excellent new medicine—in fact, it's a small patch that you wear behind your ear for about a week. If you need more medicine, you just put on a new patch. It's helped lots of people get over sickness.

Karen: Let me think about it. I'll tell you tomorrow.

Dialogue Two

A. But it's worth it, though.

B. Isn't it exciting?

C. How could I forget it?

Bill: Well, the holidays will be coming soon.

Helen: I know! (4) _____ Next week at this time, we will be traveling to the airport!

Bill: No, we won't! We will be already sitting in the plane, ready to take-off!

Helen: Yes, just think! In a few days' time we will be lying in the sun under one of those big umbrellas in Hainan.

Bill: Remember last time you were there? You got sunburnt because you stayed outside for too long.

Helen: (5) _____ So this time I'm going to take with me enough sun lotion and a big hat. In fact, I have prepared everything I can think of to protect myself from being hurt by the sun. But it doesn't mean I won't get a little browner at all.

Bill: Do you think we will like the food in the hotel? Last time we stayed in a small hotel.

The food was not so good as we expected.

Helen: Never mind. It is said that there is always a lot of fresh seafood and fruit to be sold on the street. Besides, they are cheaper than the price here. When we come back in a fortnight, we'll buy enough presents this time not only for our children, but also for our friends and neighbours.

Bill: I'm afraid it will cost us a lot of money again. (6) _____

Helen: Of course. I can't wait for the time to come! Bill, look! What's this letter? It's from the travel company! It's a warning that we haven't paid for the holiday yet! Did you forget to post that check?

Bill: Oh, my god. It must still be in my suit pocket! ... All right, don't stare at me like that. I know it's my fault. Where's my pen? I'll mail it right away.

Section B

Directions: *In this section there is one incomplete interview which has four blanks and four choices A, B, C and D, taken from the interview. Fill in each of the blanks with one of the choices to complete the interview and mark your answer on the* **Answer Sheet.**

A. Well, it seems to work.

B. I don't know about that

C. That shows how young you are.

D. You hear it everywhere

Interviewer: What do you write? Story books? Plays?

Pat: Just articles for newspapers.

Interviewer: What are you working on now?

Pat: I've just finished a piece of background music.

Interviewer: Background music? Oh, like the music they're playing here in the restaurant?

Pat: Yes. (7) _____ ... in restaurants, airports, supermarkets, chain stores and department stores. It's supposed to put you in a good mood.

Interviewer: I'm not sure I like that idea.

Pat: (8) _____ Companies pay millions of dollars every year for background music. It's supposed to give you a better feeling about yourself and the people around you.

Interviewer: Now that I think about it, I can't remember when there wasn't background music in restaurants and stores.

Pat: (9) _____ Actually, it all started during World War II when some factories had their own music band to keep workers happy and calm. Now, of course, different kinds of music are played at different time during the day. They play faster music at ten in the morning than at eight because workers seem to be slower then.

Interviewer: What about restaurants? Do they play the same music for dinner and lunch?

Pat: (10) _____, but I do know that hamburger places play fast music. When they started playing faster music, they found that a customer spent only seventeen minutes eating like mad. The time was twenty-two minutes before that. You see, 5 minutes faster merely by a change of background music.

Interviewer: Interesting. So they can prevent customers from staying too long and can have more people coming in and out to buy hamburgers.

Model Test Eight

Part One　Oral Communication (15 minutes, 10 points)

Section A

Directions: *In this section there are two incomplete dialogues and each dialogue has three blanks and three choices A, B and C, taken from the dialogue. Fill in each of the blanks with one of the choices to complete the dialogue and mark your answer on the **Answer Sheet**.*

Dialogue One

A. Try these on.

B. All right.

C. Oh, excuse me

Salesman: Good afternoon, madam. May I help you?

Pat: Yes, please. I'm interested in buying a pair of shoes to match my trousers.

Salesman: (1) _____ Do you want high heels or heels?

Pat: Well, low heels are more comfortable, but I think I should wear high heels with that pair of trousers.

Salesman: Let me measure your foot. Fine. Here are several different styles in your size, I think. (2) _____ They're on sale today.

Pat: They fit perfectly, but they aren't exactly what I want. I don't see any that I really like. Thanks anyway.

Salesman: You're welcome.

Pat: (3) _____, could you tell me where I can get a belt?

Salesman: You can find it in the Leather Goods Department on the third floor. There's in fact quite a variety of good quality belts.

Pat: Thanks a lot. Bye.

Dialogue Two

A. That would be fine.

B. Oh, one more thing.

C. I'm afraid that's unlikely.

Order clerk: Hello. Delivery Department here.

White: Good morning, this is Mr. White of G and Bs. I'm phoning about the delivery of our orders. First, what about the men's suits?

Order clerk: Yes, they will certainly be ready in March.

White: Good, and what about the sports jackets?

Order clerk: It depends on the mill, but you could get them next month.

White: (4) _____ We're running very short of blouses and swimsuits and with spring season coming, we're keen to know what the situation there is. Will they be ready in March?

Order clerk: (5) _____ But we'll probably manage them in April.

White: Lastly, how are the skirts coming along? You said that we'd have them next month.

Order clerk: I'm sorry. There's not much chance of that but they'll definitely be ready in March, two months from now, I suppose.

White: Ok, that's fine for now. (6) _____ We'd like to cancel for those jackets with fur collars. They didn't sell well.

Order clerk: Well, for that you'll have to call Mr. Parkers at 6573830.

White: Thank you. We'll no doubt be in touch again soon. Bye.

Order clerk: Bye, Mr. White.

Section B

Directions: *In this section there is one incomplete interview which has four blanks and four choices A, B, C and D, taken from the interview. Fill in each of the blanks with one of the choices to complete the interview and mark your answer on the **Answer Sheet**.*

A. The children's programs.

B. It got some quite good reviews.

C. It won't take up much of your time.

D. I think we need more international news

Visitor: Good morning, Madam! I'm from the local TV center and we're doing a survey on the popularity of different programs. I'd like to ask you a few questions on your family's viewing habits. Do you mind?

Mrs. Sears: No, I don't, but I'm rather busy at the moment.

Visitor: (7) _____ Have you got a color TV?

Mrs. Sears: Yes, we have.

Visitor: And can you tell me how many hours you watch each day, on average?

Mrs. Sears: Well, I suppose about three, three or four.

Visitor: Does anybody watch TV before 7 p.m.?

Mrs. Sears: Yes, my son Ben does. (8) _____

Visitor: And do you find them fully suitable for your child?

Mrs. Sears: Yes, I do. When I have time, I watch them with him.

Visitor: What about adult viewing? Films? Did you follow the recent detective series on

Fridays at 9?

Mrs. Sears: Yes, we did. But we didn't enjoy it very much. It's all about mentally sick and crazy people.

Visitor: You didn't? How surprising! (9) _____ Well, how about programs of current interest, politics, news commentaries, etc. ? I expect you and your husband can usually find time to keep up with the news?

Mrs. Sears: Yes, that's true. My husband is interested in discussion forums—slave issue, prison reform, gun control—whatever under discussion. (10) _____, rather than news about the Queen, the Duchesses and other people of noble blood.

Model Test Nine

Part One Oral Communication (15 minutes, 10 points)

Section A

Directions: *In this section there are two incomplete dialogues and each dialogue has three blanks and three choices A, B and C, taken from the dialogue. Fill in each of the blanks with one of the choices to complete the dialogue and mark your answer on the **Answer Sheet**.*

Dialogue One

A. Can't you give me pills?

B. Do you feel tired?

C. Probably, if you have a good rest today.

Dr. Smith: Now, what seems to be bothering you?

Simon: I've got a sore throat and a headache. My fever is gone, but I still have a cough and pains in my chest.

Dr. Smith: You're looking pale. (1) _____

Simon: Yes, my whole body feels weak. I really feel terrible.

Dr. Smith: I'm sorry to hear that. I'll have to examine you. Well, open your mouth wide so that I can look at your throat... yes, it's very red. It looks sore. I'll have to give you an injection.

Simon: (2) _____ I hate injections.

Dr. Smith: An injection is better than pills, you'd probably be ill for a few days, but if I give you an injection, you'll feel better tomorrow.

Simon: Will I be able to go out tomorrow?

Dr. Smith: (3) _____ Please get plenty of sleep and drink plenty of liquids. Oh, I almost forgot. Here's a prescription for some medicine. Take it every two hours so you won't cough.

Dialogue Two

A. It's for your cough.

B. That's all right.

C. Now here's your medicine.

Druggist: Can I help you, sir?

Wang Lin: Yes, I'd like to have these prescription filled, please.

Druggist: Ok. Wait a few minutes, and I'll have them for you. (4) _____ That'll be twenty dollars fifty-five cents please.

Wang Lin: Can you tell me how many pills to take and how many times a day?

Druggist: Certainly. Now look at the label on this bottle of red pills. Take one of these three times a day after meals. As for the white pills in that plastic bottle, take two every four hours, is that clear?

Wang Lin: Oh, yes. What is this medicine?

Druggist: (5) _____ Take as needed but don't take more than three tablespoons a day.

Wang Lin: Thank you very much for your help. Good-bye.

Druggist: Excuse me. Have you forgotten something?

Wang Lin: Forgotten something? What's that? Oh, I'm terribly sorry. I forgot to pay. You know I'm sick and I didn't mean to …

Druggist: (6) _____

Wang Lin: Here you are.

Druggist: Thank you. Here's your change. Hope you'll feel better soon. Bye.

Wang Lin: Good-bye.

Section B

Directions: *In this section there is one incomplete interview which has four blanks and four choices A, B, C and D, taken from the interview. Fill in each of the blanks with one of the choices to complete the interview and mark your answer on the **Answer Sheet**.*

A. It's as simple as that.

B. I was frightened of them.

C. Oh, I wouldn't be without one.

D. It used to take ages.

Interviewer: What did you think about computers, before you got on the Internet?

Mary: (7) _____ I knew I couldn't use them. I used to hate them.

Interviewer: We often hate the things which we don't understand, is that what you're saying?

Mary: Yes, yes it is.

Interviewer: And how do you feel about them now?

Mary: (8) _____ Before, I used to go to the shops almost every day. I had to go down all those stairs—four flights, you know, take things from the shelves and put them in the shopping cart, and then stand in queues. (9) _____ —and I'm quite slow on my legs now.

Interviewer: Yes, hmmm. And now?

Mary: Oh, now it's a different matter. I just sit down in front of my computer, with a cup of tea besides me, and with a click of the mouse I do my shopping. (10) _____ I don't have to worry about carrying several kilos of goods home—they'll be delivered at my door.

Model Test Ten

Part One   Oral Communication (15 minutes, 10 points)

Section A

Directions: *In this section there are two incomplete dialogues and each dialogue has three blanks and three choices A, B and C, taken from the dialogue. Fill in each of the blanks with one of the choices to complete the dialogue and mark your answer on the **Answer Sheet**.*

Dialogue One

A. we'll have earned it!

B. That's a good idea.

C. And what about the garage?

Mr. Curry: It's time to get the house in shape for spring. Let's decide what we can do over the weekend.

Mrs. Curry: First we should have a spring cleaning. I'll phone Doris to come over to help, all right?

Mr. Curry: (1) _____

Mrs. Curry: We have so many things to do. We have to put up the screens, and we need to air out our winter clothes and put them away.

Mr. Curry: Isn't it time to start the vegetable garden? I can go and get seeds for tomatoes, onions. I should also get more poles ready to support young bean plants.

Mrs. Curry: But before we start the garden, we'd better check the lawn mower and have it serviced. We haven't used it for eight months.

Mr. Curry: The fence has to be repaired and painted, too.

Mrs. Curry: (2) _____ Can we get by without painting it for another year?

Mr. Curry: I don't know. Let's check it tomorrow.

Mrs. Curry: So you see, we'll have a very busy weekend. But we should do something different. Shall we go to the movies Sunday night?

Mr. Curry: If we finish all these things, (3) _____

Dialogue Two

A. Oh, that's a bit cynical, isn't it?

B. Sounds like a waste of time to me.

C. Well, not necessarily.

Catherine: I've just come back from one of those weekend breaks. It was great fun.

Robert: Have you? Where did you go?

Catherine: I went on a tai chi chuan course.

Robert: A what?

Catherine: A course in tai chi, you know. It is a Chinese physical exercise designed for bodily well-being and also as an art of self-defense.

Robert: (4) _____ Why should you want to do that, to defend yourself from an attack?

Catherine: I don't really need to, but it's a good experience, and you can't spend your whole life working. You know what he say, Robert, "All work and no play." You really should get out and do something like that.

Robert: No, I've got far too much to do. Anyway, as far as I can see, there's no point in learning something like that if you can't earn some money from it.

Catherine: (5) _____

Robert: Maybe, but I couldn't see myself earning a living by doing anything like that. Anyway, you need to be a bit athletic, surely?

Catherine: (6) _____ On most of these courses you don't have to have any past experience—not really. I mean, well, on this one, as long as you can get up early…

Robert: Well, I can get up early, but I'd be no good at doing anything like that…

Section B

Directions: *In this section there is one incomplete interview which has four blanks and four choices A, B, C and D, taken from the interview. Fill in each of the blanks with one of the choices to complete the interview and mark your answer on the **Answer Sheet**.*

A. What medicines do you recommend?

B. And when you have aches and pains, aspirin may help.

C. You mean, are they bad for your teeth?

D. Yes, I'm afraid I do.

Interviewer: You seem to have a rather nasty cold yourself?

Jeremy: (7) _____

Interviewer: Is there anything you can do to make a cold go away more quickly?

Jeremy: No, there isn't. It might take some time before it can be fully cured. But a cold isn't really serious enough for a visit to your doctor.

Interviewer: What can you do in order to feel a bit better?

Jeremy: First of all, as soon as the symptoms start, you should get plenty of rest—for the first couple of days or so. (8) _____

Interviewer: Should you eat or drink anything special?

Jeremy: Lots of hot drinks may make you feel better.

Interviewer: (9) _____

Jeremy: When you just have a cold, home remedies are probably best. You can inhale steam to clear your nose; if you have a dry cough, you can take some sweets or chew gum.

Interviewer: Don't they usually contain a lot of sugar?

Jeremy: (10) _____ Yes, they are.

Interviewer: Anything else?

Jeremy: This one is obvious. Smokers should stop smoking, at least while they have the cold.

第六节　答案及解析

Model Test One

Section A

Dialogue One

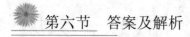 1. C   2. B   3. A

▶ 详　解

这是一段两个朋友之间谈论报纸上看到的一个正在招聘的工作岗位的对话。首先，应该明确三个答案选项的语法功能和语义。A 选项是特殊疑问句，意思是：顺便问一下，工资是多少？B 选项是特殊疑问句，意思是：他们还有什么其他的要求吗？C 选项是完整句，意思是：你可能会感兴趣。

其次，认真阅读对话，特别是仔细体会空白处的上下文的语义。由于三个选项中，只有 C 是一个肯定的完整句，可以先从它入手。第 1 题用在问题之前，因此它不可能再是问题，所以正确答案是 C。上下文联系起来的语义是：Susan 说她已经受够了自己的工作；Mike 回答说今天的报纸上有个特别适合你的工作，你可能会感兴趣；Susan 接着询问是什么工作，他们有什么要求。根据第 2 题后 Mike 的回答 Just that（就是那个）及 A university degree and three or four years of experience as a translator in a professional environment（大学学历和在专业领域 3~4 年的翻译经验），这些应该是 B 的回答，所以正确答案是 B。根据第 3 题后面 Susan 对自己问题的补充 I just hope it isn't lower than what I get now（我只希望不要比我现在拿的少）以及 Mike 的回答 It's said to be negotiable（说是可以商议的），推知两个人谈的应该是工资问题，所以正确答案是 A。

第一章 口语交际

Dialogue Two

答案 4. B　5. C　6. A

详解

　　这是一段两个朋友之间谈论彼此最好的朋友的对话。首先，应该明确三个答案选项的语法功能和语义。A 选项是省略的一般疑问句，用于进一步确定对方所说的话是否是真的；意思是：是吗？你会这么做吗？B 选项是特殊疑问句；意思是：你们是怎么认识的？C 选项是习惯用语，用来表示吃惊，意思是：你开玩笑吧？

　　其次，认真阅读对话，特别是仔细体会空白处的上下文的语义。根据第 4 题后面 Tom 的回答，可以看出他是描述了和 Harry 第一次见面时有趣的情景，因此是对 B 的回答，所以正确答案是 B。第 5 题用在刚才这段描述的后面，刚听完 Tom 讲的如此巧合的事情，Sue 的反应应该是吃惊，难以置信，因此正确答案是 C。而且随后 Tom 说的"No, no…"表示自己不是开玩笑，这一切都是真的。根据第 6 题之前 Tom 说的 I'd like to meet her sometime（我希望有机会见见她），本题的正确答案应该是 A。

Section B

答案 7. B　8. C　9. A　10. D

详解

　　这段对话是招聘者面试求职者的一段对话。首先，应该明确四个答案选项的语法功能和语义。A 选项是特殊疑问句，语义是：我应该向谁汇报？B 选项是完整句，意思是：听你这么说，我真高兴。C 选项是一般疑问句，意思是：你有什么问题吗？D 选项是一般疑问句，意思是：你还有其他问题吗？

　　其次，认真阅读对话，特别是仔细体会空白处的上下文的语义。第 7 题用在一般疑问句 Would you mind telling me a little bit about your present job?（你介意谈谈你目前的工作吗？）之前，应该不会再是问题，所以正确答案应该是 B，是对前面求职者说的 Your company has an impressive reputation and I always want to work for a smaller company（你们公司的声誉非常好，我一直愿意为小一点的公司工作）的应答。第 8～10 题都是问题，其中最容易判断的是第 9 题，根据它后面的回答 Directly to me（直接向我），应该是对 A 的回答，所以本题正确答案是 A。然后再来分析所剩的 C 和 D 两个选项的异同，两者在意思上大致相同，唯一的区别在于 D 选项中多的 other，按照对话的习惯分析，两者在对话里的合理顺序应该是 C 在前，D 在后，所以第 8 题正确答案是 C，第 10 题正确答案是 D。

　　此外，本段对话中除了面试中常有的词汇外，还出现了不少金融方面的词汇值得总结和学习，包括 financial company（金融公司）、stock（股票）、bond（债券）、broker（股票交易人）、stock market（股市）、account（账户）等。

Model Test Two

Section A

Dialogue One

答案 1. A   2. C   3. B

详解

　　这是一段朋友之间谈论一方好友的对话。首先，应该明确三个答案选项的语法功能和语义。A 选项是完整句；意思是：你跟我谈起过她。B 选项是完整句；意思是：每个人都应该有要好的朋友。C 选项是完整句，意思是：我相信你能成为她的姐妹。

　　其次，认真阅读对话，特别是仔细体会空白处的上下文的语义。第 1 题的明显提示是其后的 I did（我确实做了），据此前面的句子应该使用过去时，是 Balvir 做的一件具体的事情，因此正确答案应该是 A。根据第 2 题之前的 I'm like the sister she never had（我就像她从未有过的姐妹一样）和其后的 Sure（的确，当然），此题的正确答案应该是 C。第 3 题的答案是 B，是对这段对话的总结。

Dialogue Two

答案 4. C   5. B   6. A

详解

　　这段对话是两姐妹谈论她们对一个男孩的印象。首先，应该明确三个答案选项的语法功能和语义。A 选项是并列句，意思是：可能是这样吧，但是我觉得他自己知道这一点。B 选项是并列句，意思是：好吧，那是无礼的，但是他很穷，根本没钱。broke 的意思是：身无分文的。C 选项是完整句，意思是：他很不友好。

　　其次，认真阅读对话，特别是仔细体会空白处的上下文的语义。根据第 4 题前面的 You don't like him, do you?（你不喜欢他，是吗？）和后面的 Oh, he's just shy, that's all.（他不过是害羞，仅此而已），第 4 题应该是 Meg 提到了 Jake 的一个缺点，而 Rose 不同意，进行了纠正，据此判断正确答案应该是 C。根据第 5 题之前的 You must be joking—five minutes after meeting me he asked me to buy him a drink!（你开玩笑吧——他和我认识了才五分钟，就让我给他买饮料）以及后面的 Huh, I'm poor myself and I'm trying to save up for my holiday.（我自己也挺穷的，正为我的假期攒钱呢），第 5 题应该谈论和钱有关的事情，所以正确答案是 B，在这 Rose 竭力为 Jake 辩护。第 6 题的正确答案是 A，之前 Rose 说 Jake 长得很帅，此处尽管 Meg 不否认这点，但是她觉得 Jake 对此有充分的认识，而且觉得 Jake 是 big-headed（自负的，自大的）。

Section B

> **答案** 7. D 8. C 9. A 10. B

> **详解**

这段对话是记者对《哈利·波特》的作者 Miss Rowling 的采访。首先,应该明确四个答案选项的语法功能和语义。A 选项是完整句,语义是:而且,我希望我永远不知道。B 选项是完整句,意思是:啊,您的资源可真丰富呀。C 选项是完整句,意思是:我想我可能再写一本。D 选项是完整句,意思是:从那开始,我就一直在写。

其次,应该区分说话人的身份。A、C 和 D 应该都是 Miss Rowling——被采访人说的;而 B 应该是记者说的。因此,四个题目中,最容易判断的是第 10 题,只有它是记者说的,所以正确答案是 B。是对前面 Miss Rowling 说的 I've got one from ancient saints, maps, dictionaries, plants, war memoirs and people I met.(我从古代圣人、地图、字典、植物、战争回忆录以及我遇到的人中找我的角色的名字)的评价。第三,要认真阅读对话,特别是仔细体会空白处的上下文的语义。第 7 题是对记者提出的 how old were you when you started to write? And what was your first book?(您多大开始写作的?您的第一本小说是什么?)的回答,所以正确答案应该是 D。第 8 题和它前面的句子 My first two novels were for adults(我最早的两部小说是为成人写的)应该是对记者提出的 Do you have any plans to write books for adults?(您有没有为成人读者写小说的计划?)的回答,所以正确答案应该是 C。第 9 题的正确答案是 A,A 和它前面的 I've no ideas where the ideas came from(我不知道这些想法是从哪来的),在逻辑上是递进关系,在语义上都是对记者 where did the ideas for the "Harry Potter" books come from?(您写《哈利·波特》一书的想法从哪来的?)的回答。

Model Test Three

Section A

Dialogue One

> **答案** 1. B 2. C 3. A

> **详解**

这是老师和学生之间关于学生年龄问题展开的一段对话。首先,应该明确三个答案选项的语法功能和语义。A 选项是一般疑问句,意思是:你有没有希望过比你现在的实际年龄大点或小点? B 选项是一般疑问句,意思是:这个年纪好吗? C 选项是特殊疑问句,意思是:你更喜欢哪一个?

其次,认真阅读对话,特别是仔细体会空白处的上下文的语义;由于三个选项都是问题,所以应该更关注题目后面的句子,根据给出的答案来推断问题是什么。根据第 1 题后面的 Yeah...,可以判断,第 1 题应该是一般疑问句;此外根据其后的 you're grown up enough to be semi-independent but still young（你已经长到了能够半独立的年纪，而且也还年轻）可以判断这是对自己目前的年龄的看法，所以正确答案应该是B。根据第2题之前的At school I've just gone from being one of the oldest in my old school to being one of the youngest in secondary school.（在学校里，我刚好从原来学校里最大的变成现在中学里最小的）以及后面的 it was good being the oldest because I could boss people around but it's quite good being the youngest too because we're let out early for lunch and we can go home at two o'clock on Wednesday afternoon（当老大挺好，因为你可以指挥别人；当最小的也挺好，因为我们可以提早去吃午饭而且周三下午两点就可以回家），第2题的正确答案应该是C。第3题的正确答案是A，后面用Yeah给出了肯定回答。

Dialogue Two

答案　4. A　5. C　6. B

详解

　　这是一段租房人与房东之间关于租房问题的对话。首先，应该明确三个答案选项的语法功能和语义。A选项是主从复合句，意思是：我觉得我这刚好有适合的房子。B选项是完整句，意思是：你这个周末就可以搬过来。C选项是主从复合句，意思是：我觉得我付得起。

　　其次，应该区分说话人的身份。三个选项中，A和B应该是房东说的；C是租房人说的。因此，最容易做的是第5题，只有这句是租房人说的，所以正确的答案应该是C，而且与它前面的 I work part-time and have a fixed income（我有份兼职的工作，收入稳定）语义相符。剩下的两个题目难度也不大，第4题正确答案是A，适合用在对话开头部分，与它后面的对房子进行具体介绍的句子语义相符。第6题正确答案是B，适合用在对话结尾部分。

Section B

答案　7. B　8. A　9. C　10. D

详解

　　这段对话主要是围绕Sara的工作进行的，谈论了她工作的具体职责以及曾经做过的其他工作等。首先，应该明确四个答案选项的语法功能和语义。A选项是完整句，语义是：我做的工作和本科生没有任何关系。B选项是特殊疑问句，意思是：是吗？那会涉及什么？C选项是完整句，意思是：我一直做着相同的工作。D选项是完整句，意思是：遗憾的是我会怀念和学生的接触和联系的。

　　其次，应该区分说话人的身份。三个选项中，A、C、D应该是Sara说的；B是Interviewer说的。因此，最容易做的是第7题，只有这句是Interviewer说的，所以正确答案是 B；此外，这一问题与它后面 Sara 说的 I'm in charge of all the admissions of postgraduate students in the university（我负责整个学校研究生的招生工作）的语义完全相符。最后，认真阅读对话，特别是仔细体会空白处的上下文的语义。第 8 题和它前面的 Yes, postgraduates only.（是的，只有研究生）应该是对前面的 Only postgraduates? 这一问题的回答，所以正确答案应该是 A。第 9 题是对前面 But have you been doing just that for the last 10 years or have you done other things?（在过去 10 年里，你一直做这个工作，还是又做过其他工作？）这一问题的回答，所以正确答案是 C。第 10 题的正确答案是 D，是对它前面的 I mean more policy work, and less dealing with students（我会做更多的政策性工作，和学生接触就会少了）的进一步的补充。

Model Test Four

Section A

Dialogue One

答案 1. C 2. A 3. B

详解

在这段对话中，两个朋友主要谈论了小时候是否有独立房间的事情。首先，应该明确三个答案选项的语法功能和语义。A 选项是感叹句，意思是：我好羡慕他们呀！B 选项是 but 引导的并列句，意思是：但是，我觉得我同意你的看法。C 选项是完整句，意思是：有人跟我一起住。

其次，认真阅读对话，特别是仔细体会空白处的上下文的语义。第 1 题和它前面的句子 No, for I think the first seventeen years of my life（我觉得在我生命最初的 17 年里）合起来是对 Sharon 的问题 Did you have your own room when you were little, Wang Qiang?（王蔷，你小的时候有自己的房间吗？）的回答，所以正确答案是 C。根据第 2 题前面的句子 Well, a lot of my friends had their own rooms when they were very young, some even as babies.（我很多的朋友在他们很小的时候，甚至是婴儿的时候就有自己的房间），第 2 题的正确答案应该是 A，是对前面讲的事情表达感慨。第 3 题正确答案是 B，跟在主句后面。

Dialogue Two

答案 4. B 5. C 6. A

详解

这是一段夫妻之间为了迎接客人做准备时的对话。首先，应该明确三个答案选项的语法功能和语义。A 选项是完整句，意思是：桌子就摆成这样吧。B 选项是完整句，意思是：你最后用的它。C 选项是完整句，意思是：我找到了。

53

其次，认真阅读对话，特别是仔细体会空白处的上下文的语义。根据第4题前面的问题 Have you seen the corkscrew anywhere?（你看到螺丝锥了吗？）以及后面的问题 Don't you remember where I put it?（你记得我放哪了吗？）第4题的答案应该是B。根据第5题后的 It was in the cupboard.（在橱柜里。）本题的正确答案应该是C。第6题的正确答案是A，与其后面的句子语义相符。

Section B

答案 7. D　8. A　9. B　10. C

详解

这段对话主要探讨了如何应对工作中的压力问题。首先，应该明确四个答案选项的语法功能和语义。A选项是完整句，语义是：我总是自己做饭，不买外带的食物。B选项是主从复合句，意思是：基本上，我发现我做的事情对我自己来说是有效的。C选项是完整句，意思是：我喜欢智力方面的挑战。D选项是特殊疑问句，意思是：你晚上通常怎么休息放松呀？

其次，应该区分说话人的身份。三个选项中，A、B和C应该是 Interviewee 说的；D是 Interviewer 说的。因此，最容易做的是第7题，只有这句是 Interviewer 说的，所以正确答案是D；此外这一问题与其后的回答 I very rarely do anything work-related so it's easy to escape the markets（我很少会做和工作有关的事情，所以很容易躲开市场）相符。最后，认真阅读对话，特别是仔细体会空白处的上下文的语义。第8题和它前面的 I generally go to the gym or go for a run, especially if I had a bad day（我通常会去体育馆或者是找点其他的乐子，特别是我这一天过的很糟的话），应该都是对第7题问的晚间如何休息的回答，所以正确答案应该是A。第9题和它前面的 I don't think there is a specific rule about how to beat stress（我觉得如何应对压力，没有什么特定的方式）都是在回答 Interviewer 的问题 Do you think what you do to relax is an effective way to beat stress（你觉得你放松休闲的方式对于减压有效吗），所以正确答案应该是B，而且B中的 effective 也与前面的问题相呼应。第10题正确答案是C，C中的 I enjoy a mental challenge 与前面的 I do actually enjoy an element of uncertainty（我确实很喜欢不确定的因素）是并列和递进的关系。

Model Test Five

Section A

Dialogue One

答案 1. A　2. C　3. B

详解

在这段对话中，两个朋友主要谈论了孩子离开家后他们生活的变化。首先，应该明确三个答案选项的语法功能和语义。A 选项是完整句,意思是:我能理解这点。B 选项是完整句,意思是:看起来,我们都是忙碌的人。C 选项是完整句,意思是:我没什么特殊的园艺才能,其中 a green thumb(特殊的园艺才能)是固定的习语。

其次,认真阅读对话,特别是仔细体会空白处的上下文的语义。根据第 1 题前面 Amy 说的 You know, since Peter went off to college, it's easier to take care of the house(你知道自从彼得离开家后,收拾家变得容易多了)和它后面的 I remember when my last child moved out(我还记得我最小的孩子搬出去的时候)可以看出第 1 题是对 Amy 所说的事情有同感,所以正确答案应该是 A。根据第 2 题前面 Amy 所说的 When I'm not working in the house, I like to go outside and work in my vegetable garden. Most of the vegetables I grow are for my family. But I give a lot to my neighbors, too.(当我不忙屋子里的事时,我就会去外面我的菜园里。我的蔬菜大部分是为自己家种的,有时候也会给邻居送些)以及它后面的 I do experiment a little now and then, but with no luck. In fact, sometimes I think I can kill plants just by looking at them.(我也偶尔试验一下,但是运气不怎么样。事实上,有时我甚至觉得我只是看着那些植物,就能杀死它们。)可以看出她们谈论的是种菜、种植物的话题,而且 Mary 在这方面很不擅长,所以正确答案是 C。第 3 题正确答案是 B,与它后面的 we like to keep ourselves busy(我们愿意自己忙一点)语义相符,也是对前面这段对话的概括。

Dialogue Two

答案 4. C   5. A   6. B

详解

这是一段祖孙之间讨论音乐电视节目的对话。首先,应该明确三个答案选项的语法功能和语义。A 选项是完整句,意思是:时代不同了。B 选项是疑问句表建议,意思是:你为什么不自己看电视弄明白呢?其中,Why don't you…是表建议的常用句式,不是问原因。C 选项是完整句,意思是:我想大概没什么坏处。

其次,认真阅读对话,特别是仔细体会空白处的上下文的语义。第 4 题应该是对它前面 Paul 的提议 Why don't you sit down and watch a couple? They're really good.(你为什么不自己坐下来看几个,它们真的不错。)的回答,所以正确答案应该是 C。第 5 题和它前面的 Music today isn't just angry noise, Grandma(奶奶,今天的音乐不仅仅是愤怒的声音)是对奶奶前面发表的对今天流行音乐的评论的反驳,所以正确答案是 A。第 6 题正确答案是 B,这时 Paul 已不耐烦再给奶奶介绍节目内容了,而让她自己看。

Section B

答案 7. C   8. D   9. B   10. A

详解

这段采访对话主要涉及了 Nancy 的工作生活和个人爱好等话题。首先,应该明确四个答案选项的语法功能和语义。A 选项是完整句，语义是：我还很喜欢踢踏舞。B 选项是特殊疑问句，意思是：你靠什么谋生呢？C 选项是一般疑问句，意思是：你能再讲点你自己的事情吗？D 选项是否定回答，意思是：不，我现在住在伊比沙岛。

其次，应该区分说话人的身份。其中，A 和 D 选项应该是 Nancy 的回答；而 B 和 C 选项是 Interviewer 的问题。第三，认真阅读对话，特别是仔细体会空白处的上下文的语义。可以先做第 7、9 题，这两个都是 Interviewer 的问题，答案应该是在 B 和 C 之间选择。在具体判断的时候，应该根据 Nancy 的回答来确定具体问题是什么。根据第 7 题后面的 Sure. I was born in London.（当然。我出生在伦敦），前面的问题应该是一般疑问句，所以正确答案是 C。根据第 9 题后面的 I'm a painter, but I've recently started a jewelry business with a friend（我是个画家，但是最近我和几个朋友开始做珠宝生意），此题的正确答案应是 B。在做第 8、10 题时，应该关注前面 Interviewer 的问题。根据第 8 题前面的 Do you still live in London（你还住在伦敦吗），此题的正确答案应该是 D。根据第 10 题前面的问题 And what do you do in your free time（你空闲时间都做点什么），本题的正确答案是 A，谈及了个人爱好。

Model Test Six

Section A

Dialogue One

答案 1. C 2. A 3. B

详解

这是一段发生在餐馆里顾客和服务员之间的对话，对话中顾客表达了对餐馆服务的不满。首先，应该明确三个答案选项的语法功能和语义。A 选项是短回答，意思是：好吧，但那不是借口。B 选项是完整句，意思是：事实上，我相当失望。C 选项是省略的主从复合句，意思是：我恐怕是有。

其次，认真阅读对话，特别是仔细体会空白处的上下文的语义。根据第 1 题前面的 Is anything wrong, Madam?（夫人，有什么问题吗？）和它后面的 The service here has been terrible（服务非常差），本题的正确答案应该是 C，C 表达的完整语义应该是 I'm afraid there is something wrong。第 2 题前面的句子 The trouble is we're a bit short of hands at present. Two waitresses are ill（问题是我们现在人手很紧张，有两个服务员生病了）是服务员给出的服务差的原因解释，据此可以判断本题的正确答案是 A。第 3 题的正确答案是 B，是对前面说的 I'm afraid I'm not going to pay the service charge, or give a tip as I don't feel satisfied with it（因为我对服务不满意，所以我不会付服务费和小费）的补充解释和突出强调。

Dialogue Two

答案 4. A 5. B 6. C

详解

　　这段对话是顾客询问工作人员有关演出方面的一些问题。首先，应该明确三个答案选项的语法功能和语义。A 选项是主从复合句，意思是：我想知道现在在演什么？其中，be on（上演）是常用词组，通常指电影和演出的上演。B 选项是短回答，意思是：每天晚上，星期天除外。C 选项是完整句，意思是：你可以拿到打折的票。

　　其次，应该区分说话人的身份。其中，B 和 C 选项应该是 Clerk 的回答；而 A 选项是 Lady 的问题。因此，最容易判断的是第 4 题，只有这是顾客提出的问题，所以正确答案是 A。第三，认真阅读对话，特别是仔细体会空白处的上下文的语义。根据第 5 题前面的问题 When's it on, exactly（具体是什么时间演），本题的正确答案是 B。第 6 题正确答案是 C，与其后面的 It says here, "some tickets may be sold at half price half an hour before the performance starts."（这写着"在开演前半个小时，部分票可以半价销售"）语义相符。

Section B

答案 7. B 8. D 9. A 10. C

详解

　　这是一段招聘者面试求职者的对话。首先，应该明确四个答案选项的语法功能和语义。A 选项是完整句，语义是：我更喜欢在上午工作。B 选项是完整句，意思是：你完全能够胜任这个工作。C 选项是完整句，意思是：你下周就可以开始工作。D 选项是完整句，意思是：我意识到了这一点。

　　其次，应该区分说话人的身份。其中，显而易见，B 和 C 应该是招聘者说的话；因此，剩下的 A 和 D 选项应该是 Eddie 的回答。第三，认真阅读对话，特别是仔细体会空白处的上下文的语义。可以先判断招聘者说的第 7 和第 10 题，根据两个题目在对话中的位置可以做初步的判断，第 7 题对话开头处，正确答案应该是 B；第 10 题对话结尾处，正确答案应该是 C。此外，可以结合前后文语义做进一步的核对。B 与第 7 题后面的句子 We would be interested in having you work for us（我们有意请您为我们工作）语义相符；C 与第 10 题后面的句子 Mrs. Clarkson has got something ready for you（克拉克森女士已经为你准备好一些你要用的教具）以及 She'll show you around later（她会带你四处转转）语义相符。根据第 8 题前面招聘者所介绍的 You know that part-time employees don't get any other benefits besides their wages（你知道兼职员工是不享受工资之外的其他待遇的），本题是表示对这一情况的了解和理解，所以正确答案应该是 D。第 9 题之前谈到的是具体工作时间，之后是解释求职者要做的其他家务活，所以本题正确答案应该是 A。

Model Test Seven

Section A

Dialogue One

答案 1. C 2. B 3. A

详解

　　这是一段朋友之间关于坐船出游的对话。首先，应该明确三个答案选项的语法功能和语义。A 选项是一般疑问句；意思是：这就是全部的吗？B 选项是 but 引导的并列句；意思是：我希望我可以，但是我不能。其中，I wish I could 使用了虚拟语气。C 选项是完整句，意思是：那没什么了不起的。其中 no big deal（小事一桩）是常用习语。

　　其次，认真阅读对话，特别是仔细体会空白处的上下文的语义。根据第 1 题后面的句子 You could stay home and have the same thing（你待在家里同样可以享受这些）可以看出 Karen 对 Eddie 的建议不以为然，所以正确答案应该是 C。第 2 题前面 Eddie 所说的 We've both been working very hard and we deserve it, don't you think so?（我们工作都很努力，我们应该享受它，你不这么想吗？）是表达邀请，对于邀请的否定回答就是 B，也就是正确答案。第 3 题的正确答案是 A，这是 Eddie 在听完 Karen 描述自己晕船的感受后给出的评论。

Dialogue Two

答案 4. B 5. C 6. A

详解

　　这是一段夫妻之间在畅想假日旅行的对话。首先，应该明确三个答案选项的语法功能和语义。A 选项是完整句，意思是：尽管如此，但还是值得的。B 选项是一般疑问句，意思是：那不是很令人兴奋吗？C 选项是感叹句，意思是：我怎么能忘了呢。

　　其次，认真阅读对话，特别是仔细体会空白处的上下文的语义。根据第 4 题前面的 Well, the holidays will be coming soon（假期马上就要到了）以及后面的 Next week at this time, we will be traveling to the airport!（下周的这个时候我们已经在去机场的路上了），本题的正确答案应该是 B，表达的是对即将到来的假期旅行的兴奋和盼望。根据第 5 题前面的 Remember last time you were there? You got sunburnt because you stayed outside for too long.（记得上次你在那儿的情形吗？因为在外面待的时间太长了，你都晒黑了），本题的正确答案应该是 C；而且 C 中的 forget 和问题中 Remember 形成了词汇上的呼应。根据第 6 题前面的句子 I'm afraid it will cost us a lot of money again.（恐怕又要花掉我们一大笔钱），本题的正确答案应该是 A，和前面刚好构成转折关系，A 选项中的 it 代指的是前面的 a lot of money。

Section B

答案 7. D 8. A 9. C 10. B

详解

这段采访主要是围绕背景音乐的相关知识进行的。首先，应该明确四个答案选项的语法功能和语义。A 选项是完整句，语义是：它好像是有用的。B 选项是完整句，意思是：关于这个问题，我不太清楚。C 选项是主从复合句，意思是：这显示出你有多年轻。D 选项是完整句，意思是：到处你都能听到它。

其次，认真阅读对话，特别是仔细体会空白处的上下文的语义。在这四道题目中，最难判断的是第 8 题，应该先完成另外三道题目，最后结合排除法再来做第 8 题。根据第 7 题后面 in restaurants, airports, supermarkets, chain stores and department stores（在餐厅、机场、超市、连锁商店和百货商店）这些地点的列举可以判断，本题的正确答案应该是 D。根据第 9 题之前的句子 Now that I think about it, I can't remember when there wasn't background music in restaurants and stores（现在我想到它，几乎想不起在餐厅和商店没有背景音乐的时候）以及后面的句子 Actually, it all started during World War II when some factories had their own music band to keep workers happy and calm（实际上，它是第二次世界大战时才有的，当时一些工厂让自己的乐队演奏乐曲来使工人觉得平静和愉快），本题的正确答案应该是 C，谈到的都是时间问题。第 10 题前是一般疑问句 Do they play the same music for dinner and lunch?（他们午餐和晚餐放同样的音乐吗），本题应该给出回答，因此正确答案应该是 B，而且与其后面的 but I do know that hamburger places play fast music（但是，我确实知道快餐店放的是快节奏的音乐）语义连贯，合乎逻辑。最后，第 8 题的正确答案应该是 A，前面采访者对于 Pat 所说的背景音乐能使人保持好的情绪不以为然，而它后面的句子则说很多公司每年花很多的钱在背景音乐上，本题应该是承前启后的句子，起到转折作用，应该是肯定背景音乐的作用。

Model Test Eight

Section A

Dialogue One

答案 1. B 2. A 3. C

详解

这是一段发生在商场里顾客和售货员之间的对话。首先，应该明确三个答案选项的语法功能和语义。A 选项是祈使句，意思是：试试这双吧。B 选项是短回答，意思是：好的。C 选项是短结构，意思是：对不起。

其次，认真阅读对话，特别是仔细体会空白处的上下文的语义。根据第 1 题前面顾客所说的 I'm interested in buying a pair of shoes to match my trousers（我要买双鞋来配我的裤子）和后面的售货员接着说的 Do you want high heels or heels?（您是要高跟鞋还是普通跟），位于中间位置的适合第1题的答案应该是B。根据第2题后面顾客的回答 They fit perfectly（鞋穿着很合适），本题的正确答案应该是A。第3题的正确答案是C，excuse me 这个短语常用于向别人提问或请求别人帮助前，以示礼貌。

Dialogue Two

答案 4. A   5. C   6. B

详解

这是一段电话对话，在电话中顾客询问他所订的服装送货的问题。首先，应该明确三个答案选项的语法功能和语义。A选项是短回答，意思是：那很好。That would be fine 常常用于对建议的肯定回答。B选项是短结构，意思是：对了，还有一件事。C选项是主从复合句，意思是：恐怕那是不可能的。

其次，认真阅读对话，特别是仔细体会空白处的上下文的语义。三道题目中最难做的是第4题，可以先从后面两道题入手，最后再结合排除法来做第4题。根据第5题前面顾客的问题 Will they be ready in March?（三月份能好吗？）以及它后面订货登记员的补充回答 But we'll probably manage them in April（但是，四月可能没问题），中间应该是订货登记员给出的否定回答，所以正确答案应该是C。根据第6题前面的句子 Ok, that's fine for now（好的，现在先这样吧）以及它后面的 We'd like to cancel for those jackets with fur collars（我们要取消带毛领的夹克的订货）可以判断在对话的最后顾客在查询送货时间外又提出了其他的要求，所以本题的正确答案应该是B，起到了承上启下的作用。最后，第4题的答案应该是A，是对订货登记员给出的回答的反应，与下文中的 Ok, that's fine for now 的作用和语义相近。

Section B

答案 7. C   8. A   9. B   10. D

详解

这段对话是地方电视台的调查员登门调查观众喜爱什么样的节目。首先，应该明确四个答案选项的语法功能和语义。A选项是名词词组，语义是：儿童节目。B选项是完整句，意思是：它获得了很好的评价。C选项是完整句，意思是：不会占用您太多的时间。D选项是主从复合句，意思是：我觉得国际新闻应该再多点。

其次，认真阅读对话，特别是仔细体会空白处的上下文的语义。首先第7题位于对话的开头，而且根据它前面的被采访者说的 I'm rather busy at the moment（我现在很忙），以及后面来访者直接提出具体的问题可以判断居于中间的第7题正确答案应该是C。根据第8题前面的 Yes, my son Ben does（是的，我儿子本看）以及后面的来访者的问题 And do you find them fully suitable for your child（您觉得这些节目适合您孩子看吗），本题的正确答案是 A，介绍儿子看的什么节目，后面问题中的 them 指代的就是 The children's programs。根据第 9 题前面的对话内容，在听到被采访者不喜欢最近 9 点播放的侦探故事时，来访者觉得很惊讶，本题的正确答案应该是 B，解释了他吃惊的原因。根据第 10 题后面的 rather than news about the Queen, the Duchesses and other people of noble blood（而不是关于女王、公爵夫人或者其他的贵族的新闻），本题的正确答案应该是 D，其中 rather than（而不是）是表达对比关系的常用词组。

Model Test Nine

Section A

Dialogue One

答案 1. B　2. A　3. C

详解

这是一段发生在医院里医生和病人之间的对话，在对话中病人描述了自己的症状，医生做了检查、开了药方。首先，应该明确三个答案选项的语法功能和语义。A 选项是一般疑问句，意思是：能给我开点药吗？B 选项是一般疑问句，意思是：你觉得累吗？C 选项是短回答，意思是：可能，如果今天你能好好休息的话。

其次，应该区分说话人的身份。其中，显而易见，B 和 C 应该是医生说的话；因此，剩下的 A 应该是病人说的话。因此，3 个题目中最容易判断的是第 2 题，只有这句是病人说的，所以正确答案是 A。第三，认真阅读对话，特别是仔细体会空白处的上下文的语义。根据第 1 题前面的句子 You're looking pale（你看起来脸色苍白）以及后面的病人的回答 Yes, my whole body feels weak（是的，我全身无力），本题应该是一般疑问句，所以正确答案是 B。根据第 3 题前面病人的问题 Will I be able to go out tomorrow（我明天能出门吗），本题的正确答案应该是 C。

Dialogue Two

答案 4. C　5. A　6. B

详解

这是一段病人去药房抓药与药剂师之间的对话。首先，应该明确三个答案选项的语法功能和语义。A 选项是完整句，意思是：这是治咳嗽的。B 选项是短回答，通常是对道歉的回答，意思是：没关系。C 选项是完整句，意思是：这是你的药。

其次，认真阅读对话，特别是仔细体会空白处的上下文的语义。根据第 4 题前病人的要求 have these prescription filled（按药方抓药）以及药剂师的回答 Ok. Wait a few minutes, and I'll have them for you（好的，稍等，我给你抓），本题的正确答案应该是

C。根据第5题前面病人提出的问题 What is this medicine（这是什么药），本题的正确答案应该是 A。根据第6题前面病人认识到自己忘记付款后的道歉 Oh, I'm terribly sorry（我非常抱歉）本题的正确答案是 B。

Section B

答案 7. B 8. C 9. D 10. A

详解

  这段采访主要是关于 Mary 对计算机和网络的看法的对话。首先，应该明确四个答案选项的语法功能和语义。A 选项是完整句，语义是：就这么简单。B 选项是完整句，意思是：过去我害怕它们。C 选项是完整句，意思是：我离开它不行。D 选项是完整句，意思是：我过去要花很长时间。

  其次，认真阅读对话，特别是仔细体会空白处的上下文的语义。根据第7题前面记者的问题 What did you think about computers, before you got on the Internet（在你接触网络之前你是如何看待计算机的）以及它后面的补充回答 I knew I couldn't use them. I used to hate them（我知道我不会用。我恨它们），本题的正确答案应该是 B，表达的是过去对计算机的抵触情绪。根据第8题前面的问题 And how do you feel about them now（你现在的感觉呢），本题的正确答案是 C。第9题之前 Mary 详细地讲述了以前她需要去商店购物的经历：不得不上下楼梯，在商店里排队等，据此本题的正确答案应该是 D，是对过去购物经历的概括。第10题之前 Mary 描述了她现在如何购物，只需要坐在电脑前，点一下鼠标就可以轻松搞定，所以本题正确答案是 A。

Model Test Ten

Section A

Dialogue One

答案 1. B 2. C 3. A

详解

  这是一段夫妻之间商量如何收拾房子的对话。首先，应该明确三个答案选项的语法功能和语义。A 选项是完整句，意思是：我们将可以拥有它。B 选项是短回答，通常是对建议的回答，意思是：这个主意不错。C 选项是省略的特殊疑问句，意思是：车库怎么办呢？what about（怎么样）是常用词组。

  其次，认真阅读对话，特别是仔细体会空白处的上下文的语义。根据第1题前面 Mrs. Curry 提的建议 I'll phone Doris to come over to help, all right?（我给桃瑞丝打电话，让她来帮忙，好吗？）本题的正确答案应该是 B。根据第2题的前面 Mr. Curry 说的 The fence has to be repaired and painted, too（还需要修理和粉刷篱笆）以及它后面 Mrs. Curry

第一章 口语交际

说的 Can we get by without painting it for another year?（我们今年不粉刷它行吗?）可以判断，他们在这是讨论修理和粉刷什么地方，因此本题的正确答案是C。第3题的正确答案是A，是对前面 Shall we go to the movies Sunday night?（我们周天晚上去看电影吧?）这一建议的回答。

Dialogue Two

答案 4. B 5. A 6. C

详解

这段对话是朋友之间在讨论有没有必要通过上课来学习太极拳。首先，应该明确三个答案选项的语法功能和语义。A选项是反义疑问句，意思是：这有点愤世嫉俗了，不是吗? B选项是短回答，意思是：这对我来说就是浪费时间。C选项是短回答，意思是：不一定。

其次，认真阅读对话，特别是仔细体会空白处的上下文的语义。第4题前面 Catherine 介绍了她参加的太极拳课的内容和目标 It is a Chinese physical exercise designed for bodily well-being and also as an art of self-defense（它是中国的一种运动方式，有助于身体健康，同时也是一种自卫术），以及它后面 Robert 提出的问题 Why should you want to do that, to defend yourself from an attack?（你为什么要学这个，为了自卫吗?）可以看出 Robert 并不理解也不赞同 Catherine 的做法，所以本题的正确答案应该是B。根据第5题前面 Robert 所说的 Anyway, as far as I can see, there's no point in learning something like that if you can't earn some money from it（不管怎样，就我而言，如果你不能靠它挣钱的话，学习这个是毫无意义的），Catherine 的反应应该是A选项所表达的。第6题正确答案应该是C，是对前面问题 Anyway, you need to be a bit athletic, surely?（不管怎样，你需要身体强壮一些，对吗?）的回答。

Section B

答案 7. D 8. B 9. A 10. C

详解

这段问答是关于如何治疗感冒的对话。首先，应该明确四个答案选项的语法功能和语义。A选项是特殊疑问句，语义是：你建议吃什么药呢? B选项是主从复合句，意思是：当你觉得疼痛时，吃点阿司匹林会有帮助的。C选项是一般疑问句，意思是：你的意思是它们对牙齿不好，是吗? D选项是肯定回答，意思是：是的，恐怕是这样的。

其次，认真阅读对话，特别是仔细体会空白处的上下文的语义。根据第7题前面的一般疑问句 You seem to have a rather nasty cold yourself?（你好像感冒挺严重的吧?）

本题的正确答案应该是 D。由于第 8 题后面是采访者提出的问题，因此本题不可能是问题，所以正确答案应该是 B。根据第 9 题后面的句子 When you just have a cold, home remedies are probably best（当你感冒的时候，家庭疗法恐怕是最好的），本题应该是特殊疑问句，所以正确答案是 A。根据第 10 题后面的肯定回答 Yes, they are，本题应该是一般疑问句，所以正确答案是 C。

第二章 阅读理解

第一节 大纲要求简介

阅读理解部分在全部试卷中所占的分数比重最大,为25%,而且也是整个试卷语言难度最大的部分。第六版《大纲》对阅读理解部分的评价目标是"能综合运用英语语言知识和阅读技能,读懂一般性题材的文章、广告等应用性文本和博客及跟帖等互动形式的材料。要求能抓住大意,读懂细节,能理解上下文的逻辑关系,并能领会和分辨作者或话语参与各方的主要意图和态度及其异同等。"阅读理解部分在题型、题量、分值方面的规定是:

本部分共设25题,每题1分,考试时间为45分钟。本部分包括A、B两节,A节为段落阅读,B节的阅读形式可以是博客与跟帖或相关短文阅读、短文主题快读、广告浏览等。A节要求考生在对阅读材料理解的基础上从所给的4个备选答案中选出一个最佳答案。B节除了四选一以外,还可以在几份阅读材料的相应位置设置若干个空白,同时在它们前面提供同等数量的备选答案,要求考生根据考题指令从备选答案中为每个空白选出一个最佳答案。

第二节 大纲样题精讲

与第五版相比,第六版《大纲》和阅读理解部分的评价目标最大的不同就在于增加了对应用文题材的考查,在题型上增加了全新的题型,即B节的阅读。由于这种新题型在同等学力人员申请硕士学位英语水平全国统一考试中从未出现过,而且在全国性质的其他英语统考中也极为少见;而且像博客与跟帖、新闻报道这样的文章形式也是考生极为陌生的,对于大多数考生来说,这部分应该是难度最大的,因此下面我们就第六版《大纲》提供的三套样题进行具体的分析,帮助考生分析出题思路,明确备考要点。

样卷一

Section B

Directions: *In this section, you are required to read one quoted blog and the comments on* *it. The blog and comments are followed by questions or unfinished statements, each with four suggested answers A, B, C and D. Choose the best answer and mark your answer on the **Answer Sheet**.*

"Years ago, a friend of mine observed that 80 percent of the people in this country have too much self-esteem and 20 percent have much too little. That struck me as pretty accurate, but psychologists will tell you that self-esteem is not a constant. People's appraisal of their own worth varies...I have the impression that more people have unstable self-esteem than before. I say this because some of the traditional standards people used to measure their own worth have eroded (middle class respectability), whereas more people now seem to measure themselves against celebrities and superstars. It would be interesting to know if anybody has studied changes in the criteria we use to measure self-esteem."

Comment 1:

You bring up an interesting point because I do believe values and beliefs have changed. It would be very interesting to see the criteria used for self-worth. I find it hard to believe that only 20% of people have low self-esteem. I've been following Brene Brown's thoughts on the subject of self-worth, and low self-worth (on some level) seems much more common.

Comment 2:

If the quality of one's self-esteem is going to be judged by comparisons with those who are celebrities and superstars, then the entire exercise is really pointless.

Comment 3:

Self-esteem solution: A happy marriage.

Comment 4:

Ego (self-worth) is proportionate to wealth. The more wealth, the more self-worth.

Comment 5:

Benjamin Franklin said it best, and it applies to all facets of life. "Contentment will make a poor man rich just as discontent will make a rich man poor." It does not mean not try to do your best, or be the richest. It simply means once you've done your best be content with yourself, just as if you don't give your best effort discontent is sure to follow.

Comment 6:

I've "retired" from 30 years of expensive, if interesting, "personal growth" and "self-improvement," much probably motivated by trying to "fix" myself. Hanging out with friends at a local cafe is way more satisfying.

Comment 7:

A related concept you may be interested in is the "sociometer theory" of self-esteem, pioneered by Mark Leary (Wake Forest). Basically it states that our self-esteem is determined by the amount of perceived social acceptance/rejection, and that determination is full of cognitive biases and errors. Awesome stuff.

41. The main idea of the quoted blog is that _____.

A. most people in the country have too much self-esteem

B. it is urgent to help those who have too little self-esteem

C. the criteria for people to measure their self-worth are changing

D. the traditional standards make people feel unstable

42. Among all the comments, which of the following choices brings in authoritative sources in their discussions?

A. Comment 1 and Comment 2. B. Comment 3 and Comment 5.

C. Comment 1 and Comment 7. D. Comment 4 and Comment 6.

43. What all the commentators try to respond to in their writing is _____.

A. the respect for the traditional values

B. the standards of self-worth measurement

C. marriage, celebrities and social activities

D. ego, contentment and social judgment

44. Why does the writer of Comment 5 try to clarify Benjamin Franklin's saying?

A. Because Franklin's saying is universally applicable.

B. Because contentment means "rich" and discontent means "poor."

C. Because if you do your best, you will be the richest.

D. Because misunderstanding might occur of Franklin's saying.

45. What is the writer's attitude toward the "sociometer theory" in Comment 7?

A. Affirmative. B. Objective. C. Detached. D. Negative.

答案 41—45：CCBDD

详解

41. **主旨题。**本题做题的关键是找出博客的主题句和几个主要评论的共同点，同时可以结合排除法做题。博客的主题句应该是段尾句 It would be interesting to know if anybody has studied changes in the criteria we use to measure self-esteem.（了解是否有人研究过我们评价人的自我价值的标准所发生的变化一定是挺有趣的。）此外，but psychologists will tell you that self-esteem is not a constant. People's appraisal of their own worth varies…（但是，心理学家会告诉你自我价值不是恒定不变的。人们对自身价值的评价是变化的……）也是本段主题的体现。Comment 1 的主题句是段首的 You bring up an interesting point because I do believe values and beliefs have changed. It would be very interesting to see the criteria used for self-worth.（你提出了一个非常有趣的观点因为我确实相信价值观和信念已经发生了变化。关注评价自我价值的标准是很有趣的一件事情。）Comment 2 只有一句话，该句话体现主题的关键词是 the quality of one's self-esteem is going to be judged by…（由……来评价一个人自我价值的本质。）Comment 3 和 Comment 4 都介绍了自己对自我价值的评价标准：Comment 3 认为是 A happy marriage（幸福的婚姻），而 Comment 4 则认为 Ego (self-worth) is proportionate to wealth（自我价值和财富是成正比的），即财富越多，自我价值就越高。Comment 5 主要是讨论了富兰克林的名言 Contentment

will make a poor man rich just as discontent will make a rich man poor（满足可以让穷人觉得富有，就像不满会让富人觉得贫穷一样），这也是在讨论应该如何评价自我价值。Comment 6 是谈了评论者自己的自我价值观。Comment 7 所引用并评论的 "sociometer theory"（社会尺度理论）所信奉的 our self-esteem is determined by the amount of perceived social acceptance/rejection（我们的自我价值是由我们所接受的社会认可/拒绝所决定的），讨论的还是评价自我价值的标准。所以 C 选项 the criteria for people to measure their self-worth are changing（人们评价他们自我价值的标准在变化）是正确答案。而 A 选项 most people in the country have too much self-esteem（这个国家的大多数人对自己评价过高）只是博客中涉及的细节，其他评论中没有提及；B 选项 it is urgent to help those who have too little self-esteem（现在迫切需要帮助那些自我评价过低的人）和 D 选项 the traditional standards make people feel unstable（那些传统标准让人觉得不稳定）是原文中未涉及的内容。

42. **推断题**。做题关键是要准确理解题目的意思，特别是关键词 authoritative sources（权威观点），应该指的是名人名言或者理论。本题根据原文中人名和专有名词的线索做题最为快捷，Comment 1 中的 Brene Brown、Comment 5 中的 Benjamin Franklin 以及 Comment 7 的 "sociometer theory" 都属于 authoritative sources，而其他评论中则均未涉及，因此可以判断正确答案应该是 C。

43. **主旨题**。本题问的是所有评论中都涉及的内容，做题方法同 41 题，概括各个评论的共同主题，可以判断正确答案应该是 B 选项 the standards of self-worth measurement（自我价值的评价标准）。而 A 选项 the respect for the traditional values（对传统价值理念的尊重）是原文基本未涉及的内容；C 选项 marriage, celebrities and social activities（婚姻、名人和社会活动）只是个别评论中谈到的，例如：marriage 只有 Comment 3 中提到了；D 选项 ego, contentment and social judgment（自我，满足和社会评价）也是如此，例如 social judgment（社会评价）只是 Comment 7 的内容。

44. **推断题**。首先根据题目关键词 Benjamin Franklin's saying 在 Comment 5 中定位，找出原文中的答案，然后再进行合理的推断，同时也可以结合排除法做题。本题在原文中的答案应该是 It does not mean not try to do your best, or be the richest. It simply means once you've done your best be content with yourself, just as if you don't give your best effort discontent is sure to follow.（这句话并不意味着不用尽力做到最好，或者不要做最富有的人，而仅仅意味着一旦你尽力去做了，就应该对自己满意，就像如果你不尽力的话，你一定会对自己不满一样。）这两句话的作用应该是来解释 Franklin 的名言的真正含义，之所以需要解释应该是因为人们对此有误解，因此正确答案应该是 D 选项 Because misunderstanding might occur of Franklin's saying（因为会产生对 Franklin 的名言的误解）。尽管 A 选项 Because Benjamin Franklin's saying is universally applicable（因为 Franklin 的名言是普遍适用的）中的 Benjamin Franklin's saying is universally applicable 与原文中 it applies to all facets of life（它适用于生活的所有方面）的语义一致，但是却不是本题所问的 clarify（澄清）Franklin 的名言的原因。而 B 选项 Because contentment means "rich" and discontent means "poor"（因为满足意味着"富有"而不满足则意味着"贫穷"）和 C 选项 Because if you do your best, you will be the richest（因为如果你尽力了，你就会成

为最富有的）都和原文意思不符。

45. **主观态度推断题**。根据 Comment 7 中的评论 that determination is full of cognitive biases and errors（这一决定充满了认知的偏见和错误）以及 Awesome stuff（可怕的东西）可以判断作者对"sociometer theory"的态度是否定的，因此 D 选项 Negative（负面的，否定的）是正确答案。而 A 选项 Affirmative（肯定的）、B 选项 Objective（客观的）以及 C 选项 Detached（分离的）均与原文表达不符。

样卷二

Section B

Directions: *In this section, you are required to read several excerpts from newspapers or magazines. These excerpts are followed by four questions or unfinished statements, each with four suggested answers A, B, C and D. Choose the best answer and mark your answer on the **Answer Sheet**.*

Excerpt 1:

Sales of e-readers surged during the Christmas holiday season, according to a Pew Research Center report, which showed that the number of adults in the United States who owned tablets nearly doubled from mid-December to early January.

Excerpt 2:

Apple, based in Cupertino, California, controls 73% of the market, while Samsung Electronic Co., Sony Corp. and Toshiba Corp. are among companies making constant improvements on tablets without bringing services that cut into the market share, Sarah Rotman Epps, an analyst at Forrester, said in the report.

Excerpt 3:

Under Square's year-long pilot program, an iPad would be installed in the space where Taxi TVs currently sit, and the driver would have an iPhone to process credit-card payments. The technology would allow drivers to accept a passenger's card at any point during the ride, then enter the amount later. The system charges drivers less in credit card transaction fees than the current rates.

Excerpt 4:

When Apple introduced the iPad tablet computer in 2010, it was doing what it likes to do best: creating a new category to dominate, as it had done with the iPod and iPhone. By the end of the year, the company had sold nearly 15 million iPads, generating about $9.5 billion in revenue.

Just two years later, the chief executive of Apple, Timothy D. Cook, has a prediction: the day will come when tablet devices like the Apple iPad outsell traditional personal computers.

Excerpt 5:

Apple has made its first attempt to quantify how many American jobs can be credited to the sale of its iPads and other products, a group that includes the Apple engineers who design the devices and the drivers who deliver them—even the people who build the trucks that get them there.

On Friday, the company published the results of a study it commissioned saying that it had "created or supported" 514,000 American jobs. The study is an effort to show that Apple's benefit to the American job market goes far beyond the 47,000 people it directly employs here.

Excerpt 6:

People who read e-books on tablets like the iPad are realizing that while a book on a black-and-white Kindle is straightforward and immersive, a tablet offers a menu of distractions that can fragment the reading experience, or stop it in its tracks.

E-mail lurks tantalizingly within reach. Looking up a tricky word or unknown fact in the book is easily accomplished through a quick Google search. And if a book starts to drag, giving up on it to stream a movie over Netflix or scroll through your Twitter feed is only a few taps away.

42. What is said about Apple Inc. with its tablet devices like iPads?
 A. It doubled its sale of e-readers during the Christmas season.
 B. It controls 73% of the tablet device market.
 C. It charges customers less in credit card transaction fees.
 D. It has long been selling its traditional personal computers.

43. Which of the following choices involve the creation of tablet devices and its possible replacement of Taxi TVs?
 A. Excerpt 1 and Excerpt 5.　　　B. Excerpt 3 and Excerpt 4.
 C. Excerpt 2 and Excerpt 6.　　　D. Excerpt 3 and Excerpt 5.

44. Tablet devices can miraculously perform many functions but they also cause the problem of _____.
 A. its rivals succeeding in cutting into the market share
 B. failing to process credit-card payments with an iPhone
 C. e-book readers being distracted from their normal reading
 D. misleading the trucks that get them to the tablet market

45. It can be inferred from one of the excerpts that a successful company should take the social responsibility of _____.
 A. filing reports to the agencies like Pew Research Center
 B. installing its products in the space where Taxi TVs sit
 C. predicting the trends in product design and manufacturing
 D. creating more jobs for people to be involved in its business operation

答 案 42—45：BBCD

详 解

42. **细节题。** 根据答案选项中的关键词，逐一回原文中定位并比对。根据A选项的关键词 Christmas season 回原文定位，它在原文中的出处是 Excerpt 1 中的第一句话。A 选项 It doubled its sale of e-readers during the Christmas season（在圣诞节这段时间里苹果的电子阅读机的数量增长了一倍）与原文 the number of adults in the United States who owned tablets nearly doubled from mid-December to early January（从12月中旬到1月初美国拥有平板电脑的成人人数将近增长了一倍）意思不符。根据 B 选项的关键词73%回原文定位，它在原文中的出处是 Excerpt 2 中的第一句话。B 选项 It controls 73% of the tablet device market.（它占据了73%的平板电脑市场）与 Excerpt 2 中的第一句话的主句意思完全一致，因此是正确答案。而 C 选项 It charges customers less in credit card transaction fees（它收取消费者的信用卡的交易费较少）与原文 Excerpt 3 的最后一句 The system charges drivers less in credit card transaction fees than the current rates（这一系统收取司机信用卡的交易费要比现有利率低）语义不符。D 选项 It has long been selling its traditional personal computers（苹果销售传统的个人电脑已经很长时间了）在原文中未曾涉及。

43. **细节题**。首先应该读懂题目，本题问的是哪个选项涉及了平板电脑的发明以及它可能会取代计程车上的电视。然后根据题目关键词 Taxi TVs 回原文定位，通过速读可以发现，Taxi TVs 出现在 Excerpt 3 中，据此可以排除 A、C 两个选项。接着再判断 Excerpt 4 和 Excerpt 5 到底是哪个提及了问题所问的内容。Excerpt 5 谈到的是苹果创造的工作岗位，与本题内容无关，因此可以将 D 选项排除。

44. **细节题**。本题做题的关键是正确理解题目，并抓住题目关键词。本题的意思是：平板电脑出色地完成了多项任务，但是也引起了怎样的问题？题目关键词 cause the problem，原文中只有 Excerpt 6 第一段最后一句提到了平板电脑存在的问题。根据原文中的表述 a tablet offers a menu of distractions that can fragment the reading experience, or stop it in its tracks（平板电脑提供了可能让人分心的菜单内容，它们会割裂阅读经历或者中断阅读）可以发现正确答案是 C 选项。而 A 选项 its rivals succeeding in cutting into the market share（它的竞争对手正在侵吞它的市场份额）、B 选项 failing to process credit-card payments with an iPhone（没能通过 iPhone 进行信用卡付费）和 D 选项 misleading the trucks that get them to the tablet market（误导了将它们运送到市场的卡车）均是原文未涉及的内容，与原文不符。

45. **推断题**。首先应该正确理解题目，本题的意思是：一个成功的公司应该承担怎样的社会责任？题目关键词是 the social responsibility，这一点仅出现在 Excerpt 5 中。通过概括 Excerpt 5 两段的内容，可以判断 D 选项 creating more jobs for people to be involved in its business operation（在它的经营中为人们创造更多的工作机会）是正确答案。而 A 选项 filing reports to the agencies like Pew Research Center（像 Pew Research Center 这样的机构撰写报告）、B 选项 installing its products in the space where Taxi TVs sit（把它的产品安装在计程车电视的位置上）以及 C 选项 predicting the trends in product design and manufacturing（预计产品设计和制造的趋势）都不能算是社会责任，不符合题目要求。

样卷三

Section B

Directions: *In this section, you are required to read four pieces of news and decide which of the four titles marked A, B, C and D is best suited to each of them. Choose the best answer and mark your answer on the **Answer Sheet**.*

A. Nokia posts $1.38 bn loss in the fourth qtr

B. Gold surges to 7-week high of $1,720

C. R-Power ropes in German utility for mining

D. "We are creating, not stealing jobs in U.S., Europe"

(42) _____

LONDON: Gold prices soared Thursday to the highest level in almost seven weeks as the dollar weakened after the U.S. Federal Reserve vowed to keep interest rates near zero for more than 2 years.

The precious metal rose up to $1,720.35 an ounce on the London Bullion Market—the highest level since December 9 but still far below the record peak of $1,921.15 struck on September 6.

"With the U.S. Federal pledging to keep interest rates in check until late 2014, gold soared," said Rose Norman, boss of British-based bullion broker Sharp Pixley. "Although there was heavy speculative buying, anxious investors joined the fray who are concerned by currency depreciation as global central banks use easy monetary policies to flood markets with cash."

(43) _____

Davos: With HCL Tech announcing 10,000 jobs for locals in the U.S. and Europe, India Inc on Thursday chose the WEF meet to send a strong message that India IT firms are creating and not stealing jobs in troubled western economies. A message emerged from British PM David Cameron's advice to EU that instead of being a threat, emerging economies like India can be of great help to Europe.

Concluding FTA with India by the year-end would be in Europe's interest, he said. "There has to be FTAs, bilateral trade agreements with countries like India and Singapore along with other countries," he said.

(44) _____

Helsinki: Mobile phone maker Nokia Corp posted a fourth-quarter net loss of 1.70 billion euro ($1.38 bn) as sales slumped 21% even as the company's first Window smartphones hit markets in Europe and Asia. The loss compares with a profit of 745 million euro in the same period a year earlier.

Nokia said net revenue, including both its mobile phones and its network divisions, fell from 12.6 billion euro in the Q4 of 2010 to 10 billion, with smartphones plunging 23%. Nokia has lost its once-dominance in the global cell phone market, with Android phones and iPhones overtaking it in the growing smartphone segment. Nokia is attempting a comeback with phones using Microsoft's Window software, a struggle that CEO Stephen Elop characterized as "war of eco-systems."

(45) _____

New Delhi: Anil Ambani's R-Power has roped in RWE Power International of Germany to help the company with extracting coal from its captive mines of the Tilaiya ultra-mega power project, the third such plant the government has mandated the company to set up.

RWE Power is one of Europe's leading energy utilities and German's biggest coal miner. The company would help R-Power design and plan the engineering aspects of captive mine and procurement of equipment and ensure quality control. Government has allocated Kerendari Band C coal blocks of North Karanpura coal fields in Jharkhand to meet the fuel requirements of the Tilaiya project. These mines have reserve of over 1 billion ton. The company plans to produce 40 million tons of coal per year.

答案 42—45：BDAC

详解

首先，抓住小标题的关键词，应该是标题中最突出的人名、地名、数字及专有名词等，以此为线索回原文的新闻中比对。其次，可以核对标题意思与新闻主要意思是否一致。新闻主旨的表达基本是在新闻的第一句话中。

根据 A 选项中的 Nokia 回原文定位，应该是 44 的内容。A 选项 Nokia posts $1.38 bn loss in the fourth qtr（诺基亚宣布在第四个季度中损失了10.38亿美元）与原文首句 Mobile phone maker Nokia Corp posted a fourth-quarter net loss of 1.70 billion euro（$1.38 bn）as sales slumped 21% even as the company's first Window smartphones hit markets in Europe and Asia（手机制造商诺基亚宣布由于销售下滑公司在第四个季度中损失了10.38亿美元，尽管公司的第一款 Window 智能手机登陆欧洲及亚洲市场）语义相符。

根据 B 选项的关键词 Gold 回原文定位，应该是 42 的内容。B 选项 Gold surges to 7-week high of $1,720（黄金价位飙升至7周以来的最高值1,720美元）与原文第一句 Gold prices soared Thursday to the highest level in almost seven weeks as the dollar weakened after the U.S. Federal Reserve vowed to keep interest rates near zero for more than 2 years（由于美联储2年多前决心将存款利率维持在零利率左右，美元持续走低，因此周四黄金价位飙升至近7周以来的最高值）语义一致。

根据 C 选项中的关键词 R-Power 回原文定位，应该是 45 的内容。C 选项 R-Power ropes in German utility for mining（R-Power 劝说德国矿业公司加入）与原文第一句 Anil Ambani's R-Power has roped in RWE Power International of Germany to help the company with extracting coal from its captive mines of the Tilaiya ultra-mega power project, the third plant the government has mandated the company to set up.（Anil Ambani's R-Power 已经说服德国的 RWE Power International 加入帮助该公司在 Tilaiya 超大发电站项目中他们所取得的煤矿采煤，该项目是政府要求公司建立的第三大发电厂）语义相符。

D 选项是 43 的内容。"We are creating, not stealing jobs in U.S., Europe" 就是原文第一句话 With HCL Tech announcing 10,000 jobs for locals in the U.S. and Europe, India Inc on Thursday chose the WEF meet to send a strong message that India IT firms are creating and not stealing jobs in troubled western economies（随着 HCL Tech 宣布在美国和欧洲给当地人提供1万个工作岗位，印度有限公司选择在世界教育联谊会上明确表明印度的信息科技业正在为困境中的西方经济创造工作岗位，而不是窃取工作岗位）中的内容。

第三节　考试要点归纳

三套样卷 B 节阅读给出的三篇文章的文章特色和语言难度如下：第一，三篇都是应用文体裁的。第一篇是博客及跟帖；第二篇是报纸或杂志上的新闻摘选；第三篇是新闻报道。第二，文章长度与 A 节文章长度基本一样。第一篇是 384 个单词；第二篇是 439 个单词；第三篇是 485 个单词。第三，三篇文章的题材涉及了社会现象、社会热点以及经济民生。第一篇是关于自我评价的标准问题的探讨；第二篇是苹果平板电脑对市场和人们生活的影响；第三篇是经济方面的各种新闻报道，涉及了从黄金价格的飙升到诺基亚的亏损等话题。从选择的这些题材上，能够看出其突出的特色就是新，紧跟最新的新闻时事。第四，文章语言难度大。由于文章题材是应用文，且以新闻时事为主，因此文章中出现了大量的专业术语以及新词，甚至有不少超纲的词汇。

就出题形式而言，样卷一和样卷二沿用了 A 节阅读的四选一的选择题出题方式。就题目所考查的阅读能力而言，着重考查考生把握文章的主旨大意、具体细节以及引申推断的能力。就具体题型而言，这 9 道题目中包含 1 道主旨题、4 道细节题、1 道主观态度题、3 道逻辑推断题。能够看出这种选择题的出题思路与 A 节阅读的一致，与前些年考题中阅读部分的出题思路一致。样卷三的出题模式是小标题对应模式，这是以往阅读真题中未出现的，主要考查学生把握新闻主旨的能力。

综上，不难看出阅读 B 节新题型的增加，加大了阅读部分的考试难度。因此，考生在阅读理解备考过程中应该着重做好以下几点：第一，进行充分的知识储备。根据对样题的分析，本部分的知识储备主要包括两部分：正确的阅读习惯和有效的阅读技巧，特别是短时间内快速浏览寻找信息的技巧以及阅读核心词汇的能力。第二，掌握有效的做题方法。第三，进行有针对性的训练。本章第四节为考生提供了阅读理解所需的阅读技巧和核心词汇；第五节提供了十五套样题，即《大纲》样卷中涉及的三种不同体裁的文章各五篇；第六节样题详解中除了解释做题涉及的知识点外，还介绍了做具体每道题目最直接有效的方法，并提供了全文翻译。

第二章　阅读理解

 第四节　核心知识储备

一、阅读理解的技巧和方法

在考试中，考生需要在既定的时间内完成大量的阅读任务，因此仅有坚实的语言基础还远远不够，考生还需培养正确的阅读习惯，掌握一定的阅读技巧和方法，从而在保证阅读正确率的基础上提高阅读速度。本篇旨在帮助考生训练并养成正确的阅读习惯和阅读方法。

1. 克服不良的阅读习惯

要养成正确的阅读习惯，首先要克服不良的阅读习惯。在有效阅读时，眼的快速接受活动和脑的紧张处理活动应是一个同时进行的整体活动。一切外来的活动参与都是多余的，它对阅读非但没有帮助，反而会减慢阅读速度，分散阅读注意力。许多未受过良好阅读训练的人往往有很多不良的阅读习惯，列举如下：

（1）转头阅读。

这种不良习惯表现在阅读时，读者随着眼球视线的移动头也跟着视线移动。这种毛病主要是学生阅读时始终把自己的鼻尖对准他正在阅读的每个词。这样他顺着词一行一行往下读时，头也随之不断地移动。另外，这个毛病的出现还有可能是因读者坐姿不正确，眼睛离开书本距离过近。美国哈佛医学院眼科学教授 David Millei 提出，"正常人在阅读距离为 33 厘米时，眼睛可以看到长度中等的三个词"。因此，只要坐姿距离正确，眼球移动视线跨度完全能够扫过书本。用不着借助颈部的移动。

（2）指词阅读。

这种不良习惯表现为，学生在阅读时经常用手指、铅笔或米尺等其他东西指着词一个一个地看。这种表象多数出现在阅读能力比较差的阅读者中。他们为了集中注意力，不让视线左右复视，往往借助于某种东西控制自己的视线，并且依赖这种东西引导自己的阅读。很显然，这种阅读方式不仅会减慢阅读的速度，而且会使学生的注意力集中于一个个的单词上，很难抓住句子的实际含义。一般的读者完全不需要用手或其他东西帮助阅读。他们的眼睛完全能在书页上逐行移动。

（3）出声阅读。

它的主要表现形式是：学生在阅读时把所看到的每个词都一个一个地轻声读出来，近似喃喃自语（并非朗读）。还有一种表现形式，即读者阅读时虽然不发出轻微的声音，但是他的嘴唇、舌、喉头却默默地活动。它的弊病主要是使阅读速度受到了说话速度的限制。由于发音器官参与了阅读，读者一部分注意力转移到如何声读某个词，读错了还可能会重读。因而，逐词念出来如同指词阅读一样，容易分散阅读注意力，并且也影响对文章的篇章理解。

（4）重复阅读。

这是指读者在阅读的过程中，眼睛的视线短暂地停留在某几个词上，或者来回反复地看几个词。这种现象的发生往往是读者在阅读中碰到了生词，一下子给卡住了，或者是不理解短语或句子的意思，也有可能阅读速度过慢导致看到后面忘了前面，整个意思连不起来。为了完全搞清楚整句的意思，重读一遍是很有必要的，不过不宜过于频繁，否则很有可能养成重复阅读的不良习惯。

以上这些不良的阅读习惯都会影响考生的有效阅读，大大降低考生的阅读速度，因此考生应该首先纠正这些习惯。

2. 养成正确的阅读习惯

对考生来说，克服逐词阅读，养成按意群阅读的良好的阅读习惯是非常必要的。众所周知，一个句子的意思是由一个个相互联系的语义单位所组成。因此，一个高效的阅读者在阅读时，他两眼的注视点不是在单个的单词上，而是集中在一个具有特定意义的较大语言单位上。也就是说，他是根据句子中出现的一个个完整的、有意义的意群进行阅读。采用这种阅读法，阅读者停顿的注视点比逐词阅读大大减少，从而可以大大提高阅读速度，而且按照意群阅读，可以给读者形成一个更大更完整的句意概念，从而极大地提高了阅读理解率。一般来说，可以按照句子的一般语法结构把它划分成以下意群视读单位：

（1）短句。
    a. How are you?
    b. Here it is.
    c. It's 12 o'clock.

（2）名词短语。
    a. an old man
    b. boys and girls

（3）介词、不定式、分词短语。
    a. in the morning
    b. to be honest
    c. frankly speaking
    d. greatly influenced by his teacher

（4）动词短语。
    a. break out
    b. take the place of
    c. give up

（5）主谓结构。
    a. The boy is sitting between his father and mother.
    b. He has been studying for hours.
    c. It is supposed to be true.

（6）动宾结构。
    a. help him
    b. try to stop
    c. enjoy your time

（7）系表结构。
    a. sound interesting

b. look pretty

c. is nice

(8) 动状结构。

a. run fast

b. stand outside

c. study very hard

(9) 从句。

a. Could you tell me where the dean is?

b. If I were you, I wouldn't believe this.

c. What he told you is true.

意群单位的划分不是绝对的。初练者注视的意群单位可以小一些，注视的次数可以多一些。随着训练的增加，技能的提高，注视面可以逐渐扩大，停顿的次数逐渐减少。

训练按意群阅读的方法如下：

方法一

用挖有一个长方形孔的卡片盖住词组。

然后用卡片由上往下迅速移动，注意迅速阅读孔里露出来的词组。

这样读完一组词组后，接着回答下面的问题。用"∨"表示你所选择的答案。

你能在两分钟内读完下列十组词组，并回答六个以上的问题吗？你可以反复练习，不断提高你成语阅读的习惯。第一组例解。

all objects

    all places

    all people

    all pipes

    all lamps

       What have you learned?

    books _____

    papers _____

    places ____∨____

for example

    in general

    in conclusion

    on purpose

    in the end

    at command

       What has not been mentioned?

    instance _____

    general _____

    conclusion _____

at large
   at last
   at length
   at night
   at noon
   at random
   in common
   in abundance
   in appearance
   in addition
      What has been mentioned?
   charge _____
   combination _____
   random _____
in detail
   in English
   in earnest
   in essence
   in front
   in number
   in point
   in position
   no matter
   nothing else
      What has not been mentioned?
   number _____
   earnest _____
   abstain _____
at a disadvantage
   at a distance
   at full speed
   break the record
   by any means
   by all accounts
      What has been mentioned?
   might _____
   equation _____
   speed _____
by the hour

by the way

catch up with

close the switch

come in contact

come into fashion

　　　What has not been mentioned?

switch _____

fashion _____

reason _____

the windows are close

　　the door is open

　　the lights are off

　　at a different time

　　in a different direction

　　at a different speed

　　　　What has been mentioned?

experiment _____

room _____

lights _____

a row of columns

　　all large buildings

　　test the experimenter

　　the bottom is thick

　　the top is dark

　　the walls are stone

　　　　What has not been mentioned?

bottom _____

columns _____

stairs _____

about 3 years ago

　　a very useful metal

　　the most useful metal

　　less and less useful

　　of all the alloys

　　to make it stronger

　　　　What has been mentioned?

years _____

months _____

weeks _____

    from side to side
      oil trade of tomorrow
      synthetic food from coal
      from within the earth
      high on the list
      oil in the sea-bed
        What has not been mentioned?
      side _____
      girl _____
      food _____

方法二

将短文中句子分成若干个意群，意群与意群之间用斜线分开，这样考生可以训练自己对意群的敏感性。例如：

I

  Asia-Pacific Economic Cooperation (APEC) / should play an even more important role / in promoting regional economic growth and prosperity, /said by President Jiang Zemin/ yesterday.

  The region's biggest informal forum APEC /recognizes "the reality of diversity in the region /and holds the key to/ the success of its member economies /through closer cooperation," /he said /during the meeting of leaders/ from APEC member economies.

  The Ninth APEC Economic Leaders' Meeting /concluded yesterday /in Shanghai /as eight months of multilevel gatherings /culminated with a joint declaration/ addressing the global economic pains and efforts/ to balance globalization. The group also issued a statement /contemning terrorism/ as symbolized by the Sep. 11 terrorist attack/ on the United States.

  The leaders clad /in traditional Chinese silk attire, /concluded their annual gathering yesterday/ with a vision for a bright future/ in defiance of the current hardships /and promises for closer cooperation.

  "The meeting has attained/ all its expected goals," / Jiang told reporters/ during a press conference. "APEC members are satisfied with /the achievements of the meeting, / believing that it is a meeting /of great significance/ and far-reaching impact."

  By hosting this year's APEC meetings/ on the brink of/ its pending entry into WTO, / China has demonstrated/ its commitment to its opening up /and reform policies, /Jiang said.

II

  Exchange a glance/ with someone, /then look away. Do you realize /that you have made a statement? Hold the glance/ for a second longer, /and you have made a different statement. Hold it /for 3 seconds, /and the meaning has changed again. For every social situation, /there is a permissible time /that you can hold a person's gaze /without being intimate, rude, or aggressive. If you are on an elevator, /what gaze-time /are you permitted? To answer this question, /consider what you typically do. You are very likely to /give other passengers /a quick glance /to size them up（打量）/and to assure them/ that you mean no threat. Since being close to another person /signals the possibility of interaction, /you need to /emit a signal /telling others /you want to be left alone. So you cut off eye contact, /what sociologist Erving Goffman (1963) calls/ "a dimming of the lights." You look down /at the floor, /at the indicator lights, /anywhere but into another passenger's eyes. Should you break /the rule against staring at a stranger /on an elevator, / you will make the other person /exceedingly uncomfortable, / and you are likely to /feel a bit strange yourself.

If you hold eye contact /for more than 3 seconds, /what are you telling another person? Much depends on /the person and the situation. For instance, /a man and a woman/ communicate interest in this manner. They typically /gaze at each other /for about 3 seconds /at a time, /then drop their eyes down/ for 3 seconds, before letting their eyes meet again. But if one man/ gives another man/ a 3-second-plus stare, /he signals, "I know you," / "I am interested in you," /or "You look peculiar /and I am curious about you." This type of stare / often produces hostile feelings.

III

In the old days, /children were familiar with /birth and death/ as part of life. This is perhaps /the first generation of /American youngsters（年轻人）/who have never been close by / during the birth of a baby /and have never experienced /the death of a family member.

Nowadays /when people grow old, /we often send them to nursing homes. When they get sick, /we transfer them to a hospital, /where children are forbidden /to visit terminally ill patients /even when those patients are their parents. This deprives（剥夺）the dying patient of / significant family members/ during the last few days of his life /and it deprives the children of /an experience of death, /which is an important learning experience.

Some of my colleagues and I/ once interviewed and followed / approximately 500 terminally ill patients /in order to find out /what they could teach us /and how we could be of more benefit, /not just to them /but to the members of their families as well. We were most impressed by /the fact that /even those patients /who were not told of their serious illness /were quite aware of /its potential outcome.

It is important /for family members, and doctors and nurses /to understand these patients' communications /in order to/ truly understand their needs, fears, and fantasies（幻想）. Most of our patients/ welcomed another human being/ with whom they could talk openly, honestly, and frankly /about their trouble. Many of them /shared with us /their tremendous need /to be informed, / to be kept up-to-date on their medical condition /and to be told when the end was near. We found out /that patients who had been dealt with openly and frankly /were better able to /cope with the approach of death / and finally to reach a true stage of acceptance/ prior to death.

二、掌握正确有效的阅读方法

应试者在阅读时，除了要养成良好的阅读习惯外，还应掌握正确而有效的阅读方

法。高效的阅读者会因阅读的目的不同而采用不同的阅读方法。总的来说,一般有三种阅读方法:

(1) 第一种是略读。所谓略读,就是一种带有一般了解目的的快速阅读法。在进行略读时,阅读者不需要将文章全文看完,也不需要对文章有百分之百的理解。它只是阅读者的一种概要性浏览,抓住文章的主旨,判断有无自己感兴趣的信息或材料,这种阅读方法通常用于阅读日常报纸杂志,或查寻所需材料。在平时阅读训练时,阅读者可采用以下几种方法进行练习,来提高略读技巧。

① 略读时一定要以最快的速度进行阅读。

② 由于阅读速度快,理解水平有所降低,一般理解率能够达到百分之五十或六十即可。

③ 要特别注意文章的标题、副标题、小标题以及某些标点符号,如破折号、引号等。这些往往能够告诉我们文章大致讲了些什么内容。

④ 通常应认真地阅读文章第一、第二两段。这两段常常是引入段或总起段,作者在这两段通常都会交代写作的目的和文章的大概内容。弄清这两段,有助于弄清文章的大意、背景、作者的写作目的、风格和语气等。一旦我们抓住了中心思想就可以把注意力放在快速浏览段落的主题句或结论句上,从而抓住段落大意。段落的主题句或结论句通常会在段首或段末的位置,因此阅读时应多注意这些位置。对于具体的细节部分可以不读,只用眼睛粗略地扫视一下,注意若干的关键词、词组或数字即可。同时也要特别注意最后一段,因为最后一段往往是结论所在。

⑤ 在快速略读时还应注意文章中出现的各种连接手段。通过掌握表示对比、转折、因果、总结等不同逻辑关系的各种连接手段来把握文章的结构。

例1:

Car Running Instructions

Filling up with fuel

When filling up with fuel, avoid overfilling the tank. The fuel should not be visible in the filler intake tube. If it is and the car is left in the sun, the fuel may expand. Then there is a danger of fuel leakage. If the tank is accidentally overfilled, park the car in the shade with the filler as high as possible.

Starting

Check that the gear lever is in the neutral position and that the hand-brake is on. If the engine is cold, pull out the mixture control (choke). Switch on the ignition, check that the ignition and oil-pressure lights glow, and operate the starter. As soon as the engine starts, release the ignition key and warm up the engine. Check that oil-pressure gauge is registering or that the oil-pressure light goes out.

Warming up

Warming up the engine by allowing it to idle slowly is harmful and leads to excessive cylinder wear. The correct procedure is to let the engine run fairly fast, approximately one thousand revolutions (revs) per minute (1,000 rpm), corresponding to a speed of twenty-five kilometers per hour (25 kph) in top gear. This allows it to reach the correct working temperature as quickly as possible. Far less damage is done by driving the car from cold, than by letting the engine idle slowly.

Running in

The way a new car is looked after will have an important effect on its future life. Engine and road speeds during this early period must be limited. During the first eight hundred kilometers:

Do not exceed seventy kilometers per hour. Do not operate at full throttle in any gear. Do not allow the engine to labor in any gear.

After the running-in period, speeds should be gradually increased up to the maximum performance.

Ignition light

The light should glow when the ignition is switched on. It should go out and stay out at all times while the engine is running above normal idling speed. On cars with an alternator, the warning light should go out immediately the engine is started. Failure to do so shows a fault in the battery charging system. Check that the fan-belt is correctly tensioned, before consulting your dealer.

Temperature gauge

When the engine is running, the gauge shows the temperature of the coolant leaving the cylinder head. When the ignition is switched off, the needle returns to the 'cold' position.

这段说明文字共有六段，每一段以黑体词点出中心意思。通过阅读文章的题目《汽车运行指南》，我们就可以了解本文的体裁是说明文，文章的主要内容是关于汽车运行时的注意事项。再通过阅读各段的黑体词，我们就可知道每一段是关于汽车运行哪一方面的指令性说明。如果我们只对其中一条或数条感兴趣，则可较细心地读完有关段落，对其余的只要读一下黑体词就可以了。

例2：

Not Only for Children?

Recently, a rather sophisticated woman told me shyly that she saves up all her presents until Christmas morning and then sits up in bed and opens them, just like a child. She thought I would laugh at her and say how silly she was. **But in fact I was absolutely delighted to meet someone who treats Christmas as I do.**

Many people today have a very different attitude to Christmas. They think it's just a time when shopkeepers make a lot of money and everyone rushes round buying presents they don't want to give and food they don't want to eat. **But have they grown so far away from their own childhood that they can't remember all the good things?**

First of all, Christmas takes you out of the ordinary routine of life. For children, the fun begins weeks before when the decorations are put up, and excitement gradually increases as December the 25th approaches.

Everyone seems much friendlier to each other than usual at Christmas time. You can lean out of a car window when you are stopped at the traffic lights and say "Merry Christmas," and people will smile and respond. You probably wouldn't think of doing that at any other time of the year. Perhaps it's because most people are on holiday or because everyone knows that they are sharing a similar experience. **Giving presents can be very satisfying, too, if you plan enough in advance and really think of the right present for the right person.**

Indeed, whatever shopkeepers gain out of Christmas, it is still a "holy day," the words from which "holiday" is derived and it gives people time to pause and concentrate for a moment on non-commercial values.

这篇文章的题目《不仅仅为了孩子?》提出了一个问题。这种题目通常是论说文的题目，而且常常是驳斥型论说文的题目。这是我们通过阅读文章题目可以得到的关于文章体裁方面的信息。然后我们通过快速略读文章首尾两段、各段的段首句和段尾句就可以把握全文的主要内容和作者关于这一问题的观点和态度。这篇文章主要是探讨人们对圣诞节应持的态度。第一段通过举例表明了作者对这一问题的基本观点，即第一段最后一句话所表明的意思"事实上，我非常高兴能看到有人和我一样对待圣诞节"。第二段的段首句说明了该段的中心意思"现在很多人对待圣诞节的态度和我们十分不同"。而该段的段尾句表明了作者对这些人所持态度的评价。从这一句不难看出作者是不赞成这些人对待圣诞节的态度的。第三段和第四段分别论述了和圣诞节相关的美好的事情，即"圣诞节可以把你从循规蹈矩的日常生活中解放出来"和"在圣诞节期间大家对彼此好像比平时更为友好"，都是用段首句表达了该段的主要意思。最后一段为结尾段，既总结了圣诞节的意义——"它是神圣的节日"，又再次表明了作者对圣诞节的肯定态度。因此，在读这篇文章的时候，只要抓住这些重点部分，通过略读的方法就可以很快地了解文章的主要内容。

例3:

In bringing up children, every parent watches eagerly the child's acquisition（学会）**of each new skill—the first spoken words, the first independent steps, or the beginning of reading and writing.** It is often tempting to hurry the child beyond his natural learning rate, but **this** can set up dangerous feelings of failure and states of worry in the child. **This** might happen at any stage. A baby might be forced to use a toilet too early, a young child might be encouraged to learn to read before he knows the meaning of the words he reads. **On the other hand**, though, if a child is left alone too much, or without any learning opportunities, he loses his natural enthusiasm for life and his desire to find out new things for himself.

Parents vary greatly in their degree of strictness towards their children. Some may be especially strict in money matters. **Others** are severe over times of coming home at night or punctuality for meals. **In general**, the controls imposed represent the needs of the parents and the values of the community as much as the child's own happiness.

As regards the development of moral standards in the growing child, consistency is very important in parental teaching. To forbid a thing one day and excuse it the next is no foundation for morality（道德）. **Also**, parents should realize that "example is better than precept." If they are not sincere and do not practice what they preach（说教）, their children may grow confused, and emotionally insecure when they grow old enough to think for themselves, and realize they have been to some extent fooled.

A sudden awareness of a marked difference between their parents' principles and their morals can be a dangerous disappointment.

这篇文章主要是探讨在孩子成长过程中父母所起的作用。第一段主要谈及了父母们望子成龙的心情以及由此心情导致的种种催促孩子学习各种新技能的做法，并指出了这种做法的副作用。第二段的结构非常清晰。段首句点出了该段的主要内容"父母们在管教孩子的严格程度上有所不同"。随后用"一些人"和"另一些人"分述了父母们的不同之处。段尾用"总的来说"说明了导致这些不同之处的根结"父母在要求孩子的时候考虑的是他们自身的需要和社会的认可，而不是孩子们自身的需要"。第三段的中心意思是由段首句和"also"后面的句子共同表达的，即"在教育成长中的孩子道德标准时，父母教育上的一致性是非常重要的"和"父母的以身作则在教育成长中的孩子道德标准时同样很重要"。因此可以看到在用略读的方法阅读这篇文章时，除了应该注意到在略读中应注意的文章首尾两段及每段的段首和段尾句外，还应该注意到表示文章逻辑的转换和发展的信号词，即我们在第一篇中讲的各种表示文章关联的手段。

（2）第二种是扫读或查读。这是一种带有具体目的的速读方法。它是指读者在面临大量文献资料时，为了迅速准确地获取所需要的具体信息所采用的快速扫视定位式的阅读方法。它的特点是阅读时间少，收到的实际效果快。读者在查读时不必阅览全部材料，只需针对自己的阅读目的进行有选择的阅读，从中找出答案。它与略读有所差别，略读是阅读者对生疏的材料进行总的了解，而查读是阅读者对阅读材料在事先有所了解的情况下所进行的一种解决具体问题的阅读。具有较强的查读能力是做好阅读理解中的大量细节题目的关键。

在读者的日常生活中有很多时候会运用这种阅读方式。例如：读者在电话号码簿上查找某个特定单位的电话号码，或者在列车、轮船或航班时刻表上查寻某次车、船、航班离开或到达的具体时间以及沿途的停靠情况，若要准确迅速地做到这些，就需要对电话号码簿、车船时刻表的编排方式先有个大致的了解。那么怎样才能掌握好这一技巧呢？一般来说，读者应按照下列几点要求去做：

① 在确定了要找的具体信息后，要注意熟悉材料的编排方式以及具体内容所在的位置。有些材料是按字母顺序编排的，如词典、电话号码簿等；有些资料是按时间顺序编排的，如电视节目单、年鉴等。有些则是按内容编排的，如报纸、杂志的各种版面，书籍的目录等。不管是什么材料，它们都有自己一定的编排方式。如果想了解某事是何时发生的，那就要在材料中寻找日期线索。如果想要知道某个特定的人做了什么事，那就应顺着人名的线索来找。如果想找书中的某个章节，就要先翻看书的目录，等等。注意，与所查内容无关的信息就可以一带而过。

② 查读时，为了提高速度，要综合利用目光的各种扫视。由于查阅是一种捕捉具体信息的速读方式，寻觅时眼睛的运动可采用来回扫视型，垂直缫丝型，左下右上扫

视型和 Z 字扫视型,直至寻找到所需的内容。

③ 查读的准确性应是 100%,一旦发现所找的内容,就得仔细阅读,同时查阅也就结束。

例 4:

Evolution of the World Record for the One-Mile Run Up to the Four-Minute Mile

Year	Individual/Country	Time
1864	Charles Lawes/Britain	4:56
1865	Richard Webster/Britain	4:36.5
1868	William Chinnery/Britain	4:29
1868	W. C. Gibbs/Britain	4:28.8
1874	Walter Slade/Britain	4:26
1875	Walter Slade/Britain	4:24.5
1880	Walter George/Britain	4:23.2
1882	Walter George/Britain	4:21.4
1882	Walter George/Britain	4:19.4
1884	Walter George/Britain	4:18.4
1894	Fred Bacon/Scotland	4:18.2
1895	Fred Bacon/Scotland	4:17
1895	Thomas Conneff/U. S.	4:15.6
1911	John Paul Jones/U. S.	4:15.4
1913	John Paul Jones/U. S.	4:14.6
1915	Norman Taber/U. S.	4:12.6
1923	Paavo Nurmi/Finland	4:10.4
1931	Jules Ladoumegue/France	4:09.2
1933	Jack Lovelock/New Zealand	4:07.6
1934	Glenn Cunningham/U. S.	4:06.8
1937	Sydney Wooderson/Britain	4:06.4
1942	Gunder Haegg/Sweden	4:04.6
1943	Arne Andersson/Sweden	4:02.6
1944	Arne Andersson/Sweden	4:01.6
1945	Gunder Haegg/Sweden	4:01.4
1954	Roger Bannister/Britain	3:59.4

(Selected from Skimming and Scanning 1982)

1. How fast did Roger Bannister run the one-mile run?

2. Who broke his own record in the most time?

3. In what year was the mile run in 4:07.6 minutes?

4. How fast was the one-mile run in 1864?

5. In what years did a runner from Sweden break the record?

6. Which country broke the record most often?

7. In what year was the mile run in 4：06.8minutes?

答案　　1. 3：59.4　　2. Walter George　　3. 1933　　4. 4：56
5. 1942—1945　　6. Britain　　7. 1934

在用查读方式做这一练习时，首先要清楚阅读材料的编排方式以便迅速查找所需信息。这篇阅读材料是以表格形式按年代先后顺序编排的，左边一栏是年代，中间一栏先是个人然后是国家，右边一栏是时间（速度）。在具体做题时要注意抓住题干中最有提示作用的关键词以保证可用最快速度找到所需信息。在第一题中，最有提示意义的是大写的人名 Roger Bannister，由于人名比较复杂，可将它简化为 RB，这样查找起来就比较简单了。所需信息出现在材料最后一行，由于问题问的是速度，因此答案是3：59.4。第三题应以时间4：07.6为参照点；第四题以年代1864为参照点；第五题以国家 Sweden 为参照点；第七题以时间4：06.8为参照点。这些题目都较为简单，做题方法也比较机械。但是，剩下的第二、第四题就稍微复杂一些。这是由于没有直接的参照点可以利用，就必须明确用什么方式可以最快找到答案。所谓的哪个个人、哪个国家打破纪录的次数最多，其实就是哪个个人的人名、哪个国家的国名重复次数最高。明确了这一点，就很容易找到答案了。由此练习可以看出：正确迅速地判断具有提示作用的题干关键词是做题速度和准确性的有力保障。

（3）第三种是精读或研读。精读是读者最熟悉的一种阅读方式，它是指读者对文章进行细致的阅读，力求对文章有深层次的理解，以获得精确具体的信息。在进行精读时，读者经常要综合运用语言基本功，借助语法常识对句意进行分析，以达到精确理解的目的。这种阅读方法通常可以用来解答考试中关于作者的意图、句意的引申以及词义猜测之类的题目。

应试者在考试时应综合利用这三种阅读方法来回答各种类型的问题。首先，应试者应采用略读法，迅速浏览一遍短文，对短文的体裁及题材、文章的主题、结构等细节的分布情况有一个概括的了解。这时不可纠缠于短文中的生词或难句，应尽可能快地读完全文。同时略读法还可用来回答关于文章主题思想的问题。

然后，再阅读短文后的问题，这时用查阅的方法迅速在短文中锁定与问题相关的细节部分的位置。最后再用精读的方法，仔细阅读与题目相关的细节部分的内容，以便准确地找到答案。由此可见，正确有效的阅读方法对于提高阅读理解力和答题的正确率是十分关键的。应试者在平时的阅读训练中就应注意运用这几种阅读方法。

此外，应试者可充分利用试题册，在相关处做记号。看文章时最好随时在文章各段的关键词句上做标记，尤其对带有特殊标点符号的地方、大写的人名地名和某些重要地方，如：主题句、关联词语（因果、转折、列举、举例）等，答题时能帮助应试者理解文章，省去查找的时间。

在做题时，应试者应遵循先易后难的原则。一般来说，一篇文章的选择题的先后顺序是根据文章内容的先后安排的。除了推理性问题，跳蹦现象很少。因此，提倡一口气做完。遇到暂时做不了的，先在题上打上记号，继续往下做。这样，可大大节省时间，而将难题留在检查时再重点击破。对某词或某句不甚理解时，不要停留在原处反复阅读，应对整段迅速再读一遍，了解整体意义，结合上下文进行推测。对做不出的题，在前后上下文语言环境的烘托下再思考，找出正确答案，决不留空题。

最后，应试者应切记：一切从原文出发。回答问题一定要严格遵照文章中直述或隐含的观点，决不要根据自己的主观想象去臆断。阅读理解部分的解题方法与其他测试项目的解题方法一样，主要采用直接确定法或排除法。直接确定法适用于考生能在原文中直接找到或推测出问题答案的情况；排除法要求考生必须结合问题及原文，将四个选择项一一检验，排除各个干扰项，最后得出正确信息。特别对于难题可采取排除法，把不可能成为答案的选项逐一排除，剩下的一个可能就是正确答案。

三、阅读理解做题公式

根据最新颁布的大纲规定，阅读理解部分主要测试考生"综合运用英语语言知识和阅读技能来理解英语书面材料"的能力，要求考生"能以每分钟100~120词的速度阅读各种题材（社会生活、人物传记、科普、史地、政治、经济等）和体裁（议论文、记叙文、说明文、应用文等）的文字材料。"通过对1997年至2005年历年阅读真题的分析研究，社会生活、科普、教育、环境、人物传记等题材是考试中出现频率最高的，具体情况如下所示：

就出题方式而言，在5篇文章、25道阅读题目中，考查比率最高的是事实细节类的题目，不同题目所占的具体比例大致如下：

1. 主旨大意（2~3/25）
2. 事实细节（14~16/25）
3. 猜测生词（1/25）
4. 单句理解、句际关系（1/25）
5. 引申推断（4~5/25）
6. 意图和态度（1~3/25）

在以上几类题目中，对主旨大意的把握和事实细节的了解是核心和关键，而引申推断则是难点所在。本篇将针对这些常考题型为考生提供实用的阅读技巧、富有创意的阅读公式，旨在帮助学生在阅读理解能力上实现质的飞跃。

主旨题阅读公式
关于文章的主旨和大意的重要概念

1. 主题和大意的区别

很多专家认为在阅读理解中最重要的一项技能就是掌握和理解文章的主旨和大意，因为它通常是对全文内容的概括，也是对作者意图的反映。要成功地做到这一点，首先要明确几个概念：

第一是主题或题目（topic or subject），它是一个单词或词组，能够概括作者在文中要讨论的主要内容。通常，主题要具有概括性，要能够涵盖全文的内容，而非部分内容，而且同时要具有限定性。比如说，对某一篇文章来说，下面三个题目："Politics""Federal Politics""Corruption In Federal Politics"可能都对，但可能只有最后一个最能如实地反映出文章的主要内容。因此，在判断四个选项中哪个是文章最好的主题（which is the best topic of the passage）时，要注意选择既有概括性又很具体的题目。

例1：

Name a topic that includes all the details in the list：

Thanksgiving Day, Mother's Day, Independence Day, Lincoln's Birthday, Martin Luther King Day, Washington's Day

Topic：_____.

上述这些节日都是美国的节日：感恩节、母亲节、独立日（国庆日）、林肯纪念日、马丁·路德·金纪念日、华盛顿纪念日。因此，这组的标题应是"American Holidays"。如果用"Holidays"作为标题，概括的面就过大，不够具体，因为这组词语仅涉及美国的节日，而未涉及其他国家的节日，所以最合适的题目只能是"American Holidays"。

例2：

Courting behavior in birds is also believed to be instinctive. In one experiment Daniel Lehrman of Rutgers University found that when a male blond ring dove was isolated from females, it soon began to bow and coo to a stuffed model of a female—a model that it had previously ignored. When the model was replaced by a rolled-up cloth, he began to court the cloth; and when this was removed the sex-crazed dove directed his attention to a corner of the cage, where it could at least focus its gaze. It seems that threshold for release of the behavior pattern became increasingly lower as time went by without the sight of a live female dove. It is almost as though some specific "energy" for performing courting behavior were building up within the male ring dove.

Question：

The best topic of this paragraph is "_____."

A. A Male Blond Ring Dove

B. Courting Behavior

C. A Live Female Dove

D. Courting Behavior in Birds

这个题目的答案应该是D。这篇文章主要是通过描述对急于求偶的雄性鸽子进行的一连串实验来证明了鸟类的求偶行为是天生的、本能的（在通读全文时，一下子看到段首句 Courting behavior in birds is also believed to be instinctive。我们常常看到，段首句往往是主题句。而该段的第二句话 In one experiment Daniel Lehrman of Rutgers University found that when a male blond ring dove was isolated from females, it soon began to bow and coo to a stuffed model of a female.... 雄性鸽子仅仅是科学家用来实验鸟类求偶行为的实验罢了）。因此可以看出选项D既概括了主题，又限定了一连串实验的目的，应为正确答案。而选项A和C只选择了文中细节，而非全文内容的概括，而且由于本文也并不是对雄性或雌性鸽子的介绍性文章，故应当排除。至于选项B，虽具有概括性，但范围太大，没有突出这篇文章的主题，因此也不合适。

第二个概念是文章的大意或中心思想（main idea or controlling idea），它是作者针对所选定主题（topic）而进行的概述。作者在文中对中心思想进行明确而肯定的阐述的句子叫做主题句（topic sentence or main idea statement）。主题句一般是一个具有概括性或总结性的陈述句。文章大意或中心思想所讨论的内容不同于这里要讲的第三个概念——细节内容（supporting details）。细节内容用来支持中心思想的例证、说理和详述等。

例 3： Early Cognitive Development

Cognitive psychologists sometimes study young children to observe the very beginnings of cognitive activity. For example, when children first begin to utter words and sentences, they overgeneralize what they know and make language more consistent than it actually is.

Topic：_____．

Main idea：_____．

Detail：_____．

很明显上面这段文字的题目是"Early Cognitive Development"（早期认知的发展）。而其中心思想则是该段的段首句。其细节内容是该段第二句话所举的例子。

例 4： Compare the items within each group below and indicate whether each one is a statement of main idea (MI), a topic (T), or a specific supporting detail (D).

Group 1

a. In 1981 Henry Cisneros of San Antonio became the first Mexican-American mayor of a large city.

b. Mexican-American political gains.

c. Since 1960 Mexican-American have made impressive political gains.

Group 2

a. For poor farm families life on the plains meant a sod house or a dugout carved out of the hillside for protection from the winds.

b. One door and usually no more than a single window provided light and air.

c. Sod houses on the plains.

Group 3

a. As individuals, American tend to value the knowledge and skills transmitted by the schools, not for their own sake but because they hope to translate those skills into good jobs and money.

b. Social mobility through education.

c. As one study indicates, many students are attracted to college because of job and carrier considerations.

Group 4

a. For example, human babies require about twice as many calories per unit of body weight as adults.

b. Although children need less total food than adults, their metabolic needs exceed those of adults in proportion to their body weight.

c. Metabolic needs of children.

Group 5

a. The question of a bill of rights.

b. First, Hamilton wrote in Federalist 84 that a Bill of Rights might be necessary to restrict a king, but not a government established by the people; such a government, he said, possesses only the powers given to it by the people.

c. A serious objection raised against the Constitution by those who opposed its ratification was that it contained no Bill of Rights.

Keys:
Group 1
a. (D)　　b. (T)　　c. (MI)
Group 2
a. (MI)　　b. (D)　　c. (T)
Group 3
a. (D)　　b. (T)　　c. (MI)
Group 4
a. (D)　　b. (MI)　　c. (T)
Group 5
a. (T)　　b. (D)　　c. (MI)

---

2. 主题句的理解

由于一篇文章的主题思想往往是通过主题句来表达的，那么，能够快速而准确地找到文章的主题句对于正确理解全文的意思就非常重要了。为要快速地找到文章或段落的主题句，从而弄明白文章或段落的主要内容，考生首先要掌握主题句在段落中可能经常出现的位置。主题句在段落中的位置大致可归纳为以下几种：

① 段首主题句。
② 段末主题句。
③ 段中主题句。
④ 无明确标志的主题句。

然后应遵循以下介绍的行之有效的解题步骤去进行阅读理解：

① 仔细阅读全文，通观段落大意，重点理解段落的首句及尾句。
② 理解段首句与第二或第三句之间的语义关系。
③ 如果从第二句起开始陈述（陈述或释义）段首句内容的话，说明从第二句开始，是陈述或解释段首句内容的句子，这些句子被称为支撑句（Supporting sentence(s)），从而可确定段首句为主题句。
④ 如果从段首句起就开始论述细节，到段末句才进行概括或归纳的话，就说明段末句才是主题句。
⑤ 如果段首句是陈述句，段末句也是陈述句，而在段中出现一句概括性的句子时，就说明段中其他句子都是为这一概括性的句子服务的。显然，这个段中句就应当是主题句，是全段的中心思想。
⑥ 如果全段都是情节句，而未出现总结性的句子，就说明该段是一个无主题句的

段落。这时读者可根据段落所论述的中心思想或焦点,即论述哪一类性质的事情或人物,来进行推断,找出其共同点或核心点,进而得出结论。这样的段落就称为主旨大意隐含段。

⑦ 有时段落前两句都是较概括性的句子,第三句才开始论证或释义前两句。要辨认出哪句为主题句,读者需对前两句稍加分析,不难得出该段的第二句才是主题句,因为它的概括性强,而段首句仅起引导作用,引出段落要进行陈述的主题内容,所以就不可把第一句视为主题句。

⑧ 有时读者还会碰到段落中的重复主题句,即段首为主题句,到段末时又出现概括性的句子,即"段首主题句+段末主题句"共同陈述段落主题。这又是一种写作方法,而段末主题句往往是用来重复强调段首主题句的。一般来说,这种重复主题句不重复原句词句,而是用不同于段首句的表述形式和内容而变换说法来使段首句内容更加明确或确切,但根本意义则相同。

(1) 段首主题句。

全文主题句或段首主题句通常位于全文章或段落的开头,文章或段落的其他部分则围绕该主题句展开论述,这些论述句都用于说明或解释其具体内容或细节。掌握这种知识并熟悉这种文章结构,就能使考生更快地抓住对全文的中心思想及文章叙述的内容层次与具体细节。

例5:

American and Chinese cultures are at polar opposites. An American hostess, complimented for her cooking skills, is likely to say, "Oh, I'm so glad that you liked it. I cooked it especially for you." Not so a Chinese host or hostess (often the husband does the fancy cooking), who will instead apologize for giving you "nothing" even slightly edible and for not showing you enough honor by providing proper dishes.

Question:

The topic of this paragraph is _____.

A. American and Chinese cooking difference

B. American and Chinese cultural difference

C. American hostess

D. Chinese host

这段文章就属于典型的主题句在段首的文章。本段第一句就说明了整段的主要内容,即美国和中国的文化有着天壤之别。后面只是分别举了在请人到家里做客时美国主人和中国主人对待客人的赞扬可能作出的两种截然不同的回应,从而说明了两国在文化上的巨大差异。因此这道题的答案应是B。

例6:

Everyone seems much friendlier to each other than usual at Christmas time. You can lean out of a car window when you're stopped at the traffic lights and say "Merry Christmas," and people will smile and respond. You probably wouldn't think of doing that at any other time of the year. Perhaps it's because most people are on holiday or because everyone knows that they are sharing a similar experience. Giving presents can be very satisfying, too, if you plan far enough in advance and really think of the right present for the right person.

Question：

Which of the following sentences states the main idea of this paragraph?

A. People would smile to each other at Christmas time.

B. People usually prepare the presents before Christmas.

C. People often greet to each other while waiting for the traffic lights on Christmas.

D. People treat each other better than usual at Christmas time.

这一段主要描述了在圣诞节期间人们之间所表现出来的友好亲密的态度。这一主题思想在本段的段首句中就得到了体现。后面的文字是对这种友好亲密态度的具体的细节描写。因此不难看出这道题的答案应该是 D。而 A、B、C 三项只是细节描写。

（2）段末主题句。

这类段末主题句通常是用来归纳和总结前面所阐述的观点或情节的。这种归纳法在撰写文章时很常见。

例7：

Christmas is supposed to be a time to express our love and good will towards others. It is supposed to be a time when we perform acts of kindness for people less fortunate than ourselves. But do we think of other people when we sit down to our Christmas dinner? Of course not—we're too busy eating those delicious foods associated with Christmas. We are too busy wondering whether the presents we gave were as nice or better than the ones we received. We forget to think of the sick and the homeless. The whole idea of Christmas now is completely unchristian—I'm sure that Christ would be distressed if he could see what sort of celebrations are being carried out in his name.

Question：

The best summary of this paragraph is _____.

A. Christmas is a time for people to show love to each other.

B. The whole idea of Christmas now is completely unchristian.

C. On Christmas people can enjoy delicious food.

D. At Christmas time people are concerned about the presents they received.

这段文章是表达作者对现代人过圣诞节时对圣诞精神的体味。他先说明了圣诞节的意义应该是人们借此欢乐时刻互致爱意或善意、向不幸的人传达爱心，然后一步步分析指出了现代人在圣诞节期间只是忙于品尝美味佳肴，只关心收送的礼品，而对需要帮助的人置若罔闻，因此现在的圣诞节已不再具有原来的基督精神了。作者用本段最后一句话概括总结了本段的主要内容，因此这道题的答案是 B。

例8：

English is spoken by pilots and airport control operators on all the airways of the world. Over 70 percent of the world's mail is written in English. More than 60 percent of the radio programs are in English. Clearly, English is an international language.

Question：

Which of the following is the best title for this paragraph?

A. English—Spoken on All Airways

B. English—A Language for Mail

C. English—A Language for Broadcasting

D. English—An International Language

这是一段非常简练的文字。前三句分别从三个不同领域描述了英语使用的普遍性，即飞行员及地面控制人员使用英语。世界上70%的邮件是用英语书写的。全球60%以上的广播节目是用英语播出的。通过以上三点具体事实，作者最后向读者总结出一个结论，即英语是一门国际性的语言。因此，最后一句为本段的主题句，说明了本段的中心思想。正确答案应该是D。

（3）段中主题句。

主题句既不在段首，也不在段末，而位于段中时，它常出现的位置是该段的第二句话。为了使一篇文章结构更紧凑，意思更连贯，很多时候，一些段落的段首句只起着承上启下的过渡作用，而该段的第二句才是段落的主题句。当然这种情况不是绝对的，有时候段中主题句的位置需视具体情况而定。

例9：

The Cherokee Indians, who considered themselves the "real people," established their village along the streams and rivers of what are now the Carolines, Georgia, Virginia, and Kentucky. The building methods used by the Cherokee people reveal a unique civilization. The walls of their houses were constructed with large, sturdy posts planted at three-foot intervals. Small posts were held in place by twigs and long grasses interwoven to provide strength and protection. To insulate against the wind and cold, the woven walls were plastered with a mixture of grass and clay. This process also improved the appearance of the house and kept the posts from rooting. Many historians feel that these building techniques place the Cherokee at the forefront of early American Indians.

Questions:

1. Which of the following is the best title for this paragraph?

A. The Cherokees' Life

B. Early American Indians

C. Unique Building Technique of the Cherokees

D. Cultural Traditions of Early American Indians

2. Which sentence best states the main idea of this paragraph?

A. The Cherokee Indians believed that they were superior people.

B. The Cherokee Indians built houses along the river.

C. The Cherokee Indians used grass and clay to build houses.

D. The Cherokee Indians' architectural skill reflects a special civilization.

本段描述了切诺基印第安人早期建造家园时使用的独特建筑艺术。第一句介绍了切诺基人建造家园的位置选择，第二句指出了本段的中心思想，即他们建造房屋的艺术是他们独特文明的反映。第三句到第七句详细地介绍了他们的建筑艺术。这些均属细节内容，都是为了说明当时切诺基人建筑艺术已经达到的那种文明程度。最后一句是主题的重复,称赞切诺基部落是早期美洲印第安人文明的象征。因此,第一个问题的答案应为 C 项,第二题的答案应为 D 项。

例 10:

In back of social change lie many forces. Climate, natural resources, agriculture and manufactures serve to set in operation influences that tend to change a person's life. It is the part of good administration to adjust these forces in such fashion that changes are balanced and national experience is not left at his mercy of varying conditions. But the economic life of a person is so complicated that complete adjustment is beyond human power. Poverty in itself is seldom the cause of revolution. It is the sense of inequality in the distribution of wealth that breeds discontent. When wealth increases and at the same time tends to become monopolized in some group or class, this discontent is always keen. And, above all, when the rich are indifferent to the inequality which economic change increases, and when the burdens of the economic life from those least able to bear them, the consciousness of the inequality grows into enmity.

Question:

Which statement best expresses the central idea of this paragraph?

A. Social change is caused by many factors such as climate and agriculture.

B. Poverty is usually the cause of revolution.

C. The sense of inequality in distribution causes discontent.

D. The burdens of economic life lead to enmity between the rich and the poor.

本文探讨的是导致社会发生变化的诸多因素及政府主管部门调控这些因素和力量的制衡作用。文中分析了引起人们对社会不满的主要原因。作者认为导致社会发生变化的因素虽然很多,但政府应当履行制衡各种力量的职能,并起到运用传播媒介、宣传媒介促进人民团结的作用。作者继而指出,贫困并非导致革命的原因,财产分配不公才是引起社会不满的根本原因,而富人对于这种分配不公的麻木不仁更加剧了人们的不满和动荡。本段属于将主题句放在段落中间成为该段中心的例子。因此这道题的答案应是 C。

(4)无明显主题句。

前面已举例分析了主题句出现在段落中间的不同位置的情况,但是我们还必须认识到还有些段落没有明显的主题句。但这不等于说该段落就没有主题思想。应该说,每一段文字都有其想要表达的主题内容,只不过在这种段落里,主题思想隐藏于字里行间而已。一般来说,对于没有明显主题句的段落,考生应根据上下文,细心琢磨推敲,分析段落的主要细节,从中归纳出其论述的主题思想,切忌用辨认主题句的方法来分析这种无明显主题句的段落,因为这种段落的特征是没有对主题进行概括或总结。

例 11:

I paid \$606 for a new color TV from John Doe's Bargain Barn. For the first time, I watched all of my favorite programs in color. My every favorite star, Rock Henry, looked even more handsome than in black and white. After two days, the set went on the blink. It's been three months now, and I've taken it back three times. Doe won't fix the set and the factory doesn't pay any attention to my letters. Doe says he doesn't like the way I act and not to come back. I've complained to everybody I can think of—and still no result! I want my money back.

Question:

What is the best title for this paragraph?

A. A New Color TV

B. A Famous Star on TV

C. A TV Buyer's Complaints

D. Buyer's Unhappiness

这是一篇作者投诉刚买的新彩电质量差、售后服务差的文章。文中没有一句概括全文大意的话，但是通过分析各个细节可以找到隐含的主题思想，即作者买了新彩电两天后就发现彩电的质量问题。之后他多次将彩电送回售后服务店里修理，也未能修好。他写信到生产这种电视的厂家，而厂家也对此置之不理。由此不难看出，这段的主题思想应为"This TV buyer is complaining about what has happened to the TV since he bought it."因此，这个问题的答案应是C。A、B两项均为文中涉及的细节内容，不能概括全文，而D项虽能概括全文，但涵盖范围过大，没能点出本文的中心要素——电视。

例12：

Experiments are being carried out at the University of Arizona on ways of storing solar energy on a large scale. To satisfy a large part of the energy in a country like America, huge power stations covering 5,000 square miles would have to be built and one wonders whether this would be acceptable to environmentalist. While experiments in generating energy from the sea and the wind are interesting, neither can be considered an obvious solution to a future energy crisis; the first because a lot of energy is needed to generate energy from the sea, and the second because the amount of energy generated from the wind would only satisfy a small percentage of a nation's needs. Another source of energy which could be more widely used is that generated from hot water or steam from under the earth. This form of energy is already being used in some countries.

Question:

The controlling idea of the paragraph is _____.

A. experiments in generating energy from the sea

B. experiments on generating energy from the wind

C. experiments on new ways of solutions to a future energy crisis

D. experiments in ways of storing solar energy in a large scale

浏览上述整段文字，考生可以确定该段论述的主要对象是，能源危机及其解决方案。作者就此展开叙述。先论及太阳能利用，再讨论利用潮汐及风能发电。最后讨论地热资源的利用问题。作者平铺直叙，层层展开描述。展现于考生面前的是一篇内容翔实的资料。而考生则需要纵观全段，逐步概括出本段的中心思想来，即 Experiments on new ways of solutions to a future energy crisis 研究未来能源危机解决途径的各种实验。因此，C为正确答案。

例 13：

As many as one thousand years ago in the Southwest, the Hopi and Zuni tribes of North America were building with adobe—sun-brick plastered with mud. Their homes looked remarkably like modern apartment house. Some were four stories high and contained quarters for perhaps a thousand people, along with store rooms for grain and other goods. These buildings were usually put up against cliffs, both to make construction easier and for defense against enemies. They were really villages in themselves, as later Spanish explorers must have realized since they called them "pueblos," which is Spanish for town.

The people of the pueblos raised what are called "the three sisters" —corn, beans and squash. They made excellent pottery and wove marvelous baskets, some so fine that they could hold water. The southwest has always been a dry country, with water scarce. The Hopi and Zuni brought water from streams to their fields and gardens through irrigation ditches. Water was so important that it played a major role in their religion. They developed elaborate ceremonies and religious rituals to bring rain.

The way of life of less settled groups was simpler and more strongly influenced by nature. Small tribes such as the Shoshone and Ute wandered the dry and mountainous lands between the Rocky Mountains and the Pacific Ocean. They gathered seeds and hunted small animals such as rabbits and snakes. In the Far North the ancestors of today's Inuit hunted seals, walruses, and the great whales. They lived right on the frozen seas in shelters called igloos built of blocks of packed snow. When summer came, they fished for salmon and hunted the lordly caribou.

The Cheyenne, Pawnee, and Sioux tribes, known as tile Plains Indians, lived on the grasslands between the Rocky Mountains and the Mississippi River. They hunted the bison, commonly called the buffalo. Its meat was the chief food of these tribes, arid its hide was used to make their clothing and the covering of their tents and tepees.

Question:

Which of the following is the best title for the passage?

A. Building with Adobe
B. One Thousand Years of Hunting
C. The Hopi and Zuni Tribes
D. Early North American Societies

本文并未给出主题句，但作者的意图在前后段落的叙述中体现得非常明显。全文共分4个自然段，每段的中心内容如下：

第1段：北美"Hopi"（霍皮）和"Zuni"（朱尼）等印第安部族的住房特点。

第2段：这两个部族的生活状况。

第3段：较小的"Shoshone"（肖肖尼）和"Ute"（犹他）等印第安部族的生活居住情况。

第4段：平原印第安部族（Plains Indians）的生活居住情况。

由于第3段和第4段中都分别提到了落基山脉（the Rocky Mountains）和密西西比河（the Mississippi River）等北美洲地名，故所提到的部族无疑生活在北美洲。文章一开始便确定了时间，即所描述的事发生在一千多年前（as many as one thousand years ago）。这样，四个备选答案中，只有 D "Early North American Societies"（早期的北美洲社会）与原文相同，其中 "societies" 和 "tribes" 意思相同。

作者在第 1 段虽着重描写霍皮和朱尼部落的住房 "adobe"（用土坯和干草盖成的棚屋），但这只是他们衣食住行的一部分，况且 2、3、4 段中对此只字未提。作者在 3、4 段中分别提到了打猎 "hunting"，但也只是一带而过，属于枝节问题。C 不对，第 1、2 段的文字完全是关于霍皮和朱尼等印第安部族，但这只是前两段的中心内容，它不可代替整篇文章的中心内容。文章的中心是各个段落都围绕并与之进行描述和论证的内容，它必须具有概括性，即涉及全篇文章，这一点是至关重要的。

主旨题阅读公式及真题讲解

主旨类试题的目的是考查考生对文章中心思想的理解程度和区别主要信息和次要信息的辨别能力。这类问题的提问形式大致有以下几种：

① The key point of the passage is that _____.
② The main (central, principal) idea (topic, subject) of the passage is about _____.
③ The article is written to explain _____.
④ The passage is mainly (chiefly) concerned about _____.
⑤ Which of the following best reflects the main idea of the article?
⑥ Which statement best expresses the main idea (central thought) of the essay?
⑦ The theme of the passage is _____.
⑧ The best summary of the passage (paragraph) is _____.
⑨ What does the article (author) mainly discuss?
⑩ The passage is chiefly concerned with _____.
⑪ Which of the following statements best summarizes the main idea of the passage (paragraph)?
⑫ Which of the following is the best conclusion of the passage (paragraph)?
⑬ The original title of this passage can be probably replaced by _____.
⑭ What is the best title for this passage?
⑮ What is the passage mainly concerned about?
⑯ Where do you think the passage is taken from?
⑰ In the first paragraph, the author mainly tells us _____.
⑱ The author's main purpose in writing the passage is to _____.

这些题目虽然提问方式多种多样，但基本上体现了三种命题方式：

第一种是 Main Idea 类型。最典型、最常见的提问方式是：What is the main idea/point of this passage? 这类题目的答案选项的表达形式是陈述句。要求考生找出体现文章主要内容、中心思想的句子。

第二种是 Main Topic 类型。最典型、最常见的提问方式是：What is the main topic/subject of this passage? 和 What is the best title for this passage? 这类题目的答案选项的表达形式通常是名词性词组。

第三种是 Main Purpose 类型。最典型、最常见的提问方式是：What is the author's

main purpose in writing the passage? 这类题目的答案选项的表达形式通常是以带 to 的不定式引出的动宾结构来表达。

不论是针对文章的中心内容提问还是要求给文章选定合适的标题，还是要求选定作者的写作目的，最根本的都是要求考生能够概括文章的中心思想。下面两套主旨题做题公式可以帮助考生迅速准确地抓住文章中心思想，从而排除干扰选项。

1. 主旨题阅读公式一

文章的主旨 = 全文的主旨句（thesis）
           = 各段落主题句之和
           = 各段落段意之和

分析阅读段落的内容，迅速捕捉文脉和段落主题句，是阅读考试中概括中心思想最常用、最便捷的方法。在本章第一节中我们已经分析了辨别和捕捉段落主题句的方法以及主题句的位置和表现形式。全篇文章是放大的段落，因而全文的主旨句和段落主题句功能相同，都是用来表达全文中心思想的。文章其他的部分不论是段落还是句子，均围绕这一主旨句展开议论、描述或解释说明。它通常以陈述句的形式出现，在文章中最常见的位置是第一段首句、第一段末句和全文末句等地方。有些文章没有一个概括全文内容的主旨句，而是每一段落中有概括该段主要内容的主题句，这时只要把每段的主题句综合起来大致就可以发现全文的主旨。此外，还有少数文章全文和各段落都没有明显的主题句，这时就需要考生自己先概括每一段的主要内容，然后再将各段段意相加，就可大致归纳出全文的中心思想。

（1）文章的主旨 = 全文的主旨句（thesis）。

① 首段首句。

很多英文文章都喜欢开门见山，一开始就明确提出全文论述的主要观点或主要说明的内容。接下去的段落和句子内容就会进一步具体地阐述或说明文章的主旨。这类文章的结构通常是从一般到具体，是典型的演绎模式的文章。全文的主题句就是文章的首段首句。

例 1:

Taste is such a subjective matter that we don't usually conduct preference tests for food. The most you can say about anyone's preference, is that it's one person's opinion. But because the two big cola（可乐饮料）companies—Coca-Cola and Pepsi Cola are marketed so aggressively, we've wondered how big a role taste preference actually plays in brand loyalty. We set up a taste test that challenged people who identified themselves as either Coca-Cola or Pepsi fans: Find your brand in a blind tasting.

We invited staff volunteers who had a strong liking for either Coca-Cola Classic（传统型）or Pepsi, Diet（低糖的）Coke, or Diet Pepsi. These were people who thought they'd have no trouble telling their brand from the other brand.

We eventually located 19 regular cola drinkers and 27 diet cola drinkers. Then we fed them four unidentified samples of cola one at a time, regular colas for the one group, diet versions for the others. We asked them to tell us whether each sample was Coke or Pepsi; then we analyzed the records statistically to compare the participants' choices with what mere guess-work could have accomplished.

Getting all four samples right was a tough test, but not too tough, we thought, for people who believed they could recognize their brand. In the end, only 7 out of 19 regular cola drinkers correctly identified their brand of choice in all four trials. The diet-cola drinkers did a little worse—only 7 of 27 identified all four samples correctly.

While both groups did better than chance would predict, nearly half the participants in each group made the wrong choice two or more times. Two people got all four samples wrong. Overall, half the participants did about as well on the last round of tasting as on the first, so fatigue, or taste burnout, was not a factor. Our preference test results suggest that only a few Pepsi participants and Coke fans may really be able to tell their favorite brand by taste and price.

Question：

The author's purpose in writing this passage is to _____.

A. show that taste preference is highly subjective

B. argue that taste testing is an important marketing strategy

C. emphasize that taste and price are closely related to each other

D. recommend that blind tasting be introduced in the quality control of colas

这是一篇非常典型的实验报告性说明文，旨在通过实验说明在品尝食品上个人口味具有极强的主观性。文章开门见山，第一句就点出了全文的主旨，这一句又是全文的主题句（thesis）。后面分别介绍了所做实验的目的、对象、方法、过程及其发现和结论。这类实验报告性说明文通常会涉及实验的内容。在阅读这类文章时，把握了实验的内容就等于把握了文章的全部。在这里，最重要的是实验的目的和结论，因为这两方面是把握文章主旨的关键。通常都会有题目。本文首先介绍了所做实验的目的：个人口味在消费者对可乐品牌的忠诚度上有多大的影响。围绕这一实验目的，在对可口可乐和百事可乐的忠诚消费者中间仅凭个人口感而不知其可乐品牌的情况下测试消费者分辨自己所喜爱的品牌的能力，最后得出的结论是：仅有极少数的受测者能凭着可乐的口感和价格断定是否是自己喜爱的品牌。作者介绍该实验的目的只有一个，即想要证明全文的主旨——文章的首句。就这道题目而言，把握住全文的主旨句，就等于找到了答案。所剩的工作就是在答案选项中找与这句话表述最为相似的表述即可。本题的正确答案是 A 选项。

例2：

The media can impact current events. As a graduate student at Berkeley in the 1960s, I remember experiencing the events related to the People's Park that were occurring on campus. Some of these events were given national media coverage in the press and on TV. I found it interesting to compare my impressions of what was going on with perceptions obtained from the news media. I could begin to see events of that time feed on news coverage. This also provided me with some healthy insights into the distinctions between these realities.

Electronic media are having a greater impact on the people's lives every day. People gather more and more of their impressions from representations. Television and telephone communications are linking people to a global village, or what one writer calls the electronic city. Consider the information that television brings into your home every day. Consider also the contact you have with others simply by using telephone. These media extend your consciousness and your contact. For example, the video coverage of the 1989 San Francisco earthquake focused on "live action" such as the fires or the rescue efforts. This gave the viewer the impression of total disaster. Television coverage of the Iraqi War also developed an immediacy. CNN reported events as they happened. This coverage was distributed worldwide. Although most people were far away from these events, they developed some perception of these realities.

In 1992, many people watched in horror as riots broke out on a sad Wednesday evening in Los Angeles, seemingly fed by video coverage from helicopters. This event was triggered by the verdict（裁定）in the Rodney King beating. We are now in an age where the public can have access to information that enables it to make its own judgments, and most people, who had seen the video of this beating, could not understand how the jury（陪审团）was able to acquit（宣布无罪）the policemen involved. Media coverage of events as they occur also provides powerful feedback that influences events. This can have harmful results, as it seemed on that Wednesday night in Los Angeles. By Friday night the public got to see Rodney King on television pleading, "Can we all get along?" by Saturday, television seemed to provide positive feedback as Los Angeles riot turned out into a rally for peace. The television showed thousands of people marching with banners and cleaning tools. Because of that, many people turned out to join the peaceful event they saw unfolding（展开）on television. The real healing, of course, will take much longer, but electronic media will continue to be a part of that process. （1999年第三篇）

Question：

The best title for the passage is _____.

A. The 1989 san Francisco Earthquake and the 1992 Los Angeles Riots

B. How Media Cover Events

C. The 1992 Los Angeles Riots

D. The Impact of Media on Current Events

这是一篇典型的论说文。文章通过几个事例，清楚地表明了媒体对时事的巨大影响。在做题时，可先套用主旨＝全文主题句这一公式在 B 和 D 两个选项中作出选择。原文第一段的段首句 The media can impact current events 就是全文的主题句。B 是文章根本未涉及的内容。第二段的主题句是段首句 Electronic media are having a greater impact on the people's lives every day；第三段没有主题句，只是举了一个说明媒体对时事报道影响的具体事例。这两段的主要内容再次验证了文章的主题是探讨媒体对时事报道的影响。因此，不难看出本文最好的题目是正确答案 D。然后可再结合排除法做题，排除 A 和 C 两个选项。这两个选项都是具体例子，属于细节内容。

② 首段末句。

英文文章的结构很有规律性，除了开门见山类的文章外，还有很多文章将首段作为文章的引入部分，通过举例子、讲故事、描述某种社会现象来引出文章要探讨的主题。这类文章的全文主旨句最常出现的位置就是首段末句。它不仅是全文中心思想的概括，往往还是第一段主要内容的总结。这类文章中应当特别注意批驳型论说文的特点。文章首段往往提出一个作者反对的观点，在表示强转折的连接词 but，however，yet 等后出现的首段末句才是作者真正的观点，也是全文的主旨句。考生还应当注意：有时候这类文章的引入部分不止一段，可能是两段或三段。这时要记住全文的主旨句通常在整个引入部分的末句。

例 3：

The way people hold to the belief that a fun-filled, pain-free life equals happiness actually reduces their chances of ever attaining real happiness. If fun and pleasure are equal to happiness then pain must be equal to unhappiness. **But in fact, the opposite is true: more often than not things that lead to happiness involve some pain.**

As a result, many people avoid the very attempts that are the source of true happiness. They fear the pain inevitably brought by such things as marriage, raising children, professional achievement, religious commitment（承担的义务）, self-improvement.

Ask a bachelor（单身汉）why he resists marriage even though he finds dating to be less and less satisfying. If he is honest he will tell you that he is afraid of making a commitment. For commitment is in fact quite painful. The single life is filled with fun, adventure, excitement. Marriage has such moments, but they are not its most distinguishing features.

Couples with infant children are lucky to get a whole night's sleep or a three-day vacation. I don't know any parent who would choose the word fun to describe raising children. But couples who decide not to have children never know the joys of watching a child grow up or of playing with a grandchild.

Understanding and accepting that true happiness has nothing to do with fun is one of the most liberating realizations. It liberates time: now we can devote more hours to activities that can genuinely increase our happiness. It liberates money: buying that new car or those fancy clothes that will do nothing to increase our happiness now seems pointless. And it liberates us from envy: we now understand that all those who are always having so much fun actually may not be happy at all.

Question:

What is the author trying to tell us?

A. Happiness often goes hand in hand with pain.
B. One must know how to attain happiness.
C. It is important to make commitments.
D. It is pain that leads to happiness.

这就是一篇典型的批驳型论说文。文章首段首句提出了要批驳的观点：很多人认为充满快乐、没有痛苦的生活就是幸福，并且指出了这种观点会给人们带来的不利影响：会减少他们获得真正幸福的机会。在首段末句中表示强转折的 But 之后，作者提出了自己的观点：能给人们带来真正幸福的事情往往会带着些许痛苦。这句话才是全文的主旨句。在答案选项中和它最为相似的表述是 A 选项，意思是幸福和痛苦常常密不可分。文章首段之后的部分就是在一步一步地论证作者观点的正确性。在文章的第二、三、四段，作者从正反两面分析说明能给人们带来真正幸福的事业、婚姻、养育子女等都不能简单地用充满快乐来形容，因为这些往往就意味着承诺和付出，会给人带来一定的痛苦；但是，如果人们因为惧怕痛苦而回避它们，人们也会失去获得真正幸福的机会。在文章末段，作者有力地阐述了接受他的观点能给人们带来的好处：可以使人们节省时间金钱、摆脱嫉妒等不良的个人偏见。

例4：

Revenge is one of those things that everyone enjoys. People don't like to talk about it, though. Just the same, there is nothing more satisfying or more rewarding than revenge. The purpose is not to harm your victims but to let them know that you are upset about something that they are doing to you. **Careful plotting can provide you with relief from bothersome coworkers, gossiping friends, or nagging family members.**

Coworkers who make comments about the fact that you are always fifteen minutes late for work can be taken care of very simply. All you have to do is get up extra early one day. Before the sun comes up, drive to each coworker's house. Reach under the hood of your coworker's car and disconnect the center wire that leads to the distributor cap, the car will be unharmed, but it will not start, and your friends at work will all be late for work on the same day. If you're lucky, your boss might notice that you are the only one there and will give you a raise.

Gossiping friends at school are also perfect targets for a simple act of revenge. A way to trap either male or female friends is to leave phony messages on their lockers. If the friend that you want to get is male, leave a message that a certain girl would like him to stop by her house later that day. With any luck, her boyfriend will be there. The girl won't know what's going on, and the victim will be so embarrassed that he probably won't leave his home for a month.

When Mom and Dad and your sisters and brothers really begin to annoy you, harmless revenge may be just the way to make them quiet down for a while. The dinner table is a likely place. Just before the meal begins, throw a handful of raisins into the food. Wait about five minutes and, after everyone has begun to eat, cover your mouth with your hand and begin to make odd noises. When they ask you what the matter is, point to a raisin and yell, "Bugs!" They'll dump their food in the disposal, jump into the car, and head for McDonald's. That night, you'll have your first quiet, peaceful meal in a long time.

A well-planned revenge does not have to hurt anyone. The object is simply to let other people know that they are beginning to bother you. （1997 年第四篇）

Question：

The main topic of the passage is how to _____.

A. avoid nagging family members

B. silence gossiping friends

C. make a harmless revenge

D. deal with bothersome coworkers

本文主要介绍了如何对你不喜欢的同事、朋友、亲戚进行无害的报复，实际上，就是通过巧妙策划、精心安排来对他们搞一些恶作剧。在做题时，可套用公式：主旨＝全文主题句（thesis statement）和主旨≠文章某一部分的内容。全文的主题句就是第一段最后一句：Careful plotting can provide you with relief from bothersome coworkers, gossiping friends, or nagging family members 这句话概括了第二、三、四段的内容，由此可以看出A、B、D 选项都只是文章某一段的内容，不够全面，因此不能作为全文主旨。只有 C 选项是对全文内容的概括。

③ 全文末句。

主旨句直到全文末段才出现的情况往往是归纳模式的论说文或说明文。这类文章在同等学力人员考研英语阅读中比较少见。比较多见的是文章首、末两段都有全文主旨句，这时末段的主旨句常常是首段主旨句的重述，旨在强调文章的主旨。

例5：

Most people would agree that, although our age exceeds all previous ages in knowledge, there has been no corresponding increase in wisdom. But agreement ceases as soon as we attempt to define "wisdom" and consider means of promoting it.

There are several factors that contribute to wisdom. Of these I put first a sense of proportion: the capacity to take account of all the important factors in a problem and to attach to each its due weight. This has become more difficult than it used to be owing to the extent and complexity of the special knowledge required of various kinds of technicians. Suppose, for example, that you are engaged in research in scientific medicine. You have no time to consider the effect which your discoveries or inventions may have outside the field of medicine. You succeed (let us say) as modern medicine has succeeded, in enormously lowering the infant death-rate, not only in Europe and America, but also in Asia and Africa. This has the entirely unintended result of making the food supply inadequate and lowering the standard of life in the parts of the world that have the greatest populations. To take an even more dynamic example, which is in everybody's mind at the present time; you study the makeup of the atom from a disinterested desire for knowledge, and by chance place in hands of a powerful mad man the means of destroying the human race.

Therefore, with every increase of knowledge and skill, wisdom becomes more necessary, for every such increase augments our capacity for realizing our purposes, and therefore augments our capacity for evil, if our purposes are unwise.

Question：

What is the main idea of the passage?

A. It is unwise to place the results of scientific research in the hands of a powerful mad man.

B. The more knowledge one has, the wiser one becomes.

C. Any increase in knowledge could lead to disastrous results without the guidance of wisdom.

D. Wisdom increases in proportion to one's age.

这是一篇典型的归纳类型论说文。文章第一段首先指出：人们普遍认为我们这个时代在知识领域已经超越了以往任何时代，但在智慧方面却没有相应的增长。第二段指出：在影响智慧的诸多因素中，是否具备纵观全局、正确判断一个问题中每个重要因素的作用和地位的能力至关重要，因为如果缺乏这种能力，人们所取得的成就往往会给人们带来意想不到的恶果。文章末段是全文的主旨句，强调指出：随着知识和技能的增长，人们就更需要智慧的引导，因为如果没有智慧来引导我们的目的，这种知识和技能的增长在增强人们达到自己目的的能力的同时，也随之不可避免地增添了他们干坏事的能力。正确答案 C 选项就是对这句话的诠释。

例6：

Nowadays, we hear a lot about the growing threat of globalisation, accompanied by those warnings that the rich pattern of local life is being undermined, and many dialects and traditions are becoming extinct. **But stop and think for a moment about the many positive aspects that globalisation is bringing Read on and you are bound to feel comforted, ready to face the global future**, which is surely inevitable now.

Consider the Internet, that prime example of our shrinking world. Leaving aside the all-too-familiar worries about pornography and political extremism, even the most narrow-minded must admit that the net offers immeasurable benefits, not just in terms of education, the sector for which it was originally designed, but more importantly on a global level, the spread of news and comment. It will be increasingly difficult for politicians to maintain their regimes of misinformation, as the oppressed will not only find support and comfort, but also be able to organize themselves more effectively.

MTV is another global provider that is often criticized for imposing popular culture on the unsuspecting millions around the world. Yet the viewers' judgment on MTV is undoubtedly positive; it is regarded as indispensable by most of the global teenage generation who watch it, a vital part of growing up. And in the final analysis, what harm can a few songs and videos cause?

Is the world dominance of brands like Nike and Coca-Cola so had for us, when all is said and done? Sportswear and soft drinks are harmless products when compared to the many other things that have been globally available for a longer period of time—heroin and cocaine, for example. In any case, just because Nike shoes and Coke cans are for sale, it doesn't mean you have to buy them—even globalisation cannot deprive the individual of his free will.

Critics of globalisation can stop issuing their doom and gloom statements. Life goes on, and has more to offer for many citizens of the world than it did for their parents' generation. （2003 年第五篇）

Question：

Which of the following could be the best title of the passage?

A. Globalisation Is Standardization

B. Globalisation: Like It or Lump It

C. Globalisation: Don't Worry, Be Happy

D. Gloalisation Brings Equality

本文是一篇典型的驳斥性论说文。作者通过分析网络、MTV、运动服装和软饮料等经济全球化的标志性事物的出现会给我们生活带来的便利，表明了自己对全球化趋势的认可。全文主题句出现在第一段段末，意思是：我们应当想想全球化给我们生活带来的便利，让我们坦然面对全球化的到来。这一主旨在文章的最后一段再次得到重述。

（2）文章的主旨＝各段落主题句之和。

在没有全文主旨句的文章中，利用在本章第一节提到的抓段落主题句的阅读方法，迅速准确地找到文章各段的主题句就成了把握全文中心思想的关键。

例7：

Americans are proud of their variety and individuality, yet they love and respect few things more than a uniform, whether it is the uniform of an elevator operator or the uniform of a five-star general. **Why are uniforms so popular in the United States?**

Among the arguments for uniforms, one of the first is that in the eyes of most people they look more professional than civilian（百姓的）clothes. People have become conditioned to expect superior quality from a man who wears a uniform. The television repairman who wears a uniform tends to inspire more trust than one who appears in civilian clothes. Faith in the skill of a garage mechanic is increased by a uniform. What an easier way is there for a nurse, a policeman, a barber, or a waiter to lose professional identity（身份）than to step out of uniform?

Uniforms also have many practical benefits. They save on other clothes. They save on laundry bills. They are *tax-deductible*（可减税的）. They are often more comfortable and more durable than civilian clothes.

Primary among the arguments against uniforms is their lack of variety and the consequent loss of individuality experienced by people who must wear them. Though there are many types of uniforms, the wearer of any particular type is generally stuck with it, without change, until retirement. When people look alike, they tend to think, speak, and act similarly, on the job at least.

Uniforms also give rise to some practical problems. Though they are long-lasting, often their initial expense is greater than the cost of civilian clothes. Some uniforms are also expensive to maintain, requiring professional dry cleaning rather than the home laundering possible with many types of civilian clothes.

Question:

The best title for this passage would be _____.

A. Uniforms and Society

B. The Importance of Wearing a Uniform

C. Practical Benefits of Wearing a Uniform

D. Advantages and Disadvantages of Uniforms

本文是一篇典型的正反观点对比的论说文。首段是文章的引入部分，首先引出本文要谈论的主要话题：在美国，制服颇受人们的喜爱和尊敬。首段末句是承上启下的过渡句,引出了第二、三段的内容。第二、三段主要分析了制服深受人们喜爱和尊敬的原因。其中,第二段分析了人们格外喜欢制服的主要原因是:穿制服比穿普通衣服显得更专业一些;第三段列举了穿制服可以节省其他衣服、可以减税等许多实际的好处。第四、五两段列举了一些人反对穿制服的理由。其中,第四段谈到了这些人反对穿制服最主要的理由是:制服缺乏变化,因而穿制服会使人丧失了个性;第五段列举了穿制服可能给人带来的一些麻烦,例如:购买和养护制服都比普通的衣服要贵。其实,在做这道主旨题时不需把文章了解得如此清楚,只需抓住各段的主题句——第二、三、四、五段的段首句,就可以回答问题了。很明显,文章涉及了制服的有利之处,也谈到了制服不利的方面,因此正确答案是 D 选项。

例8:

In the USA, 85% of the population over the age of 21 approve of the death penalty. In the many states which still have the death penalty, some use the electrical chair, which can take up to 20 minutes to kill, while others use gas or lethal injection.

The first of these was the case of Ruth Ellis who was hanged for shooting her lover in what was generally regarded as a crime of passion. **The second** was hanged for murders which, it was later proved, had been committed by someone else.

The pro-hanging lobby uses four main arguments to support its call for the reintroduction of capital punishment. First, there is the deterrence theory, which argues that the potential murderers would think twice before committing the act; if they knew that they might die if they were caught. The armed bank robber might, go back to being unarmed.

The other two arguments are more suspect. The idea of retribution demands that criminals should get what they deserve: if a murderer intentionally sets out to commit a crime, he should accept the consequences. Retribution, which is just another word for revenge, is supported by the religious doctrine of an eye for an eye and a tooth for a tooth.

The arguments against the death penalty are largely humanitarian. But there are also statistical reasons for opposing it: the deterrence figure do not add up. In Britain, 1903 was the record for executions and yet in 1904 the number of murders actually rose. There was a similar occurrence in 1946 and 1947. If the deterrence theory were correct, the rate should have fallen.

The other reasons to oppose the death penalty are largely a mater of individual conscience and belief. One is that murder is murder and the state has no more right to take a life than the individual. **The other** is that Christianity advises forgiveness, not revenge. (1997 年第一篇)

Question:

The passage is mainly about _____.

A. the argument in favor of the death penalty

B. the argument against the death penalty

C. the argument about the reintroduction of the death penalty

D. the argument about the abolition of the death penalty

这是一篇关于美国人对死刑态度的说明文。从每一段的主题句可以看出第一段主要讲美国大多数人赞成执行死刑以及各种执行死刑的方式；第二段列举了历史上两个死刑执行的案例；第三、四段介绍了人们赞成重新实施死刑的依据；第五、六段介绍了人们反对实施死刑的理由。由此可以看出，本文对是否应该恢复执行死刑这一问题正反两方面的观点进行了平实客观的介绍，不掺杂任何作者个人的态度，因此应该首先排除含有作者主观意见的 A、B 两个选项。此外 D 选项说的是死刑的废除，和文章主旨不符，因此正确答案是 C 选项。

（3）文章的主旨 = 各段落段意之和。

阅读中也有少数文章的各段落中没有明显的主题句，这就给把握全文主旨增加了一定的难度。遇到这种文章时，一种办法是自己总结各段的主要内容，然后将各段内容相加得到全文主旨。另一种办法是套用下文将要提到的排除法公式做题。在总结各段的主要内容时，可以利用本书第一篇中提到的文章篇章结构的知识，特别是可以体现主题的核心词语的重复出现来把握主旨。

例 9：

Researchers have established that when people are mentally engaged, biochemical changes occur in the brain that allow it to act more effectively in cognitive areas such as attention and memory. This is true regardless of age.

People will be alert and receptive if they are faced with information that gets them to think about things they are interested in. And someone with a history of doing more rather than less will go into old age more cognitively sound than someone who has not had an active mind.

Many experts are so convinced of the benefits of challenging the brain that they are putting the theory to work in their own lives. "The idea is not necessarily to learn to memorize enormous amounts of information." says James Fozard, associate director of the National Institute on Aging. "Most of us don't need that kind of skill. Such specific training is of less interest than being able to maintain mental alertness." Fozard and others say they challenge their brains with different mental skills, both because they enjoy them and because they are sure that their range of activities will help the way their brains work.

Gene Cohen, acting director of the same institute, suggests that people in their old age should engage in mental and physical activities individually as well as in groups. Cohen says that we are frequently advised to keep physically active as we age, but older people need to keep mentally active as well. Those who do are more likely to maintain their intellectual abilities and to be generally happier and better adjusted. "The point is, you need to do both," Cohen says. Intellectual activity actually influences brain-cell health and size.

Question:

What is the passage mainly about?

A. How biochemical changes occur in the human brain.

B. Why people should keep active not only physically but also mentally.

C. How intellectual activities influence brain-cell health.

D. Why people should receive special mental training as they age.

第二章　阅读理解

本文是一篇调查研究类型的论说文。文章第一段指出研究者认为人们动脑时，脑部的注意力和记忆力等认知区域的活动会更活跃、更有效。第二段指出如果人能多思考使他们感兴趣的问题，当他们老的时候会比没这么做的人具有更强的认知能力。第三段介绍了这些研究者深信这一理论并将它付诸实践，不断用各种活动来挑战自己的大脑。第四段总结指出老年人不仅应有健康的身体，还应有健康的头脑。文章的第四段点出了全文的观点：老年人不仅应有健康的身体，还应有健康的头脑；第一、二段说明了为什么要这么做的理论依据；第三段提供了事实依据。因此，通过综合各段主要内容可以判断全文的主旨应该是 B 选项所表达的。

例 10：

Americans usually consider themselves a friendly people. Their friendships, however, tend to be shorter and more casual than friendships among people from other cultures. It is not uncommon for Americans to have only one close friend during their life-time, and consider other "friends" to be just social acquaintances. This attitude probably has something to do with American mobility and the fact that Americans do not like to be dependent on other people. They tend to "compartmentalize"（划分）friendships, having "friends at work" "friends on the softball team" "family friends", etc.

Because the United States is a highly active society, full of movement and change, people always seem to be on the go. In this highly charged atmosphere, Americans can sometimes seem brusque or impatient. They want to get to know you as quickly as possible and then move on to something else. Something, early on, they will ask you questions that you may feel are very personal. No insult is intended; the questions usually grow out of their genuine interest or curiosity, and their impatience to get to the heart of the matter. And the same does for you. If you do not understand certain American behavior or you want to know more about them, do not hesitate to ask them questions about themselves. Americans are usually more eager to explain all about their country or anything "American" in which you may be interested. So much so in fact that you may become tired of listening. It doesn't matter because Americans tend to be uncomfortable with silence during a conversation. They would rather talk about the weather or the latest sports scores, for example, than deal with silence.

On the other hand, don't expect Americans to be knowledgeable about international geography or world affairs, unless those subjects directly involve the United States. Because the United States is not surrounded by many other nations, some Americans tend to ignore the rest of the world.（2001 年第一篇）

Question：

The general topic of the passage is _____.

A. American culture　　　　　　B. American society

C. Americans' activities　　　　　D. Americans' personality

本文是一篇介绍美国人性格典型特征的论说文。由于文章主要探讨的主题，不是通过文章的主题句集中表达的，而是散落于各段当中，因此做该题应当应用主旨题答题的公式：主旨＝各段主要内容之和。本文第一段主要讲美国人对待友谊的态度；第二段主要讲美国人看似无礼、不耐烦等性格特征；第三段主要讲美国人对国际事务缺乏了解。不难看出，全文重在介绍美国人典型的性格特征，因此 D 是正确答案。A 项 American culture（美国文化）和 B 项 American society（美国社会）覆盖面过广，过于宽泛。而 C 选项 Americans' activities（美国人的活动）与各段内容不符。

2. 主旨题阅读公式二

文章的主旨 ≠ 文中的某一细节
　　　　　 ≠ 文中某一部分的主要内容
　　　　　 ≠ 覆盖面过广的表述
　　　　　 ≠ 文章未涉及的内容

这套主旨题做题公式主要用于排除法做题。特别适用于那些既没有全文主旨句又没有段落主题句的文章。对于这类文章，很多考生往往缺乏概括每一段落主要意思的能力，这时候，应当从研究答案选项入手，采取排除法做题，可以取得事半功倍的效果。本套公式就是考生用排除法做题去掉主旨题干扰项时应当参照的依据。本章第一节已经清楚界定了文章主旨的相关概念，因此在用此套公式做题时，要首先排除只涉及了文章中某个具体事例或带有具体的人名、地名的细节描述型选项；其次，要重点研究并排除最具有干扰力的一类选项，这类选项往往和主旨相关，但却不够全面，只涉及文章某一段或某几段的内容；第三，还要警惕那些放之四海而皆准的常识性表述；最后，还要排除那些文章中根本未提及的内容，这些内容往往和主题沾边，但在文章有限的范围内未能被涉及。

例 11：

The concept of "environment" is certainly difficult and may even be misunderstood; but we have no handy substitute. It seems simple enough to distinguish between the organism and the surrounding environment and to separate forces acting on an organism into those that are internal and biological and those that are external and environmental. **But in actual practice this system breaks down in many ways, because the organism and the environment are constantly interacting so that the environment is modified by the organism and vice versa**（反之亦然）.

In the case of man, the difficulties with the environmental concept are even more complicated because we have to deal with man as an animal and with man as a bearer（持有者）of culture. If we look at man as an animal and try to analyze the environmental forces that are acting on the organism, we find that we have to deal with things like climate, soil, plants, and such-like factors common to all biological situations; but we also find, always, very important environmental influences that we can only class as "cultural," which modify the physical and biological factors. But man, as we know him, is always a bearer of culture; and, if we study human culture, we find that it, in turn, is modified by the environmental factors of climate and geography. We thus easily get into great difficulties from the necessity of viewing culture, at one moment, as a part of the man and, at another moment, as a part of the environment.

Question：

In this passage, the author is primarily concerned with _____.

A. the interpretation of the term "environment"
B. the discussion on the organisms and biological environment
C. the comparison between internal and external factors influencing man
D. the evaluation of man's influence on culture

这是一篇典型的驳斥性论说文。第一段首先指出很多人对于环境这一概念的理解过于简单。第一段第二句介绍了普通人对环境的理解，这正是本文要批驳的靶子。第一段最后一句，在转折词 But 之后的部分是作者真正要表达的观点，也是文章的主旨，即生物和环境是相互影响、相互作用的，因此在现实中很难截然区分出哪些是生物链的内部因素，哪些是环境的外部因素。文章的第二段是以生物中最为复杂的人为例来进一步说明环境概念的复杂性，进一步申明作者自己的真实观点，即人和环境是相互影响、相互作用的。虽然文章中有明显的全文主旨句，但是这道主旨题的选项却是用主题（subject）的形式来概括全文内容的，而不是用主题句的形式，因此要做对这道题目，仅仅抓住了主旨句是不够的，还必须结合主旨题阅读公式二中所列举的排除法做题原则来排除干扰项。B 选项"关于生物体和生物环境的讨论"只涉及了文章中某一部分内容，而忽略了可以影响生物的外部环境因素。C 选项"关于影响人的内部因素和外部因素的比较"只涉及了文章第二段的内容，不够全面，而且对第二段的概括也不准确，因为该段根本没有对这些因素进行比较。D 选项"评价人对文化的影响"属于文章中未涉及的内容，因此，这三个选项都应予以排除。只有 A 选项"对环境概念的解释"全面、准确地概括了全文的内容，故为正确答案。

例12：

The word science is heard so often in modern times that almost everybody has some notion of its meaning. On the other hand, its definition is difficult for many people. The meaning of the term is confused, but everyone should understand its meaning and objectives. Just to make the explanation as simple as possible, suppose science is defined as classified knowledge (facts).

Even in the true sciences distinguishing fact from fiction is not always easy. For this reason great care should be taken to distinguish between beliefs and truths. There is no danger as long as a clear difference is made between temporary and proved explanations. For example, hypotheses (假设) and theories are attempts to explain natural phenomena. From these positions the scientist continues to experiment and observe until they are proved or discredited. The exact status of any explanation should be clearly labeled to avoid confusion.

The objectives of science are primarily the discovery and the subsequent understanding of the unknown. Man cannot be satisfied with recognizing that secrets exist in nature or that questions are unanswerable; he must solve them. Toward that end specialists in the field of biology and related fields of interest are directing much of their time and energy.

Actually, two basic approaches lead to the discovery of new information. One, aimed at studying curiosity, is referred to as pure science. The other is aimed at using knowledge for specific purposes—for instance, improving health, raising standards of living, or creating new consumer products. In this case knowledge is put to economic use. Such an approach is referred to as applied science.

Sometimes practical-minded people miss the point of pure science in thinking only of its immediate application for economic rewards. Chemists responsible for many of the discoveries could hardly have anticipated that their findings would one day result in application of such a practical nature as those directly related to life and death. The discovery of one bit of information opens the door to the discovery of another. Some discoveries seem so simple that one is amazed they were not made years ago; however, one should remember that the construction of the microscope had to precede the discovery of the cell. The host of scientists dedicating their lives to pure science are not apologetic about ignoring the practical side of their discoveries; they know from experience that most knowledge is eventually applied. （1999年第五篇）

Question：

The best title for the passage is _____.

A. Hypotheses and Theories　　　　　B. On distinguishing Fact from Fiction
C. The Nature of Science and Scientists　　D. Biology and the Scientific Age

这篇文章是一篇典型的说明文。文章主要通过阐述理论科学和应用科学的区别，揭示了科学本质和科学家的使命。由于文章各段没有明显的主题句可以利用，所以在做主旨题时也要用到排除法，首先根据公式排除细节内容A选项和B选项，再排除未涉及的内容D选项，所剩的就只有正确答案C选项了。

上述例子说明在利用主旨题做题公式时，同时还要利用其他方法以求达到最迅速、最准确做题的目的，说明考生应在初读文章的时候，就应当格外留意文章的首尾两段，甚至各个段落的首句和末句，并相应地做出标记。其次，在判断选项时可结合排除法原则来排除明显的干扰项，缩小考虑的范围，减少阅读量。

细节题阅读公式

1. 注意事项

确定了中心思想只是完成了正确理解文章的第一步，抓住了文章主干，并不等于全面掌握全文内容，考生还需要找出阐述主题或中心思想的相关细节，即抓住文章的枝叶，这样才能准确地理解全文，获取必要的、充分的信息。有关事实和细节（specific details），即针对文章中的某一句或几句话的考题，在阅读部分所占的比例最大，每套阅读真题的20道阅读题目中常常有一半多是细节题。我们知道，文章中的具体内容都是为了烘托主题，或是为了使主题更鲜明以便读者一目了然，或是以例证的形式来证明某个观点是正确或错误的。因此，要想迅速准确地捕捉到所需要的信息，考生在阅读时应注意以下四点：

① 中心内容和具体内容的辩证关系。只有抓住文章的主要内容才能确定有关具体内容的准确位置。同样，对文章具体内容有了较为全面的理解，才能更好地判明文章的主题。

② 文章的细节与相关内容的依存关系。即某个具体事实并不是孤立的，它总要与其他事实前后呼应，相同性质的事实总会放在一起阐述。

③ 文章的组织结构对发现相关细节的引导作用。看懂文章的段落结构对捕捉到所需要的信息也同样起着重要的作用。

④ Wh-型疑问词的引导作用。一般说来，每篇文章都会包括如下 5 个方面，即我们通常所说的"5Wh's"：Who；When；Where；What；Why（How）。

本类考题相对来说最为容易，关键是如何迅速准确地在一篇 350～400 字左右的文章中找到所需信息。绝大多数考生不可能只读一遍文章就能记清每个细节问题，但有经验的考生知道某个细节该从哪个自然段的哪一部分去找，这是因为他们在通读完文章后对每一段落的主要内容有个大致的了解。考生要严格按照先通读再做题的先后顺序，切莫为了节省时间而直接答题，这样做往往适得其反。另外，首先要把问题看清后再去文中查找，要看文中哪句话和你的问题对应，而不是哪个词。另外，文章后面问题出现的先后顺序一般与文章的顺序一致，这多少也能大致"帮助"我们确定所需内容的位置。

2. 常见的提问方式及解题要点

要掌握确定细节的阅读技能，考生首先要了解对这些事实和细节提问的方式。前面讨论过的关于细节内容的提问方式大致可以分为三大类：

第一大类是以疑问代词 when, where, what, who, how, how many 等文中细节提问的方式。常见的提问方式总结如下：

What is said about…?
Who played an important role in…?
Where can you find…?
How long does it take for…to…?
What is the chief factor influencing…?
How many possible places have been recommended for…?
According to the passage, when did…begin to…?
How does…feel about…?

在做这类题目时，可遵循前面介绍过的解题步骤，先速读全文以掌握主要内容，明确细节分布的大致情况，然后再快速浏览问题，带着问题回到原文中查找相关细节所在位置，以便准确地找到答案。在第一遍阅读时，应当注意有关人名、地点、时间、数字、形容词或副词的比较级、最高级之类的信息，适当做些标记，以便迅速查找。

例 1：

An election year is one in which all four numbers are evenly divisible by four (1944, 1948, etc.). Since 1840, American presidents elected in years ending in zero have been destined to die in office. **William H. Harrison**, the man who served the **shortest** term, died of pneumonia several weeks after his inauguration.

Abraham Lincoln was one of four presidents who were assassinated. He was elected in 1860, and his untimely death came just five years later.

James A. Garfield, a former Union army general from **Ohio**, was shot during his first year in office (1881) by a man to whom he wouldn't give a job.

While in his second term of office (1901), **William McKinley**, another Ohioan, attended the Pan-American Exposition at Buffalo, New York. During the reception, he was assassinated while shaking hands with some of the guests.

Three years after his election in **1920**, **Warren G. Harding** died in office. Although it was never proved, many believe he was poisoned.

Franklin D. Roosevelt had been elected four times (1932, 1936, 1940, and 1944), **the only man** to serve so long a term. He had contracted polio in 1921 and died of the illness in 1945.

John F. Kennedy, the last of the line, was assassinated in **1963**, only three years later his election.

Will 1980's candidate suffer the same fate?

Questions:

1. Which president served the shortest term in office?
   A. Abraham Lincoln.　　　　　　　B. Warren G. Harding.
   C. William McKinley.　　　　　　　D. William H. Harrison.
2. When did Lincoln die?
   A. 1881.　　B. 1860.　　C. 1865.　　D. 1901.
3. Who was NOT assassinated in office?
   A. John F. Kennedy.　　　　　　　B. Franklin D. Roosevelt.
   C. Abraham Lincoln.　　　　　　　D. James A. Garfield.
4. Which of the following is an election year in the U.S. ?
   A. 1982.　　B. 1984.　　C. 1991.　　D. 1923.
5. Where was McKinley assassinated?
   A. In Ohio.　　　　　　　　　　　B. In New York.
   C. In Washington.　　　　　　　　D. In Chicago.

这是一篇介绍美国自1840年以来历届在以零结尾的年份当选的总统的死亡情况。十分巧合的是他们都是死在任期中，其死因或由于疾病或遭到暗杀。这篇文章的特色是全文充满了具体的人名和地名。阅读起来难度不大，但需要考生相当细心。上面的题目都是针对这些细节而出的。考生只要回查原文相关细节就不难找到答案。

第一题的答案是 D，文章在第一段第三行有明确的表述。第二题的答案是 C，这是对具体的时间提问。首先要回到关于 Lincoln 的那段仔细阅读，然后需要做一下计算。Lincoln 是1860年当选总统，5年之后被暗杀，因此他是死于1865年。第三题的答案是 B。这道题可以用两种方法来做。第一种方法是根据第一遍速读时的印象回到有关 Roosevelt 的这段寻找答案。这段明确表述了 Roosevelt 是死于疾病。第二种方法是用排除法来做。第四道题的答案是 B。这需要根据文章的介绍做一下计算。从文章第一段可知美国大选的年份是可以被4整除的，因此首先可以排除 C 和 D，然后再计算一下 A 和 B 即可。第五道题是关于地点的问题，只要回到介绍此人的段落中去，不难发现他是生于 Ohio，死于 New York 的。

第二大类是针对导致事件发生的起因、影响事件发展的因素等方面的问题。常见的提问方式如下：

The author describes…as…because _____.

The passage seems to say that different definitions of…are given due to _____.

According to the passage,…is most probably caused by _____.

One reason why…are likely to…is that _____.

Why does the author think…?

According to the passage, the problem of…partly arises from…?

Which of the following account for…?

在回答这类问题时，应注意文章里一些表示因果关系的词语。例如：连词：so, hence, therefore, as, for, since, because 等。动词：cause, lead to, result in, result from, contribute to, induce 等。介词词组：due to, because of, owning to, thanks to 等。名词：reason, factor, cause 等。

例2：

Teenagers often spend hours shopping, especially on weekends. The fact that they are doing more shopping may **result in** their spending more money in stores they go to. **In addition**, youths often have a great deal of authority in store-selection decisions, which means that stores must attract them with an effective appeal. Although the popular belief is that young people buy products impulsively and are less rational than the market as a whole, surveys indicate that most respondents aged 14 to 25 compare prices and brands before buying.

Questions：

1. Teenagers are spending more money because _____.

    A. they are richer than before

    B. they are doing more shopping

    C. they are wasting more money

    D. they get more money from their parents

2. Why does the store want to attract the teenagers?

    A. Because they are spending more money.

    B. Because they can often decide which store to go in.

    C. Because they are less rational.

    D. Both A and B.

这段短文论述了现在的商店为什么要吸引十几岁的孩子们的注意力。文章说这主要是因为现在越来越多的孩子负责购物，他们花的钱越来越多，而且他们往往能够替父母决定在哪里购物。所以，第一题的答案应是 B，应注意原文中表示因果关系的动词词组 result in；第二题的答案应是 D，应注意表示文章结构的连接词语 In addition，由此可知商店要吸引孩子的原因不止一个。

第三大类的问题是排除式题型。这类题目包括：

Which of the following statements is true according to this passage?

According to this passage, all of the following are true except…?

Which of the following is Not true?

Which of the following is not mentioned (included) in the passage?

Which of the following can best describe…according to the text?

All of the following descriptions of…are correct except _____.

Which of the following is true concerning …?

All the following are stated in the passage except that _____.

在做这类题目时，要特别小心题中带有 not 或 except 等否定词的导向作用词，因此这些题的做题方法要使用反向思维。这种题目往往出现在文章有列举的地方，比如并列句或并列的词组。因此，在阅读时应对文章出现列举的地方做适当的标记。在解题时，最基本的做法是逐项对照原文找出肯定的内容，确定要否定的内容。也就是要采用排除法，首先排除与原文内容相同的选项，逐渐缩小范围，最后未被排除的选项就是该题的正确答案。或者可以采用较为直接和快速的做法：找出和文章中某一句话的表述正好相反的选项，那就是正确答案。这种方法往往对考生的阅读基本功有较高的要求。

例 3：

Many people agree with the ideas and goals of women's liberation. **They feel that** women ought to be considered equal to men in every way. **They feel that** a woman should be able to decide to stay home and raise a family, **or** to stay home and not raise a family, **or** to go out and work, **or** to have a job outside the home and in family as well. **They feel** a woman should be able to do anything that she wants to do and can do. Other people are opposed to women's liberation. **They do not think** that women should have the same jobs and the same pay as men. **They believe** that men should do all of the important work. **They feel** that women belong at home, taking care of men and children. Many husbands do not want their wives to work outside the home. Some women agree with these men. People who believe in women's liberation do not feel that it is bad for a woman to remain at home if she wants to. They believe that work in the home is important and should be respected. But they want to make sure that a woman works at home because she wants to, and not because she can't get a job outside the home, or because she does not believe that she can do anything useful in her community.

The women's liberation movement is trying to give women a chance to show what they can do. **Perhaps a woman will** find the cure for our most serious disease. **Perhaps a woman will** solve the energy crisis, perhaps women and men, working together, will be able to accomplish important things better and sooner than men if men were working alone. If the women's liberation movement is successful, we will have a chance to find out.

Questions：

1. Which is not the view of people who agree with women's liberation?

    A. Women ought to be considered equal to men in every way.

    B. A woman should be able to decide to stay home or to go out and work.

    C. A woman should be able to do anything that she wants to do and can do.

    D. A woman should have a job outside the home.

2. Which is not the view of people who disagree with women's liberation?

    A. Women should not have the same jobs and the same pay as men.

    B. Men should do all of the important work.

    C. Women should earn money to help their husbands.

    D. Women belong at home, taking care of men and children.

3. People who believe in women's liberation _____.

   A. feel that it is bad for a woman to remain at home even if she wants to

   B. believe that work in the home is not important and should not be respected

   C. want to make sure that a woman works at home because she wants to

   D. believe women would work better than men do

4. Which of the following might women's liberation have nothing to do with?

   A. Finding the cure for our most serious disease.

   B. Solving the energy crisis.

   C. Accomplishing important things better and sooner than men if men were working alone.

   D. Stopping the wars in the world.

5. Which of the following is true?

   A. All women agree with the ideas of women's liberation.

   B. Some women agree with the men who don't want their wives to work outside the home.

   C. All women disagree with the ideas of women's liberation.

   D. Women should be allowed to serve in the army.

这篇文章主要是介绍了人们对于妇女解放运动的不同态度，有人赞同，有人反对。支持妇女解放运动的人认为妇女应该在每一个方面都和男人平等；妇女应该能够决定自己是否要留在家里照顾丈夫和孩子；妇女可以做任何她想做而且能做的事情。而反对妇女解放运动的人则认为妇女不该和男人同工同酬；妇女就应该待在家里照顾男人和孩子。而且，很多丈夫不希望妻子外出工作。文章的最后一段还展望了妇女外出工作以后可能给社会带来的种种好处。要想回答这五道题，只要回到原文仔细阅读，采用排除法排除与题意不符的或文中未提到的即可。因此，第一题的答案是 D；第二题的答案是 C；第三题的答案是 C；第四题的答案是 D；第五题的答案是 B。

由于这一类的 NOT TRUE 或 EXCEPT 题型的细节题在阅读试题中很常见，因此对于考生来说，一定要养成一种意识：文章中有列举或并列的地方通常会有题目出现，不管是出现在一句话中的并列结构，还是散落于段落中的并列句（通常以表示并列或递进的连接词为引导）。

细节题阅读公式

1. 普通细节题阅读公式

① 题干关键词 + 正确答案 = 原文含有题干关键词的一句话

② 原文含有题干关键词的一句话 – 题干关键词 = 正确答案

阅读中细节题部分的题目很有规律性，其出题原则就是考查考生对文章中支持主旨的细节部分某一句话或相邻的某几句话的理解，而出题者就根据原文中的这些句子先编出细节题的题干和正确答案选项，然后再添加适当的干扰项。因此对于一道细节题而言，就如细节题阅读公式①中所示，其题干和正确答案之和就是原文中直接含有题干关键词的一句话或含有题干关键词的原文上下文中的某一句话。在真正解题时，考生可以利用细节题阅读公式②，并按照以下的具体做题步骤来解题即可。

具体做题步骤：第一，根据题干中具有提示作用的关键词回到原文中迅速定位，找出原文中带有该关键词或该词同义词的语句。

第二，去掉原句与题干重复的表述，所剩部分通常便是答案所在。

第三，以剩余部分为依据，在答案选项中寻找与之相似的表达。

在运用这一公式做题时，辨别题干中的哪一部分是具有提示作用的关键词和寻找与原文表述相似的答案选项是做题的关键所在。题干中具有提示作用的关键词通常是人名、地名、专有名词、时间以及与文章主题密切相关的核心词语、带有引号等特殊标点符号的词语。由于这些词语在文章中出现时都较为醒目，因此以这些词语为依据就可以迅速找到该题在原文中出处，从而节省做题时间。在同等学力阅读测试中作为正确答案的选项很少会是和原文完全相同的表述，通常会对原文答案部分进行同义词、近义词替换或句子结构方面的调整，比如：原文用的是主动语态，答案选项可能变成被动语态；原文用的是肯定句，而答案选项改成双重否定句等。这就要求考生能够具备在本书第一篇所涉及的词汇和句子基本功。

例1：

On the other hand, don't expect Americans to be knowledgeable about international geography or world affairs, unless those subjects directly involve the United States. Because **the United States is not surrounded by many other nations**, some Americans tend to ignore the rest of the world. （2001年第一篇）

Question：

According to the passage, Americans are inclined to ignore the rest of the world because _____.

A. they are not interested in other countries

B. they are too proud of themselves

C. their country does not have many neighboring nations

D. They are too busy to learn about other countries

本题中的大写字母单词是很好的提示词，可以帮助读者很快回到原文中定位，特别注意题干和答案选项中出现的同义词替换。tend to 和 are inclined to 是同义词；正确答案 C 中的 their country does not have many neighboring nations 是原文中 the United States is not surrounded by many other nations 换一句的说法。

例2：

In the 1997 general-election campaign, "Education, Education" was Tony Blair's pet phrase. Times change quickly. Education is going rapidly out of fashion. "Learning" (to be exact) is New Labour's buzzword (时髦语). The shift from "education" to "learning" **reflects more than a change**. It stems from both educational research and left-ideas. During the 1980s, British educationalists got some new American ideas. One was the notion that traditional examinations do not test the full range of people's abilities. Another was the belief that skills are not necessarily learned from teachers in an conventional classroom. People can pick them up in all sorts of ways. （2000年第六篇）

Question：

According to the writer, the shift from "education" to "learning" _____.

A. is nothing but a change of language

B. reflects the traditional ideas in education

C. reflects the government's wish to restrict choices

D. is not just a change of language

细节题中带有特殊标点的单词也是很好的信号词。正确答案选项将原文中的 more than 替换成了相似的说法 not just。

上述这些例子是细节题最普遍、最基本的出题模式。从上述例子的分析中可以发现当套用这套细节阅读公式做题时找出细节题的答案，在大多数情况下根本不需要仔细斟酌句子的含义，就像解代数题一样，只不过代数题是用数字来替换代数式中的 A、B、C 或 X、Y，而细节阅读题是同义词、同义结构来替换原文中关键部分的表述。

但是，有些细节题不像上述这些例子这么简单，考生往往不能直接从原文含有题干关键词的句子中找到答案。在这类细节题中，原文包含题干关键词的句子只是题干的重述，而正确答案在该句的相邻语句中。这时，必须找到答案在原文的正确位置，然后再套用细节题公式做题。

例3：

Although the threat of global warming known to the world for decades and all countries and leaders agree that we need to deal with the problem, we also know that the effects of measures, especially harsh measures taken in some countries, would be mollified（抵消）if other countries do not control their emissions. Whereas the UN team on climate change has found that the emissions of carbon dioxide would have to be <u>cut globally by 60%</u> to stabilize the content of CO_2, in the atmosphere, this path is <u>not feasible for several reasons</u>. **Such deep cuts would cause a breakdown of the world economy**. Important and populous low-or-medium-income countries are not willing to undertake legal commitments about their energy uses. In addition, the state of world technology would not yet permit us to make such a big leap. （1999 年第四篇）

Question：

According to the author, <u>it is impossible at present to cut 60% of carbon dioxide emissions globally</u> because _____.

A. some people are irresponsible

B. it would cause a collapse of the world economy

C. it is only a goal to be reached in the future

D. some people are lacking in imagination

最有提示作用的题干关键词应当是 cut 60% of carbon dioxide emissions globally，特别是数字 60% 的提示作用。因此很容易找到原文中的出处是在第二段第二句话。但这句话完全是题干的翻版，本身并不包含答案，要根据 this path is not feasible for several reasons 这句话的提示在下文中找答案。紧随其后的这句话 Such deep cuts would cause a breakdown of the world economy. 才是答案。B 选项中用代词 it 代替了 Such deep cuts；用 collapse 代替了 breakdown，进行了同义词替换。

例4：

<u>In 1992</u>, many people watched in horror as <u>riots broke out</u> on a sad Wednesday evening in

Los Angeles, seemingly fed by video coverage from helicopters. **This event was triggered by the verdict**(裁定)**in the Rodney King beating**. We are now in an age where the public can have access to information that enables it to make its own judgments, and most people, who had seen the video of this beating, could not understand how the jury(陪审团) was able to acquit(宣布无罪) the policemen involved. Media coverage of events as they occur also provides powerful feedback that influences events. This can have harmful results, as it seemed on that Wednesday night in Los Angeles. By Friday night the public got to see Rodney King on television pleading, "Can we all get along?" by Saturday, television seemed to provide positive feedback as Los Angeles riot turned out into a rally for peace. The television showed thousands of people marching with banners and cleaning tools. Because of that, many people turned out to join the peaceful event they saw unfolding(展开) on television. The real healing, of course, will take much longer, but electronic media will continue to be a part of that process. (1999年第三篇)

Question:

The 1992 Los Angeles riots broke out because _____.

A. video coverage from helicopters had made people angry

B. video coverage had provided powerful feedback

C. the jury acquitted the policemen who had beaten Rodney King

D. people can make their own judgments

根据题干中的关键词 The 1992 Los Angeles riots broke out 回到原文第三段段首第二句话可知正确答案应是 C 选项所表达的原因。在这里应注意原文中表示起因的动词 trigger(引起)的提示作用和 This 的指代作用。

从上面两个例子，可以看出做细节题的共同点是原文包含题干关键词的句子和其后的句子联系非常密切，而这种紧密关系都是通过运用我们在第一章中讲到的指代词的连接作用来实现的。

阅读文章细节题中的90%都可以套用本节的细节题公式来做题，在使用这一公式时要注意以下几点：第一，要准确判断题干关键词，这是做题速度的保障。因为很多时候整个题干很长，而且并非所有信息都重要，这时能准确抓住最有提示意义的关键词，就不必满篇乱找，可以节省做题时间。第二，一定要回原文中定位，这是做题正确率的保障。一定要回原文中找出包含题干部分的句子，不能只根据自己的记忆或理解来做题。一般的读者在速读完一篇文章后，可能会对文章的大意有所了解，但不太可能记清文章的所有细节，因此仅靠记忆做细节题是很不准确的。而细节题是各类阅读题目中占比重最多的也是最容易得分的，因此，一定要保证细节题的正确率。第三，要注意比对正确答案选项和原文的异同之处，这是培养语感的关键。在每次做完细节题后，拿出一点时间来比对一下正确答案和原句的说法，注意总结什么样的表达可以算做同义替换，这样，久而久之，就会培养出对正确答案的一种特殊的"好感"，也就是我们所说的语感。

2. 特殊细节题阅读公式

（1）例子说明题：正确答案＝例子之前或之后的一句概述。

第二章 阅读理解

在阅读中,除了普通的细节题之外,还有一类特殊的细节题,那就是例子说明题。这种例子说明题通常是通过运用某个事例,提问作者要说明什么。这类题目虽特殊,但并不难做。文章中任何具体事例的作用都是要说明一个较为抽象、较为概括的实例、理论或观点。做题的关键就是怎样在文章中快速准确地找到这些概括的实例、理论或观点。根据本书第一章所讲的文章段落结构可知:英文段落最常见的是先总述后分述的结构,其次就是先分述后总述的结构,也就是说,表达段落中心意思的概括语句常出现在段首或段末,段落中间通常是用来阐述这些概括语句的分述部分。而分述部分最常见的阐述技巧之一就是列举具体事例。因此,找到例子说明的内容,不能紧紧盯着例子本身研究,而应该绕过例子,找到它前面或后面的一句概括语。做题的具体步骤应当是:根据题干中的有提示意义的关键词,迅速回原文找到该例子的出处,然后再绕过例子看概述。

例5:

A status has been compared to ready-made clothes. Within certain limits the buyer can choose style and fabric. But an American is not free to choose the costume(服装)of a Chinese peasant or that of a Hindu prince. We must choose from among the clothing presented by our society. Further more, our choice is limited to a size that will fit, as well as by our pocketbook(钱包). Having made a choice within these limits we can have certain alterations made, but apart from minor adjustments, we tend to be limited to what the stores have on their racks. Statuses too come ready made, and the range of choice among them is limited.

Question:

By saying that "an American is not free to choose the costume of a Chinese peasant or that of a Hindu prince" (Lines 2-3, Para. 3), the writer means _____.

A. different people have different styles of clothes

B. ready-made clothes may need alterations

C. statuses come ready made just like clothes

D. our choice of statuses is limited

根据本题题干中的三个大写的单词American、Chinese和Hindu,很容易找到题干在文章中的位置。这句话是作为该段分述部分的一个具体例子来说明该段段首和段末表达的段落主旨:人的身份、地位是既定的,就像成衣一样,人们在做选择时,是受限的。段落是典型的总—分—总的结构。因此,正确答案应当是D选项。

例6:

While still in its early stages, welfare reform has already been judged a great success in many states—at least in getting people off welfare. It's estimated that more than 2 million people have left the rolls since 1994.

In the past four years, welfare rolls in Athens County have been out in half. But 70 percent of the people who left in the past two years took jobs that paid less than $6 an hour. The result: the Athens County poverty rate still remains at more than 30 percent—twice the national average.

For advocates(代言人) for the poor, that's an indication much more needs to be

121

done. "More people are getting jobs, but it's not making their lives any better", says Kathy Lairn, a policy analyst at the Center on Budget and Policy Priorities in Washington.

Question:

What is worth noting from the example of Athens County is that _____.

A. greater efforts should be made to improve people's living standards

B. 70 percent of the people there have been employed for two years

C. 50 percent of the population no longer relies on welfare

D. the living standards of most people are going down

根据题干关键词"Athens County",可以很快找到原文第二段是这个例子的出处。这个例子给出了具体的数字,指出了在 Athens County,虽然接受救济的人数减少了,但是该地区的贫困程度却没有改善。根据第三段第一句中"that"的指代作用,我们可以判断该句就是这个例子所说明的问题:还要做更多的工作才能真正地提高人们的生活水平。正确答案 A 选项就是该句同义的表述。

例7:

Diego Chiapello, legally blind since birth, isn't one of Italy's famous "mama's boys" who live with their parents into adulthood. The 27-year-old lives alone in Milan, works as a network administrator, loves diving and dreams of sailing across the Atlantic with a sight-impaired(有视力障碍的) crew.

Obviously, he's not your average disabled person—but especially so in Italy. The country has more barriers to integration than almost anywhere else on the Continent: among European countries, Italy ranks third from the bottom in accessibility for the disabled, ahead of only Greece and Portugal. People who use wheelchairs, especially, find it difficult to navigate the country's cobblestone(鹅卵石) streets, ride buses or visit restaurants, shops and museums. Less than a quarter of Italy's disabled hold jobs compared with 47 percent for Europe. (2004 年第三篇)

Question:

In this passage, Chiapello is cited as an example of _____.

A. unusual disabled Italians

B. courageous blind sailors

C. typical handicapped people

D. vulnerable disabled Europeans

据 Chiapello 可以回到原文中定位,但仅从第一段的例子中很难概括出正确答案,这时应当注意到第二段的第一句话"Obviously, he is not your average disabled person"这是承上启下的过渡句,根据 he 的指代作用不难判断 A 是正确答案。选项中的 unusual 是 not average 的同义词。

在运用例子说明题的公式做题时,要记住两个关键点:一是要明确例子所出现的原文的段落结构和段落主旨;二是要能区分什么是概括的表述,什么是具体的细节。还要纠正一个错误习惯,那就是不能纠缠在例子本身的叙述中,不能一叶障目。这类题目在同等学力人员考研英语阅读考试中并不多见,因此考生更重要的是能够掌握此类题目的做题思路，特别是概述和例子之间在语义上有互为说明的关系。

（2）NOT TRUE 或 EXCEPT 题：正确答案≠原文中某一句话的表达。

在前面中我们已经详细介绍过此类题目的出题特征和答题的主要思路，我们可以将主要的答题思路归纳为上面的公式，以此应对在历年阅读真题中已经出现过的绝大部分此类题目。

例 8：

Americans usually consider themselves a friendly people. Their friendships, however, tend to be shorter and more casual than friendships among people from other cultures. It is not uncommon for Americans to have only one close friend during their life-time, and consider other "friends" to be just social acquaintances. This attitude probably has something to do with American mobility and the fact that Americans do not like to be dependent on other people. They tend to "compartmentalize"（划分）friendships, having "friends at work" "friends on the softball team" "family friends", etc.

Because the United States is a highly active society, full of movement and change, people always seem to be on the go. In this highly charged atmosphere, Americans can sometimes seem brusque or impatient. They want to get to know you as quickly as possible and then move on to something else. Something, early on, they will ask you questions that you may feel are very personal. No insult is intended; the questions usually grow out of their genuine interest or curiosity, and their impatience to get to the heart of the matter. And the same does for you. If you do not understand certain American behavior or you want to know more about them, do not hesitate to ask them questions about themselves. Americans are usually more eager to explain all about their country or anything "American" in which you may be interested. So much so in fact that you may become tired of listening. It doesn't matter because Americans tend to be uncomfortable with silence during a conversation. They would rather talk about the weather or the latest sports scores, for example, than deal with silence.

On the other hand, **don't expect Americans to be knowledgeable about international geography or world affairs**, unless those subjects directly involve the United States. Because the United States is not surrounded by many other nations, some Americans tend to ignore the rest of the world. （2001 年第一篇）

Question：

Which of the following statements is NOT TRUE according to the passage?

A. American do not like to depend on other people.

B. Friendships among Americans are prone to be casual.

C. Americans know a lot about international affairs.

D. Americans always seem to be busy.

正确答案为 C 选项。它与原文中最后一段第一句话"don't expect American to be knowledgeable about international geography or world affairs"的意思正好相反。在这里关键词的替换是答案中的"know a lot about"替换了原文中的"be knowledgeable about"。而其他三个选项均与原文的表达一致。

例 9：

In the 1997 general-election campaign, "Education, Education" was Tony Blair's pet phrase. Times change quickly. Education is going rapidly out of fashion. "Learning" (to be exact) is New Labour's buzzword (时髦语). The shift from "education" to "learning" reflects more than a change. It stems from both educational research and left-ideas. During the 1980s, British educationalists got some new American ideas. One was the notion that traditional examinations do not test the full range of people's abilities. Another was the belief that skills are not necessarily learned from teachers in an conventional classroom. People can pick them up in all sorts of ways.

All this echoed left-wing ideas that traditional teaching methods were not sufficiently adaptable to the needs of individual learners. Advocates of lifelong learning argue that it merely describes what has changed in education in the past decades. And there are now hundreds of schemes in which pupils learn outside the classroom.

Until now, education has been changing from below. In the next few weeks, the government will help from above. One of its main projects for lifelong learning is about to begin its first pilot programmers. With funding of $44 million in its first year, it will coordinate a new network of "learning centers" throughout the country. Traditional institutions, such as schools and colleges, will provide training at some non-traditional places of learning, such as supermarkets, pubs, and churches. **The theory is that in such places students will feel more at ease, and therefore will be better motivated, than in a classroom.**

The new schemes allow consumers of education to exercise complete choice over where, what and when they learn. In the rest of the state-run education sectors (部门), the government still seem to be committed to restricting choices as much as possible. If these programs succeed, they could improve the skills of Britain's workforce. （2000 年第六篇）

Question：

All the following statements are true EXCEPT that _____.

A. pupils can learn skills outside the classroom

B. students will be better motivated in a classroom

C. the new schemes are intended to improve the skills of Britain's workforce

D. traditional teaching methods cannot satisfy the needs of individual learners

正确答案为 B 选项。它与原文中第三段最后一句话的意思正好相反。原文在此处指出学生在超市、酒吧或教堂这些场所学习比在教室里学习更有动力。

我们在本章的第一节中已提到过此类题目经常会针对文章中的列举部分提问。这时，首先根据答案选项的提示，在文章中找到列举部分出现的位置，然后再进行比照。

例 10：

In the USA, 85% of the population over the age of 21 approve of the death penalty. In the many states which still have the death penalty, **some use the electrical chair**, which can take up to 20 minutes to kill, while **others use gas or lethal injection**. （1997 年第一篇）

Question:

All of the following death penalty methods are mentioned in the passage EXCEPT _____.

A. the electrical chair B. the lethal injection
C. the poisonous gas D. the shooting

这道题目就出现在原文有集中列举的地方，做起来比较容易，可根据原句列举的三项方式对照答案选项，便可得知正确答案是 D 选项。考生一定要熟悉这种集中列举在文章中的体现方式，它通常是跟在以下几种结构后：

① 并列关系，如：both…and…; not only… but also…; for one thing, … for another…; one…, the other…等。

② 举例，如：such…as; including…等。

For more than 10 years there has been a bigger rise in car crime than in most other types of crime. An average of more than two cars a minute are broken into, vandalized（破坏）or stolen in the UK. Car crime accounts for almost a third of all reported offences with no signs that the trend is slowing down.

Although there are highly professional criminals involved in car theft, almost 90 percent of car crime is committed by the opportunist. Amateur thieves are aided by our carelessness. When the Automobile Association (AA) engineers **surveyed one town centre car park last year**, 10 percent of cars checked were unlocked, a figure backed up by a Home Office national survey that found 12 percent of drivers sometimes left their cars unlocked.

The vehicles are sitting in petrol stations while drivers pay for their fuel. The AA has discovered that cars are left unattended for an average of three minutes—and sometimes much longer—as drivers buy drinks, cigarettes and other consumer items—and then pay at the counter. With payment by credit card more and more common, it is not unusual for a driver to be out of his car for as long as six minutes providing the car thief with a golden opportunity.

In an exclusive AA survey, carried out at a busy garage on a main road out of London, **300 motorists were questioned over three days of the holiday period**. 24 percent admitted that they "always" or "sometimes" leave the keys in the car. This means that nationwide, a million cars daily become easy targets for the opportunist thief.

The AA recommends locking up whenever you leave the car—and for however short a period. A partially open sunroof or window is a further come-on to thieves.

Leaving valuables in view is an invitation to the criminal. A Manchester probationary（假释期）service research project, which **interviewed almost 100 car thieves last year**, found many would investigate a coat thrown on a seat. Never leave any documents showing your home address in the car. If you have a garage, use it and lock it—a garaged car is at substantially less risk. （2002 年第四篇）

Question:

The researches mentioned in the passage on car theft include all the following EXCEPT _____.

A. checking private garages
B. interviewing motorists
C. questioning car thieves
D. examining parking lots

本题属于分散列举，可按照答案选项逐一回原文中定位。只有 A 是文中没有提到过的方式。分散列举做起来相对困难一些，可借助文中一些连接手段加以辨别，例如：first…, second…, third…; to begin with…, in addition…, moreover…等。

在做细节题时，除了可以套用上面的各种公式外，考生还应该对选项有一定的辨别能力，了解干扰项和正确答案通常具备的一些特点，结合排除法做题，以确保准确率和阅读速度。

干扰项通常具有以下特征：
① 照抄原文部分信息，有意给予一些遗漏；
② 含有原文中没有涉及的内容；
③ 含有与原文相矛盾的内容；
④ 含有张冠李戴的内容（把 A 的特征加到 B 上）；
⑤ 偷梁换柱：与原文内容一半相同一半不同，即选项仍用文章中的句法结构和大部分内容，但更换关键词，造成实际意思上的改变；
⑥ 与原句内容相似，但过于绝对化，常含有 only, everything, all, none, never, always, no, entirely, absolute 等词。

正确答案选项通常具有以下特征：
① 同义词替换；
② 常含有一些不肯定的词，例如：some, sometimes, more…than…, not as…as, less 等；
③ 正确答案选项常常在两个意思相近或相反的选项中。

词汇题阅读公式

要进行成功的阅读理解，掌握一定量的词汇是必不可少的。词汇包括领会式的，即看到一个单词就能理解其词义；也包括复用式的，即看到一个单词不但能理解其词义，而且能准确地拼写与运用。但是，词汇量大并不等于就能进行成功的阅读理解。懂得一篇文章所有单词的词义，并不等于就能理解通篇文章；而透彻理解一篇文章并不一定必须懂得这篇文章的所有单词！

对照我们使用母语进行阅读理解的过程就会发现我们常常碰到生词，但对此首先我们并不感到紧张。一般情况下，我们也不会翻开词典立刻查阅生词的词义，但却能理解文章的含义。实际上，许多汉语词汇并不是在课堂上学会的，而是在日常生活中、在大量阅读中、在一定情景下自然而然地习得的。同样，对于英语的阅读理解，我们也应该充分利用我们在学习、使用母语时已习得的各种技巧，根据英语的特点，逐步养成正确、可行的阅读技巧与习惯。例如：
① 英语单词是可以分析的，所以我们可以运用构词法知识来猜测、确定词义。
② 一个单词总是出现在一个连贯完整的语篇之中，有一定的情景、上下文限制，

所以我们可以利用上下文推测、确定词义以至语义。

③ 我们还可以利用语篇中逻辑连接词来推测、确定词义与语义。必须指出，在阅读理解过程中，对有些生词是可以采取忽略不计的态度的。在一个语篇特定的上下文中，特别是由于语言所固有的冗余现象，有些生词并不影响人们对文章的理解。再者，对不同类型的读者来说，有些生词所表达的信息并不是他所感兴趣需要获取的；或者说，在阅读理解考题中，这些生词所表达的信息并没有作为问题出现，所以完全可以忽略不计的。对于有些生词，我们只需知道其大概的意义就足够了，根据理解的需要，并不一定要搞懂其确切的含义。

每位考生都有自己的阅读习惯及理解、答题的方式。最好的方法是考生本人自己重复试验用自己的实践体会得到证明是奏效的、成功的方法。以下介绍的步骤分别是从各个不同的角度来处理、猜测词义和语义的。

1. 猜词基本步骤

（1）结构、功能线索可看做是猜测词义的第一步。

主要考虑：

① 生词属于哪一词类，是动词、名词、形容词，还是其他词类？

② 这一生词是对某一事物的描述，还是某一事物的名称？

③ 就作者的用意或逻辑连接词来看，这一生词的意义是褒义的，还是贬义的？是肯定的，还是否定的？

例1： The <u>discontent</u> of the people gave rise to much trouble.

对画线的这一生词，我们至少可以获得以下信息：名词，因前有定冠词；描述人们的情绪或行为，gave rise to much trouble 说明了这一点。

（2）构词法信息。

主要考虑：

① 你是否认识生词的某一部分？

② 生词是否加了前缀，后缀，还是由两个或两个以上单词合成？

对上例的 discontent，可获得信息：content 满意，dis 前缀，意为：不，无，相反。至此，整个词义就明确了。

（3）上下文信息。

上下文可以指整个语篇，也可指一个句子。这里最重要的是遇到一个生词，不要停下来冥思苦想，而是要继续下去，设法从上下文中找出生词的含义。如有必要，在读完一个语段或语篇后再回头看这个生词。

例2：

She poured the water into a *tock*. Then, lifting the *tock*, she drank. Unfortunately, as she was setting it down again, the *tock* slipped from her hand and broke. Only the handle remained in one place.

tock 是一个生造的无意义词，代表生词。以上语段，共四个句子。从第一句到第四句，我们可以一步步推进，缩小范围来猜测确定 tock 的含义。以下数字分别代表句1至句4。

① tock 是能够盛水的容器，可能是水桶、碗、洞等。

② tock 是能够举起的，所以不可能是洞，里面的水能喝。

③ 是易碎品，制作材料可能是玻璃、瓷等。

④ 有一个手柄，所以可能是喝水的杯子。是否有可能是其他带柄的盛水容器呢？缺乏充足的证据，但我们还是可以认定 tock 最有可能是杯子。

必须指出，对推断的词义我们并不要求100%的精确词义，对大部分阅读理解题来说，只要知道一个生词的大致的意思就已足够了。

2. 利用上下文猜词的依据

在阅读中遇到生词，除了运用构词法信息来推测其词义外，还可以充分利用生词所处的具体的上下文来揣摩、发现词的语法特征，并找出作者对词义的提示以确定其词义。

（1）根据上下文解释猜测词义。

① 直接定义法。

根据上下文以生词的定义为线索猜测词义是进行快速阅读时最常见、最直接的一种猜词方法。所谓定义就是作者经常会对文章中出现的一些生词、词组或术语进行解释。作者在解释这些词时直接使用下定义的方法，而且这些定义通常伴随一些标志性的语言，如：be, mean, refer to, to be defined as, be known as, be called, be termed, be described as, the definition of...is 等。

例3：

Anthropology is the study of human beings as creatures of society.

人类学就是对作为社会产物的人类进行研究的科学。

例4：

There has been an upsurge of interest in this aspect of reading difficulty, which has been variously described as word blindness, dyslexia, or specific reading disability.

我们不认识 dyslexia 这个词，但从句子本身可得到启发，or 所引出的词组就是 dyslexia 的重述，也就是对该词的解释。在这个句子里，word blindness，dyslexia 和 specific reading disability 三者同义。

例5：

An unreasonable and lasting fear of something is called a phobia.

这句话明确地告诉了我们画线词的含义，即对某一事物莫名而持久的恐惧。

例6：

The unit of radiation is called rem.

Rem 这个词作为术语，一般的词典上都很难查到它的含义，但是却不需要担心这种词汇，因为对于这类词汇，大多数情况下作者是要作出解释的。从这句话中可以知道，rem 就是计量辐射的一个单位。

② 符号解释法。

还有一种解释的方法就是用标点符号来引出对生词的解释，如逗号、冒号、破折号、括号等。

例7：

Botany, the study of plant, occupies a peculiar position in the history of human knowledge.

两个逗号之间通常是插入语或者是同位语。在这句话中，两个逗号之间的是前面名词的同位语，因此含义是相同的。由此可知，Botany 就是植物学。

例 8：

Of these I should put forward a sense of proportion: the capacity to take account of all the important factors in a problem and to attach to each its due weight.

冒号后面的内容通常是对前面内容的解释。根据冒号后面的解释可知：a sense of proportion 就是能够全面考虑一个问题中的所有因素并按这些因素的重要性程度来区别对待的能力。

例 9：

The principal—money he put in his savings account to earn interest was safe—even though the bank was closed by the police.

此句中我们可能不知道 principal 的意思，但破折号引出的内容都是对其前面内容进行解释的确切成分：他放在存款账户上用以挣利息的钱。因此 principal 的含义即为本金。如果将这句话中的破折号换成括号，意思也是一样的。

③ 信号词解释法。

为了解释清楚文章中出现的一个较难的词，作者有时会用一个同义词或近义词来使他的意思表达得更清楚明白，这些同义词或近义词就为读者推断生词词义提供了线索；有时作者可能采取重述的方式复述一下前面的内容，也就是换一个说法。这种重述往往用比前面一种表达更为简单易懂的词语。表达重述时也有一些信号词，常用的有：similarly, consequently, that is, equally, in a like manner, in the same way, likewise, in other words, namely, like, to put it more simply, it would be better to say, that is to say, to put it another way。

例 10：

They seem to have problems with directionality. In other words, they get lost.

通过词组"In other words"（换句话说）我们能推断出这两句话的含义是一样的，即他们好像是迷路了。由此我们可断定画线词的意思为"方向、方向感"。

例 11：

Mary is bilingual, that is to say, she can speaks both English and French.

通过词组"that is to say"（也就是说）我们能推断出这两句话的含义是一样的，即 Mary 可以说两种语言——法语和英语，由此我们可以推断画线词的意思为"双语的"。

例 12：

Britain almost more than any other country in the world must seriously face the problem of building upwards, that is to say, of accommodating a considerable proportion of its population in high blocks of flats.

在这句话里，building upwards 和信号词 that is to say 后面的动名词结构意思是完全相同的，就是指相当多的人住在高楼大厦里。

④ 举例解释法。

有时为了进一步说明某一生词的词义，作者会采取举例的方式来对它进行说明和解释。通过理解这些例子的意思，便可以归纳出词的含义，表示举例的连接词有：for example, for instance, such, such as, like, especially, consist of , including 等。

例 13：

At the party we were offered various beverages including hot tea, coffee, wine, beer, lemon juice, mineral water, and so on.

在这句话里画线词显然是一个生义词，其含义涵盖了后面列举的各种具体类型的饮料，因此我们可以判断画线词即为饮料的总称。

例 14：

Extractive industries, such as mining and lumbering, use up our natural resources.

在这里如果我们不清楚画线词的含义，可以根据后面的 mining 采矿和 lumbering 伐木进行猜测可知画线词是指开采工业。

例 15：

The remuneration for many jobs can vary greatly. For example, one can earn the minimum wage at the Pizza Pub, $5.50 an hour at a department store, or $4.50 an hour at the Bargain Toy Store.

在此句中，"remuneration"是生词，但完全可以从上下文中猜测它的含义。举例连接词"for example"引出了三个例子：一个人在不同的工作地点可以挣到不同的报酬，从 $5.50 到 $4.50 不等。通过对所举范例的理解可推断出 remuneration 的大意是报酬。

（2）根据上下文中的限定关系猜测词义。

① 对比关系猜词法。

英语句子中每一个词都处于某一逻辑关系中，弄清这个关系，有助于猜到生词的含义，也便于理解全句。最能提供生词词义信息的逻辑结构莫过于对比了。让我们来看一道托福词汇题：

例 16：

One cause of the Civil War was economic and political rivalry between the agrarian South and the industrial North.

  A. prosperous   B. old fashioned

  C. agricultural   D. poorly organized

agrarian 是什么意思呢？我们也许不知道，但 industrial 却是个熟词。句中通过 rivalry between 这两个词形成对比结构，一方是"工业化的北方"，不难推想与之对应的另一方就是"从事农业的"南方了。因此答案应为 C：agricultural。

对比使不同的事物的特点更为突出，也只有明显不同的事物才能对比。

对比关系常由被我们称为"关联词"（connectors）的信号词来表示。常用的对比关联词有：although, (even) though, nevertheless, still , but, nonetheless, while, by contrast, on the contrary, yet, however, on the other hand, whereas, in the end, in fact, actually, in spite of, unlike, instead 等。

例 17：

He thought it was quite unfair to him. He was up to the eyes in his work, while others in his office chatted with each other having nothing to do.

通过这两句话可以看出，他之所以感到不满是因为办公室的其他人都无所事事地在闲聊，只有他在忙碌地工作。"while"在这里表示对比，因此只要比较一下它连接的两个分句的意思，不难发现画线词组的含义是"非常忙碌"。

例18：

Unlike his brother, who is truly a handsome person, Adam is quite <u>ill-favored</u>.

通过分析这句话，我们可以看出 Adam 和他的兄弟长得不像，在这里我们知道他的兄弟是英俊的，那 Adam 自然是丑陋的，这样画线词的意思就清楚了。

② 并列关系猜词法。

根据对并列连词 and、or、as well as 等的了解可知：并列连词前后相连的两个成分通常在结构上是相同的，在含义上相同或者相反。利用这一信息也可在上下文中猜测词义。

例19：

Preparation for this change gives the student confidence and <u>competence</u> from the beginning and makes him an effective and attentive listener.

我们可能不认识 competence 这个词，但是我们应该认识前面的 confidence 这个词，and 只连接对等的词，故可推知 competence 也是个名词。confidence 是个抽象名词，表示性质状态，我们可以推想 competence 大概也是个抽象名词，表示性质状态。这样，我们对该词的印象，就接近于实际含义了。即使不查词典，也可以读下去，而不致影响对下文的理解。

例20：

Children often try to <u>emulate</u> or copy the behavior that they see on television.

此句中，emulate 可能是生词，但其后 or 引出了它的同义词，copy 的意思为"抄写；仿效"，那 emulate 的含义就不难推测了。

③ 因果关系猜词法。

在该词出现的上下文中，如果有因果关系的表达，那么这也可以成为猜测词义的重要依据。常见的因果关系信号词有：表原因的：because, since, for, due to, owing to, thanks to, because of, as a result of, as 等；表结果的：so, therefore, hence, as a result, consequently, thus, as a consequence, accordingly 等；表示因果关系的动词词组：lead to, cause, result in, result from, contribute to, attribute to 等。

例21：

After the rent increased, he refused to pay it. Consequently, he was <u>expelled</u> by the landlord.

第一句话说明了由于房租上调他拒绝再付房租。因此我们可以猜想其结果可能是被房东赶了出去。由此可猜测画线词的意思是"驱赶、撵"。

例22：

"When making this mixture," the man said, "you don't need two teaspoons of salt, because one teaspoon is <u>sufficient</u>."

在这句话里，不需要加两勺盐的原因是因为一勺就足够了，从因果关系中可非常清晰地明确画线词的意思。

④ 常识猜词法。

如果利用上述手段还得不出生词的意思，或者你仍旧觉得把握不大，还可以使用另一个办法：运用常识进行判断。一个人的知识面越广，猜测词义的本领也就越大。

例23：

Even the gifted teacher had difficulty making clear to the secondary school classes such an abstruse subject as Einstein's theory of relativity.

从上句的谓语 had difficulty，我们可以想到 abstruse 与 difficult 相近。爱因斯坦是个伟大的科学家，他的理论一定是不平凡的，可能一般人难于接受。确切地说，abstruse 的词义是"深奥难懂的"。从这一点出发，可以推想到这门功课大概是 too difficult for the secondary school students to understand。

例24：

One of the greatest breakthroughs for professional women came in 1973 when the field of banking opened up for them.

A. most serious disappointments   B. most significant advances
C. most abrupt declines   D. most crucial situations

句中 greatest 是个带有感情色彩的词，词义积极，它的后面状语从句中的 opened up for them，也是积极的意义。因此可以推想而知，breakthroughs 必定是"成就""进步""贡献"之类的积极含义，而不会是"失望""没落"之类的消极含义。结合全句其余名词所提供的信息和四个供选择的答案，我们完全可以断定 B 是正确答案。breakthrough 一定是 advance 的同义或近义词。

词汇题阅读公式

正确答案 = 原文中含有该词的上下文对该词的解释——定义、释义、近义词、反义词

在阅读理解测试中，词汇猜测题并不是考查考生是否认识这个生词，而是考查学生能否根据上下文所提供的语境线索来推断词汇的含义，因此考生应该努力学会在上下文中寻找猜测相关词汇含义的依据和线索。

猜测词义题的常见题型如下：

In the last sentence of the first paragraph, the word "…" could best be replaced by _____.

What does the word "…" in the first paragraph most probably mean?

Which of the following could best replace the word "…" in the fourth paragraph?

What does "…" mean in the fourth paragraph?

The word "…" in the third paragraph most probably means _____.

The phrase "…" suggests that _____.

In Paragraph 5, "…" probably refers to _____.

What is the meaning of the word "…" in Line 10?

The phrase "…"（Paragraph 1）in the context means _____.

The word "…" most likely means _____.

According to the article, the word "…" is known as _____.

The author uses the phrase "…" to mean ＿＿＿＿.

In Line…, the word "…" is used to indicate ＿＿＿＿.

By "…" the writer means ＿＿＿＿.

1. 根据定义、释义猜词

例1：

You need to emit a signal telling others you want to be left alone. So **you cut off eye contact**, what sociologist Erving Goffman (1963) *calls* "a dimming of the lights." You look down at the floor, at the indicator lights, anywhere but into another passenger's eyes. Should you break the rule against staring at a stranger on an elevator, you will make the other person exceedingly uncomfortable, and you are likely to feel a bit strange yourself.

Question：

By "a dimming of the lights" Erving Goffman means "＿＿＿＿."

A. closing one's eyes   B. turning off the lights

C. ceasing to glance at others   D. reducing gaze-time to the minimum

在第一节里我们曾介绍过文章中下定义的常见方法和语言标志，其中 calls 是典型的下定义的标志，what sociologist Erving Goffman (1963) *calls* "a dimming of the lights" 是 **you cut off eye contact** 的同位语，据此不难看出"a dimming of the lights"的含义。

2. 通过具体例子猜词

例2：

There are hidden factors which scientists call "feedback mechanisms." No one knows quite how they will interact with the changing climate. Here's one example：Plants and animals adapt to climate change over centuries. At the current estimate of half a degree centigrade of warming per decade, vegetation（植物）may not keep up. Climatologist James Hansen predicts climate zones will shift toward the poles 50 to 75 kilometres a year faster than trees can naturally migrate. Species that find themselves in an unfamiliar environment will die. The 1000-kilometre-wide strip of forest running through Canada, the USSR and Scandinavia could be cut by half. Millions of dying trees would soon lead to massive forest fires, releasing tons of CO_2 and further boosting global warming. （1998 年第 4 篇）

Question：

"Feedback mechanisms" in this paragraph most probably refer to ＿＿＿＿.

A. how plants and animals adapt to hidden factors

B. how plants and animals interact with the changing climate

C. how climate changes

D. how climate zones shift

题目是：本段中的"feedback mechanisms"的意思最可能是：A. 动植物是如何适应隐含因素的；B. 动植物是如何与不断变化的气候相互作用的；C. 气候是如何变化的；D. 气候带是如何变迁的。

正确选项是 B。文章第一、二句指出，存在一些被科学家叫作"feedback mechanisms"的隐含因素，谁也不太了解这些隐含因素（feedback mechanisms）是如何与不断变化的气候相互影响的。后面举例进行了说明。植物和动物数世纪以来一直适应着气候的变化。现在，气温每10年上升半摄氏度，按此速度计算，植物就跟不上气候变化的速度。气候学家James Hansen预测：气候带每年向两极迁移50至70千米，比树木自然迁移的速度快。环境的改变会使许多物种灭绝。生长在加拿大、苏联和斯堪的纳维亚半岛上的1 000千米宽的森林带就会减半，许多濒临死亡的大树可能很快引起森林大火，释放出的二氧化碳会使全球进一步变暖。这些例子说明上述的feedback mechanisms不是一个单向影响问题，而是动植物和气候相互作用、相互影响的双向过程，从上下文来看，B是正确答案。

3. 通过同义词猜词

例3：

We also tend to believe what we want to believe. A majority of people think they are more intelligent, more fair-minded and more skilled behind the wheel of an automobile than the average person. Part of the reason we view ourselves so favorable is that we use criteria that work to our advantage. As economist Thomas Schelling explains, "Everybody ranks himself high in qualities he values: careful drivers give weight to care, skilled drivers gave weight to skill, and those who are **polite** give weight to courtesy." This way everyone ranks high on his own scale.

Question：

The word "courtesy" probably means _____.

A. good manners　　　　　　　B. appropriate speech
C. friendly relations　　　　　　D. satisfactory service

在上面的这个例子里，courtesy出现在一个并列句中。这里的三个并列的分句是为了解释前面的概括句：每个人都看中自身所具有的品质。通过分析前两个分句中形容词和名词的对应关系 careful 和 care、skilled 和 skill，可以判断第三个分句中的形容词和名词的对应关系 polite 和 courtesy 一定也是同义词的关系，所以符合这一词义的只有A选项。good manners 就是 polite 和 courtesy 的同义词，意思是有礼貌。

例4：

Because the United States is a **highly active** society, **full of movement and change**, people always seem to be on the go. In this highly charged atmosphere, Americans can sometimes seem brusque or impatient. They want to get to know you as quickly as possible and then move on to something else. Something, early on, they will ask you questions that you may feel are very personal. No insult is intended; the questions usually grow out of their genuine interest or curiosity, and their impatience to get to the heart of the matter. And the same does for you. If you do not understand certain American behavior or you want to know more about them, do not hesitate to ask them questions about themselves. Americans are usually more eager to explain all about their country or anything "American" in which you may be interested. So much so in fact that you may become tired of listening. It doesn't matter because Americans tend to be uncomfortable with silence during a conversation. They would rather talk about the weather or the latest sports scores, for example, than deal with silence. （2001年第一篇）

Question:

The phrase "highly charged" (paragraph 2) most probably means _____.
A. extremely free   B. highly responsible
C. very cheerful   D. full of mobility and change

首先，回到原文中该词出现的地方，然后仔细阅读包含该词的原句和其上一句和下一句，找出和该词相对应的解释。对于本题而言，"highly charged"出现在第二段的第二句话中，原句是"In this highly charged atmosphere, …"，基于对指代词 this 的了解可知，this 通常前指，因此应在其前一句"Because the United States is a highly active society, full of movement and change, people always seem to be on the go."找等同关系。在这里，"In this highly charged atmosphere"就等于"the United States is a highly active society, full of movement and change"。这个说法与"highly charged"功能相等，其意思相近的表达则是 highly active 和 full of movement and change，到此就不难看出正确答案应是D，它只不过是把原文中的 movement 换成了 mobility 而已。

推断题阅读公式

1. 推断简介

推断是从已知事物出发，论述未知事物的存在、发生、变化和发展的可能性。日常生活中处处需要推断。例如，很久没有接到朋友的来信了，他是出差了，还是病了？你可能根据对他过去的了解，推断他不可能是工作太忙或别的什么原因，有可能是生病了。如果你在早晨向一位老朋友致早安时他没有作出反应，你就会推断：他一定心情不好，或是在考虑什么问题，或是没有注意到你。又如，你看见一个人穿着沾满油污的工作服，手上都是油污，你就会推断，这个人一定是一名汽车修理工。街上一长串车辆被阻，开不了。如果停的时间较短，那可能是交通高潮的阻塞，如果时间长则可能是出了事故。许多人在那里排队，你可能推测到那里有便宜货或紧俏商品出售。

以上的例子说明我们在日常生活中经常对我们周围发生的情况进行推断，而这些推断都是以平时积累的经验为基础的。因此可以说推断是以掌握的知识去获取未知的信息。推断能力在阅读理解中占据很重要的位置，因为一些文章的作者有时并不是明确陈述他们的观点和描写他们想解释的事物，而是通过暗示使读者从字里行间悟出言外之意。因此在阅读过程中，读者需要借助于自己的逻辑思考能力、背景知识对文章的主题、作者的意图等作出合乎逻辑的推断。

（1）推断是阅读中达到完全理解的重要手段。

在阅读时，只有从文字表面深入到字里行间，才有可能完全理解所读的内容。我们常常可以根据上下文，推想出文章未明显提出的问题，作出自己的结论或判断，如：

① The climbing team planned to begin the ascent on the 14th May if the weather was fine. They didn't begin until June.

根据上文，我们可以推断，这段时间天气不好，登山日期往后推迟了。

作者常常不是把一切详情都叙述得一清二楚，有些地方略去了，而没有交代的东西，可通过推测而断定，如：

② The background to the development of the new towns is as follows: in 1960, the population density of the main city in the region was already one of the highest in the world and since then the population has grown by another several million.

从文中可推断出：(a) 该城市的人口密度也许仍旧是世界上最高的，然而我们不敢肯定别的城市人口是否增长得更快；(b) 此外，我们暂时可以认为该城市太拥挤，所带来的社会问题可能很大。这些情况文中虽然没有提供，但我们可以推想到。

下面的语句选自人物对话，让我们推断这些语句所表达的深层意义：

The young man quickly answered, "yes, sir." 从 quickly 和 "yes, sir"，我们可以推断：说话者似乎态度谦卑，甚至有点诚惶诚恐。

在阅读时应注意用词造句的特点，并从这些特点推断未知事物和未知情况。如：

③ A. I believe that smoking cigarettes is harmful.
   B. It is believed that smoking cigarettes is harmful.
   C. Smoking cigarettes is harmful.

三个句子都讲抽烟有害，却用不同的句型表示出来。这三个句子的语气是不同的。句 A 用的是 I believe，表明作者肯定抽烟有害。句 B 用了 It is believed 的句型，我们读后无法得知作者究竟抱何态度，只不过是"据认为""人们认为"抽烟有害而已。而句 C 这个句型传达信息则是：抽烟是有害的，是一个医学上公认的事实。

还应注意词在词典中的解释和语流或上下文中的含义的不同，后者往往有所引申、发展。Mother 这个词在词典上解释为"母亲"，而在语流中还有 live, care, warmth 和 tenderness 等的含义。又如：

④ The book really deals with applied mathematics but the emphasis is on the adjective there.

这个句子中，"adjective" 原意为"形容词"，但显然是指 applied 一词的含义。这个句子的译文应该是"本书是论述应用数学的，且重点在应用方面"。

⑤ The old man staggered along the sidewalk. He grab bed at the picket fence to keep from falling. His torn gray overcoat flapped open in the winker wind.

有人看了上文以后作出这样的推断 The old man is drunk。

显然这种推断缺乏足够的依据，staggered along…，grab bed…并不能说明这老人一定是喝醉了酒，倒有可能是"贫病"加上"老"，所以才这样虚弱。也可能有别的原因。

从上面的例子可以看出要作出正确的逻辑判断既需要注意到文中的细节又要具有一定的归纳和演绎能力。有些题目就要求读者在解答问题时根据短文中提供的信息进行归纳总结。通常，读者可在短文中找到一些有关的信息或线索。例如：

The average person in psychoanalysis is young, generally not past his thirties. This means that he has yet to encounter some of those stages of life which are so revelatory of personality. For example, he may not yet have married, have children, achieved the peak of his career, and so on. Neither the analysis nor the patient knows how the patient will react to these events. Thus, certain aspects of the patient's personality may remain inaccessible for purposes of examination and understanding.

Question：

The author implies that personality characteristics can often be most completely revealed by _____.

A. the patient's behavior as a young person
B. interviewing the patient's spouse, children and parents
C. how a patient handles life's common stages
D. exploring the patient's intellectual life

题目要求读者推断出作者暗示的怎样才能体现一个人的个性这一内容。从短文中可以看出，作者认为精神分析法的一般对象都是未过30岁的青年人。这意味着这些人还未经历有些能反映人的个性的生活阶段，如婚姻，生儿育女，达到事业的顶峰等。分析者甚至病人自己都不知道他们在面临这些问题时会作出何种反应。因此，就不可能观察到和理解病人的某些个性。作者认为精神分析法否定了所列举的事实，因此，我们可以得出结论：病人通过处理生活上所经历的几个阶段都暴露出他的个性。因此C项是正确的。

（2）推断的注意事项。

如何才能作出准确的推断呢？综合上一小节中所述，要作出合乎事实的、准确无误的推断，读者必须：a. 分析文中已提供的事实、资料；b. 注意用词造句的特点，特别是词在语流或语境中的含义；c. 阅读和思考时，必须透过表面的文字讯号而达到深层；d. 测知作者的立场观点或写作意图。

另外，根据所读材料进行判断、推理和引申要注意以下几点：

① 合乎逻辑。

逻辑是正确推断的基础。它涉及有些有效的推理所必须遵循的原则。在进行推理前必须确立正确的论断或前提。有了正确的前提才能推导出合乎逻辑的结论。推理包括演绎和归纳。

演绎是从一般到具体的推理过程。如果我们所作的结论在逻辑上符合它的前提，这个结论就有效；反之，则无效。

例1：

Jane S. is a student at our college.

All students at our college must pass a special examination.

Therefore, Jane S. must have passed the entrance examination.

这句推断的前提是"All students at our college must pass a special examination."由于Jane是我们学校的学生，因此可以根据这个前提推断出"那么她一定通过了入学考试"，推断符合逻辑，因此正确。

例2：

All bipeds are humans.

Ducks are bipeds.

Therefore, ducks are humans.

"所有的两足动物都是人"，这个前提显然是错误的，不能成立，因此，得出的结论"鸭子有两条腿，所以鸭子也是人"也无疑是错误的。

由具体到一般，对掌握的事实进行推断、总结称为归纳。正确的归纳基于可靠的数据。

例3：

Dr. Smith: "Every patient I've seen this week has symptoms of a disease that hasn't been seen for four decades."

Dr. Johnson: "I was just saying the same thing to the people at the Disease Center in Atlanta. At first I thought I was mistaken, but I have a steady stream of patients all week with the same symptoms. The people in Atlanta claim that they have been getting similar reports from all over the country."

Dr. Smith: "It appears that we have an epidemic on our hands of a disease we thought we had virtually wiped out a long time ago."

史密斯医生最后用了"It appears"来总结"多年前早已绝迹的流行病可能又死灰复燃"这一事实，并表示可能性很大。根据两人对话中说到的看到许多病人得了几十年不见的疾病，以及各地都有类似的报道这些事实，这个结论合乎逻辑，可以成立。

② 了解主题。

正确的推断取决于对原文的正确理解。在阅读文章时首先应了解文章的主旨大意，然后对作者的观点、文章论述的事实进行合乎逻辑的推断，切莫望文生义，用自己的观点代替作者的观点。

③ 注意修饰语。

推断题大都要求读者从字里行间领会作者暗示的意义。因此在阅读过程中，应特别注意作者使用的一些修饰语。忽略形容词和副词常常会导致推断错误。因此，在答题时还需仔细观察文章提供的数据前后的词语搭配和句子。

④ 领会题意。

解题时一定要看清题意和题型。如要求针对暗示的意义进行理解时，切莫把文章中列举的事实当作答案。推断能力强的读者在阅读过程中很自然地会去收集和捕捉各种线索。培养推断能力的过程也是培养好的阅读习惯的过程。它需要经过大量的实践和不懈的努力。

2. 推断的主要题型及提问方式

（1）推断的主要题型。

在掌握了解题步骤之后，阅读者还应对这类推断、引申题所针对的内容有所了解。最常出现的两种就是数字推断和逻辑推断。

① 数字推断。

数字推断要求读者在阅读文章中出现的数字时要仔细，先找到文章中题目针对的表示数字的部分，如时间、计量等，然后再进行推算。

例4：

The development of the English language falls into three reasonably distinct periods: Old English, from about A. D. 450, when the first Germanic tribes began to settle in England, until about 1100; Middle English, from about 1100 to about 1475; and Modern English, from about

1475 to the present. Of course the breaks were not as sudden and definite as these arbitrary（任意的）dates indicate. There has never been a year when the language was not changing or a time when it was spoken with anything like complete uniformity. Nevertheless, the characteristics of the three periods are so different that a person who knows both old and modern English well will find a good deal of difficulty in reading some of the Middle English writings without additional training.

Question：

According to the passage, the English language probably has a history of _____.
A. 2,575 years　　　B. 1,540 years　　　C. 1,475 years　　　D. 1,990 years

这篇短文的大意是英语的发展分为三个时期：古英语、中古英语和现代英语。没有一天英语不在变化，也没有任何时候说出来的英语是完全一样的。然而由于三个时期的英语特征完全不同，即使一个人精通了古英语和现代英语，如不经训练，在阅读一些中古英语文章时仍会有许多困难。

从短文中可以看出古英语从公元450年发展到1100年，中古英语发展时期为1100年至1475年，1475年至今为现代英语发展时期。我们用1999年减去450年便可得出英语发展的历史，因此，正确的答案为B项：1,540 years。

② 逻辑推断。

逻辑推断包含四个内容，即主题思想推断、作者态度推断、论调推断和作者思路推断。这类问题要求读者有较强的概括能力和逻辑思考能力。对作者陈述的论点和事实进行推理，从而得出合乎逻辑的推断。

以下分别就主题思想推断和作者思路推断举例说明。关于作者态度和论调推断将在第七章里进行讨论。

第一，主题思想推断。

例5：

The Greek's lofty（高傲）attitude toward scientific research and the scientists' contempt of utility was a long time dying. For a millennium（千年）after Archimedes, this separation of mechanics from geometry hindered fundamental technological progress and in some areas repressed it altogether. But there was a still greater obstacle to change until the very end of the middle ages: the organization of society. The social system of fixed class relationships that prevailed through the Middle Ages (and in some areas much longer) itself stultified（使自相矛盾）improvement. Under this system, the laboring masses, in exchange for the bare necessities of life, did all the productive work, while the privileged few—princes, nobles, and kings—concerned themselves only with ownership and maintenance of their own position. In the interest of their prerogatives（特权）they did achieve considerable progress in defense, in war-making, in government, in trade, in the arts of leisure, and in the extraction of labor from their dependents, but they had no familiarity with the processes of production. On the other hand, the laborers, who were familiar with manufacturing techniques, had no incentive to improve or increase production to the advantage of their masters. Thus, with one class possessing the requisite knowledge and experiences but lacking incentive and leisure, and the other class lacking the knowledge and experience, there was no means by which technical progress could be achieved.

Question:

We may infer that a change in class relationships after the close of the Middle Ages produced greater productivity because _____.

A. freemen had incentive to produce more

B. masters had greater incentive to work their workers harder

C. slaves never starved, no matter what they produced

D. productivity could go in only one direction

这篇短文的大意是直至中世纪末，影响生产力发展的最大障碍依然是社会组织机构。中世纪普遍存在的固定阶级关系的社会制度妨碍了技术进步。在这个制度下，劳动人民懂得生产技术，但没有为他们的主人改进和提高生产力的积极性。而享有特权的极少数人却不掌握生产知识和经验，这就使得技术无法进步。

根据短文可以推断出，中世纪后随着阶级关系的变化，获得自由的人有了积极性便可以产生更大的生产力。因此正确答案为 A 项。

第二，写作思路推断。

这类推断主要针对与短文有关的上文或下文提出的问题。在作出此类推断时首先要求读者充分理解短文的主题思想，并应着重分析短文的开头和结尾部分。

例6：

The mistake was made more than a hundred years ago in the British colony of Mauritius, a small island in the Indian Ocean. In 1847 an order for stamps was sent to a London printer—Mauritius was to become the fourth country in the world to issue stamps.

Before the order was filled and delivered, a ball was planned at Mauritius' Government House, and stamps were needed to send out the invitations. A local printer was instructed to copy the design for the stamps. He accidentally inscribed （刻写）the words "Post Office" instead of "Post Paid" on the several hundred stamps that he printed. Today there are only twenty-six of these misprinted stamps left—fourteen One Penny Orange-Reds and twelve Two penny Blues. Because of the Two penny Blue's rareness and age, collectors have paid as much as \$16,800 for it.

Question:

The paragraph preceding this one probably discusses _____.

A. what serious consequence a mistake might lead to

B. mistakes are often made unconsciously

C. any mistake made in the printing of a stamp raises its value to stamp collectors

D. mistakes are often made by the stamp printers

短文大意：

一百多年前英国殖民地毛里求斯开始成为世界上第四个发行邮票的国家，总督官邸计划在邮票发行之时举行舞会，因此需要印刷邮票散发邀请书。地方印刷商错把几百张应印"邮资已付"的邮票上印上了"邮局"两字。这些错印的邮票流传至今仅剩26张，其中两便士兰票仅存12枚，因其稀少和年份，收藏者要花高达16 800元，才能买到一枚。

纵观全文，作者列举了由于铅印造成邮票升值的例子，在文章一开始 mistake 前用了"the"表示有所指的错误。可以推断出在这篇短文前很可能是讨论任何印刷错误都会提高邮票的价值，因此正确答案应是 C 项。

（2）推断型题目的主要提问方式。

The last sentence of this passage implies that _____.

If you…, which of the following will you go into?

We can infer from the statement "…" that _____.

Which of the following is not stated but implied in the last paragraph?

It can be inferred from the passage that _____.

What would the next paragraph most likely discuss if the text continues?

The first paragraph implies that _____.

What can we infer from the figures about…in the first paragraph?

…most likely agrees that _____.

Which might be inferred about…from the sentence at the beginning of the text?

Which of the following statements best describes…?

The sentence "…" suggests that _____.

As to…, what can we infer from the passage?

If the passage continues, what is the author most likely to discuss in the next paragraph?

The passage is most probably taken from _____.

What the author tries to suggest may best be interpreted as _____.

Which of the following cannot be inferred from the passage?

The author of the passage would most probably imply _____.

Where would the paragraph most probably appear?

The passage implies that _____.

According to the author, what does the sentence in Line…suggest?

The paragraph following this article would most probably mention _____.

推断题阅读公式

推断题是阅读理解所有题目中难度最大的，也是答错率最高的一种题型。究其原因，是这种题型很难从文章中直接找到答案。通常必须找准推断的依据，然后在此前提下，进行合理的推断。考生在掌握了本章第一节介绍的推断的基本技巧后，可利用下面介绍的不同推断题的做题公式来攻破这类难题。

1. 归纳推断题阅读公式

具体事例（叙述）1
具体事例（叙述）2 =正确答案
具体事例（叙述）3

归纳推断题是推断题中较为容易的一种题型，就是要通过对具体事例或具体描述的分析来概括出它们之间的共同之处。常见的此类题目的提问方式通常是：

What can be concluded from…?

What can be learned from…?

It can be learned from… that ＿＿＿＿＿＿.

It can be inferred from…that ＿＿＿＿＿＿.

例1：

Wolong is but one example of this difficulty. This 494,000-acre preserve was declared a protected area in 1975. Yet 1,800 people, mostly Tibetans, still live in the preserve, logging trucks still roll down the narrow mountain roads, and blasting work still goes on at the site of a new 160,000-kilowatt hydroelectric plant just six miles away. （1997年第三篇）

Question：

Which of the following threatens the pandas' survival in the Wolong preserve?

A. Local population.

B. Economic development.

C. Unfavorable environment.

D. All of the above.

正确答案是 D 选项。这是归纳推断题的一种变换的问法。根据题干中非常有提示意义的地名 Wolong 可迅速在原文中找到其出处：本段第一句。仔细阅读后可以发现该段第二句话给了三方面的信息：根据"Yet 1,800 people, mostly Tibetans, still live in the preserve"可以归纳出 A 选项所举的当地人口的问题；根据"logging trucks still roll down the narrow mountain roads, and blasting work still goes on"可以归纳出 B 选项所举的经济发展方面的问题；根据"a new 160,000-kilowatt hydroelectric plant just six miles away"可以归纳出 C 选项所举的环境不利的问题。因此，最完整的答案应该是 D 选项。

例2：

In 1992, many people watched in horror as riots broke out on a sad Wednesday evening in Los Angeles, seemingly fed by video coverage from helicopters. This event was triggered by the verdict（裁定）in the Rodney King beating. We are now in an age where the public can have access to information that enables it to make its own judgments, and most people, who had seen the video of this beating, could not understand how the jury（陪审团）was able to acquit （宣布……无罪） the policemen involved. Media coverage of events as they occur also provides powerful feedback that influences events. This can have harmful results, as it seemed on that Wednesday night in los Angeles. By Friday night the public got to see Rodney King on television pleading, "Can we all get along?" By Saturday, television seemed to provide positive feedback as the Los Angeles riot turned out into a rally for peace. The television showed thousands of people marching with banners and cleaning tools. Because of that, many more people turned out to join the peaceful event they saw unfolding（展开）on television. The real healing, of course, will take much longer, but electronic media will continue to be a part of that process. （1999年第3篇第50题）

Question:

It can be inferred from the passage that _____.

A. media coverage of events as they occur can have either good or bad results

B. most people who had seen the video of the Rodney King beating agree with the verdict of the jury

C. the 1992 Los Angeles riots lasted a whole week

D. Rodney King seemed very angry when he appeared on television on Friday

上述题目问的是：从文章中能够推断出_____。A. 媒体对事件的现场报道可以产生好的或不良的结果；B. 大多数看过殴打 Rodney King 录像的人同意陪审团的判决；C. 1992 年洛杉矶骚乱事件持续了整整一周；D. Rodney King 星期五在电视采访中显得很气愤。

正确答案是 A。典型的归纳推断题。必须从文章的几处细节入手才能得出答案。文章第五句指出 "This (media coverage of events) can have harmful results…"（媒体对事件的报道产生了有害的结果），后面第七句又指出，"…provide positive feedback…a rally for peace"（随着洛杉矶骚乱转为一场和平集会，电视似乎产生积极作用）。A 项综合表述了这两句的内容，原文中的 positive 及 harmful 换成了 A 项中的 good 和 bad，所以 A 项是可以从文章推断出来的正确内容，为本题的正确选项。本段前半段指出，多数看过殴打录像的人不明白，陪审团怎么会判定参与殴打的警察无罪（…could not understand how the jury was able to acquit the policemen involved），这表明他们不同意审判团的判决，所以 B 项是错误的。本段第一句指出骚乱发生于星期三晚上，第七句指出到星期六骚乱转变成了和平示威，整个事件何时结束没有提到，所以 C 项的说法不确切。本段第六句"星期五晚上，Rodney King 在电视上露面，向公众恳求说，我们大家能否和平相处呢？"可见，此时他是一种心平气和的态度，所以 D 项也是错误的。

2. 演绎推断题阅读公式

原文中与题干相关的概括表述（推断的前提）

↓

具体事例的个别情况

↓

正确答案

典型的演绎推断题在历年阅读真题中并不多见，其出题的特点是题干中涉及的往往是一个具体的事例或情况，有时这个事例或情况在原文中可能并未出现，在原文中能够找到的是相对较为概括的定义或论述，考生需要据此对事例或情况作出合理的推断。

例 3：

Actually, two basic approaches lead to the discovery of new information. One, aimed at studying curiosity, is referred to as pure science. The other is aimed at using knowledge for specific purposes—for instance, improving health, raising standards of living, or creating new consumer products. In this case knowledge is put to economic use. Such an approach is referred to as applied science. （1999年第五篇）

Question：

A scientist interested in adding to our general knowledge about oxygen would probably call his approach _____.

  A. pure science   B. environmental science

  C. applied science   D. agricultural science

本题是历年阅读真题中唯一一道典型的演绎推断题。本题属于由一般到具体的推断题型。做这一题目首先要根据四个答案选项回读原文，找到相应信息的位置，然后再根据文中给出的理论科学与应用科学的定义来推断题干中的例子符合哪个定义即是。而 oxygen 在文中并未出现。正确答案是 A。

3. 事实推断题公式

正确答案 = 原文中含有题干关键词的一句话

事实推断题的做题方法和细节题的做题方法大致相同，只不过细节题的正确答案就是对含有题干关键词的一句话的同义表述（paraphrase），而事实推断题的正确答案要在原句的基础上做进一步的逻辑推理。这类题目的常见提问方式有：

It can be inferred from…that _____.

It is implied/indicated…that _____.

The author implies that _____.

例 4：

At the Kyoto conference on global warming in December 1997, **it became abundantly clear how complex it has become to work out international agreements relating to the environment** because of economic concerns unique to each country. It is no longer enough to try to forbid certain activities or to reduce emissions of certain substances. The global challenges of the interlink between the environment and development increasingly bring us to the core of the economic life of states. During the late 1980s we were able, through international agreements, to make deep cuts in emissions harmful to the ozone layer. These reductions were made possible because substitutions had been found for many of the harmful chemicals and, more important, because the harmful substances could be replaced without negative effects on employment and the economies of states. （1999年第四篇）

Question：

In the passage the author implies that _____.

  A. the world has recently become aware of the threat of global warming

  B. the problem of global warming has largely been solved

  C. it is always difficult to work out international agreements to cut down emissions harmful to the ozone layer

  D. it is no longer easy to reach international agreements relating to the environment

正确答案是 D 选项。将它与原文的第一句相比较，不难发现两者的相似之处，原文中说由于各国追求的经济利益不同,在 1997 年那次关于全球变暖问题的会议上,已经看出各国很难就限制自己国家二氧化碳的排放量达成协议。再加上对本段倒数第二句的理解,可以发现以前这种协议还是能够达成的,所以 D 是最合适的推断。

例 5:

The other reasons to oppose the death penalty are largely a mater of individual conscience and belief. One is that murder is murder and the state has no more right to take a life than the individual. The other is that Christianity advises forgiveness, not revenge. (1997 年第一篇)

Question:

We can learn from the last paragraph that _____.

A. neither state nor the individual has the right to take a life

B. the state has the right to take a life but the individual does not

C. the death penalty has nothing to do with individual conscience and belief

D. the deterrence figures have added up and the execution rate has fallen

正确答案是 A 选项。本题主要是考查对该段第二句话的理解。其中有一较难的句型 "A is no more X than B",根据第一篇语言基础中介绍过的特殊句型,它的意思是:A 和 B 都不……X。本题的意思就是政府和个人都无权夺走一个人的生命。A 选项是和原文完全相同的表述。

4. 逻辑推断题阅读公式

正确答案 = 根据原文可以分析得出的原因、条件、结果、行为

例 6:

Although the threat of global warming known to the world for decades and all countries and leaders agree that we need to deal with the problem, we also know that the effects of measures, especially harsh measures taken in some countries, would be mollified (抵消) if other countries do not control their emissions. Whereas the UN team on climate change has found that the emissions of carbon dioxide would have to be cut globally by 60% to stabilize the content of CO_2, in the atmosphere, this path is not feasible for several reasons. Such deep cuts would cause a breakdown of the world economy. Important and populous low-or-medium-income countries are not willing to undertake legal commitments about their energy uses. In addition, the state of world technology would not yet permit us to make such a big leap. (1999 年第四篇)

Question:

What should all countries do to help solve the problem of global warming?

A. They should hold another world conference on climate change.

B. They should provide advanced technology.

C. They should replace all the harmful substances.

D. They should willingly undertake legal commitments about their energy uses.

本段第四句话明确指出全球变暖这一问题之所以难以解决,主要是因为很多国家不愿意承担控制本国能源使用的法律义务,由此可以依据逻辑推断,要解决这一问题的方法必然是各国自觉承担控制本国能源使用的法律义务。因此,正确答案是 D 选项。

例 7：

In the United States, most education dollars are spent in elementary schools. But the lessons are aimed at a too limited audience; just 9 percent of all fire deaths are caused by children playing with matches. （1998 年第二篇）

Question：

It can be inferred from the passage that _____.

A. fire safety lessons should be aimed at American adults

B. American children have not received enough education of fire safety lesson

C. Japan is better equipped with fire facilities than the United States

D. America's large population accounts for high fire frequency

根据原文本段最后一句话 But the lessons are aimed at a too limited audience; just 9 percent of all fire deaths are caused by children playing with matches 可以推出防火教育不应仅针对孩子，也应面向成人，因此 A 是正确答案。

5. 作者态度推断题阅读公式

正确答案 = 原文主旨 + 表达主旨的用词

这类题型要求考生对文章作者的态度和语调作出推断。如作者对所陈述的事件、观点是赞同还是反对，对所描写的人或事物是表示赞颂、同情、冷淡还是厌恶。通常作者对所述事物的态度不直接表露出来，而是通过他所使用的语气、语调来体现。为此在回答此类问题时必须仔细阅读文章的开头，了解短文的主旨大意，并特别注意作者使用的修饰语。常见的提问方式现总结如下：

Which of the following statements could fully express the author's view towards…?

Which of the following best describes the author's attitude?

The author holds different opinions from other people in that _____.

What is the main purpose of the last paragraph?

What is the main purpose of the passage?

What is the author's attitude towards…?

Why does the author mention…in the passage?

The author wrote the passage in order to _____.

The author's main purpose in writing this article is to _____.

The author of the article quotes…'s words to _____.

Why does the author mainly emphasize about…?

What does the author seem to suggest about…?

Which of the following statements best describes the author's view of…?

The tone of this article can be best described as _____.

The writer most likely thinks (holds, believes, insists) that _____.

Which of the following best describes the tone of the whole passage?

According to the passage, which of the following best characterizes the writer's attitude towards…?

What is the author's opinion (point of view) about…?

例 8：

A new atomic clock being developed for navigation satellites will perform better than previous devices. The clock, which incorporates a hydrogen maser, will use a new microwave cavity design to provide a compact and light weight package, and new electronic techniques to maintain long-term stability. The clock can provide precise navigation information because it is stable to one second in three million years. The differences in the time when signals from four satellites arrive at one location can be used to calculate that position to within a few yards.

Question：

What is the primary purpose of the passage?

A. To teach a lesson.

B. To sell a product.

C. To support a theory.

D. To provide information.

这篇文章的体裁是说明文，它介绍了一种用在导航卫星上的一种新的原子钟所具有的种种特殊的功能，这些功能和以前的同类装置相比要具有很大的优越性。由此不难看出这篇文章的主要目的是给读者提供关于这种新的原子钟的一些有用的信息。因此这道题的答案是 D。

例 9：

The over dependence of modern man on machines could have disastrous consequences on the future of mankind. Such a dependence leads to an excessive forfeiture of the basic reasoning faculties of thought to **mindless** machines. This in turn could lead to a **dehumanized** society and mechanized approaches to problems and solutions. If we continue to surrender our natural intelligence to unnatural mechanical contrivances we may even **ultimately lose our capacity** for creative thought.

Questions：

1. What is the author's attitude toward machines?

A. Immoral.　　　B. Indifferent.　　　C. Laudatory.　　　D. Deprecatory.

2. The writer is of the opinion that _____.

A. man's capacity for creativity may be lost

B. machines will take over the world by force

C. man's dependence on machine will enhance his lifestyle

D. our ability to think is dependent on machine

这篇文章的主要内容是指出了人们过度依赖机器将给人类的将来带来的严重后果。如果人们仍然如此依赖机器，将来人们解决问题的所有方法将都依赖于机器，而且我们的社会将变成非人类的社会，并最终导致人类失去创造性思维的能力。由此可以看出作者对待机器的态度是批评谴责的，因此，第一题的答案是 D。第二题的答案应是 A。文中黑体突出的都是具有贬义色彩的词汇和否定的表述。

例 10：

Icebergs（冰山）are among nature's most spectacular creations, and yet most people have never seen one. A vague air of mystery envelops them. They come into being somewhere—in faraway, line frigid waters, amid thunderous noise and splashing turbulence, which in most eases no one hears or sees, they exist only a short time and then slowly waste away just as unnoticed.

Objects of sheerest beauty, they have been called. Appearing in an endless variety of shapes, they may be dazzlingly white, or they may be glassy blue, green, or purple, tinted faintly or in darker hues. They are graceful, stately, inspiring—in calm, sunlit seas.

Question：

The attitude of the author toward icebergs is one of _____.

A. disappointment B. humor C. disinterest D. wonder

作者对"icebergs"的看法完全体现在他的选词上。作者先后用了 spectacular（壮观的）、mystery（神秘）、sheerest beauty（绝美）、graceful（高雅）、stately（雄伟）和 inspiring（令人鼓舞）等感情色彩非常强烈的词汇，故作者对冰山的看法应该是惊叹的（wonder），选项 D 为正确答案。

在做这类作者对某一问题的态度的题目时，应注意积累一些有关的词汇。例如：indifferent 冷漠的、laudatory 赞成的、agreeable 同意的、deprecatory 谴责的、ironical 讽刺的、traditional 传统的、creative 有创意的、objective 客观的、subjective 主观的、critical 批判的、favorable 赞同的、prejudiced 有偏见的、positive 肯定的、negative 否定的、humorous 幽默的、neutral 中立的、optimistic 乐观的、pessimistic 悲观的、concerned 关心的、sympathetic 同情的等。

二、阅读核心词汇

（一）环境保护

protect the environment 保护环境	ecology 生态	in/off balance 平衡/失去平衡	natural resources 自然资源
release carbon dioxide 排放二氧化碳	pollution/pollute 污染	pollutant 污染物	extinction 灭绝
industrial/domestic sewage 工业/生活污水	toxic smog 有毒气体	contaminate 污染	overgraze 过度放牧
waste/rubbish 垃圾	recycle 循环	energy conservation 能源节约	drought 干旱
flood 洪水	water shortage 缺水	greenhouse effect 温室效应	global warming 全球变暖
gas emission 气体排放	energy consumption 能源消耗	atmosphere 大气	fertile 肥沃的
natural environment 自然环境	barren 贫瘠的	ecological 生态的	soil erosion 水土流失
cut down trees 砍伐树木	vegetation 植被	natural disaster 自然灾难	habitat 栖息地

excessive exploitation	air quality	reduce pollution	species
过度开采	空气质量	减少污染	物种
earthquake	typhoon	tsunami	tornado
地震	台风	海啸	龙卷风
cyclone	storm	hurricane	whirlwind
龙卷风、旋风	风暴	飓风	旋风
hail	garbage disposal	low-carbon	exhaust
冰雹	垃圾处理	低碳	废气，尾气

（二）司法犯罪

commit a crime	criminal	suspect	witness
犯罪	罪犯	嫌疑犯	证人
death penalty	punishment	sentence	accuse
死刑	惩罚	判刑	指控
arrest	murder	evidence	convict
逮捕	谋杀	证据	宣告有罪
execution	investigate	attack	victim
死刑，执行	调查	攻击	被害者
criminal law	civil law	testimony	court
刑法	民法	证词	法庭
imprisonment	jury	judicial	hijack
入狱	陪审团	司法的	劫持
warrant	trial	wanted	smuggle
逮捕令	审讯	通缉	走私
kidnap	armed robbery	fraud	innocent
绑架	持械抢劫	诈骗	无辜的
capital punishment	theft	accuser	deter
死刑	偷窃	原告	震慑
guilty	burgle	defendant	attorney
有罪	入室抢劫	被告	律师
rape	assault	assassination	hostage
强奸	攻击	暗杀	人质
massacre	pirate	slaughter	verdict
残杀	盗版	残杀	判决
terrorism	terrorist attack	bombing	homicide
恐怖主义	恐怖袭击	轰炸	凶杀
hijack	shoplift	pickpocket	prosecute
劫机	入店行窃	扒手	起诉
testify			
作证			

（三）电脑科技

science and technology	科学技术	cyberspace	电脑空间
high-tech	高科技	information age	信息时代
internet	互联网	attachment	附件
soft/hard ware	软件/硬件	lap top	笔记本电脑
log on	上网	surf on the net	网上冲浪
e-mails	电子邮件	PC games	电子游戏
desk top	台式机	digital camera	数码照相机
download	下载	virus	病毒
hacker/cracker	黑客	firewalls	防火墙
web-site	网址	chat-room	聊天室
netizen	网民	invention	发明
information exchange	信息交换	on line fee	上网费
artificial intelligence	人工智能	clone	克隆
innovation	创新	biotechnology	生物技术
scanner	扫描仪	printer	打印机
upgrade	升级	chip	芯片
data	数据	memory	存储器
disk drive	驱动器	click the mouse	点击鼠标
blog	博客	twitter	推特
post	帖子	seckill	秒杀
human-powered search	人肉搜索	spam	垃圾邮件
junk mail	垃圾邮件	broadband	宽带
tablet	平板电脑	palmtop	掌上电脑

（四）市场经济

economy/economic	经济	market management	市场管理
market competition	市场竞争	advertising campaign	广告、促销活动
commercial	商业的	promotion	促销
awarding sales	有奖销售	fake commodities	假冒伪劣产品
consumers rights and interests	消费者利益	complain	投诉
daily articles	日用品	make a profit	赢利
tourism	旅游业	investment	投资
stock broker	股票经纪人	stock holder	股东
demand/supply	需求/供给	boom	繁荣
recreation	娱乐	taxpayer	纳税人
stock exchange	股票交易	gross	毛利
productive forces	生产力	enterprises	企业

economic prosperity	经济繁荣	globalization	全球化	manufacturer	生产商	sales	销售
brand loyalty	品牌忠诚	holiday economy	假日经济	production	生产	cost	成本
material wealth	物质财富	ownership	所有权	trade	贸易	protectionism	保护主义
economist	经济学家	socialist economy	社会主义经济	planned economy	计划经济	private sector	私营部门
public sector	公共部门	economic balance	经济平衡	economic fluctuation	经济波动	economic depression	经济衰退
economic stability	经济稳定	economic policy	经济政策	economic recovery	经济复原	holding company	控股公司
economic trend	经济趋势	infrastructure	基本建设	standard of living	生活水平	purchasing power	购买力
scarcity	短缺	stagnation	停滞，萧条，不景气	underdevelopment	不发达	free trade	自由贸易
tariff	关税	audit	审计	bonus	红利	budget	预算
balance	结余，余额	closing rate	收盘汇率	currency	货币	commission	佣金，提成
deficit	赤字	deposit	存款，押金	recession	衰退	downturn	低迷，衰退
Dow-Jones average	道琼斯工业指数	economic sanction	经济制裁	bailout	救援	exchange	兑换，交易
Federal Reserve	联邦储备	futures	期货	idle money	闲散资金	depreciation	贬值
face value	面值	fixed asset	固定资产	real estate	房地产	housing bubble	房地产泡沫
freeze	冻结	inflation	通货膨胀	joint venture	合资企业	multinational	跨国公司
mortgage	抵押贷款	loan	贷款	monetary	资金的，货币的	financial crisis	金融危机
quota	配给	refund	退货	retail	零售	wholesale	批发
revenue	收入	securities	有价证券	margin	利润	monopoly	垄断
oil reserve	石油储备	premium	额外费用，奖金	speculation	投机	surplus	剩余

transfer	turnover	merge	sub-prime mortgage crisis
转账，过户	营业额	合并	次贷危机
Euro	debt ceiling	net	
欧元	债务上限	净利	

（五）交通运输

1. Means of transport 交通工具

（1）Around-city transport 跨城市交通

train	coach	ship	maglev	airplane/flight
火车	长途巴士	轮船	磁力悬浮火车	飞机

（2）Urban transport 市内交通

① Public transport 公共交通

bus	minibus	trolley	subway/underground/tube
公共汽车	小型公共汽车	电车	地铁
light rail transit	taxi/cab	double-decker	fare
轻轨	出租车	双层巴士	车票费

② Private transport 私人交通

vehicle	van	motorbike	bike
汽车	货车	摩托车	自行车

2. Road conditions 道路状况

roundabout	fast lane	underpass	expressway
环岛	快行线	地下通道	高速道路
highway	overpass	corner	sign
干道	过街天桥	路口	标志
ring road	traffic light	one-way lane	parking lot
环路	交通指示灯	单行线	停车场
toll booth	zebra-crossing	T-junction	crossroads
收费亭	斑马线	丁字路口	十字路口

3. Traffic jam 交通堵塞

（1）Heavy traffic 交通拥堵

congested	rush hour	traffic jam	held up in the heavy traffic
拥堵	高峰时段	交通事故	交通堵塞

（2）Traffic accidents 交通事故

injury	casualty	damage	crash	collide
受伤	伤亡	损害	撞车	撞车

（3）Traffic offense 交通违规

speeding	drunk driving	suspend the driver's license	
超速	酒后开车	吊销驾照	
fine	ticket	exceed the speed limit	
罚款	罚单	超速	

（六）文化教育

quality education	higher education	full-time education	curriculum
素质教育	高等教育	全日制教育	课程
syllabus	moral	mental pressure	exam-oriented education
大纲	道德	精神压力	应试教育
educationalist	preach	principle	psychological obstruction
教育家	说教	原则	心理障碍
motivation	on-the-job study	academic	job-hunting
学习动机	在职学习	学术的	求职
seminar	vocational education	primary education	secondary education
研讨会	职业教育	初等教育	中等教育
Oriental culture	Western culture	culture shock	compulsory education
东方文化	西方文化	文化差异	义务教育
mass media	cross-culture communication	diversity/variety	individualism/materialism
大众传媒	跨文化交际	多样性	个人主义/物质主义
manners	tradition/convention	religion	Christianity
礼貌	传统	宗教	基督教
Buddhism	Catholicism	Islamism	Judaism
佛教	天主教	伊斯兰教	犹太教
Puritanism			
清教主义			

（七）体育运动

1. 奥运会

The Olympic bid/bid to hold the Summer Olympics	logo	motto	
申奥/申请举办夏季奥运会	会徽	口号	
An Olympic host city	Olympic torch relay	Five-ring Olympic flag	
奥运会主办城市	奥运火炬接力	奥运五环旗	
manager	instructor	guide	trainer
经纪人	教练，技术指导	领队	助理教练

contestant, competitor 运动员	referee 裁判	professional 职业运动员	enthusiast, fan 迷，爱好者
amateur 业余运动员	favourite 可望取胜者	outsider 无取胜希望者	championship 冠军赛
tournament 锦标赛	champion 冠军	record 纪录	stadium 运动场
record holder 纪录创造者	track 跑道	ring 圈	pitch （足球、橄榄球）场地
field 场地	court 网球场	team, side 队	

2. Athletics 田径运动

race 跑	middle-distance race 中长跑	long-distance running 长跑运动	marathon 马拉松
sprint 短跑（dash）	the 110 metre hurdles 110米栏	decathlon 十项全能	cross-country race 越野跑
jump 跳跃	pole vault 撑竿跳	long jump 跳远	(broad jump) high jump 跳高
triple jump, hop step and jump 三级跳	throw 投掷	putting the shot, shot put 推铅球	throwing the discus 掷铁饼
throwing the hammer 掷链锤	throwing the javelin 掷标枪		

3. Sporting Events 体育项目

gymnastics 体操	gymnastic apparatus 体操器械	horizontal bar 单杠	parallel bars 双杠
rings 吊环	side horse, pommelled horse 鞍马	weight-lifting 举重	weights 重量级
boxing 拳击	Greece-Roman wrestling 古典式摔跤	judo 柔道	fencing 击剑
skiing 滑雪	downhill race 速降滑雪赛，滑降	ice skating 滑冰	figure skating 花样滑冰
roller skating 滑旱冰	bobsleigh, bobsled 雪橇		

4. Ball Games 球类运动

football 足球	rugby 橄榄球	basketball 篮球	volleyball 排球
tennis 网球	baseball 垒球	handball 手球	hockey 曲棍球

golf	cricket	ice hockey	goalkeeper
高尔夫球	板球	冰球	球门员

（八）航天航空词汇

launch a satellite	launch pad	multistage rocket	second stage
发射卫星	发射台	多级火箭	第二级
third stage	orbit	artificial satellite	telstar
第三级	轨道	人造卫星	通信卫星
antenna	solar cell	spacecraft	lunar module
天线	太阳电池	航天器	登月舱
landing pad	LM-maneuvering rockets	service module	directional antenna
着陆架	登月舱机动火箭	服务舱	定向天线
lunar module	nozzle of the main engine	ascent stage	descent stage
登月舱	主发动机喷嘴	上升段	下降段
hatch	ladder	command module	service module
舱口	扶梯	指令舱	服务舱
astronaut	space suit	access flap	
航天员	航天服	接口盖	
emergency oxygen apparatus			
应急供氧装置			

（九）医疗卫生

disease	illness	bird flu	mad cow
疾病	疾病	禽流感	疯牛病
AIDS	swine flu	epidemic	allergy
艾滋病	猪流感	流行病	过敏
hypertension	acute disease	chronic disease	heart attack
高血压	急性病	慢性病	心脏病发作
malaria	obesity	diabetes	dementia
疟疾	肥胖症	糖尿病	痴呆症
virus	bacteria	inflect	gene
病毒	细菌	感染	基因
cell	antibody	antibiotic	organism
细胞	抗体	抗生的	有机体，生物体
symptom	diagnosis	prescription	treatment
病症	诊断	药方	治疗
syndrome	acupuncture	transplant	vaccine
综合征	针灸	移植	疫苗
immune system	therapy	operation life support system	
免疫系统	治疗	手术生命维持系统	

第五节 模拟试题精练

Model test 1

Section B

Directions: *In this section, you are required to read four pieces of news and decide which of the following four titles marked A, B, C and D is best suited to each of them. Choose the best answer and mark your answer on the* **Answer Sheet.**

A. Isaac, the tropical storm, is on its way

B. The dispute between the Chicago Teachers Union and the school board

C. Texas was hit hardest by the spread of West Nile virus

D. U.S. national debt surged to a new high

1. _____

The mayor of Dallas, says his city is facing an emergency. The problem is West Nile Virus. There is an outbreak of it happening around the U.S. It's the biggest jump in the number of reported cases of West Nile since 2004, and the outbreak is spreading. This map shows some of the states that have been hit the hardest. By far, Texas has had it the worst: More than 380 confirmed cases of West Nile there. Officials are trying to fight the outbreak by using a spray to kill infected mosquitoes. The insects spread the disease after they get it from birds.

West Nile started in Africa. No one knows how it got to the U.S., but we do know when it arrived: 1999. Most people who get West Nile don't get seriously sick. Dr. Sanjay Gupta runs through some of the symptoms of this disease. The vast majority of people who get West Nile won't have hardly any symptoms at all, or so mild that they won't realize that in fact they have West Nile.

2. _____

Early Sunday, this was listed as a tropical storm with wind speeds up to 65 miles per hour. But forecasters were saying Isaac could strengthen to a hurricane today. And that's when it was expected to move across the Florida Keys. Around Florida, people started getting ready for the storm last week. They filled sandbags and stocked stuck up on supplies, things like bottled water, butteries and flashlights.

The storm's projected path showed it moving up into the Gulf of Mexico, west of Tampa. That's why the start of the Republican National Convention which is happening in Tampa is being delayed until tomorrow. Officials are hoping that'll make it safer for delegates. Tropical storm Isaac moved across the Caribbean over the weekend, one of the countries it hit there was Haiti.

3. _____

U.S. national debt has hit a new milestone, and it's not a good one. The government now owes more than $16 trillion. That's 16 with 12 zeroes after it, and still counting. We can put it this way, if you spend a million dollars a day, it would take you almost 44,000 years to spend

16 trillion.

For this debt many Republicans blame Democrats and President Barack Obama. Many Democrats blame Republicans and former president George W. Bush. Two things we can say for sure. One, the government is spending a lot of money, and two, it's taking in a lot less tax revenue because of the struggling economy, so you can count on this number increasing in the months ahead.

4. _____

Three hundred and fifty thousand students in America's largest school district are not back in class today. The earliest that could happen is Wednesday, and the standoff between the Chicago Teachers Union and the school board has not been resolved. School officials took legal action on Monday trying to force teachers off the picket lines and in the classrooms.

The city calls the dispute dangerous and says it's against the law while the Teachers Union accused Chicago Mayor Rahm Emaneul of trying to bully teachers into accepting a deal. Now, there is a deal. It's a tentative one, but many members of the Chicago Teachers Union aren't happy with it, they want more time to look it over before they sign on. The big issue is here, how long the school day is, how teachers are evaluated, and how secure their jobs are.

Model test 2

Section B

Directions: *In this section, you are required to read four pieces of news and decide which of the following four titles marked A, B, C and D is best suited to each of them. Choose the best answer and mark your answer on the **Answer Sheet**.*

A. The exit of Greece from the euro area met opposition

B. An American gossip website published photos of naked Prince Harry

C. Women were first admitted to Augusta National, the master's golf tournament

D. Apple has become the most valuable corporation on the Dow Jones share index

1. _____

The technology giant Apple has become the biggest company ever valued at more than $620bn on the Dow Jones share index in New York. A rise in its share price took the maker of iPhones, iPads and iPods, through the mark set by Microsoft in 1999. Apple shares have enjoyed significant gains since last week rising to more than $664bn at the Nasdaq market amid speculation it will shortly unveil new versions of its iconic iphone and iPad, as well as a TV device.

Apple is now worth 50% more than the oil company ExxonMobil, the second most valuable corporation with share listed in New York. The surge in Apple's stock underlines investors' belief that the next generation of its products will keep ahead of the competition, as well as the hopes they will be in the shops by Christmas.

2. _____

The hope of the master's golf tournament, Augusta National in the American state of Georgia, has admitted women members for the first time in its 80-year history. The former U. S. Secretary of State Condoleezza Rice and the South Carolina financer Darla Moore have accepted the invitation to join. Augusta has come under increasing criticism for its failure to admit women. This is, said Augusta National chairman Billy Payne, a joyous occasion.

The campaigns to have women joined the club kicked off a decade ago. The former chairman responded that one day the club might have women but not, he said, at the point of a bayonet. The club only has around 300 members, all by invitation only. The first black member was admitted in 1990. For many years all the golf caddies were black. Female caddies were however allowed well before women members.

3. _____

The head of the Eurogroup Jean-Claude Juncker says he's totally opposed to Greece being forced out of the single currency. Mr Juncker said the priority was for the country to come up with a robust and critical strategy for closing the gap on its debt. "I'm totally opposed to the exit of Greece from the euro area. This would be of no help for Greece, and this would entail major risks for the whole euro area. And if those who are advocating day after day the exit of Greece would keep them off, it would be easier to make the progress that's needed in the privatization of those enterprises which have to be privatized."

4. _____

Photographs showing Queen Elizabeth's grandson Prince Harry and a young woman cavorting naked in a Las Vegas hotel room have been published on a U. S. website. Harry had gone to Las Vegas with friends on a short break from his military duties. At some point last weekend in what should have been the privacy of his hotel suit, he evidently decided to play a game of "strip billiards" with some women he and his friends had met in the hotel bar. Photographs were taken—it's thought by someone with a mobile phone; and these pictures, showing Harry naked, were then published by an American gossip website and some sections of the mainstream U. S. media. Friends of Prince Harry say this was a young soldier letting his hair down before returning to duty; whether his family sees it in those straightforward terms may be open to question.

Model test 3

Section B

Directions: *In this section, you are required to read four pieces of news and decide which of the following four titles marked A, B, C and D is best suited to each of them. Choose the best answer and mark your answer on the **Answer Sheet**.*

A. Commemoration of Neil Armstrong, the first man to set foot on the moon

B. Greece was urged to hang onto its commitments and reforms

C. Torrential rains and floods caused great losses in Niger

D. An emergency response is called for the outbreak of cholera in Sierra Leone

1. _____

The French and German leaders have urged Greece to carry on with its painful reforms. Chancellor Angela Merkel and President Francois Hollande presented a united front as they held talks in advance of their meeting with the Greek Prime Minister Antonis Samaras on Friday and Saturday. The two leaders with a real power in the eurozone presented a united front as they prepared to meet the Greek prime minister who comes to Berlin on Friday and then onto Paris on Saturday.

Chancellor Merkel said it was important that everybody stuck to their commitments, and President Hollande said that Greece had to do what was necessary in order to stay in the eurozone. They now wait for the all-important official assessment of Greek progress on reform to be done in September by inspectors from the donor organizations.

2. _____

The British government is organizing an emergency response to a cholera epidemic in Sierra Leone which has killed more than 200 people. It plans to help provide clean water and sanitation for some 2 million people. The British government's aid arm the Department for International Development has earmarked 2.5 million dollars to tackle the cholera epidemic in Sierra Leone which has already taken over 200 lives. It could threaten many thousands more if not brought under control.

Cholera is a sort of extreme diarrhea. It can kill people within hours if rehydration is not administered quickly. It's relatively simple to treat if clean facilities and trained staff were available. But Sierra Leone is a poor country with overstretched hospitals.

3. _____

The first man to set foot on the moon Neil Armstrong has died at the age of 82. He'd undergone heart bypass surgery earlier this month. As commander of the Apollo 11 mission in July 1969, Armstrong made the first footprint on the dusty surface. "It is one small step for man, one giant leap for mankind."

Thousands of people were involved in the Apollo missions that led to this moment, but it was Neil Armstrong's ice cool nerves that ensure that lunar module Eagle landed safely. He had to take manual control of the spacecraft as it descended toward the surface, taking it toward region's drone with boulders and craters. He and his fellow crew members returned to earth to a hero's welcome. But Neil Armstrong soon retreated from the lime light, preferring the quieter life as a professor of engineering.

4. _____

An aid operation has begun in the West African state of Niger following floods that have left more than 125,000 people homeless. The aid agency Plan International says at least 65 people died when heavy rains hit the capital Niamey earlier this month.

The torrential rains which swept across the country earlier this month resulted in the River Niger rising to levels not seen since the 1920s. Sixty-five people were drowned as villages along the banks were inundated by the brown, swirling water. Homes collapsed, farm animals were killed and thousands of families lost almost everything they owned. Now the first help has arrived. The UN is calling for further donations of food, tents and household goods.

Model test 4

Section B

Directions: *In this section, you are required to read four pieces of news and decide which of the following four titles marked A, B, C and D is best suited to each of them. Choose the best answer and mark your answer on the **Answer Sheet**.*

A. Further efforts are needed to improve America's present economic situation

B. A fishing boat carrying illegal immigrants heading for Europe sank

C. Food wastage was responsible for the rising food price

D. Uranium enrichment activity in Iran is the chief concern of the IAEA

1. _____

The head of the United Nations food agency has called for coordinated action by the world's richest countries to ease worries about rising food crisis. He said the owners were on the G20 because they produce about 90% of the crops worst affected by price rises.

The conference has also urged to help reduce food wastage. Delegates to the conference in Sweden were told that about a quarter of the food were produced worldwide never reaches our plates. This increases the prices we pay in the shops and puts unnecessary pressure on land and water supplies. The way food is wasted varies. In richer countries, consumers expect their food to look so perfect that slightly blemished though perfectly nutritious food and vegetables never reach the supermarkets; in poorer developing countries, most of the waste is on farms.

2. _____

At least 40 Egyptians believed to be illegal immigrants heading for Europe are feared drown after their boat sank off the coast of neighboring Libya. One of those on the boat survived to raise the alert. Egypt launched a major search and rescue operation. An official said that five more survivors had been pulled from the water as well as three bodies.

The fishing boat was close to the maritime border between Egypt and Libya. Those on board are thought to have been headed for Europe. That's also possible they could have been looking for work in Libya itself. Since the fall of Colonel Gaddafi, Libya has demanded visas for the many Egyptians looking for work in the country.

3. _____

The UN Nuclear Watchdog says Iran has greatly increased its capacity to enrich uranium, it might have fortified underground site. The agency also accused Iran of hampering efforts to investigate whether another site to have been used to develop nuclear weapons. The Nuclear Watchdog says in the past three months Iran has more than double the number of uranium enriching centrifuges in its underground bank known as Fordo. That's in defiant of United Nations resolutions and pressure from Israel and the United States.

The Agency also complains that Iran has dismissed its concerns about the Parchin military site, where it says recent satellite images show a shroud over a containment vessel where explosives may have been tested. Power lines and roads have been removed from the site in what the IAEA suspects it's a clean up operation designed to hide previous nuclear activities.

4. _____

The Chairman of the U. S. Federal Reserve Ben Bernanke has described the America's economic situation as far from satisfactory. Mr. Bernanke told the gathering central bankers and academics that the FED would be taking additional steps to prompt a stronger recovery. Mr. Bernanke's speech was not quite a promise to take any particular immediate action, but it was a strong suggestion that the FED is ready to try further stimulus.

He described the stagnation in the job's market as a grave concern. He also said that without previous FED actions, the recession would be in deeper and recovery slower. The options include further purchases in the markets of financial assets such as government debt with newly created money. A policy is known as quantitative easing. Critics say it could lead to sharply higher inflation.

Model test 5

Section B

Directions: *In this section, you are required to read four pieces of news and decide which of the following four titles marked A, B, C and D is best suited to each of them. Choose the best answer and mark your answer on the **Answer Sheet**.*

A. A new bond-buying program to help the weak members of eurozone

B. Performances on the closing ceremony of the 2012 Paralympics

C. A large sum of money pumped into economy to reduce unemployment

D. The death of a controversial religious figure

1. _____

Officials in South Korea say the founder of the controversial Unification Church, Sun Myung Moon, has died at the age of 92. Rev Moon's church gained hundreds of thousands of followers known as "Moonies." Rev Moon had been in a critical condition for two weeks since being hospitalized with pneumonia in his home in South Korea. His children who have been carrying out most of the church duties for a while now decided keeping visual at his bedside. Rev Moon was a controversial figure. Born in 1920 in what is now North Korea, he said Jesus Christ had appealed to him as a teenager, and asked him to continue his work. Famous for holding mass weddings involving thousands of people, he also created an international business empire.

2. _____

The European Central Bank has unveiled its new program to buy government bonds from struggling countries in the eurozone. Stock markets in Europe and the United States rose sharply in response. The bond-buying plan aims to make it cheaper for countries such as Spain and Italy to raise the funds they need.

The Italian prime minister Mario Monti welcomed the ECB's announcement as an important step forward. Italy's problems are not quite severe as Spain's. But it is still in difficult and dangerous financial waters. For months, prime minister Monti has called for measures to help shield the eurozone's weaker economies from unbearable pressures on the money markets. And he is clearly relieved that the European Central Bank will now play a more robust role in this area. But Mr Monti is determined to try to do everything he can to avoid having to turn to the bank for help.

3. _____

The closing ceremony of the 2012 Paralympics is taking place in London. Based on the theme of the four seasons, acrobats and dancers have been performing to live music from the band Coldplay. In a spectacular "festival of fire" at the Olympic Stadium, the organizers say the ceremony is an emotional farewell to what has been the most successful contest in the history of the Games. Drummers and acrobats, flame-throwers and motorbikes—all performing to the sound of Coldplay; thousands of competitors seated on the infield—what a close-up view of an extraordinary closing ceremony. Dancers and musicians from Brazil will perform later to look ahead to the arrival of the Games in Rio in four years time.

4. _____

The United States Federal Reserve says it is to resume pumping billions of dollars into the American economy to try to stimulate growth and bring down unemployment. The Fed says it will spend $40m a month buying mortgage backed securities. By buying up housing debt, the Fed hopes to persuade existing holders of that debt into investments that create more jobs. It says it will carry on buying bonds in this way until unemployment is substantially lowered so long as price rise is contained. A recent round of poor economic data had made this decision seem almost inevitable. But critics say unconventional polices of this type don't work and cause inflation.

Model test 6

Section B

Directions: *In this section, you are required to read several excerpts from newspapers and/or magazines. These excerpts are followed by questions or unfinished statements, each with four suggested answers A, B, C and D. Choose the best answer and mark your answer on the* **Answer Sheet**.

Excerpt 1:

American employers cut back sharply on hiring last month, crushing hopes that the job market was improving and putting more pressure on the Federal Reserve to give the sluggish economy another push.

The Labor Department said Friday that employers added just 96,000 jobs in August, down from 141,000 in July and too few to keep up with population growth. The unemployment rate fell to 8.1 percent from 8.3 percent, but only because many people gave up looking for work and therefore weren't counted in the government's calculation.

Excerpt 2:

The percentage of Americans in the workforce dropped to its lowest level in 31 years.

The latest numbers were "downright dismal," TD Economics senior economist James Marple said in a description echoed by many others.

The economy remains hobbled in the aftermath of the deepest recession since the 1930s and simply isn't expanding fast enough to spark more hiring.

Consumers, whose spending accounts for more than two-thirds of economic activity, have been cutting down debts and spending cautiously. The government reported last week that economic growth clocked a disappointing 1.7 percent annual pace in the April-June quarter.

Excerpt 3:

The disappointing numbers are a blow to President Barack Obama's reelection campaign. Unemployment is down from a peak of 10 percent in October 2009, but no incumbent (现任的) president since Franklin D. Roosevelt has faced re-election with unemployment higher than 7.8 percent.

Republican presidential challenger Mitt Romney declared that "the weak jobs report is devastating news for American workers and American families… a harsh accusation of the president's handling of the economy."

Obama said August's hiring was "not good enough" and that it's "a long tough journey" to recover from the recession that officially ended more than three years ago.

Excerpt 4:

The job market got off to a strong start this year. Employers added an average 226,000 jobs a month from January through March. But they couldn't sustain that pace, and hiring slowed to a monthly average of 67,000 from April through June.

It looked like things got back on track in July, when the government initially reported 163,000 new jobs, but the Labor Department revised those gains down by 22,000 on Friday.

The August jobs report looks even uglier upon closer inspection. The unemployment rate fell because 368,000 Americans dropped out of the workforce.

Excerpt 5:

"A declining labor force is not (a) sign of an improving economy," says Joel Naroff, president of Naroff Economic Advisors.

Hourly pay fell. Manufacturers cut 15,000 jobs, the most in two years. And temporary help jobs, which often signal where the job market is headed, dropped by 4,900 in August.

The economy lost 7,000 more government jobs last month. Since the recession ended in June 2009, federal, state and local governments have slashed 670,000 jobs, partially offsetting hiring by private companies.

1. What is the common topic covered by all the excerpts?

  A. The annual pace of economic growth.   B. Consumers' cautious spending.

  C. A significant decline in hiring.   D. Economic recession and recovery.

2. According to Excerpt 1, the drop of unemployment rate is simply due to the fact that _____.

  A. the Federal Reserve gives the economy another push

B. fewer people keep on looking for work

C. more jobs have been added by employers

D. the economy is expanding fast enough

3. Which of the excerpts discusses the political consequence of high unemployment rate?

  A. Excerpt 1.   B. Excerpt 2.   C. Excerpt 3.   D. Excerpt 4.

4. Which of the following is NOT a factor causing the weak job market?

A. Governments at different levels cut down jobs since the recession ended.

B. Nearly 400 thousand Americans dropped out of the workforce.

C. The economy isn't improving enough to create more jobs.

D. The jobs added by American employers were in sharp decline in August.

Model test 7

Section B

Directions: *In this section, you are required to read several excerpts from newspapers and/or magazines. These excerpts are followed by questions or unfinished statements, each with four suggested answers A, B, C and D. Choose the best answer and mark your answer on the **Answer Sheet**.*

Excerpt 1:

In a now familiar global ritual, Apple fans jammed shops across the globe to pick up the tech juggernaut's (盲目崇拜的) latest iPhone 5. Eager buyers formed long lines Friday at Apple Inc. stores in Asia, Europe and North America to be the first to get their hands on the latest version of the smartphone.

The handset has become a hot seller despite a new map application that early users have deemed inferior to Google Maps, the software it replaces. Apple received two million orders in the first 24 hours of announcing its release date, more than twice the number for the iPhone 4s in the same period when that phone launched a year ago.

Excerpt 2:

Some fans went to extremes to be among the first buyers by arriving at Apple's flagship stores day ahead of the release of latest iPhone 5.

In downtown Sydney, Todd Foot, 24, showed up three days early to nab the coveted first spot. He spent about 18 hours a day in a folding chair, catching a few hours' sleep each night in a tent on the sidewalk.

Excerpt 3:

In Paris, the phone launch was accompanied by a workers' protest—a couple of dozen former and current Apple employees demonstrated peacefully to demand better work benefits. Some criticized what they called Apple's transformation from an offbeat company into a multinational powerhouse.

But the protesters—urged by a small labor union to demonstrate at Apple stores around France—were far outnumbered by lines of would-be buyers on the sidewalk outside the store near the city's gilded opera house.

Excerpt 4:

Not everyone lining up at the various Apple stores was an enthusiast, though. In Hong Kong, university student Kevin Wong, waiting to buy a black 16 gigabyte model for 5,588 Hong Kong dollars ($720), said he was getting one "for the cash." He planned to immediately resell it to one of the numerous grey market retailers catering to mainland Chinese buyers. China is one of Apple's fastest growing markets but a release date for the iPhone 5 there has not yet been set.

Excerpt 5:

In New York, several hundred people lined up outside Apple's 5th Avenue store. Jimmy Peralta, a 30 year-old business management student, waited three hours before getting the chance to buy his new gadget. Was it worth the wait?

"Definitely," he said, noting that the new phone's larger screen and lighter weight compelled him to upgrade from the iPhone 4. "It's just such a smart phone it does all the thinking for you, you can't get any easier than that."

Excerpt 6:

In a sign of the intense demand, police in Osaka, Japan, were investigating the theft of nearly 200 iPhone 5s, including 116 from one shop alone. In London, police sought help finding a man wanted in connection with the theft of 252 iPhone 5s from a shop in Wimbledon early Friday morning.

Excerpt 7:

In London, some shoppers had camped out for a week in a queue that snaked around the block. In Hong Kong, the first customers were greeted by staff cheering, clapping, chanting "iPhone 5! iPhone 5!" and high-fiving them as they were escorted through the front door.

1. Eager buyers were lining for the release of iPhone 5 in the following places EXCEPT _____.

   A. Beijing　　　　B. New York　　　　C. Paris　　　　D. Sydney

2. Which Excerpt mentions the merits of iPhone 5 in particular?

   A. Excerpt 1.　　B. Excerpt 3.　　C. Excerpt 5.　　D. Excerpt 7.

3. Which of the following choices involve Apple employees?

   A. Excerpt 1 and Excerpt 3.　　　　B. Excerpt 2 and Excerpt 7.

   C. Excerpt 3 and Excerpt 7.　　　　D. Excerpt 4 and Excerpt 6.

4. Which of the following statements is NOT TRUE according to the excerpts?

   A. The map application of Apple is thought to be not as good as Google Maps by early users.

   B. In Paris, the demonstration of former and current Apple employees turned to violence.

   C. The main purpose of protesters in Paris was to improve their work benefits.

   D. Not all people who queue up at the Apple stores are eager buyers.

5. Which excerpt deals with the negative side of the popularity of iPhone 5?

A. Excerpt 2.	B. Excerpt 3.	C. Excerpt 5.	D. Excerpt 6.

Model test 8

Section B

Directions: *In this section, you are required to read several excerpts from newspapers and/or magazines. These excerpts are followed by questions or unfinished statements, each with four suggested answers A, B, C and D. Choose the best answer and mark your answer on the* **Answer Sheet.**

Excerpt 1:

A wave of Apple iPhone 5 buyers is bound to boost the stocks of Apple's mobile partners.

Apple stock has risen 6% since Sept. 11, the day before the company unveiled the sixth generation of the iPhone, which hits stores on Friday. Apple shares reached an all-time high of $702.10 Wednesday.

Excerpt 2:

Investors are trading on Apple's announcement that it sold more than 2 million phones last weekend in preorders and on analysts' increased sales expectations. But Apple stock—up 73% this year—isn't the only investment play. The rising tide of iPhone 5 sales is positioned to boost the stocks of businesses whose technologies are packed inside the smartphone and of wireless carriers that will sell the phone.

"If iPhone 5 shipments are stronger than anyone expects, you'll certainly see Apple's stock go up and all of the component suppliers go up," says Cantor Fitzgerald analyst Dale Pfau.

Excerpt 3:

According to Bilton, analysts and investors think a reasonable assumption given the current trends is that Apple will crack the $1 trillion plateau on April 9, 2015, at around 11 a.m., which seems strangely specific all things considered. But, Bilton warns, there are other analysts who think Apple could do it within the year. Yes, they think Apple could do it by August 16, 2013. No specific time was given.

Excerpt 4:

Having Apple skyrocket up the stock market charts with a bullet to the tune of another $350 billion is unlikely. "It's hard to imagine Apple growing any faster," said Michael E. Driscoll, chief executive a big data and predictive analytics company, who thinks the 2015 guesstimate is right. But with the new iPhone in an hour, well, anything is possible. When the original iPhone came out, it was better looking and performing than anything else out there. The iPhone 5 gave us features offered in other phones with a smaller screen than competitors.

Excerpt 5:

There is a chance Apple never reaches a $1 trillion valuation, though. As Bilton, Microsoft was once worth $616 billion. They never made it. Could Apple be the next tech giant to collapse? "Every kingdom must crumble, right? What could be the downfall of such a mighty tech company? Their maps app. Indeed, the flap over the poor-quality maps on the iPhone 5 has led some people to wonder if Apple has already jumped the shark," Bilton warns.

Excerpt 6:

Some analysts expect Apple to sell up to 10 million iPhone 5 models before the end of September. JP Morgan estimates the phone could provide a $3.2-billion boost to the U.S. economy in the fourth quarter.

Apple's rival and component supplier, Samsung, moved to spoil the party, saying it plans to add the iPhone 5 to its existing patent lawsuits against Apple.

1. As a result of the hot sale of iPhone 5, the stocks of the following companies will rise EXCEPT _____.

    A. Apple's mobile partners   B. mighty tech companies like Microsoft

    C. Apple's component suppliers   D. wireless carriers that will sell the phone

2. What is Michael E. Driscoll's attitude towards the assumption that Apple will crack the $1 trillion plateau by 2013?

    A. Critical.   B. Neutral.   C. Supportive.   D. Doubtful.

3. Which of the following choices cite analysts' assumptions about Apple's valuation?

    A. Excerpt 1 and Excerpt 3.   B. Excerpt 2 and Excerpt 3.

    C. Excerpt 3 and Excerpt 5.   D. Excerpt 5 and Excerpt 6.

4. Which of the following statements might Bilton agree on?

    A. Apple will crack the $1 trillion plateau by August 16, 2013.

    B. Like Microsoft, Apple might not reach a $1 trillion valuation.

    C. It is natural for analysts and investors to specify the exact time.

    D. The phone could provide a $3.2-billion boost to the U.S. economy.

Model test 9

Section B

Directions: *In this section, you are required to read several excerpts from newspapers and/or magazines. These excerpts are followed by questions or unfinished statements, each with four suggested answers A, B, C and D. Choose the best answer and mark your answer on the* **Answer Sheet**.

Excerpt 1:

The Council of Mortgage Lenders says more eurozone uncertainty is "not a particularly comforting backdrop" for the UK's housing and mortgage markets. More bad eurozone news could affect mortgage costs, availability and activity.

Excerpt 2:

More turbulence in the eurozone would mean banks were likely to take a more cautious approach to lending money, in part because they would not have as much to hand out.

That could mean even tougher conditions for first-time buyers, who will again require a large deposit to secure a mortgage—perhaps about 20% of the value of the home they want to buy. Some may not want to buy anyway at a time when their jobs could be at risk. Fewer first-time buyers mean more tenants—and rising rents.

Excerpt 3:

These mortgages may also go up. Investors from Greece and Italy have already shown interest in buying homes in the UK because they think that it is a safe haven for their money. These sales have made the London market operate on a different level from the rest of the country, with prices going up in the capital but falling—sometimes sharply—elsewhere. Prices rose by 5.1% in London in the year to the end of April, Land Registry figures show. That compares with a fall of 1% across the whole of England and Wales.

Excerpt 4:

As with housing, pensions would be affected by the UK being seen as a safe shelter amid eurozone disturbance. Pension funds are big investors in UK government bonds. If the cost of buying them rises, and the return on holding them falls, pension funds would not be in such a healthy position. That might mean more businesses closing their final-salary pensions—the most generous workplace pension schemes—to new or existing staff.

Excerpt 5:

The eurozone is the UK's biggest trading partner. A long-term spiral of decline in the economies of Europe would mean less demand for UK good and services, and that could mean job cuts, especially in manufacturing.

Governments have been pushing for a growth agenda, but eurozone uncertainty leads to a lack of confidence among businesses. That means a pause in new investment and new jobs, most notably for younger workers.

Excerpt 6:

UK holidaymakers are finding that their pound is buying more euros than at any time in the past three years. Worries about the eurozone have weakened Europe's single currency. Meanwhile, the pound is recovering value that it lost in a market rout during the 2008 financial crisis. Pensioners from the UK who live in Europe during the winter will see increased spending power in their UK pension.

1. Which of the following is NOT the impact of more turbulence in the eurozone on the UK's housing and mortgage markets?

    A. Banks' hesitation to lend money.

    B. More difficult situations for first-time house buyers.

    C. The decrease of the house value in London.

    D. More lodgers and increasing rents.

2. What does the word "haven" in Line 2 of Excerpt 3 mean?

    A. Shelter.   B. Prevention.   C. Approach.   D. Operation.

3. How pensions of the UK would be affected by the eurozone uncertainty?

    A. Negatively.   B. Positively.   C. Irregularly.   D. Inevitably.

4. Who can benefit from the current disturbance in eurozone?
   A. First-time house buyers.
   B. Younger workers.
   C. Investors from Greece.
   D. UK holidaymakers.

Model test 10

Section B

Directions: *In this section, you are required to read several excerpts from newspapers and/or magazines. These excerpts are followed by questions or unfinished statements, each with four suggested answers A, B, C and D. Choose the best answer and mark your answer on the* **Answer Sheet**.

Excerpt 1:

What does an economist think of that? A lot depends on whether the economist is a man or a woman. A new study shows a large gender gap on economic policy among the nation's professional economists, a divide similar—and in some cases bigger—than the gender divide found in the general public. Differences extend to core professional beliefs—such as the effect of minimum wage laws—not just matters of political opinion.

Excerpt 2:

Opinion differences between men and women are well-documented in the general public. President Obama leads Mitt Romney by 10 percentage points among women. Romney leads Obama by 3 percentage points among men, according to the latest Gallup Poll.

Excerpt 3:

Liberal economist Dean Baker, co-founder of the Center for Economic Policy and Research, says male economists have been on the inside of the profession, confirming each other's anti-regulation views. Women, as outsiders, "are more likely to think independently or at least see people outside of the economics profession as forming their peer group," he says.

Excerpt 4:

A native of France, de Rugy supported government intervention early in her life but changed her mind after studying economics. "We want many of the same things as liberals—less poverty, more health care—but have radically different ideas on how to achieve it."

Excerpt 5:

Female economists tend to favor a bigger role for government while male economists have greater faith in business and the marketplace. Is the U. S. economy excessively regulated? Sixty-five percent of female economists said "no"—24 percentage points higher than male economists. "It's very puzzling," says free-market economist Veronique de Rugy of the Mercatus Center at George Mason University in Fairfax, Va. "Not a day goes by that I don't ask myself why there are so few women economists on the free-market side."

Excerpt 6:

The gender balance in economics is changing. One-third of economics doctorates now go to women. The chair of the White House Council of Economic Advisers has been a woman three of

27 times since 1946—one advising Obama and two advising Bill Clinton. The Federal Reserve Board of Governors has three women, bringing the total to eight of 90 members since 1914.

Excerpt 7:

The genders are most divorced from each other on the question of equality for women. Male economists overwhelmingly think the wage gap between men and women is largely the result of individuals' skills, experience and voluntary choices while female economists overwhelmingly disagree. The biggest disagreement: 76% of women say faculty opportunities in economics favor men. Male economists point the opposite way: 80% say women are favored or the process is neutral.

1. Gender differences between male and female economists can be observed in the following aspects EXCEPT _____.

 A. core professional beliefs

 B. political preferences in presidential election

 C. equality for women

 D. the role of government in economy

2. The majority of female economists tend to agree that _____.

 A. business and the marketplace should play a bigger role in economy

 B. the U. S. economy is excessively regulated by the government

 C. free market should be greatly encouraged to boost the U. S. economy

 D. the wage gap between men and women might be caused by the gender difference

3. According to de Rugy, the difference between her and liberals is _____.

 A. their attitudes towards government intervention

 B. the goals they hope to achieve

 C. how to reduce poverty and improve health care

 D. the role of government in economy

4. Which Excerpt discusses the difference of male and female economists in the relationship with their profession?

 A. Excerpt 2.   B. Excerpt 3.   C. Excerpt 6.   D. Excerpt 7.

Model test 11

Section B

Directions: *In this section, you are required to read one quoted blog and the comments on it. The blog and comments are followed by questions or unfinished statements, each with four suggested answers A, B, C and D. Choose the best answer and mark your answer on the **Answer Sheet**.*

"Twitter, like Facebook, is a popular way for many people to learn about news, and some Twitter users have used it as a way to report news live, before websites do. Businesses also prosper from Twitter by keeping in constant contact with their customers. Yet, for the rest of the world, it can be a waste of time that doesn't get the message out to people it wants to reach. And for some, it's no more a bunch of nonsense limited to 140 characters. Besides, having thousands of followers may still be a big waste of time, especially since 20 percent of Twitter's users produce at least 80 percent of the site's content. It looks like a few are preaching to the masses."

Comment 1:

I've said it before and I'll say it again, Twitter seems like the Emperor's new clothes to me! It seems that almost everything can be done better through different media: Want to reach out to an audience? I bet you'll get more eyes on your message through email. Want to stay in touch with friends? Facebook does that great—with some privacy too! Got something to say? Start a blog. I just can't see that it offers more value than other forms of communication.

Comment 2:

Twitter is an excellent communication tool. If used properly and responsibly it can be a vital marketing tool for reaching 1,000s of individuals quickly and efficiently. So use it wisely and carefully!

Comment 3:

I'm new to the whole twitter thing. I must admit that I find twitter WAY more informative than I thought I would. I do find that by being selective with the people that I follow on twitter I am able to keep track of current happenings and find information relative to my life and my business.

Comment 4:

Yes, I do think both Twitter and Facebook are a waste of time. I prefer the forums myself.

Comment 5:

I don't think Twitter is a waste of time. However, keep in mind that, just like everything else, it has its limitations. As a new website owner and developer, I found that it is helpful as a means of getting my content out there as well as being exposed to similar sites from which I can learn something. Its biggest drawback is the 140 character rule but, then again, you could look at that as a way to learn to be more precise in your communication.

Comment 6:

I concluded that Twitter is nothing if not the biggest spam engine ever created. Certainly it has value for prominent people with a following but as the data presented above shows, much Tweeting goes into the void.

Comment 7:

I believe you are missing one thing about Twitter when comparing it to Facebook: it can give you feedback. On Facebook, one must "Like" you in order to communicate with you. On Twitter, on the other hand, a business can search for their products and keywords, giving them the ability to offer help, see trends, see issues, and easily get feedback.

1. What's the writer's attitude towards Twitter in the blog?
  A. Positive.   B. Negative.   C. Neutral.   D. Informational.

2. Which of the following choices holds the negative attitude towards Twitter?
   A. Comment 1 and Comment 6.
   B. Comment 2 and Comment 4.
   C. Comment 3 and Comment 7.
   D. Comment 5 and Comment 6.
3. What is the biggest weakness of Twitter revealed in the comments?
   A. It's a waste of time.
   B. It's just meaningless nonsense.
   C. It fails to provide privacy.
   D. Its length is confined to 140 characters.
4. Which of the following choices mentions the differences between Twitter and Facebook?
   A. Comment 1 and Comment 7.
   B. Comment 4 and Comment 7.
   C. Comment 1 and Comment 4.
   D. Comment 2 and Comment 3.

Model test 12

Section B

Directions: *In this section, you are required to read one quoted blog and the comments on it. The blog and comments are followed by questions or unfinished statements, each with four suggested answers A, B, C and D. Choose the best answer and mark your answer on the **Answer Sheet**.*

"Abortion is a personal issue. No one actually knows what they would do until they are actually in a position to have to decide. I am not saying I am for or against abortion. What I AM for is a women's right to decide for herself. No group, organization, or political party has the right to decide for her. This should not be a political issue. The far right wingers feel they have the right to cram their beliefs down everyone's throats. These are the same people you see standing in front of abortions clinics screaming at the women going in. The more insane of them kill abortion doctors in the name of their God. Ironically, these are the same people who tell a woman she HAS to bear a child, yet go out of their way to vote down funding for the healthcare and food she is going to need to give that child a decent life."

Comment 1:

It is the right of the woman to decide. If it's made illegal, the women wanting it will get it one way or the other placing their lives in jeopardy. Thousands of illegal "clinics" will pop up charging them excessive fees.

Comment 2:

In religious circles, we are endowed with "free will." I may disagree with you, but you are in control of your own destiny. Morally, abusing, mutilating or killing any being for an unjustifiable reason, is never right.

Comment 3:

As to the rightness—I believe an unborn baby is no less of a person than any other person; but I also understand that there are times when a doctor must make the tough decision to lose one life to save another. It is those who view abortion as an acceptable birth control plan who I feel are wrong.

Comment 4:

Human life begins at awareness of self. Abortion is up to the individual. It shouldn't dominate politics since it is a right of the individual WOMAN to choose.

Comment 5:

How do you feel about all of the children parents kill with their bare hands, or the hundreds of children laying alone in orphanages? Why aren't all of those fighting against freedom of choice not going and saving those kids? Is eradicating a few cells that a soul hasn't even entered into really such a terrible thing in comparison?

Comment 6:

There was a time earlier in my life when I decided that the Catholic approach was the right one. That is how I became a parent, unintentionally. As a parent for almost 14 years now, I know that everyone is NOT well suited for the job. Like everything else about this particular issue, there is no absolute truth that we can see.

Comment 7:

I believe it is legally sanctioned murder, especially late term abortions that are sometimes minutes or seconds from being infanticide.

1. Which of the following is NOT the kind of people criticized in the blog?

    A. The far right wingers who force their ideas on others.

    B. The crazy people who kill abortion doctors.

    C. Those people who veto funding for healthcare and food.

    D. Those women who have decided to take abortion.

2. What does the word "mutilating" in Comment 2 mean?

    A. Condemning.　　B. Hurting.　　C. Protecting.　　D. Raising.

3. In which comment one's personal experience is used to illustrate the writer's view?

    A. Comment 4.　　B. Comment 5.　　C. Comment 6.　　D. Comment 7.

4. For those who are against abortion, which of the following is NOT the reason for their negative attitude in this issue?

    A. The life of those women who need abortion will be endangered.

    B. It is morally incorrect to kill any being for unjustifiable reason.

    C. An unborn baby should also be regarded as a human being.

    D. It is wrong for people to use abortion as a means of birth control.

Model test 13

Section B

Directions: *In this section, you are required to read one quoted blog and the comments on it. The blog and comments are followed by questions or unfinished statements, each with four suggested answers A, B, C and D. Choose the best answer and mark your answer on the **Answer Sheet**.*

"In Oregon, they are attempting to be the model for healthcare reform. They have now made it possible to insure 80,000 more children and 35,000 more adults. How...You ask? Taxing the insurance companies with a 1% tax. Seems a small price for them to pay, but they did not pay it. They passed this tax on to the insured immediately. I am willing to pay 1% for helping others, but it was intended to be the insurance companies' responsibility. I do not see insurance companies competing to provide affordable coverage unless they are forced to do so by competing against a public option."

Comment 1:

The government option is not about competition. If you had followed this debate for any amount of time you would realize those who now try to promote the "government option" using the words "choice" and "competition," just a short time ago, and some still now, were talking SINGLE PAYER. SINGLE PAYER is their goal, single payer means MONOPOLY, single payer means NO CHOICE, NO COMPETION, one option which is the GOVERNMENT! They only use the words "choice" and "competition" because they have taken polls and know these words are popular, they use these words like bait for fish (us) which they wish to FRY!

Comment 2:

If Government has total control they can save money, HOW? By denying care, putting people to sleep like dogs! Making people stand in line, not allowing even cash payments. They would have total control over our lives, that is what the government option is about—Totalitarian RULE—a nations of slaves and few elite government RULERS!

Comment 3:

We all know it will take some compromise. What many forget is that this is the negotiating phase. This is when we decide how much each group will pay and everyone wants the "upper hand." So there is something to fight for and we are fighting for it.

Comment 4:

That's pretty much what will happen nationally unless something is done to foster more competition. The big insurers have no incentive to hold the line on premiums otherwise, which is why they're likely to drop their objections to the reform bill if it gets out of committee without at least a trigger provision for a public option.

Comment 5:

Some Op-Ed I read this morning—and I've been reading too much of it—suggests that the subsequent increases in premiums that will be brought on by taxing insurance companies will ultimately drive down costs, because employers will be compelled to buy less coverage or raise employee contributions. That seems nonsense to me.

Comment 6:

The best way to encourage CHOICE and COMPETITION is to lift government regulation and let the thousands of insurance companies that exist in the United States compete across state lines. Right now, that is not allowed and this restriction greatly hinders competition as each state allows only certain insurance companies access to the people, why, because Government wants CONTROL!

1. According to the writer of the blog, who will pay the 1% tax?
    A. Insurance companies.　　　　B. State government.
    C. The insured.　　　　　　　　D. The writer.
2. What's the attitude of the writer of Comment 2 towards government option?
    A. Favorable.　　B. Critical.　　C. Objective.　　D. Concerned.
3. According to Comment 5, which of the following might NOT be the results of taxing insurance companies?
    A. The increase in premiums.　　B. The rise in the costs.
    C. Less coverage bought.　　　　D. More employee contributions.
4. What is the best way to encourage CHOICE and COMPETITION?
    A. To reinforce government regulations and control.
    B. To increase the number of insurance companies available.
    C. To let existing insurance companies to compete within the state.
    D. To encourage insurance companies' competition on the national level.

Model test 14

Section B

Directions: *In this section, you are required to read one quoted blog and the comments on it. The blog and comments are followed by questions or unfinished statements, each with four suggested answers A, B, C and D. Choose the best answer and mark your answer on the **Answer Sheet**.*

"Recently Japan's legislature has approved a bill revising the nation's Copyright Law to add criminal penalties for downloading copyrighted material making DVD backups and maybe watching YouTube illegal. The penalties will come into effect in October. You know, there's a fairly constant pattern in the world of copyright enforcement. The media companies claim that piracy is 'destroying' their industries, although they never offer any independent evidence to back this up. They 'demand' that governments 'do something' —by which they mean introduce harsher penalties for unauthorized downloads. After the laws come in to force, online sharing may dip for a while, but soon returns to previous levels, so the media companies start complaining again, and demand yet tougher penalties."

Comment 1:

If any of those participants in this never-ending cycle stood back and looked at what was happening, they would see that the very fact the copyright companies keep coming back for more and harsher copyright laws offers clear proof that the current approach just isn't working.

Comment 2:

To make it illegal to sell a device that enables playback of copied data would mean making illegal computers in general, since that's what a computer at the most basic level is—a copy machine. This is why I am against copyright law. The only way to make an effective copyright law would be to severely enforce a law that says computers and all other tools that can be used to copy are illegal, which is too high a price to pay.

Comment 3:

What should happen is the entertainment industries on the whole should be totally banned from the internet, from owning or operating any web site and from having any of their material available for download from anywhere. ISPs seem to be ignorant of the fact that the more these industries demand, the more they get but it is never enough and will never be enough.

Comment 4:

This is just making sure there are only two types of people in Japan. Those that are in prison, and those that will soon be on their way to prison.

Comment 5:

The act of viewing anything online is downloading. Even though it is temporary, the act of loading a webpage would technically be illegal.

Comment 6:

I suggest someone should start a petition against this law immediately just to give those copyright jerks a reminder of what happens when they demand stupid and useless laws.

Comment 7:

Given that media industries are able to make exaggerated claims without proof, can we not turn the tables on them? Get a grass roots movement going, get some momentum and take it to congress. Demand more piracy to encourage creativity and increase sales and profits.

1. According to the writer of the blog, what might be the result of the enforcement of the new bill?

　　A. The online sharing will be greatly reduced.

　　B. It won't have any impact on unauthorized downloads on line.

　　C. The media companies won't be satisfied with its temporary effect.

　　D. Penalties for unauthorized downloads will become less severe.

2. According to the writer of Comment 3, ISPs fails to notice that _____.

　　A. the entertainment industries will never get what they demand

　　B. the entertainment industries' demands seem to be endless

　　C. the entertainment industries should be banned from the net

　　D. the entertainment industries shouldn't get what they demand

3. What can be inferred from Comment 4?

　　A. There are too many potential criminals in Japan.

　　B. People in Japan are prone to commit crimes.

　　C. The offense of Japan's new bill will be inevitable.

　　D. Japan has to set up enough prisons to hold criminals.

4. What does the phrase "turn the tables" mean in Comment 7?

　　A. Take actions to alter the situation.

B. Make exaggerated claims as well.

C. Prohibit the media industries from the net.

D. Start a petition against the law.

Model test 15

Section B

Directions: *In this section, you are required to read one quoted blog and the comments on it. The blog and comments are followed by questions or unfinished statements, each with four suggested answers A, B, C and D. Choose the best answer and mark your answer on the* **Answer Sheet**.

"Across the rest of America, packing for college usually means gathering up books, clothes and maybe an iPod. Here in gun-loving Texas, it could soon mean packing **heat**. That's because a bill heading for likely approval in the state Legislature would allow gun owners who are licensed to carry concealed weapons to bring their firearms onto the state's college and university campuses—zones where the carrying of any weapons is now strictly prohibited. What a horrible idea! A college campus is supposed to be a special environment, not an armed camp. For me, introducing firearms into college environments already saturated with youthful impulsiveness, social anxieties and alcohol is an invitation for trouble."

Comment 1:

Risky. Main issue I had at college was not enough lights and campus police around. If that were solved, I'd feel safer.

Comment 2:

I believe that doing so is asking for more gun violence on campuses. Just because you have the right to carry doesn't mean you should.

Comment 3:

Risky. It is a heavy responsibility that leaves no room for error.

Comment 4:

Concealed weapons can enable other crimes such as sexual assault. Just equip each classroom with an alarm.

Comment 5:

Please point out a single case of a concealed permit holder committing a crime on a college campus where it was legal to carry. I'll help you, you won't find one because it hasn't happened. I studied this while I was in college and spoke to the public safety directors of every college which allowed concealed carry at the time. None of them were aware of a single incident by a concealed permit holder.

Comment 6:

Do we believe that allowing students to carry loaded firearms on campus will REDUCE gun violence on campus? Only a fool would think so. And while you may be able to point to a rare event where guns might have prevented a violent incident, the risk you run in allowing students to walk around armed far outweighs the possible benefits. It's just crazy to arm college students.

Comment 7:

As for your "rare event where guns may have prevented a violent incident," what you really mean is "rarely publicized and not tracked by law enforcement like a crime is." It is estimated that there are 100 million legally, privately owned handguns in the U. S. and that handguns may be used as often as 2 million times per year in legal defense incidents. Handguns are used illegally to kill people about 30,000 times per year. That means that each year, 99,970,000 handguns didn't kill anyone.

1. What's the writer's attitude towards allowing students to carry guns legally on campus in the blog?
    A. Critical.　　　　B. Favorable.　　　　C. Objective.　　　　D. Indifferent.
2. What does "heat" in Line 2 of the blog mean?
    A. Electric stoves.　　　　　　　　　　B. Heating devices.
    C. Handguns.　　　　　　　　　　　　D. Electronic devices.
3. Which of the following choices holds the supportive attitude towards gun ownership?
    A. Comment 1 and Comment 3.　　　　B. Comment 2 and Comment 4.
    C. Comment 4 and Comment 6.　　　　D. Comment 5 and Comment 7.
4. Those opposing carrying guns on campus are worried about the possible consequences EXCEPT _____.
    A. more gun violence　　　　　　　　B. other crimes like rapes
    C. more security troubles　　　　　　　D. more defense incidents

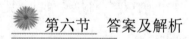

第六节　答案及解析

Model Test 1

1. 正确答案：C。

标题译文： 西尼罗河病毒重创德克萨斯州

新闻译文：

德克萨斯州达拉斯的市长称他的城市正面临紧急情况。问题是西尼罗河病毒。该病毒在美国突然爆发。这是自2004年以来西尼罗河报告的病例数出现最多的情况，且疫情正在蔓延。这张地图显示了一些遭受重大打击的州。到目前为止，德克萨斯州的情况最为糟糕：已经有超过380例西尼罗河病毒确诊病例。官员们试图通过使用喷雾杀死被感染的蚊子来对抗病毒。这些昆虫在与鸟类接触后传播疾病。

西尼罗河病毒始于非洲。没有人知道它如何到达美国，但是我们确实知道它在美国开始传播的日期：1999年。身染西尼罗河病毒的大多数人不会患上重病。桑杰·古普塔会告诉你这种病的一些症状。身染西尼罗河病毒的绝大多数人几乎没有任何症状，或者只有些轻微的症状，以至于他们意识不到自己已经身染西尼罗病毒。

2. 正确答案：A。

标题译文：热带风暴艾萨克即将登陆

新闻译文：

周日早些时候，它被称为热带风暴，风速高达每小时65英里①。但是天气预报员称艾萨克今天会变成飓风。而那个时候它将登陆佛罗里达。而在佛罗里达，人们开始准备应对上周的风暴。他们装填沙袋并储存食品，诸如瓶装水，电池和手电筒等。

风暴预计路径显示它会登陆到墨西哥湾西部的坦帕。这就是在坦帕召开的共和党全国代表大会被推迟到明天的原因。官员希望代表们更为安全。而上周末热带风暴艾萨克穿过加勒比海，并且袭击了加勒比海域的国家海地。

3. 正确答案：D。

标题译文：美国国债增长到新的高度

新闻译文：

美国的国家债务已达到一个新的里程碑，当然这不是好的那种。现在政府欠款超过16万亿美元。就是说16后面有12个零，而且这个数字还在继续增长。我们可以这样说，如果你一天花一百万美元，你需要44 000年才能花光这16万亿。

对于这笔债务许多共和党人指责民主党和贝拉克·奥巴马总统。而许多民主党人指责共和党人和前总统乔治·W·布什。但有两件事我们可以肯定。首先，政府正在花费一大笔钱，第二，因为经济困难，税收收入少之又少，所以你能想到的是这个数字在未来几个月内会继续增长。

4. 正确答案：B。

标题译文：芝加哥教师工会和学校董事会的争端

新闻译文：

美国最大学区的350 000名学生今天仍然没有回到学校上课。这起事件最早可能发生在星期三，芝加哥教师工会和学校董事会之间的僵局仍没有化解。学校官员在周一采取了法律行动试图强迫教师退出纠察线回到教室。

该市市民称这起争端十分危险，并且是违反法律的，而教师联盟则指责芝加哥市长拉姆·艾曼努尔，他试图强迫教师接受一项交易。现在，有一项协议出台。这是一项试探性的协议，但芝加哥教师工会的许多成员对此并不满意，在签字之前他们想要有更多的时间考虑。最大的问题就在这里，课时有多长，如何评估教师，以及如何确保工作的稳定。

Model Test 2

1. 正确答案：D。

标题译文：根据道琼斯股价指数，苹果成为价值最大的公司

新闻译文：

根据纽约道琼斯股价指数，科技巨头苹果成为价值最大的公司，价值6 200亿美元。这家生产iPhone，iPads和iPods的公司股价上涨，超过1999年微软的股价。有猜测称

---

① 1英里 = 1 609.344米。

苹果将很快推出新版本的标志性iPhone和iPad，以及一款电视设备，因此自上周开始，苹果在纳斯达克市场上的股价就取得了显著的增长，上升至6 640多亿美元。

苹果目前的价值比石油公司埃克森美孚国际公司高50%，美孚是在纽约上市的第二大最具价值的公司。苹果在股市的上升使投资者更加相信新一代产品能在圣诞节前上市，而且更具竞争力。

2. **正确答案：C。**

标题译文： 奥古斯塔国家高尔夫球俱乐部首次接纳女性会员

新闻译文：

美国高尔夫名人赛的希望，位于美国佐治亚州有80年历史的奥古斯塔国家高尔夫球俱乐部首次接纳女性会员。美国前国务卿康多莉扎·赖斯和南卡罗来纳州财长达拉·穆尔已接受邀请加入该俱乐部。奥古斯塔一直因不接纳女性会员而备受指责。奥古斯塔国家高尔夫球俱乐部主席比利·佩恩称，这是一个令人欢欣的时刻。

要求女性加入俱乐部的运动十年前就开始了，前主席对此表示，俱乐部总有一天会接纳女性的，但绝不是在被逼之下。该俱乐部目前大约有300名会员，所有都是邀请而来的。首位黑人会员是1990年加入的。多年来所有的球童都是黑人，接纳女性会员之前就有了女球童。

3. **正确答案：A。**

标题译文： 要求希腊退出欧元区的建议遭到反对

新闻译文：

欧元集团主席让·克洛德·容克称，他坚决反对希腊被迫退出该单一货币体系。容克说，希腊目前的当务之急是制定强健关键的战略来弥补债务缺口。"我完全反对希腊从欧元区退出，这对希腊毫无益处，会对整个欧元区构成重大风险。如果那些一直支持希腊退出的人能走开，那么对那些必须进行私有化的企业来说，其私有化过程就可以更容易取得进展"。

4. **正确答案：B。**

标题译文： 美国一家八卦网站刊登了英国王子哈里的裸照

新闻译文：

美国一家网站发布的照片显示，伊丽莎白女王的孙子哈里王子和一名年轻女子赤身裸体在拉斯维加斯酒店房间里狂欢。哈里是在服兵役的短暂假期和朋友去了拉斯维加斯。上周某个时候，他决定和一些他和朋友在酒店酒吧认识的女子玩脱衣台球游戏，这本来应该是酒店房间里的隐私。据说这些照片是有人用手机拍的，上面显示哈里赤身裸体，然后这些照片就出现在美国一家八卦网站和美国主流媒体的一些版面上。哈里王子的朋友说，这个年轻士兵是在回去服兵役之前狂欢一下，哈里的家人是否能看到这些尚不得而知。

Model Test 3

1. **正确答案：B。**

标题译文： 敦促希腊坚持自己的承诺和改革

新闻译文：

法国和德国领导人敦促希腊实施大刀阔斧的改革。总理安吉拉·默克尔和总统弗朗索瓦·奥朗德已在会谈中形成统一战线，随后他们将于周五和周六与希腊总理安东尼斯·萨马拉斯举行会谈。这两位欧元区真正有实力的领导人形成了统一战线，随后他们将于周五与前往柏林的希腊总理会谈，然后周六在巴黎会谈。

总理默克尔说人人都履行承诺是很重要的，总统奥朗德说，希腊要想留在欧元区，必须尽一切努力。他们正在等待一份很重要的来自捐助组织的监督者对希腊改革进展的评估报告，这项评估将于九月份完成。

2. **正确答案**：D。

标题译文：采取紧急措施应对塞拉利昂爆发的霍乱

新闻译文：

塞拉利昂爆发霍乱，已有 200 多人失去生命，英国政府对此采取紧急应对措施，计划为大约 200 万人提供洁净水和卫生服务。英国政府的援助机构国际发展部已拨款 250 万美元来应对塞拉利昂的这场已夺去 200 多人生命的霍乱。如果不加以控制，将会威胁数千人的安危。

霍乱是一种极端的疟疾，如果不能及时补充水分，病人就会在数小时内死亡。如果有清洁的设备和训练有素的医务人员，治疗就相对简单些。但塞拉利昂是个贫困国家，医院资源紧张。

3. **正确答案**：A。

标题译文：缅怀第一位登上月球的宇航员阿姆斯特朗

新闻译文：

第一位登上月球宇航员阿姆斯特朗辞世，享年 82 岁。他于本月初做了心脏搭桥手术。1969 年作为阿波罗 11 任务团的指挥官，阿姆斯特朗在月球上留下了人类的第一次足迹。"这是一个人迈出的一小步，却是整个人类跨出的一大步。"

上千人参与了阿波罗号任务，才使其成功实现，但是，是阿姆斯特朗的异常冷静确保了鹰号登月舱的安全着陆。他手动控制了航空飞机，使其成功降落于布满陨石和巨石坑的月球表面。人们向返回地球的阿姆斯特朗和其他宇航员致以英雄般的欢迎。但阿姆斯特朗很快从这种聚光灯下的生活全身撤退，从事了更为喜爱的一种安静的生活：工程学的一名教授。

4. **正确答案**：C。

标题译文：热带风暴和洪灾给尼日尔造成了巨大损失

新闻译文：

西非国家尼日尔发生洪灾，导致超过 12.5 万人无家可归，目前援助行动已经开始。援助机构国际计划称，本月初大雨袭击首都尼亚美，导致至少 65 人丧生。

本月初，这场暴雨袭击了整个国家，导致尼罗河水位上涨到 20 世纪 20 年代以来的最高点。河岸两边的村庄都被褐黄色漩涡流水冲毁，65 人被淹死。家园被毁，农场动物淹死，几千户人家几乎失去了一切。目前第一批援助已经到达，联合国正呼吁捐赠更多食物、帐篷和日常用品。

Model Test 4

1. **正确答案：C。**

   标题译文： 粮食浪费是造成粮食价格上升的原因之一

   新闻译文：

   联合国粮食机构主席呼吁全世界最富裕国家协作起来缓解人们对粮食危机的担心。他说G20国家是主人，因为最易受粮价上涨影响的作物中，其中有90%的就是这些国家生产的。

   会议还呼吁减少粮食浪费。来瑞士参加大会的代表们了解到，全世界生产的粮食中大约有1/4没有到达餐桌，这样我们就得在商店里支付更多的钱，并对土地和水供给构成不必要的压力。浪费食物的途径很多，在富裕国家，消费者希望自己吃的食物看起来完美无缺，那些营养完美的食物和蔬菜只要有一点缺损，就不会上到超市。而在贫困的发展中国家，大多数食物是在农场里浪费掉的。

2. **正确答案：B。**

   标题译文： 一艘载有去往欧洲的非法移民的渔船沉没

   新闻译文：

   据悉，至少40名非法移民的埃及人乘船赶往欧洲，他们的船在利比亚附近海域沉没，这些人很可能已经淹死。船上有一人幸存下来报了警，埃及开始进行大搜救，一名官员说，另外5名幸存者和3具尸体被从水中拖出。

   这艘渔船靠近埃及和利比亚的海域边界线，据说船上的人本要赶往欧洲，他们可能在利比亚找过工作。自从卡扎菲上校倒台以来，利比亚要求许多来该国找工作的埃及人提供签证。

3. **正确答案：D。**

   标题译文： 伊朗浓缩铀引起了国际原子能机构的高度关注

   新闻译文：

   联合国核观察机构称伊朗大大提高了浓缩铀的能力，这可能会加强了地下场所的防御。该机构还指责伊朗阻碍其调查该国是否利用另一地点来开发核武器的工作。核观察机构称在过去三个月内，伊朗弗多地下储备库的核浓缩离心机数量已经翻倍，全然不顾联合国决议以及来自以色列和美国的压力。

   该机构还指责伊朗不顾它对帕琴军事基地的担忧，该机构称卫星图片显示这里有一处被遮盖的安全壳，伊朗可能在这里进行炸弹测试。这里的输电线和道路已经撤去，国际原子能组织怀疑这是在清理现场，意在掩藏之前的核活动。

4. **正确答案：A。**

   标题译文： 改善美国目前的经济状况尚需更多努力

   新闻译文：

   美联储主席本·伯南克称美国的经济局势远远不能让人满意。伯南克向央行银行家和学者们表示，联邦政府官员们必须采取别的措施来促进经济更有力的恢复。伯南克的讲话并不意味着一定会采取快速的专门措施，但很有力地表明，联邦官员们准备采取进一步的刺激手段。

   伯南克称就业市场不景气是最令人关心的事。他还说，如果联邦官员没有采取之前的行动，衰退会更深，恢复会更缓慢。可采取的措施包括用新发行货币购买政府债务等财政资产，这就是所谓的量化宽松政策，批评者称这会使通胀水平更高。

Model Test 5

1. **正确答案**：D。
   标题译文：一位有争议的宗教人物去世
   新闻译文：
   韩国官员称争议颇多的统一教会创立者文鲜明去世，终年92岁。他的教堂吸引了上万名追随者，人称"统一教"。文鲜明在韩国的家中因肺炎而入院就医，两周来状况一直很糟。他那些一直履行教会大部分职责的子女现在决定守候在他的病床前。文鲜明一直是个富有争议的人物，他1920年出生于现在的朝鲜，他说耶稣基督曾在他少年时感召过他，请他继续自己的事业。他因举办上千人的集体婚礼而闻名，还建立了一个国际商业帝国。

2. **正确答案**：A。
   标题译文：一个帮助欧元区困境国家的债券购买新方案
   新闻译文：
   欧洲央行推出购买欧元区困境国家政府债券的新方案，欧洲和美国股市随之急剧上涨。这个债券购买计划意在使诸如西班牙和意大利这样的国家以较低的成本筹得所需的资金。
   意大利总理马里奥·蒙蒂对欧洲央行的宣布表示欢迎，称这是向前迈的一大步。意大利的问题不及西班牙严重，但财政状况已经很艰难很危险了。几个月来，总理马里奥·蒙蒂呼吁采取措施保护欧元区贫弱国家免受货币市场过大的压力。他坚信欧洲央行将在该地区发挥有利作用。但马里奥·蒙蒂决心尽一切努力免于向银行求助。

3. **正确答案**：B。
   标题译文：2012残奥会闭幕式的表演
   新闻译文：
   2012残奥会闭幕式正在伦敦举行，闭幕式以四季为主题，来自Coldplay乐队的杂技演员和舞蹈家们伴随音乐进行表演。伦敦体育馆举行的这场闭幕式名为"火之节日"，组织者称这是对残奥会史上这场最成功赛事的深情告别。鼓手、杂技演员、喷火者和摩托车，所有这些都随着Coldplay的音乐表演。几千名选手坐在赛场内，这是这场精彩闭幕式的特写镜头。来自巴西的舞者和音乐家稍后将举行表演，畅想4年后里约的赛事。

4. **正确答案**：C。
   标题译文：大笔资金注入美国经济以减少失业率
   新闻译文：
   美国联邦储备称将继续向美国经济注入数十亿美元以刺激发展并降低失业率。美联储称将每月支出4 000万美元购买抵押贷款证券。通过购买家庭债务，美联储希望能够劝说现有债务持有人进行投资以创造更多就业岗位，美联储称将继续这样购买债券，直到失业率大幅度降低并实现稳定物价为止。最近一轮不景气的经济数据使得该决定更加不可避免，但批评家称这种非传统政策不会起作用，还会引起通胀。

Model Test 6

1. 正确答案：C。

详解

主旨题。可套用公式：主旨≠文章某一部分的内容，以及文章的主旨≠文中的某一细节，利用排除法做题。A、B 选项只是 Excerpt 2 中涉及的内容；而 D 选项尽管在多个摘录中都提到了，但是 Excerpt 4 却未曾提及。只有 C 选项才是每个摘录都涉及的内容，也是全篇的主旨，尽管每个摘录中用的词不尽相同。各个摘录中表达就业率下降的语句如下：Excerpt 1 中的 American employers cut back sharply on hiring last month；Excerpt 2 中的 The percentage of Americans in the workforce dropped to its lowest level in 31 years；Excerpt 3 中的 The disappointing numbers 以及 the weak jobs report 和 August's hiring was "not good enough"；Excerpt 4 中的 hiring slowed to a monthly average of 67,000 from April through June 以及 The August jobs report looks even uglier upon closer inspection；Excerpt 5 中的 Manufacturers cut 15,000 jobs, the most in two years 以及 The economy lost 7,000 more government jobs last month 等。

2. 正确答案：B。

详解

细节题。可套用公式：正确答案＝原文中含有题干关键词的一句话——题干关键词。根据题干关键词 the drop of unemployment rate 回到 Excerpt 1 中的最后一句，原文中的正确答案就是 only because 之后的 many people gave up looking for work，据此可以判断本题的正确答案是 B。

3. 正确答案：C。

详解

推断题。首先，要读懂题目，本题问的是哪个摘录中讨论了高失业率引发的政治方面的后果；题目关键词是 the political consequence。其次，可以套用概括推断题的做题公式，通过概括 Excerpt 3 中的关键词来判断这部分涉及了政治方面的后果。这部分中和政治有关的词汇如下：reelection campaign（竞选连任）；president（总统）；Republican（共和党的）；presidential challenger（总统竞选的挑战者）等。

4. 正确答案：B。

详解

细节题中的 NOT TRUE 题型或 EXCEPT 题型。首先，要读懂题目，本题问的是哪个选项不是引发就业市场疲软的原因。可套用公式：正确答案≠原文中某一句话的表达。A 选项的意思是：自衰退结束后，各级政府削减了工作岗位；与 Excerpt 5 中的最后一句话相符，而且是导致失业率高的原因，因此可以排除。根据 B 选项中的数字和关键词 dropped out of the workforce 回原文中定位，原文中的出处是 Excerpt 4 中的最后一句：The unemployment rate fell because 368,000 Americans dropped out of the workforce；

据此可以判断 B 选项是失业率下降的原因，而不是引发就业市场疲软的原因，因此 B 是本题的正确答案。C 和 D 选项均与原文表述相符，而且都是造成就业市场疲软的原因。C 选项在原文中的出处是：Excerpt 2 中的 The economy...and simply isn't expanding fast enough to spark more hiring。D 选项在原文中的出处是：Excerpt 1 中的第一句。

全文翻译

摘录 1：

上个月美国员工雇用率大幅削减，粉碎了就业市场有所好转的希望，给美国联邦贮备局增加了更大的压力来设法振兴疲软的经济。

周五劳工部指出 8 月新增的工作岗位仅为 9.6 万个，比 7 月份的 14.1 万个下降了不少；新增的工作岗位太少了，无法跟上人口的增长。失业率从 8.3% 下降到 8.1%，这仅仅是因为很多人不再找工作，因此没包括在政府的统计数据里。

摘录 2：

美国就业率降到了 31 年来的最低水平。

一位资深经济学家 James Marple 在一篇文章中指出最近的数据是"彻底的惨淡"，他的说法得到了很多人的赞同。

在经历了自 20 世纪 30 年代以来最为严重的衰退后，经济一直萎靡不振，发展的速度根本不足以创造更多的就业机会。

消费者的消费构成了经济活动的 2/3，但是现在消费者却削减债务、谨慎消费。根据政府上周的报告，在 4~6 月这个季度经济的年增长率仅为 1.7%，令人失望。

摘录 3：

这些令人失望的数字是对奥巴马总统竞选连任的一大打击。尽管失业率相比 2009 年 10 月最高点的 10% 有所下降，但是自罗斯福总统以后没有哪一位现任的总统在竞选连任时面临高于 7.8% 的失业率。

共和党的总统候选人罗姆尼宣称："就业疲软的报告对于美国劳动者和他们的家人来说是灾难性的消息……是对总统应对经济问题能力的严厉指控。"

奥巴马承认 8 月份的就业率不够好，认为要想让经济从 3 年前正式结束的衰退中恢复起来是一件长期而艰难的工作。

摘录 4：

今年就业市场开头十分顺利。从 1~3 月每月平均增加了 22.6 万个工作岗位。但是，这种速度却没能保持下来，从 4~6 月每月的平均新增岗位数下降为 6.7 万个。

到了 7 月份当政府最初宣布新增 16.3 万个工作岗位时，事情看上去好像重新上了轨道，但是，周五劳工部重新修正了这些数字，工作岗位减少了 2.2 万个。

如果仔细审视的话，8 月份的数字就更令人失望。失业率的下降是因为有 36.8 万人不再计算在劳动力里面。

摘录 5：

Naroff 经济顾问机构的总裁 Joel Naroff 认为"劳动力的减少不是经济复苏的迹象。"

小时工资减少。制造商削减了 1.5 万个工作岗位，这是近两年里最多的一次。通常能够显示就业市场发展方向的临时用工在 8 月减少了 4 900 个。

上月，7 000多位政府人员丢掉了工作岗位。自2009年6月经济萧条结束以来，联邦、各州及地方政府削减了67万个工作岗位，从某种程度上抵消了私有企业增加的工作岗位。

Model Test 7

1. 正确答案：A。

详解

细节题中的NOT TRUE题型或EXCEPT题型。可套用公式：正确答案≠原文中某一句话的表达。根据Excerpt 4的最后一句China is one of Apple's fastest growing markets but a release date for the iPhone 5 there has not yet been set可知iPhone 5在中国大陆地区的销售日期还未确定，因此应该没有人在商店门前排队购买。此外，也可通过排除法做题，在各个摘录谈及各个iPhone 5热销地点中，没有提及A选项。

2. 正确答案：C。

详解

推断题。首先，要读懂题目，本题问的是哪个摘录中特别讨论了iPhone 5的优点；题目关键词是merit（优点，长处）。其次，可以套用概括推断题的做题公式，通过概括Excerpt 5中的关键词来判断这部分涉及了iPhone 5的优点。Excerpt 5中的关键语句包括：the new phone's larger screen and lighter weight 以及 "It's just such a smart phone it does all the thinking for you, you can't get any easier than that." 据此可以判断本题的正确答案是C。

3. 正确答案：C。

详解

细节题。首先，要读懂题目，本题问的是哪个摘录中涉及了苹果的员工。根据题目关键词Apple employees回原文中定位，并结合排除法做题。Excerpt 3涉及了正在参与示威的苹果之前的和现有的员工；Excerpt 7介绍了在香港，第一批顾客受到了店员的热烈欢迎，并详细描写了店员的动作。

4. 正确答案：B。

详解

细节题中的NOT TRUE题型或EXCEPT题型。可套用公式：正确答案≠原文中某一句话的表达。A选项的意思是：苹果的地图应用被早期用户认为不如谷歌的好；与Excerpt 1中的第2段第一句话相符，因此可以排除。根据B选项关键词former and current Apple employees回原文中定位，原文中的出处是Excerpt 3中的第一句：a couple of dozen former and current Apple employees demonstrated peacefully不符，因此B是本题的正确答案。

5. 正确答案：D。

详解

推断题。首先，要读懂题目，本题问的是哪个摘录中涉及了iPhone 5的热销的负面影响；题目关键词是negative side（负面）。其次，可以套用概括推断题的做题公式，通过概括 Excerpt 6 中的具体例子来判断这部分涉及了 iPhone 5 的负面影响。Excerpt 6 中提及的日本大阪和英国伦敦都出现了 iPhone 5 盗窃案。Excerpt 6 中的关键词是 theft（盗窃），据此可以判断本题的正确答案是 C。

全文翻译

摘录1：

全球的苹果迷们拥挤到商店里购买让人顶礼膜拜的最新科技产品 iPhone 5，这已经成为人们所熟悉的全球流行仪式。周五，热切的购买者在亚洲、欧洲以及北美各地的苹果商店排起了长队，都想成为第一个将最新款智能手机握在手里的人。

这款手机已经成为热门的畅销货，尽管早先的一些用户认为新的地图应用部分不如它所取代的原先的谷歌地图好。在刚刚宣布销售日期的 24 小时内苹果就接到了 200 万份订单，比一年前宣布销售 iPhone 4s 时收到的订单高出了两倍还多。

摘录2：

有一些粉丝非常极端，在最新的 iPhone 5 开始销售前几天就到苹果的旗舰店等候希望成为第一批购买者。

在悉尼市中心，为了占据令人垂涎的第一名的位置，24 岁的 Todd Foot 三天前就到了。他一天 18 个小时都坐在折叠椅里，晚上就在人行道的帐篷里睡几个小时。

摘录3：

在巴黎，与手机销售同时进行的是工人的抗议活动——几十名苹果先前的及现在的员工和平示威，要求提高工资待遇。一些人指责苹果的转变，他们称这一转变为从一个不规则的公司发展成为跨国大公司的转变。

但是，由一个小型工会煽动在全法国境内苹果商店示威的抗议者人数远低于城市镀金歌剧院附近的商店门外人行道上排队想要买手机的人数。

摘录4：

但是，并非每个在各个苹果商店门口排队的人都是狂热的购买者。香港的一名大学生 Kevin Wong 排队等着买一部价值5 588港元（720 美金）的黑色 16 兆节的手机，他说他是为了挣钱。他准备马上将它转手卖给众多半黑市零售商之一，这些人的客户都是中国内地的买家。中国是苹果发展速度最快的市场，但是在那 iPhone 5 的销售日期还没有确定。

摘录5：

在纽约，几百人在第五大道苹果商店门口排队。Jimmy Peralta 是一名 30 岁左右学工商管理专业的学生，他等了三个小时才有机会购买到他的新玩意。值得等这么久吗？

"当然，"他说，并解释说新手机更大的屏幕以及更轻的重量促使他要把他的 iPhone 4 升级。"它真是一部智能手机，可以替你思考，不可能有比它更轻松省力的了。"

摘录6：

有鉴于巨大的需求，日本大阪警方着手调查将近 200 部 iPhone 5 手机的盗窃案，包括仅从一家商店就盗取的 116 部。伦敦警方正寻求帮助搜捕一名与温布尔登周五早上 252 部 iPhone 5 手机失窃案有关的通缉犯。

摘录7：

在伦敦，一些购买者已经在商店外宿营了一周，排起的长队蜿蜒在整个街区。在香港，第一批顾客受到了店员的热烈欢迎，店员们欢呼拍手，高喊"iPhone 5！iPhone 5"，并和被簇拥通过大门的顾客击掌相庆。

Model Test 8

1. **正确答案：B。**

▶ **详解**

细节题中的 NOT TRUE 题型或 EXCEPT 题型。首先，要读懂题目，本题问的是由于 iPhone 5 的热销，以下哪个公司的股票不会随之上涨。然后，根据各答案选项中的关键词逐一回原文中定位，再结合排除法做题。A 选项 Apple's mobile partners（苹果手机的合作伙伴）出现在 Excerpt 1 的第一句中，根据 A wave of Apple iPhone 5 buyers is bound to boost the stocks of Apple's mobile partners 的语义，苹果手机合作伙伴的股票一定会随之上涨，与题目要求不符，应该排除。C、D 两个选项集中出现在 Excerpt 2 中。C 选项 Apple's component suppliers（苹果的零件供应商）出现在第二段的第一句里；D 选项 wireless carriers that will sell the phone（卖手机的无线运营商）出现在第一段的最后一句中。根据原文这两句话可以排除这两个选项。而 B 选项 mighty tech companies like Microsoft（像微软这样强大的科技公司）则出现在 Excerpt 5 中关于苹果价值能否突破 1 万亿美元大关的讨论，未涉及此类公司的股票涨跌问题，因此 B 是正确答案。

2. **正确答案：D。**

▶ **详解**

态度推断题。可以套用公式：正确答案＝原文话题＋表达话题的用词。根据题干关键词 Michael E. Driscoll 回到原文 Excerpt 4 中，根据介绍 Michael E. Driscoll 的定语从句 who thinks the 2015 guesstimate is right 可以看出，Michael E. Driscoll 同意的是关于苹果 2015 年能突破万亿大关的推断，对于 2013 年实现这一目标的推断可以从 Michael E. Driscoll 所说的"It's hard to imagine Apple growing any faster,"来判断，从这句话看出 Michael E. Driscoll 是持怀疑态度的。因此可以判断正确答案是 D 选项，而 A 选项 critical（批评、批判的）尽管也是负面态度，但与原文表述不符。

3. **正确答案：C。**

▶ **详解**

细节题。做题的关键是要读懂题目。本题问的是哪些摘录引用了分析家们对苹果估价的推断。首先根据题干关键词 analysts' assumptions about Apple's valuation 回原文定位，结合排除法做题。Excerpt 1、Excerpt 2、Excerpt 6 根本未涉及这一话题，因此含有这几个摘录的答案选项应该排除，所以正确答案是 C，Excerpt 3 主要探讨的就是这一推断，而 Excerpt 5 第一句也引用了这一推断的内容。

4. **正确答案：B。**

▶ **详解**

推断题。本题做题的关键是根据 Bilton 回原文中定位，能正确理解 Bilton 的观点态度，并结合排除法做题。Bilton 的观点集中出现在 Excerpt 3 和 Excerpt 5 中，根据 Excerpt 3 中第一段的最后两句，可以看出 Bilton 对于 A 选项的态度是否定的，关键词是这句中的 warn（警告）。C 选项 It is natural for analysts and investors to specify the exact time（分析家和投资者能够精确说出苹果实现这一目标的具体时间是很自然的事情）与 Excerpt 3 中第一句话中的 which seems strangely specific all things considered 语义不符。而 D 选项是 Excerpt 6 中 JP Morgan 的推断，与 Bilton 无关，因此这三个选项都可以排除。正确答案是 B 选项 Like Microsoft, Apple might not reach a $1 trillion valuation（像微软一样，苹果有可能达不到 1 万亿美元）。这一点可以从 Excerpt 5 中 Bilton 的警告"Every kingdom must crumble, right? What could be the downfall of such a mighty tech company? Their maps app. Indeed, the flap over the poor-quality maps on the iPhone 5 has led some people to wonder if Apple has already jumped the shark"得到证实和支持。

全文翻译

摘录 1：
众多的 iPhone 5 买家注定会推高苹果手机合作伙伴的股票。
自 9 月 11 日公司揭开第六代 iPhone（周五将登陆各大商店）的面纱以来，苹果的股票上涨了 6%。周三苹果的股份涨到了空前的高度：702.10 美元。

摘录 2：
投资者正在利用苹果公司的声明和分析家对销售增长的预期做交易，声明称上周末苹果通过预定已销售了 200 万部手机。但是，苹果股票——今年上涨了 73%——并不是唯一的投资活动。iPhone 5 销售的上升趋势势必会推高那些技术应用于此款智能手机的公司以及销售手机的无线运营商的股票。
Cantor Fitzgerald 的分析师 Dale Pfau 说："如果 iPhone 5 的出货高于所有人的预期，你肯定能看到苹果股票上涨，以及所有零件供货商的股票上涨。"

摘录 3：
在比尔顿看来，分析家和投资者认为在当前趋势下的合理设想是：在 2015 年 4 月 9 日 11 点左右，苹果将突破 1 万亿美元大关；当考虑到所有因素时，这一设想就具体到令人奇怪的程度了。但是，比尔顿警告说还有一些分析家认为苹果在年内就能实现这一目标。是的，他们认为在 2013 年 8 月 16 日前就能做到这一点。没有给出具体的时间。

摘录 4：
让苹果的股票在股票市场分析图上直线上升到另外 3 500 亿美元是不太可能的。"很难想象苹果还能增长得更快"，一家大型数据预测分析公司的执行官 Michael E. Driscoll 说。他觉得 2015 年的估计是对的。但是，能在短时间内推出新的 iPhone，一切皆有可能。当最初的 iPhone 问世的时候，它比市场上其他手机外观更漂亮、功能更强大。iPhone 5 在比其他竞争者小的屏幕上具有了其他手机有的所有特征。

摘录 5：
但是，在一种情况下苹果的价值永远不能达到 1 万亿美元。像比尔顿一样，微软一度价值为 6 160 亿美元。但是，却从来没能突破万亿大关。苹果会成为下一个垮掉的科技巨人吗？"每个王国都会衰败，对吗？这样一个强大的科技公司的衰败会是什么呢？他们的地图应用系统。事实上，iPhone 5 提供的地图质量不高这一缺陷已经使一些人猜想苹果是否已经开始走下坡路了，"比尔顿警告说。

摘录6：

一些分析家预期在9月底前苹果能销售1 000万部iPhone 5。摩根大通估计 iPhone 5 能为第四季度的美国经济带来32亿美元的收益。

苹果的竞争对手兼零件供货商三星公司已经开始破坏这一盛宴了，三星公司表示，它计划将 iPhone 5 列入已经进行的针对苹果的专利诉讼案中。

Model Test 9

1．正确答案：C。

> 详解

细节题中的 NOT TRUE 题型或 EXCEPT 题型。首先，根据题干关键词 more turbulence in the eurozone 及 UK's housing and mortgage markets 回原文中定位，A、B、D 三个选项集中出现在 Excerpt 2 中。A 选项 banks' hesitation to lend money（不太愿意借钱）与 Excerpt 2 的第一段表述相符，银行在贷款方面采取了更为谨慎的态度；B 选项 More difficult situations for first-time house buyers（首次买房者面临更为困难的情形）与第二段第一句语义一致；D 选项 More lodgers and increasing rents（更多的租房人，更高的租金）与第二段最后一句语义一致。因此可以判断这三个选项都是欧元区的动荡对英国房地产和抵押信贷市场的影响，通过排除法，正确答案是 C 选项。此外，也可套用公式：正确答案≠原文中某一句话的表达。C 选项 The decrease of the house value in London（伦敦房产价值下滑）与原文 Excerpt 3 中对伦敦房价的描述不符，据此也可以判断 C 是正确答案。

2．正确答案：A。

> 详解

猜词题。根据原文 Investors from Greece and Italy have already shown interest in buying homes in the UK because they think that it is a safe haven for their money 句子，可以把答案选项的词汇带回到原文这句话中，一要判断答案选项的词汇能否用在 safe 之后，受 safe 的修饰，还要和钱相关，据此可以先将 B、C 两个选项排除；第二还要判断新组成的表述能否符合这句话所表达的因果关系，符合这两个要求的只有 A 选项 shelter（保护，庇护所）。也可以套用猜词题公式：正确答案＝原文中含有该词的上下文对该词的解释——定义、释义、近义词、反义词。根据 Excerpt 4 中的 the UK being seen as a safe shelter amid eurozone disturbance，可以找到 haven 的同义词 shelter，在这两句话中这两个词语义和用法相同，都是描述英国被认为是动荡的欧元区中的安全避风港。

3．正确答案：A。

> 详解

推断题。首先根据题干关键词 pensions of the UK 和 the eurozone uncertainty 回原文中定位，可以发现出现在 Excerpt 4 中。可套用概括推断题的公式，从 Excerpt 4 对 pensions 所受影响的具体分析中进行提炼和概括。特别关键的有两句话：pension funds would not be in such a healthy position 以及 more businesses closing their final-salary pensions—the most generous workplace pension schemes—to new or existing staff，据此可以看出欧元区的不确定性对养老金的影响是负面的。B 选项 positively（正面地）与这两句话的语义刚好相反；C 选项 irregularly（不规律地）是无关选项；D 选项 inevitably（不可避免地）与原文中 If the cost of buying them rises, and the return on holding them falls 所表达的假设不符。所以正确答案是 A 选项。

4. **正确答案**：D。

▶ **详 解**

细节题。做题的关键是要读懂题目。本题问的是哪些人能在目前欧元区的动荡中获益，可以根据各个答案选项中的关键词逐一回原文中定位。Excerpt 2 指出了目前形势对 A 选项 first-time house buyers（首次买房者）不利；Excerpt 5 指出由于欧元区的动荡，使得商界信心不足，这就意味着 a pause in new investment and new jobs, most notably for younger workers，据此可以看出 B 选项 younger workers（年轻劳动者）所受的明显影响应该是没有工作机会，所以他们受到的是负面影响。Excerpt 3 指出 C 选项 Investors from Greece（希腊的投资者）有意购买英国的房产，为了他们的钱能保值，因此也不能说他们是明显从中获益的。只有 D 选项 UK holidaymakers（英国的度假者）根据 Excerpt 6 中的描述可以用英镑兑换更多的欧元，因此可以获益。

全文翻译

摘录 1：

按揭机构协会指出欧元区更多的不确定性对于英国的房地产和按揭市场不是一个特别令人舒服的背景。欧元区更多的坏消息会影响按揭的成本、可能性和活跃性。

摘录 2：

欧元区更多的动荡就意味着银行可能在贷款时采取更为谨慎的措施，这样做的一部分原因是银行没有那么多可以借出的钱。

这对于首次购房者就变得更为困难，要想按揭成功，他们将支付大笔的首付，大概相当于他们所购房子总价值的 20%。有些人可能根本不想买房，因为他们能否保住自己的工作还是个问题。首次购房者人数的减少就意味着有更多租房的人，租金会不断上涨。

摘录 3：

这些按揭抵押的房产还有增值的可能。希腊和意大利的投资者已经显示出对在英国买房的兴趣，因为他们觉得这是他们财富的安全避风港。此类销售使得伦敦的市场运作水平不同于英国的其他地区；伦敦地区房价上涨，而其他地区房价下降，有时还是大幅下滑。根据地政局的数字，今年前四个月伦敦的房价上涨了 5.1%。而整个英格兰和威尔士的房价下跌了 1%。

摘录 4：

养老金像房地产一样，也受到了认为英国是动荡的欧元区安全避风港这一观念的影响。养老金是英国政府债券的重要投资者。如果购买债券的成本高了，而持有债券的回报低了,那么养老金的前景就不那么乐观了。这就意味着更多的企业会取消他们新员工或者现有员工的最后薪水养老金——最慷慨的养老金体制。

摘录5:

欧元区是英国最大的贸易伙伴。欧洲经济长期不断衰退意味着对英国商品和服务的需求减少,这也就意味着工作岗位的减少,特别是在制造业。

人们敦促政府出台增长计划,但是欧元区的不确定性使得商界缺乏信心。这就意味着新投资和新增工作岗位会暂停,特别是针对年轻劳动者。

摘录6:

英国度假者发现,现在他们的英镑可以兑换比过去三年里任何时候都要多的欧元。对于欧元区的担忧削弱了欧洲的单一货币。同时,英镑正在恢复它在2008年金融危机中市场溃败时缩水的价值。冬季生活在欧洲的英国退休人员将会看到他们英国退休金的购买力的增长。

Model Test 10

1. 正确答案:B。

▶ **详解**

细节题中的 NOT TRUE 题型或 EXCEPT 题型。可套用公式:正确答案≠原文中某一句话的表达。首先,根据题干关键词 Gender differences between male and female economists 回原文中定位,A 选项出现在 Excerpt 1 的最后一句中,C 选项出现在 Excerpt 7 的第一句中,D 选项出现在 Excerpt 5 的第一句中,这三个选项都是男性、女性经济学家的差异所在,因此都可以排除。根据 B 选项 political preferences in presidential election(总统选举中的政治倾向)回到原文 Excerpt 2 中可以发现这是在普通大众身上体现出来的性别差异,不符合题目要求,所以 B 是正确答案。

2. 正确答案:D。

▶ **详解**

推断题。首先,要读懂题目,本题问的是大多数女性经济学家会赞同哪种观点。其次,要抓住本题的做题关键,即能够准确区分哪些是男性经济学家的观点,哪些是女性经济学家的观点,然后可以结合排除法做题。根据答案选项中的题干关键词分别回原文中定位可以发现:Excerpt 5 的第一句表明了 A 选项 business and the marketplace should play a bigger role in economy(商界和市场可以在经济中发挥更大的作用)是男性经济学家的观点,而女性经济学家则认为政府该扮演更重要的角色,与此不符。根据 Excerpt 5 中的 Is the U. S. economy excessively regulated? Sixty-five percent of female economists said "no" 这一问一答可以发现提到的 B 选项 the U. S. economy is excessively regulated by the government(美国经济受到了政府的过度调控)与原文表述不符,不是女性经济学家的观点。根据 Excerpt 5 中的最后一句 Not a day goes by that I don't ask myself why there are so few women economists on the free-market side 可以判断大多数女性经济学家是不支持自由市场的,所以 C 选项 free market should be greatly encouraged to boost the U. S. economy(应该大力发展自由市场来振兴美国经济)也不是女性经济学家的观点。根据

D 选项中的关键词 the wage gap between men and women 回原文中定位,可以发现它出现在 Excerpt 7 中,根据原文的表述 Male economists overwhelmingly think the wage gap between men and women is largely the result of individuals' skills, experience and voluntary choices while female economists overwhelmingly disagree,以及 Excerpt 7 主要讨论的男女经济学家最大的差异是在对待 equality for women(男女平等问题)上,结合逻辑推断题公式可以得出以下结论:女经济学家认为男女工资的差异主要不是由个人能力等原因引起的,而是由于男女差异、男女不平等引起的,所以 D 是正确答案。

3. **正确答案**:C。

> **详 解**

细节题。可套用公式:正确答案=原文中含有题干关键词的一句话—题干关键词。根据题干关键词 de Rugy 回原文中定位,可以发现出现在 Excerpt 4 中,根据原文的表述 We want many of the same things as liberals—less poverty, more health care—but have radically different ideas on how to achieve it 可以看出原文的正确答案是 how to achieve it,其中 it 应该代指 less poverty, more health care,所以正确答案是 C 选项。

4. **正确答案**:B。

> **详 解**

细节题。做题的关键是要读懂题目。本题问的是哪个摘录中涉及了男女经济学家在与自身职业关系上的不同,关键词是 the relationship with their profession。在 Excerpt 3 中 Dean Baker 提到了男性经济学家是 on the inside of the profession 而女性经济学家则是 outsiders,据此可以判断正确答案应该是 B。

全文翻译

摘录1:

经济学家如何看待这一问题?这在很大程度上取决于经济学家是男性还是女性。一项新研究表明专业经济学家们在经济政策上的观点有明显的性别差异,这种差异与在普通大众中发现的差异相似,甚至在某些方面还要更大。分歧已经扩大到一些核心专业理念例如最低工资法案的作用——不仅仅限于政治观念方面。

摘录2:

在公众领域,男女之间的观念差异已经有了充分记录和显示。根据最新的盖洛普民意调查,奥巴马总统在女性中的支持率领先罗姆尼 10 个百分点;而罗姆尼在男性中的支持率领先奥巴马 3 个百分点。

摘录3:

自由经济学家 Dean Baker 是经济政策及研究中心的创始人之一,他认为男性经济学家已经深入这个职业里面,会确认彼此的反规则观点。而女性则是外部的旁观者,更能独立思考,或者至少认为经济学圈子外的人们有着自己的小圈子。

摘录4:

de Rugy 是一个土生土长的法国人,她早期支持政府干预,但是后来在学了经济学后改变了她的观点。"我们和自由主义者渴求相同的东西——减少贫穷、改善医疗——

但是在如何获得这些方面却有着截然不同的观点。

摘录 5：

女性经济学家倾向于支持政府发挥更大的作用，而男性经济学家则对商界和市场抱有更大的信心。美国经济受到了过度调控吗？对于这个问题，65% 的女性经济学家的答案是否定的，高出男性经济学家 24 个百分点。位于弗吉尼亚州费尔斐可斯的乔治·梅森大学 Mercatus 中心的自由市场经济学家 Veronique de Rugy 说："这很令人困惑，我每天都问自己为什么支持自由市场的女经济学家这么少？"

摘录 6：

在经济学领域，性别平衡正在发生变化。1/3 的经济学博士头衔为女性获得。自 1946 年以来 27 届白宫经济顾问委员会的主席中有三届是女性——一位是奥巴马的顾问，两位是克林顿的顾问。美联储董事会有 3 位女性，这就意味着自 1914 年以来总数为 90 名成员中有 8 名是女性。

摘录 7：

在男女平等问题上，性别差别是最为明显的。绝大多数男性经济学家认为男女工资上的差异主要是由个人能力、经验和自愿选择引起的。绝大多数女性经济学家不同意这一观点。最大的分歧在于：76% 的女性认为经济学领域的职业机会更青睐男性。男性经济学家则持相反观点：80% 的人认为女性更受青睐，或者过程是不偏不倚的。

Model Test 11

1. **正确答案**：B。

   详解

   态度推断题。 可以套用公式：正确答案＝原文话题＋表达话题的用词。博客中 Yet 之后的信息才是作者真正观点及主观态度的表述，这之后讲的都是微博的不足之处，关键性的表述如：for the rest of the world, it can be a waste of time, it's no more a bunch of nonsense 和 It looks like a few are preaching to the masses。因此，可以判断作者对微博是负面的态度。

2. **正确答案**：A。

   详解

   态度推断题。 首先要抓住问题的重点，本题的核心词是 negative attitude（负面态度）；此外，可以套用公式：正确答案＝原文话题＋表达话题的用词。根据评论 1 中的关键表述 Twitter seems like the Emperor's new clothes to me, almost everything can be done better through different media 以及 I just can't see that it offers more value than other forms of communication 可以判断，作者是负面态度。根据评论 2 中的关键表述 Twitter is an excellent communication tool，作者是正面态度。根据评论 3 中的 I find twitter WAY more informative than I thought 可以判断作者是正面态度。据此排除 B 和 C 选项。根据评论 5 中的表述 I don't think Twitter is a waste of time，作者不是负面态度，因此 D 选项也可以排除。根据评论 6 中 Twitter is nothing if not the biggest spam engine ever created 和 much Tweeting goes into the void 可以判断，作者是负面观点，所以正确答案是 A。

3. 正确答案：D。

详解

细节题。可套用公式：正确答案＝原文中含有题干关键词的一句话－题干关键词。根据题干关键词 the biggest weakness of Twitter 回原文中定位，可以发现出现在评论5中，根据原文的表述 Its biggest drawback is the 140 character rule，可以初步判断正确答案是 D 选项，至于在这谈到的 140 字规定指什么，可以从博客中获得解释，根据博客中的表述 it's no more a bunch of nonsense limited to 140 characters，可以看出 140 字的规定应该指微博的长度限制。另外三个答案选项尽管都是微博的缺点，却不能对应 the biggest，因此应该予以排除。

4. 正确答案：A。

详解

细节题。首先要读懂题目，本题问的是哪些评论涉及了微博和脸谱网站的区别，然后根据本题的关键词 Facebook 回原文定位，再结合排除法做题。评论 2 和 3 根本就没有提及 Facebook，所以可以排除 D 选项。评论 4 中虽然出现了 Facebook，但是谈到的是它和微博的共同点而不是区别，所以 B 和 C 选项也可以排除。评论 7 的主要内容就是在介绍这两者的区别；评论 1 中涉及两者区别的句子是 Facebook does that great—with some privacy too，由此可以看出脸谱网站的隐私性更好。

全文翻译

"微博像脸谱网站一样，是受很多人欢迎的了解新闻的方式，一些微博用户也会用它在网站报道之前来现场报道新闻。商业企业也可以通过它和顾客保持联系，并从中获益。但是，对于所有其他人来说，它可能就是浪费时间，因为它不可能将信息传递给它所希望传递的人。而且，对于一些人来说，它不过就是最多用 140 个字来表达的一堆废话。此外，拥有成千上万的追随者也是浪费时间，当 20% 的微博用户提供了 80% 的微博内容，那就更是如此。这就像几个人在对大众说教一样。"

评论1：

正如我以前说过的，我现在再说一遍。对我来说，微博就像皇帝的新衣。好像它所有的功能都可以通过其他媒体来更好地实现：想和读者接触吗？我敢打赌用电子邮件可以让更多的人关注你的信息。想和朋友保持联系吗？脸谱网站做得很好，而且还可以保有一定的隐私。想说点什么吗？那就写博客吧。我根本看不出它比其他的交流方式有更多的好处。

评论2：

微博是极好的交流工具。如果能恰当地、负责任地使用它的话，它会成为至关重要的推销工具，可以快速有效地联系到成千上万的个人。所以，要小心明智地使用它。

评论3：

就微博而言，我是个新手。我必须承认我觉得微博的信息比我想得要丰富许多。我确实发现通过选择在微博上我要追随的人群，我可以了解时事，获得与我的生活和事业有关的信息。

评论4：

是的，我确实认为上微博和脸谱网都是浪费时间。我个人更喜欢论坛。

评论5：

我认为上微博不是浪费时间。但是，应该记住就像所有事物一样，微博也有它的局限性。作为一名新的网站所有者和开发者，我觉得它有助于我把信息传递出去，也可以使我接触到可供我学习的相似网站。它最大的缺陷就是140个字的限制，但是你也可以把这个当作使你的交流更为精准的方式。

评论6：

我的结论是微博就是人类所创造的最大的制造垃圾信息的工具。当然对于那些有追随者的名人来说，它还是有价值的，但是正如上面的信息所显示，很多微博内容是空洞无物的。

评论7：

我觉得当你把微博和脸谱网站相提并论时，你忽略了一点，那就是微博可以给你反馈。在脸谱网站上，人们必须要"喜欢"你才能和你交流。但是，在微博上，一个企业可以寻找产品和关键词，赋予它们提供帮助、观察潮流、分析问题的能力，而且很容易获得反馈。

Model Test 12

1. **正确答案：** D。

详解

细节题中的 NOT TRUE 题型或 EXCEPT 题型。可套用公式：正确答案≠原文中某一句话的表达。首先要读懂题目，本题问的是以下哪种人不是博客的作者所批评的。第二，要把握博客作者的主观态度。根据博客的前5句话可以看出作者是同意堕胎的，认为这是女性个人的权利。因此，D 选项 Those women who have decided to take abortion（那些已经决定要堕胎的人）不是作者所批评的。博客的作者反对和批评的人应该是原文第5句话之后一直到段末的那些人，包括 A 选项 The far right wingers who force their ideas on others（那些将自己的观点强加给别人的极右翼分子）、B 选项 The crazy people who kill abortion doctors（杀害堕胎医生的疯子）以及 C 选项 Those people who veto funding for healthcare and food（那些否决对医疗和食物资助的人）。

2. **正确答案：** B。

详解

猜词题。可以套用猜词题公式：正确答案=原文中含有该词的上下文对该词的解释——定义、释义、近义词、反义词。根据该词在原文中的出处 Morally, abusing, mutilating or killing any being for an unjustifiable reason, is never right 可以找到并列连词 or 所连接的 mutilating 的两个近义词 abusing（虐待）和 killing（杀害），因此可以判断 C 选项 protecting（保护）和 D 选项 raising（养育）与原文语义和逻辑均不符，应该排除。尽管 A 选项 condemning（谴责）是负面语义，但是与两个近义词的语义仍有较大的差距，所以正确答案应该是 B 选项 hurting（伤害）。

3. 正确答案：C。

> 详解

细节题。首先要读懂题目，把握题目的关键点。本题问的是哪个评论中作者引用了个人的经历来阐述自己的观点；本题的关键词是 personal experience。只有评论6中，作者通过讲述自己如何成为父母的经历来说明不是每个人都适合为人父母的，因此正确答案是C选项。

4. 正确答案：A。

> 详解

细节题中的 NOT TRUE 题型或 EXCEPT 题型。可套用公式：正确答案≠原文中某一句话的表达。首先要读懂题目，本题的意思是：对于那些反对堕胎的人来说，哪个不是他们反对堕胎的理由。A选项的出处是评论1中的 If it's made illegal, the women wanting it will get it one way or the other placing their lives in jeopardy。而这句话及整个评论1的观点都是同意堕胎的，所以是本题的正确答案。而B选项 It is morally incorrect to kill any being for unjustifiable reason（因为不合理的原因而杀人在道德上是不对的）与评论2的最后一句语义相同；C选项 An unborn baby should also be regarded as a human being（未出生的孩子也应被当作人来看待）与评论3的第一句语义相同；D选项 It is wrong for people to use abortion as a means of birth control（人们把堕胎作为节育手段是错误的）与评论3最后一句语义相同，这三个选项都是反对堕胎的原因。

全文翻译

"堕胎是个人问题。在还未到必须做决定的时候没有人确切地知道他们想怎么做。我不是想说我是赞成还是反对堕胎。我所赞成的是女性有权自己决定。没有哪个团体、组织或者政党有权替她决定。这不应该是政治问题。一些极右翼分子认为他们有权利把自己的想法强加给别人。这些人和你在堕胎诊所门前看到的冲着进去的女性大喊大叫的人士是一样的。甚至他们中间还有更疯狂的人打着上帝的旗号杀死堕胎的医生。讽刺的是，还是这批人一面告诉妇女生育孩子是她们的义务，一面故意否决对医疗和食物的资助，而医疗和食物正是给这个孩子提供体面生活的妇女所必需的。"

评论1：

妇女应该有权决定。如果认定堕胎是违法的，那么需要堕胎的女性就会以这样或那样的方式使自己的生命受到威胁。成千上万的非法"诊所"就会纷纷涌现，向她们收取过高的费用。

评论2：

在宗教方面，我们被赋予"自由意志"。我可能不同意你的看法，但是你可以掌握自己的命运。在道德层面，因为不合理的原因虐待、伤害或杀害任何一个生命都是不对的。

评论3：

至于公平公正，我认为一个未出生的孩子和其他任何人一样也是人，但是我也理解会有这样的时候医生必须做出艰难的选择来放弃一个生命以挽救另一个生命。我认为有错的是那些把堕胎当作可以接受的节育方案的人。

评论4：

人的生命始于自我意识。堕胎应该由个人来决定。它不应该左右政治，因为它是女性个人的选择权利。

评论5：

你怎么看待那些父母用手杀死的孩子，还有孤儿院里成千上万的儿童？为什么那些反对自由选择的人不去拯救这些孩子？相比之下，根除一些还没能真正形成心灵的细胞就是这么可怕的事情吗？

评论6：

我早年的时候曾经一度认为天主教的做法是正确的。这就是我怎样在无心的情况下为人父母的。现在我已经为人父母14年了，我意识到并非每个人都适合这个工作。关于这个具体的问题，就像其他所有事情一样，没有什么我们能发现的绝对真理。

评论7：

我觉得法律应该裁定堕胎为谋杀，特别是怀孕晚期的堕胎，有时只是比谋杀婴儿早几分钟或几秒钟而已。

Model Test 13

1. **正确答案：C。**

   ▶ **详解**

   细节题。可套用公式：正确答案＝原文中含有题干中心词的一句话－题干中心词。根据题干中的关键词 pay the 1% tax 回到博客中，找到该题在原文的出处 Seems a small price for them to pay, but they did not pay it. They passed this tax on to the insured immediately。根据这两句话可以看出，纳税的不是保险公司，而是保户，因此正确答案是C选项。原文中的关键词组是 pass sth. on to sb.，意思是把某事转嫁或传递给某人。

2. **正确答案：B。**

   ▶ **详解**

   态度推断题。可以套用公式：正确答案＝原文话题＋表达话题的用词。根据Comment 2 中的 single payer means MONOPOLY、single payer means NO CHOICE, NO COMPETION 以及 They only use the words "choice" and "competition" because they have taken polls and know these words are popular, they use these words like bait for fish (us) which they wish to FRY 等表述，可以看出作者认为 government option 就意味着垄断，没有选择和竞争，作者认为政府之所以使用这些字眼，是出于应对民调的需要，是对民众的愚弄，因此可以判断作者是批判的态度。A选项 favorable（赞同的）、C选项 objective（客观的）以及D选项 concerned（关注的）均与原文观点不符。

3. **正确答案：B。**

   ▶ **详解**

   细节题中的 NOT TRUE 题型或 EXCEPT 题型。可套用公式：正确答案≠原文中某一句话的表达。首先要读懂题目，题目的意思是哪个选项不是向保险公司征税可能引起的后果,然后回到原文中认真阅读,理解原文因果关系的表述。做题的关键是理解 the subsequent increases in premiums that will be brought on by taxing insurance companies will ultimately drive down costs 这句的含义。这句话有两层意思:一层是向保险公司征税会引起保险金的相应上升;另一层意思是保险金的相应上升最终会压低成本。因此,可以看出 B 选项 the rise in the costs(成本上升)与原文表述不符。

4. **正确答案**:D。

→ **详解**

细节题。可套用公式:正确答案=原文中含有题干中心词的一句话-题干中心词。根据题干中的关键词 the best way to encourage CHOICE and COMPETITION 回原文中定位,出现在 Comment 6 中,本题在原文中的出处是 lift government regulation and let the thousands of insurance companies that exist in the United States compete across state lines。做题的关键是对这句话中两个语言点的理解。一是 lift 的语义,另一个是 across state lines 的意思。Lift 在这里的语义是撤销,据此可以判断 A 选项 To reinforce government regulations and control(加强政府的管制管控)与原文语义不符,应予以排除。across state lines 的意思是跨洲,据此可以判断 C 选项 To let existing insurance companies to compete within the state(让现存的保险公司在各州内部竞争)的语义与原文不符;而 D 选项 To encourage insurance companies' competition on the national level(鼓励保险公司在全国范围进行竞争)符合原文的语义,是本题的正确答案。而 B 选项 To increase the number of insurance companies available(增加现有保险公司的数量)是无关选项,原文未曾涉及。

全文翻译

"俄勒冈正在努力成为医疗改革的榜样。现在那里的 8 万多位孩子以及超过 3.5 万位成人可以获得医疗保险。你可能会问,如何做到这一点?那就是收取保险公司 1% 的税。对保险公司来说,这是个很小的数目,即便如此,他们也没有付。他们立刻把这笔税转嫁给了投保人。为了帮助别人,我愿意付这 1%,但是,这本应该是保险公司的责任。我认为除非通过公众选择权带来的竞争强迫他们这么做,不然他们是不会相互竞争以便提供投保人负担得起的保险金。"

评论1:

政府的选择权和竞争无关。如果你关注这一争论一段时间的话,你就会发现那些正在努力推动"政府选择权"的人不久前才开始使用"选择"和"竞争"这样的词汇,而且一些人现在仍在讨论单一付款人。单一付款人是他们的目标,单一付款人意味着垄断,单一付款人意味着没有选择,没有竞争,就一个选择,那就是政府。他们只是因为要参与民意调查,知道"选择"和"竞争"这样的词汇为公众所喜欢才用它们的,他们用这些词来当诱饵引他们想炸的鱼(我们)上钩。

评论2:

如果政府能够全面控制,他们就可以省钱,怎样做到呢?通过剥夺人们的医疗,让人们像狗一样生活。让人们排着队,而且不允许现金支付。他们将完全控制我们的生活,这就是政府选择权的全部,极权统治——一个由极少数的精英政府统治者和奴隶构成的国家。

评论3：

我们都知道我们不得不做出一些让步。但是很多人忘了这是协商的阶段。这是我们决定每个群体支付多少的时候，是每个人都想占上风的时候。因此，还是有需要我们为之奋斗的东西，而且我们正在争取它。

评论4：

除非能做点什么来鼓励更多的竞争，不然全国会发生相当多的事情。不然，大保险公司没有动力来维持保险费，这就是他们为什么可能会放弃反对改革法案，如果在没有引发公众选择权条款的情况下，委员会出台法案的话。

评论5：

今天早上我读的一些专栏文章——最近我读得有点多——显示由于向保险公司征税所引起的保险金的相应上升最终会压低成本，因为雇主们会被迫购买覆盖较少的保险，或者增加雇员应付的份额。这一切对我来说都是胡说八道。

评论6：

鼓励选择和竞争的最佳方式是取消政府的管治，让美国现有的成千上万的保险公司可以跨州相互竞争。目前，这一点是不允许的，因为政府想要控制，所以每个州只允许特定的一些保险公司接触到民众，这一限制大大阻碍了竞争。

Model Test 14

1. 正确答案：C。

▶ 详解

细节题。可套用公式：正确答案＝原文中含有题干中心词的一句话－题干中心词。根据题干中的关键词 the result of the enforcement of the new bill 回到原文定位，本题在原文的出处是博客的最后一句话。去掉该句与关键词意思相同的 After the laws come in to force 后，所剩的 online sharing may dip for a while, but soon returns to previous levels, so the media companies start complaining again, and demand yet tougher penalties 就是本题的答案。根据前半句，可以排除 A 选项 The online sharing will be greatly reduced（网络共享会大大减少）及 B 选项 It won't have any impact on unauthorized downloads on line（对未经授权的下载不会有任何影响）都与原文表述不符，应予以排除。根据后半句话可以看出 C 选项 The media companies won't be satisfied with its temporary effect（媒体公司对法律起到的短暂效果不满意）与原文表述相符，因此是正确答案；同时可以判断 D 选项 Penalties for unauthorized downloads will become less severe（对未经授权的下载的处罚会减轻）与原文语义不符。

2. 正确答案：B。

▶ 详解

细节题。可套用公式：正确答案＝原文中含有题干中心词的一句话－题干中心词。根据题干中的关键词 ISPs 回原文定位，本题在原文的出处是 Comment 3 的最后一句，去掉该句中与题干语义相同的 ISPs seem to be ignorant of the fact that 后，句子所剩的 the more these industries demand, the more they get but it is never enough and will never be enough 就是答案所在。据此可以判断 A 选项 the entertainment industries will never get what they demand（娱乐业永远无法得到他们所需要的）与原文语义不符，而 C 选项 the entertainment industries should be banned from the net（应该禁止娱乐业进入网络）是本评论作者的观点，是在这个题目之前的信息，不符合题目要求；D 选项 the entertainment industries shouldn't get what they demand（娱乐业不应该得到他们所需要的）与原文表述不符，没有选择的依据。因此，只有 B 选项 the entertainment industries' demands seem to be endless（娱乐业的要求好像是没有止境的）是对原文语义的正确概括提炼。

3. **正确答案：C。**

> **详 解**

推断题。本题的关键是对原文 This is just making sure there are only two types of people in Japan. Those that are in prison, and those that will soon be on their way to prison 这句话的准确理解。这句话的意思是：这么做就是在确保日本只有两种人。那些已经关进监狱的人，以及那些即将要入狱的人。据此可以得出的合理推断应该是 C 选项 The offense of Japan's new bill will be inevitable（违反日本的这项新法律将是不可避免的）。而 A 选项 There are too many potential criminals in Japan（日本有太多的潜在罪犯）、B 选项 People in Japan are prone to commit crimes（日本人容易犯罪）以及 D 选项 Japan has to set up enough prisons to hold criminals（日本应该建立更多的监狱来关押罪犯）均是将原文的意思扩大化，并有一定程度的歪曲。

4. **正确答案：A。**

> **详 解**

猜词题。可以套用猜词题公式：正确答案＝原文中含有该词的上下文对该词的解释——定义、释义、近义词、反义词。根据该词在原文中的出处，可以看出本词组应该表示针对 media industries 的行为，根据后面具体的做法 Get a grass roots movement going, get some momentum and take it to congress. Demand more piracy to encourage creativity and increase sales and profits（发起草根阶级的运动，来点动力，把这个问题提到国会里。要求更多的盗版来鼓励创新、提高销售和扩大收益）可以概括出 A 选项 Take actions to alter the situation（采取行动扭转局面）是正确答案。而 B 选项 Make exaggerated claims as well（同样发表夸张的声明）、C 选项 Prohibit the media industries from the net（禁止媒体业进入网络）以及 D 选项 Start a petition against the law（发起反对法律的请愿活动）与原文语义均不符，因此应该排除。

全文翻译

"最近日本立法机构通过了一项修改国家版权法的法案，增加了对下载受版权保护的材料的刑事处罚，使得做 DVD 备份甚至可能是观看 YouTube 成为非法的行为。处罚将于 10 月份生效。你知道，在版权执行领域，一直有种相当稳定的模式。媒体公司声称盗版摧毁了他们的行业，尽管他们从未提供任何独立证据来证明这一点。他们要求政府要有所作为——说作为，他们是指对于未经授权的下载要进行更为严厉的惩罚。在法律生效以后，网络共享会沉寂一阵，但是很快就会恢复到原来的水平，因此媒体公司就又开始抱怨,并且要求更为严厉的处罚。"

评论1:

如果参与这一永无休止的循环的人能够停下来,回头看一下的话,他们就会发现,版权公司反复要求颁布更多更为严厉的法律这一事实明确地证明了当前的方法不起作用。

评论2:

认定销售可以重放复制信息的设备是违法的,那就意味着认定所有的计算机都是违法的,因为从最基本的层面来说,计算机就是一台复制机。这就是我反对版权法的原因。有效贯彻版权法的唯一方式就是严格地执行法律,规定计算机和所有其他能用来复制信息的工具都是违法的,可没人能付如此高的代价。

评论3:

应该做的事情是在互联网禁止整个娱乐业,禁止娱乐业拥有或运营任何网站,禁止娱乐业在任何地方提供可供下载的材料。网络服务提供者似乎不清楚这样的事实:这些行业要求得越多,他们就获得的越多,而他们从不满足,而且永远不会觉得满足。

评论4:

这么做就是在确保日本只有两种人。那些已经关进监狱的人,以及那些即将要入狱的人。

评论5:

在网上浏览任何东西都是下载行为。尽管是暂时的行为,但是确切来说,加载网页也是违法的。

评论6:

我希望立即有人请愿反对这一法律,给那些版权疯子们提个醒,当他们要求愚蠢和无用的法律时会发生什么事情。

评论7:

当媒体行业可以毫无根据地发表夸张的声明时,我们能否扭转局面呢?发起草根阶级的运动,来点动力,把这个问题提到国会里。要求更多的盗版来鼓励创新、提高销售和扩大收益。

Model Test 15

1. 正确答案:A。

详解

态度推断题。可以套用公式:正确答案 = 原文话题 + 表达话题的用词。作者在博客中将个人态度表达得非常充分。最能体现作者态度的表述包括:What a horrible idea! A college campus is supposed to be a special environment, not an armed camp. For me, introducing firearms into college environments already saturated with youthful impulsiveness, social anxieties and alcohol is an invitation for trouble. 其中,horrible(可怕的)以及an invitation for trouble(招惹麻烦)是非常明确的负面态度的表述词,因此本题的正确答案是A选项。

第二章 阅读理解

2. 正确答案：C。

> 详解

猜词题。可以套用猜词题公式：正确答案＝原文中含有该词的上下文对该词的解释——定义、释义、近义词、反义词。根据该词在原文中的出处 Here in gun-loving Texas, it could soon mean packing **heat** 可以找到该词的同义词 gun，而且也可以从文章后面的论述中得到证实，在德克萨斯州，大学生可以带枪去学校，因此 C 选项 handguns（手枪）是正确答案。而 A 选项 electric stoves（电炉）、B 选项 heating devices（供暖装置）以及 D 选项 electronic devices（电子设备）都是围绕 **heat** 最常用的语义设置的干扰项。

3. 正确答案：D。

> 详解

态度推断题。首先读懂题目，本题问的是对枪支拥有持正面态度的评论。然后可以套用公式：正确答案＝原文话题＋表达话题的用词，对涉及的评论逐一概括作者的主观态度，并结合排除法做题。两个答案选项中都有的 Comment 4，可首先判断 Comment 4 的观点，根据评论中的表述 Concealed weapons can enable other crimes such as sexual assault（隐藏武器可以引发其他的一些犯罪，例如：性侵犯）可以判断本评论对拥有枪支持否定态度，因此可以据此将 B 和 C 两个选项排除。然后判断 A 选项，根据 Comment 1 and Comment 3 中共同的用词 Risky（危险的）可以看出这两个评论也是负面态度，因此本题符合要求的正确答案应该是 D 选项。Comment 5 和 Comment 7 都是从拥有枪支不一定会引发犯罪这个角度，为拥有枪支进行了辩护。

4. 正确答案：D。

> 详解

细节题中的 NOT TRUE 题型或 EXCEPT 题型。可套用公式：正确答案≠原文中某一句话的表达。首先要读懂题目，题目的意思是：反对将枪支带入校园的人担忧可能发生的后果不包括哪一个。A 选项 more gun violence（更多的暴力）出现在 Comment 2 I believe that doing so is asking for more gun violence on campuses 中；B 选项 other crimes like rapes（其他犯罪，例如强奸）是 Comment 4 中 Concealed weapons can enable other crimes such as sexual assault 中提到的，sexual assault 是性侵犯；C 选项 more security troubles（更多的安全问题）是可以通过全文概括出来的，这些均是令人担忧的拥有枪支可能引发的问题。只有 D 选项 more defense incidents（更多自卫事件）与问题要求不符，这是枪支的正面用途。

全文翻译

"在美国其他地方，打包整理上大学的东西可能就意味着收拾书本、衣服，可能还有 iPod。但是，在热爱枪支的德克萨斯州，很快就意味着打包手枪了。这是因为州立法机构很可能会通过允许有执照的枪支拥有者携带武器进入大学校园的法案。而大学校园现在是严禁携带任何武器入内的。多可怕的想法呀！大学校园应该是一种特殊的环境，而不应成为武装的军营。就我而言，允许武器进入已经充斥着年轻人的冲动、社会的焦虑和酒精的大学校园就是自找麻烦。"

评论1：

太危险了。我在大学遇到的主要问题是缺乏足够的路灯和校园警察。如果这个解决了，我就觉得安全多了。

评论2：

我觉得这么做就是在校园里制造更多的暴力。只是因为你有权携带，并不意味着你应该携带。

评论3：

太危险。这么做责任太重大了，不允许出任何差错。

评论4：

隐藏武器可以引发其他的一些犯罪，例如：性侵犯。只要给每个教室安上警报装置就行。

评论5：

请举出一个获准携带枪支的人在带枪合法的大学校园里犯罪的例子来。我可以帮助你一下，你找不出来，因为根本就没有发生过。我在上大学时研究过这个问题，并和当时允许秘密携带枪支的每个大学的公共安全主管咨询过。他们没人发现合法的枪支拥有者有任何违法的事情。

评论6：

我们该相信在校园里允许学生携带装好子弹的枪支会减少校园的枪支暴力吗？只有傻子才相信呢。尽管你可以举出很罕见的枪支阻止暴力事件的例子来，但是允许学生带着枪在校园里走动，其风险要远远超过它的好处。武装大学生就是疯狂的行为。

评论7：

关于你所说的"枪支可以阻止暴力事件的罕见例子"，你真正的意思是说"极少曝光的，就像没被法律执行机构监测到的犯罪案件一样"。据估计，美国目前有1亿支合法的私人拥有的手枪，每年用于合法自卫的手枪使用次数是200万次。而每年手枪用于非法杀人的次数是3万次。这就意味着每年9 997万支手枪根本没有杀人。

第三章

短 文 完 成

第一节 大纲要求简介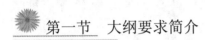

短文完成是全新的考试形式,在整个试卷所占的比重仅次于阅读,占20%。第六版《大纲》对短文完成部分的评价目标是"在理解阅读材料的基础上能综合运用词汇、语法、搭配、语段、篇章逻辑等方面的知识和上下文对语篇各层次的信息进行正确判断和完形处理。"对于短文完成部分在题型、题量、分值方面的规定是:

本部分共设20题,每题1分,考试时间为20分钟。本部分共有3篇短文,每篇短文自身有3~4个空白。同时,每篇短文前面又设有3~4个带有1个空白的语言段。这些语言段前设有方框,其中为每个语言段的空白提供了相应的备选答案。本部分要求考生在理解短文和语言段的基础上完成两项任务:一是从语言段前面的方框中所设的备选答案中选出一个最佳答案分别填入各个语言段的空白处,使相应的语言段完整;二是从短文前3~4个语言段选项中选出一个最佳答案分别填入短文的相应空白处。两项任务完成后应该使短文完整。

第二节 大纲样题精讲

由于短文完成这种新题型在同等学力人员申请硕士学位英语水平全国统一考试中从未出现过,而且在全国性质的其他英语统考中也未曾见过,所以很多考生对此题型应该是完全不了解的;而且整个做题过程属于做两次补全填空,做题步骤比较复杂,因此下面我们就第六版《大纲》提供的三套样题进行具体的分析,帮助考生分析出题思路,明确备考要点。

样卷一

Directions:In this part there are three short texts. For each text, you should first fill in the blank in the choices A, B, C (and D) with the best answer provided in the rectangle. Then, complete the text itself by filling in each of the blanks with the completed A, or B, or C (or D). Write your answer on the Answer Sheet.

Text One

```
           learn to    on    or not
```

A. Whether we like it (56) _____

B. have to (57) _____ accept

C. that exists (58) _____ planet Earth

The film shows how wonderfully gentle and caring elephants are, and just how intelligent and "human" they are as well. People (59) _____ that we humans are, in fact, animals. (60) _____, we are still part of the whole. Every species (61) _____ has a role to play. The role of humans has, on the whole, been destructive. Humans need to have more respect for nature.

答案 56. or not   57. learn to   58. on   59. B   60. A   61. C

详解

首先判断三个语言段空白处的句子成分是什么，与其前后的文字是否构成固定的词组或常见的搭配。然后再确定填好后的句子语义是否通顺，逻辑是否合理，整个语言段的语法成分是什么，既可以检查所选的词汇是否合适，又可为后面将句子填回文章中做好准备。在 Whether we like it (56) _____ 中，空白处应该是状语，而且 Whether 有常见的搭配，本题的考点是固定搭配。Whether 经常与 or 或 or not 搭配使用。在 have to (57) _____ accept 中，缺的是不定式后的动词，本题考点是 have to do（不得不做某事），不定式 to 后要跟动词原形。在 that exists (58) _____ planet Earth 中，exist 是不及物动词，后面跟介词词组作状语，本题考点是介词的用法。

三个语段填好后完整的语义和语法功能如下，A 的语法成分是：状语从句；意思是：不论我们喜欢与否。B 的语法成分是：谓语；意思是：不得不学会接受。C 的语法成分是：定语从句；意思是：地球上存在的。

由于我们已经清楚了三个语言段的语法功能和基本语义，因此在我们把它们填回文章中时应该先把握段落的主要内容，这一点主要通过阅读段首句来把握；其次，作语法判断，把握带有题目的几句话中，需要补全的部分应该是什么语法成分；第三，确定填好后的句子本身语义是否通顺，逻辑是否合理，此外，它们与其前后文相连接是否合理通顺。

这篇短文主要是讲述人与自然的关系。59 题前面是名词，后面是 that 引导的从句，根据句法知识可以判断，59 题应该是主句的谓语部分，B 是正确答案；整句话的意思是：我们不得不学会接受人类事实上就是动物。60 题位于句首，逗号与后面分割，其后是句子的主语，从语法上判断，所缺部分应该是状语，因此正确答案应该是 A；整句话的意思是：不论我们喜欢与否，我们都是整体的一部分。61 题之前是名词词组作的主语，之后是谓语动词，按照语法判断，61 题应该是起到修饰名词作用的后置定语，因此正确答案是 C；整句话的意思是：地球上存在的每个物种都起了一定的作用。

Text Two

> watch   information   with

A. associated (62) _____ a 22-minute reduction in their life expectancy
B. lived an average 4.8 years less than those who didn't (63) _____ any television
C. when they collected TV viewing (64) _____

Sitting in front of the television may be relaxing, but spending too much time in front of the tube may take years off your life. That's what Australian researchers found (65) _____ from more than 11,000 people older than 25 years. The study found that people who watched an average six hours of TV a day (66) _____. Also, every hour of TV that participants watched after age 25 was (67) _____. The more TV you watch, the less physically active you are. And the less exercise you get, the more likely you are to develop diseases such as diabetes or heart **disease.**

答案 62. with   63. watch   64. information   65. C   66. B   67. A

详解

62 题之前是动词，之后是名词短语，空白处应该是连接两者的介词，本题考点是动词词组，associate …with（联合，联系）。63 题之前是助动词，之后是名词词组，所缺的应该是谓语动词的原形，而且 watch television（看电视）也是常见搭配。64 题和它前面的 TV viewing 合起来作的是 collected 的宾语，64 题的空白应该是填名词。这三道题难度不大，只要能把握好各语言段空白处的成分，很快就可以把它们补全。

三个语段填好后完整的语义和语法功能如下：A 的语法成分是：过去分词，可以作谓语动词的被动语态，还可以在句子中作后置定语，意思是：与寿命缩短 22 分钟相联系。B 的语法成分是：谓语动词主动式的过去式，意思是：比不看电视的人平均少活 4.8 年。C 的语法成分是：状语从句，意思是：当他们收集电视收看的信息时。

这篇短文的主要内容是探讨看电视时间过长会缩短我们的寿命。65~67 三个题目中，容易判断的是 66 和 67 题，所缺的语法成分很明确。66 题在句子中的作用是作 that 引导的宾语从句中的谓语，该从句的主语是 people，66 题和 people 之间的是修饰 people 的定语从句，因此，本题的正确答案应该是 B，整句话的意思是：研究发现每天平均看 6 个小时电视的人比不看电视的人平均少活 4.8 年。67 题之前是系动词，那么 67 题需要填的要么是表语，要么是被动语态的过去分词，在这里，正确答案应该是 A；整句话的意思是：参与调查的人在 25 岁以后，每天每看 1 个小时的电视，就意味着寿命要缩短 22 分钟。至此，根据排除法可以确定 65 题正确答案是 C。之所以要这么做，是因为对于很多考生而言，直接判断 65 题在句子中作什么成分是比较困难的。整句话的意思是：这就是澳大利亚研究者在收集了 11 000 多个大于 25 岁的人收看电视的信息时发现的事实。填好后，可以发现 collect…from…的搭配。

Text Three

> hard economic times
> carbon accounting
> qualified workers
> large and active student clubs

A. like team projects, (68) _____

B. offering electives in topics like (69) _____

C. (70) _____ have not tempered this demand

D. To meet this demand will require (71) _____

The demand for workers with sustainability-related job skills has been rising sharply these years. (72) _____. So, a growing number of graduate business programs are (73) _____, corporate social responsibility and lean manufacturing techniques to reduce waste and environmental impact.

The top program will also offer a variety of learning experiences, (74) _____, and hands-on field experience as well as classes in policy and environmental management. Demand from students is also driving business schools to include more social and environmental topics in their curriculum, and (75) _____. The economic downturn has caused some deep soul searching among this generation and they want to incorporate their desires to change the world into their careers now.

答案
68. large and active student clubs　　69. carbon accounting
70. hard economic times　　71. qualified workers
72. D　　73. B　　74. A　　75. C

详解

这篇文章主要是介绍对劳动者掌握相关技能的要求不断提高。上面这四个语言段填起来比较有难度，因为所缺的全部是名词成分，方框中给出的选择也全部是名词词组，这种情况下，语法就起不到什么作用了，就只能从语义和搭配方面入手了。此外，四个语言段本身的语义信息是非常有限的，仅靠它们很难判断正确答案到底应该是什么。这就意味着必须从更大的语言环境入手，所以只能回到文章中，把两部分题目结合起来完成。

72题处缺少的是完整的一句话，符合这一要求的有两个选项C和D。要想确定到底应该选哪一个，还要参考72题后面的句子，因此，只能接着往下读，先做73题。73题在句子中充当的是谓语，使用的是现在进行时，缺少的是谓语里的实义动词部分，符合这一要求的只有B。下一步填的是69题，应该从其前后词汇语义的连贯来考虑。现在69题前的词汇提示是electives in topics，即选修课的课程内容，后面的词汇提示是corporate social responsibility and lean manufacturing techniques to reduce waste and environmental impact，意思是企业的社会责任和能够减少浪费和环境影响的节约型生产工艺，这是并列课程内容举例。在方框内的四个词组中，既可以是一门课程名称，又能和后面的课程并列的应该是 carbon accounting（碳计算）。

74 题所在的句子所缺的是并列的名词词组的中间内容，因此不可能是完整的句子，所以正确答案应该是 A。接下来要完成的是 68 题，68 题前的提示信息是 a variety of learning experiences like team projects（各种各样的学习经历，例如团队项目），后面相关的信息是动手操作的实际体验，嵌在这两者中间合适的名词词组应该是 large and active student clubs（大型活跃的学生社团）。

75 题之前是并列连词 and，所以 75 题可以是完整的一句话，即在 C 和 D 中选择。下一步应该是先把 C 和 D 的内容补全。71 题更容易判断，它之前的信息是 To meet this demand will require，语义是：要满足这种需求就需要，此处不可能填 hard economic times（经济不景气），所以正确答案只能是 qualified workers（称职的员工）。这样，72 题的正确答案就是 hard economic times，补全后 C 的语义是：经济不景气没能缓和这种需求。根据 75 题后面的 The economic downturn（经济低迷），我们可以判断 75 题的正确答案应该是 C，这样前后语义才能连贯。72 题的正确答案是 D。这时可以检查一下 72 题前后语义是否一致。它之前的句子意思是：近几年来，对可持续发展的职业技能的需求越来越大；之后的这句话完整的语义是：越来越多的研究生商务培训项目提供了诸如碳计算、企业的社会责任和能够减少浪费和环境影响的节约型生产工艺等选修课程。D 选项放在这两句话中间，刚好合适，起到了承上启下的作用。

样卷二

Directions：*In this part there are three short texts. For each text, you should first fill in the blank in the choices A, B, C (and D) with the best answer provided in the rectangle. Then, complete the text itself by filling in each of the blanks with the completed A, or B, or C (or D). Write your answer on the Answer Sheet.*

Text One

| pitch in | agenda | recycled |

A. a greater demand for the (56) _____ materials

B. seems to be the (57) _____

C. feels moved to (58) _____ and help

We hear it a lot in the news these days: "Recycle newspapers and save a tree. Collect bottles and cans so they can be reused in the manufacturing of new products."

Protecting our delicate environment (59) _____ of politicians, government leaders, and citizens in many parts of the world to show support for mother nature. The concept of green consumerism has gained momentum more and more over the last decade, and the public (60) _____. However, three essential keys needed to power this movement include a more informed public, the development of improved technology and (61) _____.

答案   56. recycled   57. agenda   58. pitch in   59. B   60. C   61. A

> 详解

当看到这个练习中方框内的词汇时，应该可以立刻发现它们的词性各不相同，所以可以利用语法知识将 56~58 题完成。56 题之前是定冠词 the，之后是名词，在这缺的是名词的定语，正确答案是 recycled，考点是过去分词作定语。57 题出现在定冠词 the 之后，应该用名词，正确答案是 agenda。58 题的答案是 pitch in 与 help 并列，考点是不定式后跟动词原形。

三个语段填好后完整的语义和语法功能如下：A 的语法成分是：名词词组，在句子中可以做主语、宾语或表语，意思是：对再循环材料越来越大的需求。B 的语法成分是：谓语动词一般现在时第三人称单数形式，意思是：似乎是议题。C 的语法成分是：谓语动词一般现在时第三人称单数形式，意思是：受到了鼓舞，要努力投入和给予帮助。

这篇文章的主要内容是关于绿色消费问题，特别是对再循环材料的利用问题。59 题所在的句子缺少的是谓语，应该在 B 和 C 中选择；此外，59 题之后跟的是介词而 C 的结尾词是动词 help，其后是不可能跟介词的，因此正确答案应该是 B。完成之后，该句的语义是：保护我们脆弱的环境似乎成为世界各地的政治家、政府官员和普通公民关注的话题。60 题之前是 the public，充当的是 and 引导的并列句中的主语，所以 60 题处还应该填谓语，本题的正确答案应该是 C，句子补全后，整句话的语义是：在过去的十年里，绿色消费的理念获得了越来越多的支持，公众受到了鼓舞，要努力投入和给予帮助。61 题在该句中的语法功能是 and 连接的并列宾语的最后一个，应该用名词词组，所以正确答案是 A，整句话的意思是：推动绿色消费运动发展的三大基本要素是公众知识的增长、技术的发展和对再循环材料越来越大的需求。

Text Two

| beautiful   street art   had trouble with |

A. galleries are collecting the work of (62) _____

B. others think it is a very (63) _____ new form of culture

C. (64) _____ the police and the local government

Street art is a very popular form of art that is spreading quickly all over the world. You can find it on buildings, sidewalks, street signs, and trash cans from Tokyo to Paris, from Moscow to Cape Town. Street art has become a global culture and even art museums and (65) _____.

Street art started out very secretly because it is illegal to paint public and private property without permission. People often have different opinions about street art. Some think it is a crime and (66) _____.

Art experts claim that the movement began in New York in the 1960s. Young adults sprayed words and other images on walls and trains. This colorful, energetic style of writing became known as graffiti（涂鸦）. Graffiti art showed that young people wanted to rebel against society. They didn't want to accept rules and travelled around cities to create paintings that everyone could see. In many cases they (67) _____.

答案

62. street art   63. beautiful   64. had trouble with
65. A   66. B   67. C

详解

这篇的做题方法与上篇大致相同。当看到方框内的词汇时，可以判断它们的词性各不相同，所以利用语法知识将 62~64 题完成。62 题之前是 the work of，其后应该跟的是名词性质的成分，正确答案是 street art（街头艺术）。63 题之前是 a very，其后是 new form 空白处应该是形容词，正确答案是 beautiful。64 题的答案是 had trouble with。

三个语段填好后完整的语义和语法功能如下：A 的语法成分是：完整句，意思是：艺术馆正在收集街头艺术作品。B 的语法成分是：完整句，意思是：其他人认为它是很新、很漂亮的文化形式。C 的语法成分是：谓语动词过去式，意思是：与警察和当地政府有矛盾。

本篇文章主要介绍的是街头艺术的发展和人们对它的态度。65 题应该是 and 引导的并列句，A 和 B 中，语义相符的应该是 A，补全后这个并列句的语义是：甚至于很多博物馆和艺术馆都在收集街头艺术作品。在本段中，还没有谈及不同的人对街头艺术的态度，所以不能选 B。66 题所在的这段才探讨了人们对街头艺术的不同态度。66 题之前的 Some 刚好对应 B 中的 others，整句话表达的是一些人认为它是违法行为，而另一些人认为它是很新、很漂亮的文化形式。本题是在考句子之间的关联。67 题的正确答案是 C，该句与前文的内容刚好相符。之前的句子主要讲的是街头涂鸦艺术表现了年轻人对社会的反叛，他们不愿接受规则的约束。

Text Three

| rise above challenges |
| in spite of the challenges |
| a positive influence |
| with each inspiring page |

A. we can derive strength and positivity（68）_____ that come our way

B. you can have ideas on how he was able to（69）_____

C. to nourish your mind and soul（70）_____

D. evolve into（71）_____ for millions of his admirers

We live in a world that is complex and chaotic, and if we're not careful, we can easily lose inspiration and motivation to carry on with our lives. All is not lost, though, for there are still plenty of sources from which（72）_____. A biography of a successful person is always a great source of inspiration, especially if that person is someone you truly respect. In that narrative,（73）_____, address his critics, and ascertain what tools and skills he needed to make it in his chosen field and（74）_____. A biography can also give you an insider's look at the industry you're hoping to break into, so go ahead and invest in one（75）_____.

答案

68. in spite of the challenges　　69. rise above challenges
70. with each inspiring page　　71. a positive influence
72. A　　73. B　　74. D　　75. C

详解

首先区别方框内的词汇在语法性质上的异同，其中 in spite of the challenges 和 with each inspiring page 是介词词组，rise above challenges 是动词词组，a positive influence 是名词词组。下面应该先从缺名词和动词成分的语言段入手。69 题应该是用动词原形，考点是不定式 be able to 的用法，因此正确答案应该是 rise above challenges。71 题用在介词之后，应该是名词成分，所以答案是 a positive influence。在判断 68 和 70 题时，最为直接简单的办法是根据 68 题后面的定语从句谓语动词的复数形式，这说明它前面的先行词应该是名词的复数形式，所以正确答案应该是 in spite of the challenges。70 题的答案则是剩下的 with each inspiring page。

四个语段填好后完整的语义和语法功能如下：A 的语法成分是：完整句，意思是：尽管会遇到挑战，但我们仍然能获得力量和鼓励。B 的语法成分是：完整句，意思是：你就会知道他是如何战胜挑战的。C 的语法成分是：不定式，意思是：用每一页令人鼓舞的文字来滋润你的心灵。D 的语法成分是：动词原形，可作谓语也可用在不定式后面作其他成分，意思是：发展成为对他的成千上万的崇拜者的巨大影响。

这篇文章主要是讲传记能够给人灵感和动力。72 题就语法判断而言，缺的是完整句，所以应该在 A 和 B 中选择；就搭配和上下文的语义而言，符合的应该是 B。首先，derive…from…（从……中获得/得到……）是常见的固定搭配。其次，就上下文语义而言也是恰当的，因为前一句意思是：我们现在生活的这个世界是复杂且混乱的，如果我们不小心的话，就会丧失激励我们继续生活下去的灵感和动力。72 题补全后的意思是：但是，这一切都没有丧失，因为生活中有很多可以让我们从中获得力量和鼓励的源泉，尽管会遇到挑战。下文具体讲成功人士的传记正是这样的源泉。73 题之前是状语 In that narrative，之后是并列的动词词组，就此可以判断 73 题应该是主语加谓语的结构，正确答案应该是 B，而且 73 题后面出现的 his 和 he 也和 B 相符。74 题用在 and 之后，应该是与 to make it in his chosen field 并列的不定式，由于前面已经有了 to，后面的可以直接用动词原形，因此正确答案应该是 D。73 题和 74 题填完后，这句话完整的语义是：在你所读的传记中，你就会知道他是如何战胜挑战，应对他的批评者，确定他在自己选择的领域中获得成功进而对他的成千上万的崇拜者产生巨大影响所需的手段和能力。75 题的正确答案是 C。最后一句话完整的语义是：由于传记可以给你内行人对你想进入的领域的观点，所以你应该买一本传记，用每一页令人鼓舞的文字滋润你的心灵。

样卷三

Directions: In this part there are three short texts. For each text, you should first fill in the blank in the choices A, B, C (and D) with the best answer provided in the rectangle. Then, complete the text itself by filling in each of the blanks with the completed A, or B, or C (or D).

Write your answer on the Answer Sheet.

Text One

| number   released   to |

A. it offers BCom courses (56) _____ students throughout India

B. was (57) _____ in Dec. 2011 and asked the perspective students to avoid these self-styled universities

C. the second highest (58) _____ of such varsities

Believe it or not, a "university" is being run from a cramped 20 × 20-foot on the second floor of a building at Daryaganji in Old Delhi. The owner of the establishment claims (59) _____.

Commercial University Ltd, as the place is called, is one of six "universities" in the capital that have been branded by the University Grants Commission. The list (60) _____.

Delhi has (61) _____ in the list, after Uttar Pradesh which has eight.

答案 56. to   57. released   58. number   59. A   60. B   61. C

详解

这篇所有的题目都比较简单。当看到方框内的词汇时，可以判断它们的词性各不相同，所以可以利用语法知识将56~58题完成。56题缺的是介词，正确答案是to，本题考点是offer sth. to sb.（给某人提供某物）。57题缺的是被动语态中的过去分词，正确答案是released。58题之前是形容词的最高级，所以此处缺的是名词，正确答案是number。

三个语段填好后完整的语义和语法功能如下：A的语法成分是：完整句，意思是：它给整个印度的学生提供了商学士的课程。B的语法成分是：谓语，意思是：2011年12月公布，并要求未来的学生不要选择这些自封的大学。C的语法成分是：名词词组，意思是：这种大学的数量位居第二。

这篇文章主要介绍了印度旧德里出现的"微型"大学。首先根据语法进行判断，比较好做的是60和61题。60题所在的句子缺的是谓语，正确答案应该是B。61题前面是谓语动词has，所以该处应该是宾语，正确答案是C。59题正确答案是A，出现在动词claims之后，考的是宾语从句的用法。

Text Two

| how   because of   another |

A. has 650 employees in Coventry and (62) _____ 200 at a center in Manchester

B. shows (63) _____ popular our phone banking service is with our customer

C. (64) _____ the growth of its phone banking service

Barclays Bank is setting up a call center in Sunderland (65) _____. This is a welcome decision for the north-east, which companies considered less attractive than regions such as London and Scotland in their list of the best locations for all centers. Opening early next year, the center is expected to employ 2,000 people over next three years.

Barclaycall, the phone banking service, was introduced in 1994 and has more than 600,000 customers. The service (66) _____. Barclaycall is attracting 25,000 new customers every month and the bank expects one million customers over the next two years. One director said: "Opening another call center (67) _____. Barclays will continue to invest to satisfy their needs."

答案 62. another   63. how   64. because of   65. C   66. A   67. B

详解

首先区别方框内的词汇在语法性质上的异同，其中 another 是形容词，how 是疑问副词，because of 是介词词组。62 题用在数词 200 前，作数字的修饰词，答案应该是 another。63 题之后是形容词 popular，能修饰形容词的只能是副词，正确答案应该是 how，这是 how 引导的宾语从句。64 题放在名词词组之前，可以是动词或者介词，正确答案是 because of。

三个语段填好后完整的语义和语法功能如下：A 的语法成分是：谓语加宾语，意思是：在考文垂有 650 名雇员，在曼彻斯特还有另外 200 名。B 的语法成分是：谓语加宾语从句，意思是：显示了我们的电话银行服务是多么受我们的消费者欢迎。C 的语法成分是：介词词组，可以作原因状语，意思是：由于它的电话银行服务的增长。

这篇文章主要内容是讲（英国）巴克莱银行提供的电话银行服务。首先还是先作语法判断，66 题和 67 题所在的句子都缺少谓语，因此都不能是 C，所以 C 只能是 65 题的答案，补全后该句的语义是：由于巴克莱银行的电话银行服务的增长，它在森德兰建立了一个电话服务中心。所剩的两道题中，比较容易确定的是 67 题，主语 Opening another call center（开设另一个电话服务中心）是不可能跟 has 650 employees（有 650 名员工）这样的谓语和宾语的，因此正确答案应该是 B。而且，根据 66 题之前和之后的句子可以判断，这部分是在介绍电话银行服务的规模和现状，所以正确答案是 A。

Text Three

| while | range | Furthermore | into |

A. It will fit (68) _____ the smallest space

B. (69) _____ the machine is performing another one

C. the latest addition to our extensive (70) _____ of fax machines

D. (71) _____, the laser printing gives you high quality pictures.

The answer to all your communication problems? The KR 700 is (72) _____. It is a more advanced version of the KR 600 with an answerphone facility and many other special features. One of these means that you can perform one operation (73) _____. There several dialing techniques allow you send faxes easily, quickly and cheaply. It takes just fifteen seconds to fax an A4 page.

(74) _____. The answerphone has fourteen minutes' recording time, which is a bonus for any business. Although it is such a flexible machine, it is compact. (75) _____ in the office or at home.

答案 68. into   69. while   70. range   71. Furthermore
72. C   73. B   74. D   75. A

详解

首先区别方框内的词汇在语法性质上的异同，其中 into 是介词，while 是连词，range 是名词，furthermore 是副词。68 题所缺的应该是介词，正确答案是 into，考点是常用词组 fit into（适合）。69 题后面是完整句，不缺任何必要的语法成分，由于没有逗号与后面文字分割，所以正确答案应该是连词 while。70 题前面是形容词，因此缺的是名词，正确答案是 range，而且 extensive range（广泛的范围）是常见的词汇搭配。71 题位于句首，逗号与后面文字分割，这是典型的状语成分，正确答案是副词 furthermore。

三个语段填好后完整的语义和语法功能如下：A 的语法成分是：完整句，意思是：它刚好适合最小的空间。B 的语法成分是：状语从句，意思是：机器刚好做了另一个。C 的语法成分是：名词词组，意思是：我们已然很丰富的传真机种类里又添了新款式。D 的语法成分是：完整句，意思是：此外，激光打印机可以给你高质量的图片。

这篇文章主要是介绍一款新型的传真机。72 题用在系动词后，作的是句子的表语，正确答案应该是 C，名词词组作表语。这句话是对 KR 700 作的基本介绍。73 题正确答案是 B。73 之前的 you can perform one operation（你可以进行一个操作）和 B 选项刚好构成对比关系，while 引导让步状语从句，表对比。74 和 75 题都应该用完整句，根据 75 题之前的句子 it is compact（它是小型的），可以判断与 75 题语义相符的应该是 A。74 题正确答案是 D，继续介绍这款传真机的优点，起到了承上启下的作用。

第三节　考试要点归纳

三套样卷共涉及了 9 个短的语篇，语篇的长度从 70 个单词至 160 个单词不等。文章的体裁一致，都是说明文；而文章涉及的题材则十分广泛，包括了环境保护、劳动就业、文学艺术、文化教育、科学技术以及社会生活等方面的内容。文章的语言难度适中，与前些年考题中的中等难度的阅读理解和完形填空基本相同。

就答案选项的设置而言，基本体现了《大纲》的考查目标，那就是对考生能否综合运用词汇、语法、搭配、语段、篇章逻辑等方面的知识和上下文对语篇各层次的信息进行正确判断和完形处理的综合语言能力进行了考查。由答案选项中可以总结出以下考点：词汇的语义和词性、常用的词组和固定搭配、语法知识、篇章的联结手段等。

考生在短文完成的备考过程中应该着重做好以下几点：第一，进行充分的知识储备。根据对样题的分析，本部分的知识储备主要包括三部分：常用的词组和固定搭配、语法知识、篇章的联结手段。第二，掌握有效的做题方法。第三，进行有针对性的训练。本章第五节提供了十套样题；第六节样题详解中除了解释做题涉及的知识点，还介绍了具体做每道题目最直接有效的方法。

第四节 核心知识储备

一、常用词组及固定搭配

A

a few 少许，少数	a good/great deal/many 大量	a little/few（of） 少量，少许
a lot（of）/lots of 非常多	a number of 许多的	a series of 一连串的
above all 最重要，首先	account for 说明，占，解决，得分	adapt… to 使适应，改编
add（up）to 总计	agree on/upon with/to 对……达成协议	after all 毕竟
all at once 突然	all of a sudden 突然	all over 全部结束，到处，浑身
all right 好，良好，顺利，确实	all the same 仍然	all the time 始终
allow for 虑及，体谅	and so on/forth 等等	anything but 决不
apart from 远离，除……之外	appeal to 呼吁，要求，上诉，有吸引力	apply to 将……应用于
as a matter of fact 事实上	as a result 结果	as a rule 通常
as far as 远到，直到，至于	as far as…. be concerned 就……而言	as follows 如下
as for 至于/就……方面说来	as good as 和……一样，实际上 相当于……	as if/though 好像，仿佛……一样
as（so）long as 只要	at the spot 当场	as regards 关于，至于
as soon as 一……就	as to 关于，至于，谈到	as usual 照常
as well as 也，又	aside from 除……以外	ask after 探问

续表

ask for 请求，寻找	at a loss 困惑，亏本地	at a time 每次，在某时
at all costs 不惜任何代价，无论如何	at (all) time 偶尔	at any rate 无论如何，至少
at best 最多	at first 起先	at first sight 乍一看
at hand 在手边，在附近，即将到来	at heart 在内心里	at home 在家，在本地，在国内，熟悉
at intervals 不时，相隔一定距离	at large 详尽，普遍	at last 终于
at least/most 至少/多	at length 最后，详细地	at once 立刻
at one time 同时，曾经	at sb's disposal 受……支配	attend to 照料，照顾
at the cost of 以……为代价	at the mercy of 受……支配	at the moment 此刻
at the same time 同时，但是		

B

back and forth 来来往往地，来回地	back up 支持，倒退，裱	back off 后退
be about to 将要，正打算	believe in 信仰	be made up of 由……组成
benefit from 受益于	bear in mind 记住	because of 因为
before long 不久以后	beyond question 无可争辩	break away 突然离开，脱离，放弃
break down 毁掉，倒塌，垮掉，分解	break in (into) 闯入，打断，开始工作	break off 中断，突然停止，脱落，解除
break out 突发，爆发	break through 突围，突破	break up 打碎，破碎，分裂，结束
bring about 使发生，致使	bring down 打倒，击落，打死，降低	bring forward 提出，提前，显示
bring/come/put into effect 实行，实施，使生效，实现	bring out 使显示，出版，生产，说出	bring up 教育，培养

续表

bring/come/put into operation/practice 使生效，实现	build up 树立，增进，增大，堵塞	burn out 烧坏，烧掉，烧尽
burn up 烧起来，烧掉，发怒	burst into 闯入，开出，突然开始	but for 要不是
by accident/chance 偶然	by all means 尽一切办法，一定	by air 通过航空
by and by 不久以后	by far 到目前为止	by hand 用手
by means of 依靠	by mistake 错误地	by reason of 由于，因为
by the way 在途中，顺便	by way of 经由，作为，为了	by no means 决不

C

call for 要求，提倡	call off 取消，放弃	call on/upon 号召，呼吁，邀请
call up 召唤，使想起，打电话给	calm/cool down 变凉，平静下来	cannot but 不得不，必然，不能不
cannot help 不得不	capable of 有能力做	care about 担心
carry off 获得，成功对付	carry on 继续开展，坚持	carry out 完成，实现，贯彻，执行
cast light on 使……清晰起来	catch up with 赶上，逮捕，处罚	care for 关怀，照顾，愿意
catch sight of 瞥见	check in 登记，报到	check up 核对，检验
cheer up 使振奋，感到振奋	clear away 清除，消失	clear up 整理，消除，放晴
come about 发生，产生，改变方向	come across 偶遇，不期而遇	come around 恢复知觉，回来
come off 离开，举行，实现，成为	come out 出来，长出，出现，真相大白	come over 过来
come to 达到，继承，复苏，共计	come true 实现，达到	come up 走近，上来，发芽，流行
come up with 赶上，提出	compare…to / with 把……比作/与……相比	consult with…about 咨询

续表

contribute to 导致，引起	cope with 与……竞争，应付	count on 依靠，指望
count out 点数，拳击中判输	cover up 掩盖	check out 付账后离开
cross out 删去，注销	cut across 抄近路通过	cut down 削减，删节
cut in 插嘴，插入，把……插进	cut off 切断，断绝，剥夺继承权	cut out 切掉，取代，停止
cut short 打断，缩减		

D

deal in 经营	deal with 安排，处理，涉及，做生意	dedicate…to 献（身），致力，
deprive…of 剥夺，使丧失	devote…to 投入于，献身	die down 变弱，逐渐停止，渐渐消失
die out 灭绝	differ from 不同	distinguish…from 区别，辨别
divide into 分成	do away with 废除	do/try one's best 尽最大的努力
do/go without 没有……也行	draw in 收，引诱，紧缩开支	draw up 草拟，停住，逼近
dress up 盛装，打扮，装饰，伪装	drop by/in 随便访问	drop off 离开，散去，逐渐减少
drop out 不参与，离去，放弃	due to 由于，应归于	

E

each other 彼此，互相	either…or 或者	end up (with) 结束
ever so 非常	ever now and then 偶尔	except for/that 除……以外

F

face to face 面对面地	face up to 勇敢地面对	fall back on 求助于，退到，回头再说
fall behind 落在……的后面，拖欠	fall in love (with) 爱上	fall out 争吵，吵架

续表

fall through 失败，成为泡影	far from 远离，远非	feel at home 感觉自在
feel like 意欲，摸上去如同	figure out 计算出，解决，断定，领会到	fill in / out 填充，填写，填满
focus on 集中	for ever 永远，总是	for example/instance 例如
for good 永久地，一劳永逸地	for the time being 暂时	for the moment 暂时，目前
for the sake of 为了	from time to time 有时	

G

gaze at 盯住	get along with 进展，走开	get at 到达，够到，了解
get away from 逃离	get back（to）…(from) 回来，恢复，找回（失物等）	get by 通过，混过
get down to 开始认真考虑	get in 进入，到达，收获，插入	get in the way 妨碍
get into 进入，陷入，穿上	get on 生活，融洽相处，进展	get out 出去，离开，逃脱，泄露
get over 克服，熬过，恢复，原谅	get rid of 摆脱，除去	get the better of 打败，智胜
get through 到达，做完，通过，打通	get to 到达，接触到，开始	get together 聚集，收集，积累
get up 起床	give away 送掉，分发，放弃，泄露	give in 投降，屈服，让步，交上
give up 放弃（念头、希望等），停止	go after 追逐，追求	go ahead 前进
go around/round 走来走去，供应	go back on/upon/ from 背弃	go for 去找，努力获取，主张，拥护
go in for 参加，追求，从事，赞成	go into 进入，加入，探究，变得	go off 离开，去世，爆炸，被发射
go out 出去，熄灭，过时，罢工	go over 仔细检查，润色，复习	go up 上升，增长
go through with 完成，把……进行到底	go wrong 走错路，(机器等)发生故障	be good at 擅长……
guard against 提防，预防		

H

had better 最好	hand down 传下来，宣布	hand in hand 手拉手地，联合地
hand out 把……拿出来，分发，施舍	hand over 移交	hang about 徘徊，闲荡
hang on 坚持，不挂断	hang up 挂断，拖延，把……挂起来	happen to 发生在……人身上
have an advantage over 胜过，优于	have sth. in mind 记住某事，想做某事	have nothing to do with 与……无关
head for/on 出发，动身，前往	heart and soul 全心全意地	hear about/of 听说，接到消息
hear from 接到……的信	hold back 踌躇，阻止，抑制，隐瞒	hold on（to） 继续，不挂断，停止
hold out 伸出，提供，维持，阻止	hold up 举起，支撑，阻挡，拦截	how about 怎么样
hurry up 赶快，使赶快		

I

if only 只要	in a hurry 匆忙	in a moment 立刻
in a sense 在某种意义上	in a way 在某种程度上，稍稍	in a word 总之，总而言之
in accordance with 与……一致，依照	in addition（to） 另外	in advance 预先
in all 总共	in any case 无论如何	in any event 无论如何
in case 万一	in charge of 负全责，经管，照顾	in common 共有
in consequence of 由于……的缘故	in debt 负债	in detail 详细地
in difficulty 有困难	in effect 有效，事实上	in fact 事实上
in favor of 赞同，有利于	in front of 在……前面	in future 今后，往后
in general 通常，大体上，一般而言	in case of 假设，在……情况下	in honor of 向……表示敬意，为祝贺……

续表

in itself 在本质上，完全地	in (the) light of 按照，根据	in line with 符合
in memory of 纪念，追念	in no case 决不	in no time 立刻
in no way 决不	in order to/that 为了……	in other words 换句话说
in part 适当，在恰当的位置	in particular 特别	in person 亲自，外貌上
in place 部分地	in practice 在实践中，实际上，熟练	in public 当众，公开地，公然地
in question 正被讨论，被怀疑	in regard to 关于	in return 作为报答
in spite of 尽管	in short 简而言之	in step (with) 步调一致
in the course of 在……期间	in the distance 在远处，在很远的那边	in the end 最后，终于
in the event of 如果……发生	in the face of 面对	in the first place 首先
in the future 未来，将来，往后	in the least 丝毫	in the long run 最后，长远看来
in the way 挡道	in time 及时	in turn 依次，轮流
in vain 徒然	inquire into 探究	insist on/upon 坚持，坚决要求
instead of 代替，而不是……	interfere in/with 干涉，干预	in place of 代替
in the short run 从短期看		

K

keep back 落在后面，阻止，隐瞒，留下	keep down 卧下，镇压，控制，缩减	keep in mind 谨记
keep off 让开，不接近	keep on 继续，穿着……不脱	keep one's word 遵守诺言
keep pace (with) 跟上，赶上	keep to 遵循	keep up (with) 跟上，维持，继续
knock down 击倒，拆卸，拍卖出	knock out 遵循	

L

lack of 缺乏，缺少	laugh at 嘲笑，漠视，因……发笑	lay aside 搁置，积蓄
lay down 放下，放弃	lay off 解雇，停止工作，休息，划出	lay out 摆开，展示，布置，安排
lead to 导致，通向	lean on 靠着	learn by heart 记住
leave alone 不管	leave behind 留下，遗留，超过	leave out 省去，遗漏，不考虑
let alone 不管，不打扰	let down 放下，使失望，辜负	let go 放开，释放，发射
let out 放掉，泄露，放大，出租	line up (for) 排队，排列起	light up 点燃
listen to 听	little by little 渐渐	live on 以……为主食，靠……生活
live through 度过，经受过	live up to 不辜负，做到	long for 渴望
look after 照顾，关心	look at 看，考虑，着眼于	look back 回顾，倒退
look down upon 蔑视，瞧不起	look for 寻找，期待	look forward to 期望，期待
look in 看望，顺道访问	look into 窥视，浏览，观察	look on 观看，面向，旁观，看待
look over 从……上面看，察看	look through 看穿，审核，浏览	look up (to) 向上看，尊敬
lose heart 丧失勇气	lose one's temper 发脾气	

M

make clear 解释，使清楚	make for （尤指匆匆地）走向，有利于	make friends 交朋友
make fun of 取笑	make a face 做鬼脸	make out 说明，理解，辨认出
make sense 有意义	make sure 确定，证实	make the best/most of 充分利用

续表

make the difference 有区别，有不同	make up 弥补，虚构，缝制	make up for 弥补
make up one's mind 下决心	make use of 使用，利用	make way 前进，让路
many a/an 很多	may/might as well 最好	mistake for 错认
mix up 混合，混淆	more or less 或多或少	make a fuss 大惊小怪

N

neither…nor 既不……又不	never mind 没关系，不用担心	no doubt 无疑地
no longer / more 不再	no more than 只是	not only…but also 不仅……而且
nothing but 只，仅仅	now and then 偶尔	

O

occur to 想起，想到	of course 当然	off and on 断断续续地
on a large (small) scale 大（小）规模地	on account of 由于	on average 由于
on behalf of 代表……	on board 到船上，在船上	on business 因公
on condition that 如果	on/off duty 上/下班	on earth 在世上，究竟
on foot 走路	on hand 在手头，即将发生，在场	on occasion(s) 有时
on (one's) guard 警戒，值勤	on one's own 独自，自己	on purpose 故意
on sale 待售	on schedule 按时	on second thoughts 进一步考虑后
on the contrary 正相反	on the grounds of (that) 依据，根据	on the one/other hand 一方面……另一方面
on the point of 正要……的时候	on the road 在旅途中	on the side 作为兼职，另外
on the spot 当场，在危险中	on the whole 大体上，基本上	on time 按时，准时

续表

once again 再一次	once and for all 断然地，坚决地	once in a while 偶尔
once more 再一次	once upon a time 从前	one another 偶尔
or else 否则	or so 大约	other than 不同于，除了
over and over（again） 反复，再三	out of breath 上气不接下气	out of control 不受控制
out of date 过时的，废弃的	out of order 次序颠倒，不整齐，状态不好	out of place 不在适当的位置，不合适
out of practice 过时的，废弃的	out of sight 在看不见的地方	out of the question 不可能

P

pass away 去世	pass on 去世，传递	pay back 偿还（借款），报答，报复
pay attention to 注意	pay for 偿还，赔偿	pay off 还清，报复，获得回报
pick out 挑选	pick up 捡起，获得，认识，加速	piece together 拼凑
play a part（in） 扮演一个角色，参与，起作用	point out 指出	prefer…to 更喜欢，宁愿
prior to 在前，居先	pull down 摧毁，推翻	pull in 进站，靠岸
pull off 脱，努力实现，赢得	pull on 穿，戴，继续拉	pull up 拔起，停下，阻止
put across 圆满完成，使被接受	put aside 撇开，储存……备用	put away 放好，储存……备用
put down 放下，拒绝，镇压	put forward 放出，拿出，提出，推举出	put in 放进，提出，提交，插入
put out 放出，生产，消除	put over 把……放在上面，使转向	put to use 使用，利用
put up with 忍受，容忍	pull out 撤退，拔，拉，离去	

Q

queue up 排队等候	quite a few 相当多的	

R

rather than 胜于，而不是	refer to…as 把……当作	reflect on / upon 思考，反省，怀疑
relieve…from 减轻，解除	regardless of 不管，不顾	rely on 依赖，依靠
remind sb. of 提醒，使想起	rest on 被搁在，停留在，信赖	result from 由……引起
ring off/up 挂断电话，停止谈话	run across 偶遇，跑着穿过	run against 撞上，偶遇，违反
run for 竞选，赶快去请	run into 跑进，撞上，偶遇，陷入	run out of 用完
run over 溢出，超过限度，辗过	result in 导致	

S

search for 搜查，搜索	see about 查询，留意于	see after 照顾，负责处理
see into 调查，检查	see off 送行	see through 看穿，识破
see (to it) that 保证	seek after/for 寻找，追求，探索	send off 寄出，派遣，解雇，给……送行
set aside 留出，不顾，取消，驳回	set about 开始，散布，攻击，着手	set apart 使分离，留出时间，金钱等
set off 出发，动身，使爆炸，引起	set down 放下，使着陆，登记，记下	set forth 阐明，宣布，提出，出发
set out 出发，开始，装饰，陈列	set up 设立，竖立，架起，升起	settle down 定居，平静下来，专心于
shake off 抖落，摆脱	show off 炫耀，卖弄，使显眼	show up 揭露，露出，露面
shut down 放下关下，关闭，停车	shut off 关掉，切断	shut up 关闭，监禁，住口，保藏
side by side 并排，并肩	sit/stay up 不睡觉	slow down/up （使）慢下来

续表

so as to 使得，以致，为了	so far 迄今为止	so far as…be concerned 就……而言
so long as 只要	sooner or later 迟早	spring up 跳起来
speak of 谈及，说到	speak out 大胆地说，大声地说	stand by 袖手旁观，准备行动
stand for 代表，代替，象征，支持	stand out 站出来，突出，坚持抵抗	stand up for 支持
step up 走近，逐步增加，提升，提高	stick to 粘住，坚持	substitute for 代替……，替换……
step down 走下，逐步减低，辞职，下台	suffer from 忍受，遭受	sum up 计算……的总数，概括，总结
such as 例如……，像这种的	switch on/off 打开/关上	

T

take advantage of 利用	take after 像，学样	take apart 拆开，粗暴对待，剖析
take away 取走	take care（of） 当心	take charge（of） 看管，负责，主持
take delight in 乐于	take down 拿下，记下，拆卸，病倒	take effect 见效，生效，实施，实行
take for 认为，以为	take for granted 想当然地认为	take in 接受，接待，吸收，欺骗
take into account/consideration 考虑	take off 拿掉，取消，脱衣，起飞	take on 披上，呈现，具有，雇用
take over 把……从一地带到另一地，接管	take part in 参与，参加	take place 发生
take the place of 代替	take turns 轮流，依次	take up 拿起，开始从事，占据
thanks to 由于	that is to say 即，就是，换句话说	the moment（that） 当……的时候
the same as 与……同样的	think highly of 尊重，赞扬	think over 仔细考虑，重新考虑

续表

throw light on/upon 使……显得清晰起来	to the point 中肯，扼要	try on 试穿，试验
try out 试验，考验，提炼	turn down 将声音调小，拒绝	turn in 上缴，出卖，告发
turn on 开启，变得兴奋，开始	turn over 打翻，移交给，折腾，翻阅	turn to 转向，变成，求助于
turn up 发现，出现，突然发生	turn off 关掉，避开，使转变方向	

U

up to 一直到，等于	up to date 最近的，最新的，新式的	use up 用完，耗尽

W

wait on 服侍，招待，拜访	warm up 热身，重新煮热，变暖	wash up 洗餐具
watch out（for） 密切注视，当心，提防	wear off 逐渐减弱，消失，磨损，耗损	wear out 穿破，用坏，消磨，疲劳
what about 怎样	what if 如果发生……该怎样	whether…or 是……还是
wind up 卷起，上紧……发条，结束	wipe out 消灭，垮台	with regard to 关于
with respect to 关于，至于	with the exception of 除……以外	without question 毫无疑问
word for word 逐字地	work at 从事，致力于，钻研	work out 可以解决，设计出，作出
write off 一口气写成，注销，取消	would rather…than 宁愿……而非……	

二、必备语法知识

（一）句子的基本概念

1. 简单句

句子只含有一个主谓结构，而句子各部分都只由单词或短语表示。简单句具有五个基本句型。

（1）主语＋谓语（不及物动词）（＋状语）。例如：

① He gets up at six every morning. 他每天早晨六点起床。

② You must leave now. 你现在必须走。

（2）主语＋系动词＋表语（状语）。例如：

① Their method of counting is different from ours. 他们数数的方式和我们的不同。

② The soup tastes good. 汤的味道不错。

（3）主语＋谓语＋宾语。例如：

① She is writing a letter. 她正写信呢。

② I saw that man again yesterday. 昨天我又看见那个人了。

（4）主语＋谓语＋间接宾语＋直接宾语。例如：

① His grandfather gave him a bicycle on his birthday. 他爷爷给他一辆自行车作为生日礼物。

② The young lady teaches us maths. 那位年轻的女士教我们数学。

（5）主语＋谓语＋宾语＋宾语补足语。例如：

① I thought him a very suitable person for that job. 我认为他是那份工作的合适人选。

② We heard someone knocking at the door. 我们听见有人敲门。

2. 并列句

由两个或者两个以上独立的主谓结构组成，通常由并列连词连接。

例如：

① Hurry up, otherwise we will miss the train. 快点，要不然我们就赶不上火车了。

② It's raining outside, so you needn't go to work today. 外面下雨了，今天你就不必去上班了。

3. 复合句

（1）概念：一个主句加上一个或多个从句构成，从句充当句子的某一成分，如主语、宾语、定语、表语、状语、同位语等。例如：

① Everyone will not forget the day when those young men died.

② What I want to know is how many people will be present.

（2）从句的概念：主句是句子的主体，从句是句子中一个相关的成分，但不能独立成句，虽然它有主语和谓语。引导从句一般是关联词的功能在起作用。在复合句中，从句可作主语、宾语、表语、定语及状语等成分。根据其所作成分及特征，可分为名词从句、定语从句和状语从句。而名词从句又包括主语从句、宾语从句及表语从句，也可包括同位语从句。

（3）常用关联词。

在英语中常用的关联词有如下几种：从属连词、疑问代词、疑问副词、关系代词及关系副词等。

① 从属连词：that（无词义），if（假如，是否），whether（是否），although（虽然），because（因为），since（既然，自从），before（在……前），after（在……后），as soon as（一……就），as long as（只要），when（当），as（表示原因，表示伴随等）。

② 疑问代词：who，which，what，whose，whom。

③ 疑问副词：why，when，where，how。

④ 关系代词：who，which，whom，that，whose。

⑤ 关系副词：when，where，why。

并列句中的一个分句可能含有一个或多个从句,这种句子叫做并列复合句。例如:
We must finish the task before next week, or we'll have to put off the meeting which is to be held next week. 我们必须在下周前完成这项工作,否则我们就不得不推迟下周要举办的会议。

(二)词汇在句子中的基本功能

序 号	基本单位	语法功能
1	名 词	主语
		宾语
2	动 词	谓语
		非谓语动词
3	介宾结构	状语
		定语
4	连 词	前后的关系

(三)词汇之间的关系

序号	系列	连 接	关 系
1	名词系列	名词+名词	N_1 修饰 N_2
		名词+名词+名词	双宾语
			名词作宾补
		名词+名词+名词	省略了连词的定语从句
		名词+介宾结构	名词扩展
		名词+连词+定从	名词扩展
		名词+连词+同位从	名词扩展
		名词+不定式	名词扩展
		名词+分词	名词扩展
		名词+形容词短语	名词扩展
2	动词系列	动词+名词	动宾短语
		动词+副词	
		动词+不定式	
		动词+动名词	
		动词+介宾	

续表

序 号	系 列	连 接	关 系
3	介宾结构	句首	状语
		名词后	定语或状语
		动词后	状语或宾语
4	形容词系列	形容词+名词	定语
		系动词+形容词	系表结构
5	副词系列	副词+形容词+名词	副词修饰形容词
		状语系列	
6	连词	并列关系	如何找并列
7	特殊结构	独立主格	
		N_1，N_2+名扩	

1. 名词

名词在句子中有以下几种重要作用，如作主语、宾语、表语、补足语等。它是句子中最主要的词。

（1）主语。

Father is working on the farm. / **Mary** visited her teacher yesterday. / A beautiful **ship** will sail on this river tomorrow. / Some **goods** have arrived.

句子中的黑体字均表示"谁……"或"什么……"，即动作的执行者。一般都放在句首。

（2）宾语。

① He has a pretty **cat**. / Teacher can help **Rose**. / The sailor crossed the dangerous **river** easily. / Students should do their **homework** alone.

句子中的黑体字均表示动作的承受者，通常放在及物动词的后面。

② She gave **John** a bag. / The grandmother is telling **children** a story. / The little boy brought **mother** an orange. / The wife cooked her **husband** a big **fish**.

句子中的黑体字均为双宾动词的宾语，其中，指人的为间接宾语，如：John，mother 等；指物的为直接宾语，如：bag，fish 等。

（3）主语的补足语。

My sister is a **doctor**. / He has become an **artist**. / The ruins have been a famous **building**.

句子中的黑体字均为主语补足语，表示主语是谁，成为什么。主语和其补足语往往指同一个人或同样东西。句子的动词多为系动词，主补多置其后。

（4）宾语的补足语。

Many people now consider the family a **school**. / They elected him **president**. / All the students in that class knew their monitor a **coward**.

句子中的黑体字均为宾语补足语，对宾语进行补充说明，表示它成为什么、被认为如何等。它和宾语有密切关系，通常紧跟宾语其后。

（5）介词的宾语。

I went to **school** everyday. / They are talking about the traffic **accident**. / On **Friday**, we always have our English lessons.

句子中的黑体字均为介词的宾语，表示与介词有关的东西，和介词一起表达一个完整的意思。这种宾语一般跟在介词后边，它和介词一起构成介词短语。

（6）状语。

He will arrive here **next week**. / We have walked **eight miles**. / He will be back **Monday**.

句子中的黑体字均为状语，这些状语用来修饰动词或形容词，表长度时间等，在多种情况下其前面有修饰语，有时也可以单独作状语。

（7）同位语。

My friend **John** is a pleasant person. / This is Mr. Smith, **headmaster** of No. 3 Middle School. / My roommate bought many things：**books**, **pencils** and **stamps**.

句子中的黑体字均为同位语，表示其前面名词或代词究竟指什么，或对其前面的名词或代词作补充说明，如 John, headmaster 和 books, pencils and stamps 分别对 friend, Mr. Smith, things 作进一步说明。

（8）定语。

My family lives in a **country** house. / They are at the **harvest** festival. / He often visits **night** club. / His uncle met a **silver** smith that day.

句子中的黑体字均为定语，修饰其后面的另一个名词，或与另一个名词构成合成词。

（9）动名词逻辑上的主语。

They thought **Tom**'s going there a mistake. / **Mary**'s getting married will be announced next month.

句子中的黑体字均为动名词逻辑上的主语，表示动名词 going, getting 的执行者。

（10）分词逻辑上的主语。

Peter being ill, his mother has to stay at home. / The **sun** having set, children went home. / She came into the classroom, her **face** covered with sweat.

句子中的黑体字均为分词逻辑上的主语，表示这是谁的情况，如 Peter 生病，太阳落山等。

2. 形容词

（1）形容词作定语。

① 形容词作定语时通常是放在它所修饰的词的前面。如：It is a **historical** fact that in 1920 women in the United States were granted the right to vote. 在1920年美国妇女获得选举权是一个历史事实。The top of a table is a **horizontal** surface. 桌面是水平的。

② 有的形容词作定语既可以前置，也可以后置。但有的形容词作定语却只能前置。

如：Can you imagine journeys to **outer** space? 你能想象去太空旅行是什么样吗? Tom is a **firm** friend of my family. 汤姆是我家的忠实朋友。

③ 有的形容词只能后置, 大致有以下几种情况：

第一, 在一些固定用法中, 如一些正式的命名或头衔中。He was elected Secretary **General**. 他当选为秘书长。His was happiness **incarnate**. 他是幸福的化身。

第二, 当修饰不定代词时。The customer wants to try on something **smaller**. 顾客想试一下再小一点的。I saw something **interesting**. 我看见一些有趣的事情。

第三, 以 a-开头的某些形容词, 往往表示当时或现在的情况。The house **ablaze** is next door to his. 那个着火的房子就在他的隔壁。Who do you think is the most famous star **alive**? 你认为谁是现今最著名的明星? 但 aloof（远离的）和 alert（警觉的）可以放在修饰词前。He is an **alert** young man. 他是一个警觉的年轻人。He went to the **aloof** church to see the carvings. 他到很远的教堂去看雕刻。如果前面带有副词修饰语, 绝大多数以 a-开头的形容词也可以作前置修饰语。如：a fast **asleep** child; a really **alive** student; a very **ashamed** girl; a wide **awake** patient。

第四, 如果是形容词短语, 通常只能作后置定语, 表示具体的状态或特征。She is a girl **good** at singing. 她是一个唱歌非常好的女孩。I know an actress **suitable** for the position. 我认识一个女演员, 她非常适合这个职位。

④ 有的形容词作定语, 前置或后置时, 含义不同。如：a man **able**（to do sth.）（能够做某事）, an **able** man（能干的）; the member **present**（出席的）, the **present** member（现有的）; the problems **involved**（有牵连的）, the **involved** problems（复杂的）; the man **responsible**（**for**）（负责某事的）, the **responsible** man（可靠的）

从上面的例子我们可以看出, 同一形容词作前置定语时通常表示一种内在的状态或特征, 而作后置定语时, 往往是"就事论事"。

（2）形容词作表语, 例：

It is **natural** that they should have different views. 他们之间有不同观点是很自然的。

① 以 a- 开头的形容词单独使用时, 通常只能作表语, 如：I have lain **awake** all night thinking of them. 我想念他们, 一夜都不能入睡。

② 有些形容词表示某人的身体状况时, 总是作表语。作其他成分时含义不同, 词性也可能不同, 如：—How are you? —I'm **fine**, thanks. —你好吗? —我很好, 谢谢。She is a **fine** woman. 她是一个优秀的妇女。Climbing those stairs caused her to feel **faint**. 爬上这些台阶使她感到很虚弱。I haven't the **faintest** idea what you are talking about. 我一点也不能理解你所谈论的东西。类似的如：a **faint** hope（微弱的希望）; a **faint** chance（很小的可能）; a **faint** sound（微弱的声音）。

（3）形容词作主语的补足语。

形容词作主语的补足语可以看作是一个被省略的分句, 其逻辑主语是主句的主语, 所处位置也比较灵活：**Glad** to accept, the boy nodded his agreement. 这个小男孩儿点了点头, 非常高兴地接受了。The chairman, **anxious** for a quick decision, called for a vote. 主席迫切希望迅速作出决定, 要求进行投票表决。

3. 副词

（1）副词的分类。

副词是用于修饰动词、形容词、其他副词的词，表示时间、地点、程度、方式等概念。可分为以下几类：

① 时间副词，是表示确定的时间，用于回答"什么时间？"的副词，如：now 现在，then 那时，today 今天，yesterday 昨天，tomorrow 明天，ago 以前，before 从前，just now 刚才，tonight 今晚，lately 最近，recently 最近。这类副词还可用来表示频率，称为频度副词。如：often 经常，usually 经常，sometimes 有时，seldom 很少，never 从来不，frequently 经常、频繁，hardly 几乎不，ever 曾经，rarely 很少不，continually 持续地。

② 地点副词，表示地点和位置关系。如：here 在这儿，there 在那儿，home 在家，somewhere 在某地，nowhere 任何地方都不，elsewhere 在别处，above 在上面，over 超过，down 在下面，out 在外面，in 在里面。

这类副词中有的可以用作介词（如上面的 above，over，down，out，in）。如：May I come in?（in 作副词）；I live in a hill village.（in 作介词）。

③ 方式副词，是一类最为典型的副词，用于回答"怎么样"，其中绝大部分是由形容词加 -ly 构成的。如：quickly 很快，badly 非常，warmly 温和地，carefully 仔细地，difficultly 困难地，nervously 紧张地，politely 礼貌地。也有少数副词不以 -ly 结尾，如：fast 快，slow 慢，hard 困难，well 好，high 高，straight 笔直，deep 深。

④ 程度副词，如：much 非常，little 少，very 很，too 太，quite 十分，extremely 极端，terribly 非常，almost 几乎，nearly 几乎，utterly 完全。

⑤ 疑问、连接和关系副词。疑问副词用来引导一个特殊疑问句，连接副词用来引导主语、宾语或表语从句，而关系副词是用来引导一个定语从句的，如：**How** are you getting on with your friend? 你与你的朋友处得怎么样？Is this the place **where** the accident happened? 这就是事故发生的地方吗？Can you tell me **why** you didn't come yesterday? 你能告诉我你昨天为什么没来吗？

⑥ 其他性质的副词，这一类副词不修饰谓语动词，而是对句子进行说明或承接上下文。这类副词一般可以用逗号与前文分开。如：**Generally**, it's wrong to do such a thing. 一般来说，做这样的事情是错误的。**Unfortunately**, he hurt his leg when playing basketball. 不幸的是，他打篮球时伤了腿。**Besides**, I must think of the feelings of others. 除此之外，我们必须考虑他人的感情。**Therefore**, we went out to look for the lost boy. 因此，我们出去寻找那个走失的男孩。

（2）副词的作用。

① 副词主要用来作状语，修饰动词、形容词、副词，有时也可以修饰整个句子。如：We should **often** clean our dormitory. 我们应该经常打扫宿舍。He **usually** goes to work by bus. 他通常乘车去上班。I can't run so **fast** as he. 我不能跑得跟他一样快。You speak rather **fast** for us to understand. 你说得太快了，我们听不懂。**Obviously** someone broke into the house and stole the equipment. 很显然，有人破门而入并偷走了设备。

② 有些副词也可以作表语。如：My brother is **out** working. 我哥哥在外面工作。Is there someone **in**? 里面有人吗？We will be **back** in three months. 我们将在三个月之内回

来。Why didn't you be **away** earlier? 你为什么不早一点离开呢？

③ 偶尔副词也可以用作定语或复合宾语。如：The students **here** all study hard. 这儿的学生学习都非常刻苦。I met your father on my way **home**. 我在回家的路上遇到了你爸爸。Let me show you **around**. 我带你转转吧。

④ 副词还可以修饰介词或用作副词的介词。如：We are left **well** behind by others. 我们被其他人远远地甩在了后面。He was beaten **right** out. 他被彻底打败了。

⑤ 有的副词可以修饰某些不定代词或数词。如：**Nearly** everybody knew the news that he had entered Harvard. 几乎所有人都知道他进了哈佛大学。**Almost** all the students passed the test. 几乎所有的学生都考试及格了。

⑥ 副词还有一些其他的用法：It is **quite** a painting. 这是一幅不错的画。It was **rather** a difficulty for such a boy. 对这样一个男孩来说太难了。

（3）副词的位置。

① 副词的位置比较灵活，多数副词都可以放在动词后面，如果是及物动词，一般放在宾语的后面：He works **hard.** 他工作努力。We must set out **quickly**, or we'll be late. 我们必须快点出发，否则我们会迟到的。He didn't do it **intentionally**. 他不是有意这么做的。

有时如果副词在句子中的地位并不重要，只是对动作加以描绘，那么副词也可以放在动词之前，如：She **happily** accepted our invitation. 她很高兴地接受了我们的邀请。

② 频度副词通常放在动词前面，但如句子中有情态动词、助动词或动词 to be，就放在此类动词的后面，如 often，always，occasionally，seldom，hardly 等。例如：I **often** drive to school. 我经常开车去学校。**Sometimes** I drive to school. 有时我开车去学校。

还有一些副词可放在此位置，如 already，yet，once，almost，just，really，suddenly，still，surely，soon ，still，certainly 等。

③ 程度副词一般放在它所修饰的词的前面，如 awfully，definitely，quite，almost，fairly 等。例如：I'm **awfully** sorry for coming late. 非常抱歉我来晚了。I **almost** fell asleep when the lecture was over. 讲座结束时，我快要睡着了。

④ 疑问副词、连接副词、关系副词和一些修饰整个句子的副词，如 actually，fortunately，obviously，of course，first 等通常放在句子（或从句）的开头。如：**How** are the things there? 那里的情况怎么样？**Certainly** our team won the first prize. 不出所料，我们队得了一等奖。

⑤ 在疑问句中，副词一般放在句中或句末。如：Is he **usually** head of those boys? 他是不是那群男孩的头？Has he been **severely** criticized? 他是不是被严厉地批评了？

⑥ 在祈使句中，副词一般放在句末。如：Go quickly, **please**. 快点。

enough 作副词时放在所修饰形容词的后面，作形容词时放在所修饰名词的前后均可。如：It is cool **enough** now. 现在够凉了。We have eaten **enough** food. 我已经吃饱了。

4. 代词

代词是用来代替名词以及起名词作用的短语、分句和句子的词。主要分为人称代词、物主代词、指示代词、不定代词、关系代词、疑问代词等几大类。在这，重点讲与文章逻辑、前后连接有直接作用的代词的指代问题。为了更清楚地说明问题，请先看下面的例子。

①One day the sun and the wind had a quarrel.

②The sun said he was stronger than the wind.

③And the wind said he was stronger than the sun.

在这个例子中，第②句中的 he 指的是 the sun，第③句中的 he 指的却是 the wind。he 是代词，the sun 和 the wind 是它的所指对象。如果不找到 he 的所指对象，那就无法对它作语义上的解释，要对它作语义解释，就得在上下文中寻找和它所指代的词语。

（1）人称代词（如 I，you，he，she，they，him，her，them 等）、所属限定词（如 your，his，her，their 等）和物主代词（如 mine，his，hers，theirs 等）在文章中用来代替前文已经出现或提到过的人或物。其中使用频率较高的是第三人称代词、第三人称形容词性和名词性物主代词。复数第一、二人称代词（we，you［你们］）也可用来指代包括第一、二人称在内的词组。例如：

① My wife and I are leaving for Beijing next Monday. We have booked the tickets already.

在这个例子中，we 指代的是前一句的 My wife and I。

② You and Jane can stay here, I'm sure you'll enjoy yourselves.

在这里，后半句中的 you（你们）指代的是前半句中的 you（你）和 Jane。单数第一、二人称代词（I，you）一般不能起照应作用，因为 I 指的是发话者自己，you（你）则指受话者。I 和 you（你）的照应对象是不言而喻的，因而意义也是清楚的。

用于人称照应的词分为三类（即人称代词、人称形容词性物主代词和名词性物主代词），这些词在句中有不同的句法功能，但这一点并不影响它们所起的衔接作用。例如：

③ Peter married a Chinese girl.

a. He met her in Hong Kong.

b. His parents were not pleased.

c. They visited her parents, but not his.

上面 a、b、c 三个句子中，he，his 和 his 的句法作用各不相同。但它们都能与前面的 Peter 构成照应关系。又如：

④ a. John has got a new car.

b. John's car is expensive.

c. That new car is John's.

在这里，虽然 John，John's（b 句）和 John's（c 句）的句法作用各不相同，但它们都可以与下句的 he 构成照应关系。

⑤ He bought it last month.

（2）指示代词的指代。指示代词主要指 this，that，these，those 这四个代词。就其所指的时间和空间概念来说，this 和 these 近一些；that 和 those 远一些。试比较：

① There seems to have been a great deal of sheer carelessness. *This* is what I can't understand.

② A：There seems to have been a great deal of sheer carelessness.

B：Yes, *that*'s what I can't understand.

例①中第二句用了 this 与上一句照应，因为第一句和第二句都是同一个人说的，"距离"近一些；例②中的 B 用了 that 与 A 的话语照应，因为这一句与 A 句是两个人讲的，"距离"远一些。

③ We went to the opera last night. *That* was our first outing for months.

④ We're going to the opera tonight. *This*'ll be our first outing for months.

从时间角度看，人们趋向于用 that 指过去时间，this 指现在或将来时间。

this，that，these 和 those 既可作为某个句子的中心词，也可作为限定词。一般说来，this 和 these 既可用于前照应用法，又可用于后照应，但 that 和 those 通常只用于前照应。例如：

⑤ I heard Friday's meeting has been cancelled. If *this* is so, I shall protest very strongly. (this 代指 Fridays meeting has been cancelled)

⑥ Mary had a bad cold yesterday. *That* was why she didn't go to the meeting. (that 代指 Mary had a bad cold)

⑦ He told the story like *this*，"Long long ago, there lived in Greece a king whose name was Midas. He was a greedy man and loved gold better than anything else in the world…"(this 代指 Long long ago, there…)

⑧ *These* language options are open to our students：Spanish, French and German.

⑨ I longed to play the piano when I was a child；but in *those* days my parents could not afford an instrument.

例⑤、⑥、⑦中的 this、that 充当中心词，例⑧、⑨中的 these 和 those 充当限定词；例⑧中的 these language options 是指 Spanish, French 和 German；例⑨中的 those days 是指 the days when I was a child。此外，these 和 those 的所指对象还可能是带有复数意义的几个并列结构，如：

⑩ "Where do you come from?" said the Red Queen. "And where are you going? Look up, speak nicely, and don't twiddle your fingers all the time."

Alice attended to all *these* directions, and explained, as well as she could, that she had lost her way.

在这个例子中，these directions 这些"指令"指的是前面 the Red Queen 所说的 look up, speak nicely 和 and don't twiddle your fingers all the time。

有时，由于句子中其他成分的语义限制，指示的范围也受到限制，例如：

⑪ They broke a Chinese vase. *That* was valuable.

⑫ They broke a Chinese vase. *That* was careless.

这两个例子只有一个单词不相同：例⑪的 valuable 和例⑫的 careless，但这已限制了 that 的指代范围，例⑪的 that 所指对象是 a (the) Chinese vase，而⑫中的 that 则指代 their breaking of the vase。

（3）指代句子的用法。

某些代词或名词词组的所指对象不是词或短语，而是分句、句子、句组或语篇。有此功能的词语可分为三类：here, it, this（这一类既可用于前指，又可用于后指）；that,（the）above, the foregoing（这一类只用于前指）；as follows, the following, below, thus（这一类只用于后指）。

① *Here* is the news I heard from the radio: Two Japanese air force pilots were missing after their training jet crashed into the sea off southern Japan yesterday. The T-2 jet plunged into the sea 144 kilometres east of its Nyutabaru base on the island of Kyushu while on a fighter training session.

在这里，here …Two… yesterday 和 The T-2… session 在这两个句子中，属于后照应用法。here 也可用于前照应。下面看 it 用于前照应和后照应的例子：

② Many students never improve oral English. They get no advice and therefore they keep repeating the same mistakes. *It*'s a terrible shame.

在这里，it 照应的是它前面的两个句子，Many …improve… They …mistakes。

③ It should never have happened. She went out and left the baby unattended.

It 在这个例子中指的是它后面的句子，She… unattended；这里的 it 是用于后指。

④ Many years ago their wives quarreled over some trivial matter, now long forgotten. But one word led to another and the quarrel developed into a permanent rupture between them. *That*'s why the two men never visit each other's house.

上述例子中的 that 照应的是分句 the quarrel developed into a permanent rupture。从这个意义上看，例④中的 that 可能相当于 that the quarrel developed into a permanent rupture between them。所以，上面的 That's why…house 表示的意义相当于 That the quarrel developed into a permanent rupture between them is why the two men never visit each other's house。

above 除了可以用来指代单词、短语外，还可以指代分句、句子、句组成语篇。此外，above 与定冠词 the 连用时，它便可充当名词中心词，这时，the above 也可作为分句照应的短语。the foregoing 主要用于正式语体的语篇中，而且较为少见。as follows 和 the following 用于后照应的例子俯拾即是，这里就不举例了。below 除了可用来照应单词、短语外，还可用来照应分句中更大的语言单位，例如：

⑤ *Below* is an example of an informal letter:

Dear Fred,

Thanks a lot for the invitation. I'm afraid Sue is ill so we won't be able to come. See you soon.

All the best,

Tom

These 有时也可用来照应分句或更大的语言单位，例如：

⑥ Carol likes living in a private house better than in a dormitory for a number of reasons. First and foremost, it costs less. Second, …Third, …Finally, she can keep her car at a house. At campus dorms, there are no parking spaces for student cars. For *these* reasons, Carol prefers to live off-campus.

在这个例子中，these reasons 指上述的几个句子（First and foremost, it costs less）。

（4）其他词语的指代。

除上面所谈的照应词语外，英语中还有其他一些词语也可用来表示指代关系。

例如：

① Ann and Mary both took part in the play. Only, *the former* has had any real experience of acting. *The latter* had never even been on the stage before.

在这里，the former 指的是 Ann，the latter 指的则是 Mary。former 和 latter 的照应对象也可以是动词，例如：

② A：Did he walk or swim?

B：*The former* seems more likely.

（*The latter* seems unlikely.）

在这里，the former 指的是 walk，the latter 的指的则是 swim。

此外，the aforesaid 和 aforementioned 也可用来表示前照应，主要出现在正式语体中。

（四）复合句的基本知识

1. 名词从句

名词从句是指在句子中起名词作用的主谓结构。在整个复合句中，它可作主语、宾语、同位语、表语或介词宾语。由于在句子中充当的句子成分不同，名词从句又可分为主语从句、表语从句、宾语从句以及同位语从句。这四种从句有以下共同之处：

① 关联词相同。一般连词用 that，whether，if；疑问副词用 when，where，why，how（用以引导间接疑问句）；疑问代词用 who，what，which 等。

② 前三种从句一般与主句或其他部分之间不能有分隔，即一般不用逗号（同位语从句有时可用逗号与句子的其他部分分开，但因其与前面名词作用相同，故亦划入名词从句中）。

（1）主语从句。

① 主语从句在句子中作主语，位置与陈述句基本结构中的主语相同。例如：

Whoever wants to have this dictionary can get it from me. 不管是谁想要这本字典都可以从我这儿拿到。

That the match will be cancelled is now certain. 比赛将被取消已是确定无疑的了。（that 引导主语从句是不能省略）

When he did it is a mystery. 他什么时候做了这件事是个谜。

② 主语从句一般放在句首，但主语从句过长放在句首时难免使整个复合句有点头重脚轻，因此常把它移到句子末尾，用引导词 it 作形式主语。例如：

It soon became obvious **that instead of being trained to sing she would be trained as a spy**. 她将被训练成一个间谍而不是去唱歌，这是显而易见的。（it 作形式主语，真正的主语是后边的黑体部分。）

It is essential **that people be psychologically able to resist the impact brought about by the transition from planned economy to market economy**. 人们从心理上抵制从计划经济到市场经济转变的影响是必然的。

（2）宾语从句。

宾语从句和主语从句相类似，只是在句中充当宾语。

① 由连词 that、疑问代词或副词（如 how，why，where 等）引出的宾语从句（从

属连词 that 在非正式文件中常省略）。例如：

I know (**that**) **he is friendly and hospitable**. 我知道他是友好热情的人。

Can you tell me **why we have put off our meeting till next week**? 你能告诉我为什么会议推迟到了下周吗？

② 宾语从句不仅可以充当动词宾语，而且还可以充当介词宾语或宾语补足语。例如：

I was surprised **at what she said**. 我对她所说的觉得很吃惊。

The enemy walked up **to where he stood**. 敌人向他站着的地方走去。

③ 连接副词或连接代词（who, which, whom, when, where, how, what, whose）以及 whether, if 引导的宾语从句一般只是跟在某些动词后面，这些动词常见的有：see, say, tell, answer, find out, know, imagine, suggest, wonder, show, discover, discuss, understand 等。例如：

The authorities cannot figure out **why the plane landed at the wrong airport**. 有关部门不清楚飞机降错飞机场的原因。

I cannot describe **what I felt** at that moment. 我不能描述我在那一刻的感受。

宾语从句是指在复杂句中充当宾语的名词性从句，它通常由从属连词 that 以及 wh-疑问词来引导。需要注意的是由 wh-疑问词所引导的宾语分句的语序在现代英语中通常采用正常语序，不能用倒装语序。

④ 在以 think, believe, suppose, expect 等动词引起的宾语从句中，尽管从句中是否定意义，一般却是通过否定主句谓语动词来否定从句。例如：

I **don't believe** that they **could** finish the work within this week.

I **don't expect** that he **will come** here in time next Sunday.

（3）表语从句。

表语从句一般由 that，关系代词 what（表示 the thing which 之意）或其他连接代词或副词引导。例如：

The main reason why he lost his job was **that he drank**.

The question **is whether we can finish our work by tomorrow evening.**

（4）同位语从句。

同位语：一个名词或代词后面有时可跟一个名词或名词性结构，对前者作进一步解释，说明它指的是谁或是什么等，这叫同位语。名词作同位语的情况最多，当然也有较复杂的结构。例如：

We communists seek not official posts, but revolution.

The lay out plan was completed within **three months**, **half the usual time**.

Wei Fang, normally a timid girl, argued heatedly with them about it.

通过以上举例，我们已了解同位语在具体句子中的功能作用。下面将讲述同位语从句出现的两种情况：

① 某些词通常为抽象名词，如：idea, fact, hope, belief, news, rumor, thought, doubt 等，后面常加 that 从句或连接代（副）词引导的从句作同位语，解释说明一个名词，这叫同位语从句。通常连词 **that** 不能省。例如：

Few people know the **fact that he is seriously ill**.

They were surprised at the **news that their American friends had a car accident on highway** 13.

There is no **doubt that he is the best choice for this post**.

② 有些同位语从句不一定紧跟在它说明的名词后面，有可能被其他词隔开，只是这种情况并非常见。例如：

The idea occurred to him **that he might work it out in other ways** when he was tired of this problem.

The story goes **that the king was killed by the beauty he loved**.

The news spread quickly **that the president was assassinated last night**.

2. 定语从句

（1）定语从句的功用及其一般结构。

定语从句在句中作定语，修饰某一名词或代词。从句所修饰的词叫先行词，定语从句必定是要放在先行词之后的。定语从句由关系代词或关系副词引导。其中关系代词为 who，whom，whose，which 和 that。关系副词为 when，why，where 等。例如：

① We went to the park **which / that we often visited**.

② I can never forget the day **when I began my studies in Beijing University**.

③ The ladder **on which I was standing** began to slip.

④ The wine, **which was in the cellar**, was all ruined.

（2）定语从句的种类。

定语从句可分为限制性定语从句和非限制性定语从句。

① 限制性定语从句：从句和主句中的被修饰词关系密切，如去掉从句，主句的意思就不完整或者逻辑上不成立；它的作用是通过对特定对象的限定，起到区别它与其他的作用。引导从句的关系代词如果在从句作宾语，可省略；书写时，主句和从句之间不需逗号分开。例如：

A man **who doesn't try to learn from others** can't hope to achieve much.

② 非限制性定语从句：非限制性定语从句只对所修饰的词起附加说明，或进一步描述、补充的作用，有一定的独立性，去掉之后，其他部分仍然可以成立，从句和主句之间常用逗号分开。所用的关系代词和限制性定语从句基本相同，但不能用关系代词 that 来引导。例如：

The most important form of energy is electrical energy, **which is widely used in our everyday life.**

I have many foreign friends, **some of whom are Russian.**

非限制性定语从句除了修饰主句的名词或代词外，还可以修饰整个句子。这时从句中的谓语动词用单数第三人称，并且用 which 来引导。例如：

The sun heats the earth, **which makes** it possible for plants to grow.

（3）关系代词和关系副词。在句中关系代词与关系副词有两个作用：第一，指代主句中的一个名词或代词（修饰限定它）；第二，在从句中承担一定的语法成分。关系代词在从句中作主语、宾语；关系副词在从句中作状语。

① 作主语时需要注意的是，关系代词在从句中作主语，其谓语动词在人称和数上必须与先行词保持一致。例如：

Do you know **the girl** who **is** talking with the teacher?

Wei Fang is one of the **students** who **have** studied Japanese before. 该句的先行词是 students。

② 作宾语。关系代词 whom，that，which 在从句中作宾语，在非正式文体中可以省略。例如：

This is the girl（whom）you've been looking for.

Such people **as** you describe are rare nowadays.

③ 作定语。关系代词 whose 在从句中用作定语。例如：

Thomas Edison is **a great inventor whose** fame is world-wide.

The Smiths, **whose** house had been destroyed in the explosion, were given rooms in the hotel.

④ 作状语。关系副词 when，where，why 在定语从句中分别作时间状语、地点状语和原因状语。当然先行词相应地也应分别是表示时间、地点、原因的名词。例如：

We may discuss the question **when** we meet again.

That is the place **where** the famous poet was born.

That he is too busy is **the reason why** he can't do it now.

（4）具体情况分析和特殊用法说明。

① 关系代词 who 指人，在从句中作主语（有关从句中主谓一致已在前面提到，请注意）；whom 指人，在从句中作宾语，在限制性定语从句中常常省略；whose 指人，作定语；which 指物，在从句中作主语或宾语，作宾语时常可省略；that 可指物或人，在从句中可作主语或宾语，指物时用法和 which 大致一样。

第一，which 作主语。例如：

Every intellectual revolution which has ever stirred humanity into greatness has been a passionate protest against inert ideas.

A dictionary is **a book which gives** the meaning and usage of words.

第二，which 作宾语。例如：

That is the house **in which** Mr. Wang lives.

This is **the novel which** Mr. Zhang mentioned this morning.

第三，that 的用法。（注意它在限制性定语从句中指物或指人，指物时和 which 差不多，但不能作从句中的介词宾语）

Could you lend me the novel **about which** you were talking the other day?

All **that glitters is** not gold.

② 关系副词 when，where，why 在从句中均作状语。

③ whom，which 在定语从句中充当介宾时，介词的位置一般来讲，如果是含有介词的短语动词，介词仍要在动词之后，而 which，whom 的位置不变，但如果介词短语独立于从句谓语动词之外，这时介词应置于 which，whom 之前。例如：

While still a young boy, Bizet knew how to play the piano well and as he grew older, he wrote operas, the most famous **of which** is Carmen.

　　Your carelessness, **which** we have **put up with** for a long time, is beginning to annoy the director.

　　④ 关系代词 who，that 亦可用作现在或过去分词的宾语（who 指人，that 指物或人），但分词必须放在从句之末，而 who 在非正式文体中可省略。

　　⑤ 关系代词 which 的特殊用法。

　　which 的先行词有时不是一个单词，而是前面整个主句或主句的一部分所表达的概念，which 在这时意同 and this。例如：

　　They have invited me to take part in the party, **which** is very kind of them.

　　Wei Fang helped me with my English, **which was** kind of her.

　　⑥ that 和 which 均指物时，一般没什么区别，但在一些特殊情况下不可混用。

　　如在下列情况下，一般须用 that。

　　第一，先行词是 all，everything，nothing，something，anything，little 等不定代词。例如：

　　All that you have to do is to make a clean copy of the draft.

　　Everything that the teacher said seemed quite reasonable if you had mastered the main meaning of his words.

　　第二，先行词为形容词最高级序数词修饰时（that 也可省）。例如：

　　This is t**he first thing that** I want to say.

　　This is **the best step that** can be taken.

　　还有以"as"引起的定语从句，多和 such 连用。例如：

　　Such people **as described in the novel** are rare nowadays.

　　Hearing the **news that** her husband had a heavy sentence, she left with a **weight** on her mind **such as** she had never had before.

　　She opposed our idea, as could be expected.

3. 状语从句

　　起状语作用的主谓结构就是状语从句，可修饰主句中的动词、形容词和副词等。状语从句由从属连词引导。从属连词除了起连接主句和从句的作用外，它本身的词义体现主从句间的逻辑关系，所以不能省略。

　　状语从句必须紧跟在从属连词之后，其位置比较灵活，可在主句之前或之后，甚至可在主句句中，但要用逗号与主句隔开。如下面同样的状语从句位置就有三种。

　　① The little boys from countryside are very interested in the computer since they have never seen any of them before.

　　② Since they have never seen any of them before, the little boys from countryside are very interested in the computer.

　　③ The little boys from countryside, since they have never seen any of them before, are very interested in the computer.

　　引导状语从句的一般是从属连词，但有时也可能由一个起从属连词作用的词组引导。如：now that，as soon as，in case 等。

根据状语从句的含义，可分为时间、地点、原因、目的、结果、方式、让步和条件等八种状语从句。

① 时间状语从句可以由 when（当……时），whenever（任何时候），as（当，一边……一边），while（在……其之间），before（在……之前）after（在……之后）till until（直到），since，ever since（自从），as soon as（一……就……），now that（一……就），once（一旦），instantly（一……就）等。例如：

When I **saw** her, she **was watching** closely at the photo on the wall.

Whenever there was a football match, Aioli, being a football fan, would surely go and watch.

While he stood there, he heard what they were talking about.

Before he came to China, the American had studied Chinese for several years.

After we finished a day of hard work, the boss planned to have a party to let us take it easy.

Let's wait **until** the rain stops if there is enough time.

Not until he came, **did we begin** the experiment.

I haven't seen her **since** she left for the U. S.

I called him **as soon as** I got the latest information.

Scarcely had the film started **when** they came.

No sooner had the meeting started **than** they came.

Every time he went to Beijing, he was used to visiting the Great Wall.

Storming applause broke forth **the moment** he appeared on the stage.

Once you understand this, you will surely make rapid progress in your study.

② 地点状语从句由 where 或 wherever 引起。例如：

Wherever you are, you should follow the laws and customs there.

I think the teacher will start **where** he stopped last time.

③ 原因状语从句。

第一，表示原因的状语从句可以由 because, as, since, now that, seeing (that) considering that, in that 等引导。例如：

I think Wei Fang should be able to pass the examination **because** she works hard and she is clever too.

Since the weather has been improved, we can go now.

As he was already late, we had to go without him.

The days are long **for** it is now July.

Now that you are all here let's discuss the possibility of building a new library.

Considering that they revealed their unwillingness to help, we needn't say anything more.

Seeing (**that**) they are busy with their homework, we don't need to ask them to play football.

A preposition differs from a conjunction **in that** it introduces a phrase while the latter introduces a clause.

第二，也有人将 be + 形容词 + that 从句（that 可省略）这一结构归入状语从句，本书将其归入了宾语从句，即 that 从句作形容词的宾语从句，但是它有表示原因的作用，that 可省，但单个 that 不能体现逻辑关系，只有从从句的意思上理解出来。例如：

I **am glad that** all of you have arrived at the place on time. 大家按时到这个地方，我感到很高兴。

④ 结果状语从句一般由 so that 或 that 引导，也可见于 so（such）…that 句型中。例如：

The wind was **so** fierce **that** we could not continue the journey and stopped.

The boy left in **such** a hurry **that** he forgot to take his train ticket.

He didn't plan well, **so that** he didn't finish the work as request.

⑤ 目的状语从句。

目的状语从句一般由 that（以便），so that（以便），in order that（以便），lest（以免），for fear that（以免），in case（以防）等引起。例如：

Give me your telephone number **in case** I need your help.

Helen listened carefully **in order that** she might discover exactly what John wanted.

⑥ 方式（或比较）状语从句（主要修饰形容词或副词）。

一般由 as（正如），than（比），as…as（和……一样），not so…as（和……不样），as though, as if（好像）等引导。这种从句由于一些成分往往可以省略，应加注意。

第一，as, as…as, than 引出的方式状语从句。例如：

You may do **as** you please.

The young worker worked **as** fast **as** a skilled worker did.

It is said that football is much **more** exciting **than** basketball is.

第二，其他。例如：

At that time I couldn't move my legs, **as if** they had been filled with lead.

The more we can do for the people, **the happier** we will be.

⑦ 让步状语从句。由 though（虽然），although（虽然），as（尽管），even 让（即使），even though（即使），no matter…（不管），however（无论如何），whatever（不论什么）来引导。例如：

Though my father was angry, he listened to me patiently.

The workers will try to finish the task in time **although** they were short of manpower.

Patient **as** she was, she had no intention to listen to your complaining for three hours.

However much advice you give him, they will fall deaf ears.

While I admit his good points, I can see his shortcomings.

⑧ 条件状语从句。

条件状语从句可由 if（假如），unless（除非，若不），suppose（假设），supposing（假设，仅用于问句），provided（假如），as（so）long as（只要）等引导。例如：

You can borrow this book **as long as** you keep it well.

If you heat the ice, it will be melted.

You can get the job **on condition that** you have Master's degree.

（五）非谓语动词

1. 非谓语动词构成

（1）不定式。

	主动形式	被动形式
一般式	(not) to make	(not) to be made
完成式	(not) to have made	(not) to have been made
进行式	(not) to be making	
完成进行式	(not) to have been making	

（2）动词的 ing 形式（动名词、现在分词）。

	主动形式	被动形式
一般式	building	being built
完成式	having built	having been built

（3）过去分词。

2. 非谓语动词的句法作用一览表

非谓语动词句子成分		不定式	动名词	分词（现在、过去）
主　语		√	√	
宾语	直接宾语	√	√	
	短语动词宾语	√	√	
	宾语补语	√	√	√
	介词宾语		√	
	形容词宾语	√	√	
表　语		√	√	√
定　语		√	√	√
状　语		√		√
同谓语		√	√	
插入语		√		√

3. 非谓语动词实际用法上的差异

（1）动词不定式。

① 在某些表示人物性格、特征等形容词作表语时，不定式后可以加 of 来引导出其

逻辑主语。常见的这类形容词有：absurd（荒唐的），clever（聪明的），bold（大胆的），good（友善的），brave（勇敢的），considerate（考虑周到的），courageous（有勇气的），grateful（感激的），careful（细心的），careless（粗心的），cruel（残忍的），polite（有礼貌的），thoughtful（考虑周到的），wise（明智的），wicked（邪恶的），rude（无礼的）等。

② 动词+带to的不定式结构。

只能跟动词不定式的动词，常见的有：afford（负担得起），agree（同意），aim（目的在于），appear（显得、看起来），arrange（安排），ask（要求），believe（相信），care（愿意），claim（声称），decide（决定），decline（拒绝），demand（要求），desire（渴望），determine（决定），endeavor（努力），expect（期望），fail（未能），hesitate（犹豫），hope（希望），intend（打算），learn（学会），long（渴望），manage（设法），mean（想要），offer（表示愿意做……），pretend（假装），promise（保证），refuse（拒绝），struggle（努力），seek（试图），swear（发誓），undertake（承担），wish（想要）等。

③ 动词+疑问代（副）词+不定式。

这类常见的动词有：advise（建议），decide（决定），discuss（讨论），find out（找出），discover（发现），forget（忘记），inquire（询问），know（知道），learn（学会），regard（认为，把……看作），remember（记得），see（查看），settle（决定），teach（教），tell（告诉、说出），think（考虑），consider（考虑），understand（理解、明白），wonder（想知道），show（说明）等。这些疑问代（副）词有 what, when, where, which, how, whether 等，但不包括 why。

④ 不定式作表语。

一种情况为主语是不定式（表示条件），表语也是不定式（表示结果）。

主语是以表示目的、意图、计划、方法、理由、功能、责任之意的名词如：aim（目标），duty（责任），hope（希望），idea（意见），reason（原因），happiness（幸福），job（工作），plan（计划），problem（问题），purpose（目的），function（功能），thing（事情），wish（希望、愿望）等为中心的名词，或以 what 引导的名词性从句不定式表语对主语起补充说明作用。

⑤ 不定式作定语。

不定式作定语修饰名词或代词，它只能放在所修饰的名词或代词后面。这时被修饰的词与不定式之间既可以是主谓关系，如：the first person to think of the ideas, the pictures to remind me of my childhood；又可以是动宾关系，如：letters to write, problems to solve；也可以仅仅是同位的关系，如：no chance to speak, no right to learn。

在一些表示企图、努力、倾向、目的、愿望、打算、能力、意向等名词之后，常要求接不定式作定语，这类词多是由同源的动词或形容词转化而来，如：ability（能力），failure（失败），refusal（拒绝），reluctance（不情愿），resolution（决定），tendency（倾向），threat（威胁），willingness（愿意），wish（希望），readiness（愿意），promise（诺言），plan（计划），need（需要），hope（希望），intention（打算），determination（决心），decision（决定），claim（声明），attempt（意图），anxiety（焦急），

ambition（雄心），agreement（同意）等。

由 only，last，next，序数词或形容词最高级修饰的名词常用不定式作定语。

⑥ 不定式作状语（注意作状语的动词不定式要与其逻辑主语在意义上和数上一致。）

表示目的，这时不定式中发生的动作的时间常在谓语动词动作之后。作目的状语的不定式前可以加上"in order"或"so as"来加强说话人的口气。为了突出表示目的，可以把不定式短语或"in order to"短语放在句首。但"so as to"短语则不能放在句首。

表示结果，在这种情况下，不定式的逻辑主语也是全句的主语。不定式短语作结果状语时还有其他几种方式。如：so + 形容词或副词 + as to…，such + 名词 + as to…，too… to…，enough to…，such as to…等。表示结果的不定式动作常发生在谓语动词之后。

注意：不定式常用在作表语用的形容词和-ed 分词后面作状语，说明产生这种情绪的原因。这些形容词主要有：angry（生气的），kind（善良的），happy（高兴的），a-shamed（感到害臊的），surprised（惊讶的），grieved（悲痛的），frightened（害怕的），shocked（震惊的），glad（高兴的），delighted（高兴的），disappointed（失望的）等。

表示伴随状况。在表示能力、倾向、愿望等意义的形容词后面也要接不定式，如：able（但其同义词 capable 后面要接 of + ing 分词），anxious（焦急的），eager（急切的），glad（高兴的），inclined（倾向于），liable（有可能的），likely（倾向于，有可能的），ready（愿意的），afraid（害怕的），considerate（考虑周到的），thoughtful（考虑周全的），thoughtless（粗心的），unwilling（不乐意的），lucky（幸运的），fortunate（侥幸的），clever（聪明的），naughty（顽皮的），rude（粗鲁的），cruel（残忍的）等。

⑦ 独立成分，如：To tell the truth，To be fair，to be exact。不定式有时和句子在句法上没有任何关系，作为一个独立成分附在句子的某一位置（有时居中，有时置前，有时居尾）。

⑧ 在复合结构中的不定式。

不定式的复合结构是指有些动词带宾语后再加不定式，作宾语的补足语，在这种结构中宾语是不定式的逻辑主语。

有很多这样的动词可以跟宾语及其补足语不定式，如：advise（劝告），allow（允许），ask（要求），beg（请求），compel（强迫），cause（引得），drive（驱使），encourage（鼓励），expect（期望），enable（使能够），forbid（禁止），force（迫使），hate（讨厌），get（使得），intend（打算要），qualify（使胜任），invite（邀请），like（喜欢），permit（允许），persuade（说服），remind（提醒），say（说），teach（教授），tell（要求，告之），trust（相信），urge（激励），lead（引导），want（想要），warn（警告），tempt（引诱），request（请求），prefer（宁愿），order（命令），oblige（迫使），promise（保证），recommend（劝告、建议）等。

在某些成语动词如：arrange for，call on，care for，count on，count upon，depend upon，long for，prepare for，prevail upon，rely on，vote for，wait for 等后面，也可以跟宾

语加不定式的复合结构。注意：在 listen to 和 look at 后面的复合宾语中，不定式常不带 to。

表示感觉的动词如 see，hear，feel，watch，notice，observe 和 have，let，make 等使役动词后的宾语可接不带 to 的不定式（help 后的不定式可以带 to，也可以不带 to）。

不定式还用在以 be said，be reported，be known，seem，happen，prove，appear 等构成谓语的复合结构中。不定式的逻辑主语便是句子的主语。

⑨ 不带 to 的不定式。

在带有复合宾语的某些动词，如 make，let，watch，see，notice，hear，feel，listen to，have 等后面的不定式的形式，在 why 或 why not 引起的句子中。

介词 except 和 but（作"只有……，只能……"讲时）跟不定式结构，当介词前的句子谓语出现了任何形式的实义动词 do 时，介词后的不定式要省略 to。

(2) 动名词。

① 动名词作主语。

It（**There**）**is no use**（**good**）+ 动词的 **-ing** 形式，表示"无用"，是固定用法，= **It is of no use**（**good**）**to** + 动词原形。

It is not much good **developing** the computer industry if we pay no attention to the work on software.

It（**There**）**is no use**（**good**）+ 动词的 **-ing** 形式，表示"无用"，是固定用法，= **It is of no use**（**good**）**to** + 动词原形。

动名词亦可在"there be no"结构中作主语。

② 动名词作宾语。

一类是动词或短语后面跟作宾语的非限定性动词只能是动名词，如：acknowledge，admit（坦白，承认），advise，advocate，anticipate，appreciate，avoid，can't help，consider，contemplate（深思），delay，deny，dislike，enjoy，escape（躲过，避开），excuse，fancy，finish，give up，imagine，include，keep on，justify，mean（意味着，等于），mind（在乎），miss，postpone，practise，prohibit，put off，quit，recall，resist，resume，risk（冒险于……），suggest，threaten 等。

表示征询意见的"How about + 动名词？"，"What about + 动名词？"

前面省略了介词 in 的动名词的惯用法。如：There be no point(in)（没有必要……），spend time/money/energy(in)（花费……做某事），There be no use(in)，have difficulty (in)，be busy(in)，have a difficult time(in) 等。

三、语篇知识

语篇通常是指在交际功能上相对独立，在逻辑上自成一体，在内容上相对完整的语言片段。语篇虽然可长可短，但是必须符合两个条件：在意义上相互关联，在结构上互相黏着，这两个条件缺一不可。英语考试中的阅读文章虽大多是节选，但是却相对独立地讨论某个话题，有自己独立的论点、论据、较完整的论证过程，因此也是自成一体的语篇。英语正式文体的典型文章架构非常固定，特别是用于阅读考试中的，绝大多数都采用先总述、后分述的结构，而且大多数段落的内部结构也是如此，因此就每篇阅读文章而言，最重要的是文章的第一段，就段落而言，最重要的是段首句。

词汇衔接与逻辑联系语

在第一节中我们已讨论了用于连句成篇的语法语义手段。在这一节中，我们将讨论词汇衔接和逻辑联系语的连接作用以及语法、词汇与逻辑联系语的配合使用问题。

（一）词汇衔接

词汇衔接指通过词的重复、同义、反义、上下义、互补、整体与部分等关系，来使语篇语义连贯。英语词汇衔接关系通常分为两大类：复现关系和同现关系。

1. 词汇的复现关系

复现指的是某一词以原词、同义词、近义词、上义词，下义词、概括词或其他形式重复出现在语篇中，语篇中的句子通过这种复现手段的使用达到了相互衔接。词汇的复现关系可分为四种：① 原词复现；② 同义词、近义词复现；③ 上下义词复现；④ 概括词复现。下面试举例说明：

（1）原词复现。

① The two men at the counter read the menu. From the other end of the counter Nick Adams watched them.

② The history of plastics is longer than you might expect. In fact that the first man-made plastic ever to appear on the market was made over a hundred years ago.

在例子①中，counter 一词反复出现提示了事件发生的地点；在例子②中 plastic 一词反复出现突出了文章的中心内容是与 plastic 有关。这两个例子都利用原词复现手段的使用实现了文章语义的连贯。

（2）同义词、近义词复现。

③ He got a lot of presents from his friends and family. All the gifts were wrapped in colored paper.

④ Grades are the first concern of most Chinese senior high school students. They work hard to get high marks.

⑤ Everything faded into mist. The past was erased, the erasure was forgotten, the lie became truth.

⑥ Some students have the false belief that they will make good grades even if they don't study. But the illusion, some teachers say, is very harmful to the students' future.

在这里，例子③和④是通过使用同义词复现的手法，例子⑤和⑥是通过使用近义词复现的手法，既实现了语义的连贯，又避免了重复。在例③中，gifts 是 presents 的同义词，均指礼物。在例④中，grades 是 marks 的同义词，均指分数。在例⑤中，faded，erased 和 forgotten 是近义词，均表示逝去、忘掉的含义。在例⑥中，the false belief 和 the illusion 是近义词，均表示错误的想法。

（3）上下义词复现。

上义词指的是那些表示意义较概括，从含义分类讲更高一类的词，通常其词义包括了下义词的词义。例如，animal 是 sheep, tiger, wolf, dog 等的上义词，sheep, tiger 等词则是 animal 的下义词。下面是几个通过上下义词而形成的复现关系的例子：

⑦ Yesterday, a pigeon carried the first message from Pinhurst to Silbury. The bird covered the distance in three minutes.

第二句的 bird 是第一句的 pigeon 的上义词，这样就出现了上义词复现关系。

⑧ Steve and Deborah are both doctors. She is a surgeon…

在这里，surgeon 是 doctor 的下义词，因而就构成了下义词复现关系。又如：

⑨ You will need to take some tools with you. You can get a hammer, a saw and a screwdriver from most big department stores.

在这个例子中，hammer, saw 和 screwdriver 都可看作是 tool 的下义词。

（4）概括词复现。

概括词指的是那些表示一般意义的词。例如，people, man, woman, thing, place, do, make 等都是概括词。概括词与其所指的词构成的衔接是通过概括词复现关系。例如：

⑩ A：What shall I do with all this crockery?
B：Leave the stuff there; someone will come to put it away.

⑪ Can you tell me where to stay in Geneva? I've never been to the place.

在这两个例子中，后一句中的概括词（stuff, place）分别和前面的 crockery 和 Geneva 构成相互衔接关系。stuff 的下义词为 crockery，而 place 的下义词则为 Geneva（日内瓦）这个地方。

在有些句组中，某一词的反复出现不但能起到衔接句子的作用，而且能使句组获得一定的文体效果。下面这段关于 fog 就是一个好例子：

⑫ Fog everywhere. Fog up the river, where it flows among green aits and meadows; fog down the river, where it rolls defiled among the tiers of shipping, and the waterside pollutions of a great (and dirty) city. Fog on the Essex marshes, fog on the Kentish heights. Fog creeping into the cabooses of collier-brigs; fog lying out on the yards and hovering in the rigging of great ships; fog drooping on the gunwales of barges and small boats. Fog in the eyes and throats of ancient Greenwich pensioners, wheezing by the firesides of their wards; fog in the stem and bowl of the afternoon pipe of the wrathful skipper, down in his close cabin; fog cruelly pinching the toes and fingers of his shivering little prentice boy on deck. Chance people on the bridges peeing over the parapets into a nether sky of fog, with fog all round them…

这是选自英国著名小说家狄更斯的作品"Bleak House"的一段文字。在这一段里，fog 一词共重复出现 13 次，不仅使得文义连贯、一气呵成，而且极为生动地描述了浓雾弥漫的情景，取得了极好的文体效果。

2. 词汇的同现关系

同现关系指的是词汇共同出现的倾向性（此定义不能成立→同现关系指的是语篇中语法手段或词汇手段共同出现在同一或临近句子中的现象）。在语篇中，围绕着一定的话题，一定的词语就往往会同时出现，而其他一些词语就不大可能会出现或根本不会出现。例如，在一篇探讨汉语词的分类的文章中，可以预料会出现"名词""动词""形容词""副词"等词语，但不大可能会出现"叫号电话""叫人电话""传呼电话"

这种词语；但如果文章谈的是有关长途电话的种类，那就会出现"叫号电话"这类词语，而不会出现"名词"这类词语。这种词的同现关系与语篇范围关系密切。词汇的同现关系包括反义关系、互补关系等。例如：

⑬ Jane is a good teacher, but she is a bad wife.

⑭ In money I'm penniless, but in peace of mind I'm very rich.

在这个例子中，good 和 bad 是一对反义词，因而构成了反义同现。

互补词的互补性指的是非彼即此或非此即彼，所以互补词不同于反义词。反义词的两极之间可以有表示不同程度性质的词语，体现对立的层次性，如 hot-cold 这对反义词之间可加进 warm, tepid, lukewarm, cool 等词。互补词在意义上是相互排斥的，如 single-married, dead-alive, husband-wife, male-female, man-woman 等，互补词之间不能加入其他词。下面是一个通过互补词而形成互补同现的例子：

⑮ Discrimination is undoubtedly practised against women in the field of scientific research. We don't find men complaining that they are not being interviewed for positions that they are clearly qualified to fill.

在这个例子中，两句之间的衔接主要是依靠互补词 men 和 women 的对照表现出来的。

⑯ John Smith says he feels very sorry for millionaires, who, instead of being masters of their wealth, are slaves of their millions.

在这个例子中，masters 和 slaves 是一对互补词，形成了互补关系。

语言中有些项目的排列是有一定规律的，比如星期一要排在星期二前面，一月份要排在二、三月……十二月前面。这些位于同一序列的词语也可起到衔接句子的作用。例如：

⑰ But spring and summer did mot come. Autumn gave golden fruit to every garden, but she did not give any to the Giants. "He is too selfish," she said. So it was always winter there, and the north wind, the frost and the snow danced among the trees.

在这个例子中，spring, summer, autumn, winter 属于同一个序列，因而也是同现关系，也起了衔接作用。

在语言实践中，人们发现有些在意义上相互联系的词语常常同时出现在同一语篇中，这些词语属于同一个词汇群类，形成了词汇链，因而，当人们遇到其中一个（些）词语时，便会联想到同一词汇群类中的另一些词。如，听（读）到"邮局"时，人们通常会联想到"寄信""汇款""打电报""挂号信""邮票""包裹"等词语。所以，当一个词汇套的词语出现在一个语篇中时，这些词语就能衔接句子，起着连句成篇的作用。例如：

⑱ A great number of high school graduates continue their education in one of the many colleges or universities in the country. After four years, they receive a bachelor's degree. Some continue studying for a master's degree and perhaps a doctor's degree.

这里的话题是高中毕业后的教育，所以出现了这么一个词汇群类：

high school, graduates, education, colleges, universities, a bachelor's degree, studying, a master's degree, a doctor's degree.

⑲ When you go to the doctor, you like to come away with a prescription. It makes you feel better to know you will get some medicine. But the doctor knows that medicine is not always needed. Some times all a sick person needs is some reassurance that all will be well. In such cases the doctor may prescribe a placebo.

在这段文字里集中出现了一批和医院、疾病相关的词汇（doctor，prescription，medicine，sick，prescribe，placebo），给读者提供了一个看病的背景，突出了这段文字的中心话题。

（二）逻辑联系语

逻辑联系语指的是表示各种逻辑意义的句子连接手段。逻辑联系语的功能是表示两个或更多的句子之间的某种逻辑关系，并指出句子是在什么意义上相互联系起来的。逻辑联系语还可用来表明语篇中的各个组成部分之间语义上的联系。

从形式上看，逻辑联系语可以由以下三类语言手段充当：① 词语（包括连词和副词），如 and，but，for，then，yet，so，therefore，anyway 等；② 短语，如 in addition，as a result，on the contrary，in other words 等；③ 分词独立主格结构或插入语，如 considering all that，to conclude，all things considered，that is to say，what is more，what is more important 等。

从意义上看，逻辑联系语可以表示很多种不同语义关系，在讨论逻辑联系语时语言学家们通常把它们表示的关系分为四大类：增补；转折；原因；时间。在这四大类下面又分出若干小类。例如在"增补"这一大类下，又分出了"增补"（and，and also，furthermore，besides，in addition），"否定"（nor，and...not），"选择"（or，or else，alternatively），"说明"（that is，I mean，in other words），"示例"（for instance，thus），"相似"（likewise，similarly，in the same way），"反意"（on the other hand，by contrast），"事后补充"（incidentally，by the way）等几个小类。

逻辑联系语表示的语义关系是多样的。下面我们举例说明几类比较常见的逻辑联系语所表示的语义关系。

1. 表示列举

列举这一语义关系通常由连接性状语表示，它们对所叙述的事情逐一列举。例如：

⑳ I want to give just two pieces of advice. One, there is no reason why he should know about your decision. Two, it would be better if you acted before he finds out.

在这里，one 和 two 表示了列举这一语义关系。能用于表示列举的词语很多，常见的有 first，second，...；first (ly)，secondly，...；one，two，...；for one thing... (and) for another (thing); in the first place，first of all to begin with，to start with，for a start; next，then，last，finally，in conclusion，last of all，to conclude 等。

2. 表示增补

增补这一语义关系可以由 and，and also，also，too，and...too，furthermore，in addition，besides，moreover，what is more 等来表示，例如：

㉑ I'm not looking for a job. Furthermore, I am not going to look for a job.

㉒ The public can see the paintings next week. What is more, they can buy them for as little as ten dollars upwards.

㉓ The house faces north, so it never gets the sun. Also, it is rather damp.

3. 表示转折或对比

转折或对比可用 still, but, yet, nevertheless, thorough, instead, anyhow, on the contrary, all the same, in fact, at the same time, on the other hand, as a matter of fact, by contrast, while, whereas 等词语来表示。例如：

㉔ There will still be difficulties. But they can be overcome.

㉕ You weren't boring me. On the contrary, you're interesting me frightfully.

㉖ He did not show anyone the papers. Instead, as soon as he got a chance, he burnt them.

4. 表示解释

解释指的是逻辑联系语引导的分句，对前面已讲到的内容加以澄清、举例说明或进行精确的描述。能用于表示这一语义关系的有：that is, that is to say, namely, for example, for instance, such as, in other words, to put it another way 等。例如：

㉗ He is a scholar who is devoted to his research to a reprehensible extent. That is to say, he neglects his family and does not fulfill his responsibilities as a citizen.

㉘ It is important that young children should see things, and not merely read about them. For example, it is valuable experience to take them on a trip to a farm.

5. 表示等同

等同指的是逻辑联系语所引导的上文和下文所表示的意义相同或相似，或在重要性上差不多。因而，有时也可把这种语义关系称为同位。用于表示等同的逻辑联系语很多，常见的有：equally, likewise, namely, similarly, in the same way, in other words, that is, I mean, that is to say 等。例如：

㉙ You must pack plenty of food for the journey. Likewise, you'll need warm clothes, so pack them too.

㉚ He is being a fool. In other words, he is behaving foolishly.

表示等同这一语义的逻辑联系语有些（如 equally, likewise, similarly）可归入"比较照应"。

6. 表示原因结果

（1）表示原因。

表示原因（reason）的逻辑联系语不多，常见的有连词 for, since, because, as; 介词词组 due to, because of, on account of, owing to, thanks to 等。例如：

㉛ Mrs. Cox's favorite subject is literature, and her most exciting classes are those on the literature of Black Americans. For Mrs. Cox, like most of the students in her school, is Black.

㉜ When I saw her in the river I was frightened. For at that point the currents were dangerous.

（2）表示结果。

结果这一语义关系可以用 accordingly, consequently, hence, now, so, therefore, thus, as a consequence, in consequence, for that reason, as a result, of course 等词语表示。例如：

㉝ He was too sick to stay. Accordingly, we sent him home.

㉞ The documents were not ready. Consequently, we could not sign them.

㉟ They refused to pay the higher rent when an increase was announced. As a result, they were evicted from their apartment.

7. 表示推论

推论这一语义关系可以由下列词语表示：else, otherwise, then in other words, in that case 等。例如：

㊱ A: Please give my regards to John.

B: Then you're not coming with me?

㊲ You must get some more petrol. *Otherwise*, we will not have enough to get us to the next town.

㊳ You say your father might object? *In that case* I will not press the matter.

8. 表示总结

表示总结的联系语主要是用在句、段或语篇的最后部分，对前面的内容作出概括或总结。能表示这一意义的有：altogether, overall, then, therefore, thus, (all) in all, in conclusion, in sum, in short, in brief, on the whole, to conclude, to sum up, to summarize 等。例如：

㊴ He lost his watch, his car broke down, and he got a letter of complaint from a customer : *all in all*, he had a bad day.

㊵ The film has a very unusual plot, with plenty of action. Both the acting and photography are excellent. *To sum up*, this is a film you should not miss.

9. 表示替换转题

（1）表示替换。

替换这一语义关系可用 again, alternatively, or, rather, better (still), worse, on the other hand, or at least, or rather 等词语来表示。替换的目的可能是纠正前面的说法，也可能是用肯定的叙述来替代否定的叙述，或用真实的结果来替代原先的预料。例如：

㊶ You can walk home, if you wish. *Or rather*, I can give you a lift in my car.

㊷ If things get any worse, we might have to arrange a public meeting to discuss the matter. *Better still*, we could even organize a demonstration.

（2）表示转题。

转题指引进新的一层意思或引进新的话题。能用来表示转题的逻辑联系语有：now, incidentally, by the way, to change the subject 等。例如：

㊸ We have settled that at last. *Now*, what was the other thing we wanted to discuss?

㊹ I must go now. *Incidentally* if you want that book I'll bring it next time.

第五节 模拟试题精练

Model Test 1

Directions: *In this part there are three short texts. For each text, you should first fill in the blank in the choices A, B, C (and D) with the best answer provided in the rectangle. Then, complete the text itself by filling in each of the blanks with the completed A, or B, or C (or D). Write your answer on the Answer Sheet.*

Text One

evidently	at times of	like

A. look (1) _____ a fool

B. (2) _____ to a significant degree

C. the way it would (3) _____ physical danger

Why is stage fright so universal when it does not pose a physical threat?

Our self-confidence and self-esteem are threatened, (4) _____. No normal person wants to (5) _____. Consequently, a speaking situation does involve threat, not physical but psychological. The brain instructs the body to react exactly (6) _____. In essence, the brain tells the body, "get ready to fight off the danger or to run away from it."

Text Two

far	selling	largely

A. it is (7) _____ too soon

B. so reports of sales are (8) _____ inaccurate

C. (9) _____ everything from computer gear to income tax preparation services

The Internet offers, among other things, "an electronic mall" with scores of retailers, (10) _____. As with anything on the Internet, it is highly decentralized, with no one authority keeping track of transactions, (11) _____. But many of the reports are discouraging.

But (12) _____ to sound the death knell (丧钟声) for electronic retailing. One reason, say analysts and service providers, is that consumers are only beginning to understand the possibilities of the new technology.

Text Three

| as fast as |
| outscoring them |
| less and less |
| concentrate on |

A. he stumbles (13) _____

B. who were reading almost three times (14) _____ the other children

C. still (15) _____ on accuracy, comprehension and vocabulary

D. so he can (16) _____ the meaning of the text

A child learns to read by sounding out the letters and decoding the words. With practice, (17) _____, reading by the phrase. With automaticity, he doesn't have to think about decoding the words, (18) _____.

It can begin as early as first grade. In a recent study of children in Illinois schools, Alan Rossman of Northwestern University found automatic readers in the first grade (19) _____ and scoring twice as high on comprehension tests. At fifth grade, the automatic readers were reading twice as fast as the others, and (20) _____.

Model Test 2

Directions: *In this part there are three short texts. For each text, you should first fill in the blank in the choices A, B, C (and D) with the best answer provided in the rectangle. Then, complete the text itself by filling in each of the blanks with the completed A, or B, or C (or D). Write your answer on the Answer Sheet.*

Text One

| to   scope   with |

A. a large population gives more (1) _____ for

B. (2) _____ feed a large population

C. could be obtained (3) _____ a smaller population

The advantages and disadvantages of a large population have long been a subject of discussion among economists. It has been argued that the supply of good land is limited. (4) _____, inferior land must be cultivated and the good land worked intensively. Thus, each person produces less and this means a lower average income than (5) _____. Other economists have argued that (6) _____ specialization and the development of facilities such as ports, roads and railways, which are not likely to be built unless there is a big demand to justify them.

Text Two

| likely   conclusive   susceptible |

A. is not (7) _____ about

B. also were (8) _____ to alcoholism

C. was more (9) _____ to take up

This evidence in itself (10) _____ anything. After all, it may be the constant exposure and easy access to alcohol that cause the children of alcoholics to become alcoholics themselves. But there is more evidence. The study found that children born to alcoholic parents but raised by non-drinking foster parents (11) _____. This group of offspring (12) _____ drinking than youngsters who were born of and raised by non-drinking parents.

Text Three

| What we need |
| all the credit |
| in the home |
| of the child |

A. to the healthy development (13) _____

B. (14) _____, rather, is

C. to analyze men's place (15) _____

D. should not receive (16) _____ —nor all the blame

It is time to reassess the role of the man in the American family. We are getting a little tired of "Momism"—but we don't want to exchange it for a "neo-Popism." (17) _____ the recognition that bringing up children involves a partnership of equals. There are signs that psychiatrists, psychologists, social workers, and specialists on the family are becoming more aware of the part men play and that they have decided that women (18) _____. We have almost given up saying that a woman's place is in the home. We are beginning, however, (19) _____ and to insist that he does have a place in it. Nor is that place irrelevant (20) _____.

Model Test 3

Directions: *In this part there are three short texts. For each text, you should first fill in the blank in the choices A, B, C (and D) with the best answer provided in the rectangle. Then, complete the text itself by filling in each of the blanks with the completed A, or B, or C (or D). Write your answer on the Answer Sheet.*

Text One

| those   much   rather |

A. most of us perform it (1) _____ effortlessly

B. (2) _____ of social interaction consists of

C. This means that we fit our actions to (3) _____

The statuses we assume often vary with the people we encounter, and change throughout life. Most of us can, at very high speed, assume the statuses that various situations require. (4) _____ identifying and selecting among appropriate statuses and allowing other people to assume their statuses in relation to us. (5) _____ of other people based on a constant mental process of appraisal and interpretation. Although some of us find the task more difficult than others, (6) _____.

Text Two

| over   only   completely |

A. wanting (7) _____ to sleep

B. cleaned out all her closets (8) _____

C. becoming so (9) _____ energized

Some people seem to lose all their energy and drive, (10) _____. Others react in exactly the opposite way, (11) _____ that they can't find enough activity to burn off their excess energy. For instance, one woman said she (12) _____ and was ready to go next door to start on her neighbor's. Both these extremes, however, eventually level off. The symptoms may be intense for two or three days, but within 10 to 14 days after quitting, most subside. The truth is that after people quit smoking, they have more energy, they generally will need less sleep, and feel better about themselves.

Text Three

| in family shelters |
| on a regular basis |
| cast off |
| less than |

A. who have been (13) _____ their homes

B. a third of whom do not attend school (14) _____

C. that (15) _____ half of them attend school regularly

D. because they do not stay (16) _____

Estimates of the number of homeless Americans range from 350,000 to three million. Likewise, estimates of the number of homeless school children vary radically. A U.S. Department of Education report, based on state estimates, states that there are 220,000 homeless school-age children, about (17) _____. But the National Coalition for the Homeless estimates that there are at least two times as many homeless children, and (18) _____.

One part of the homeless population that is particularly difficult to count consists of the "throwaway" youths (19) _____. The Elementary School Center in New York City estimates that there are 1.5 million of them, many of whom are not counted as children (20) _____ and tend to live by themselves on the streets.

Model Test 4

Directions: *In this part there are three short texts. For each text, you should first fill in the blank in the choices A, B, C (and D) with the best answer provided in the rectangle. Then, complete the text itself by filling in each of the blanks with the completed A, or B, or C (or D). Write your answer on the Answer Sheet.*

Text One

| checks   reap   walk |

A. can (1) _____ big reward

B. no one (2) _____ up on

C. may (3) _____ away not only unpunished

More and more, the operations of our businesses, governments, and financial institutions are controlled by information that exists only inside computer memories. Anyone clever enough to modify this information for his own purposes (4) _____. Even worse, a number of people who have done this and been caught at it have managed to get away without punishment. It's easy for computer crimes to go undetected if (5) _____ what the computer is doing. But even if the crime is detected, the criminal (6) _____ but with a glowing recommendation from his former employers.

Text Two

| astonishingly   available   embarrassed |

A. readily (7) _____ by pushing a button

B. that people are easily (8) _____

C. human beings are (9) _____ lazy

There are two reasons for this sad decline: One, (10) _____. Put a lift in a building, and people would rather take it than climb even two flights of steps. Similarly, invent a machine that sings, and people would rather let the machine sing than sing themselves. The other reason is (11) _____. When there is a famous, talented musician (12) _____, which amateur violinist or pianist would want to try to entertain family or family or friends by himself?

Text Three

| personal independence |
| the process |
| the parents' culture |
| prevailing values |

A. these (13) _____ in their children

B. the customs and values of (14) _____

C. In (15) _____ of their socialization

D. a first step toward (16) _____

Acculturation (文化传承), which begins at birth, is the process of teaching new generations of children (17) _____. How people treat newborns, for example, can be indicative of cultural values. In the United States it is not uncommon for parents to put a newborn in a separate room that belongs only to the child. This helps to preserve parents' privacy and allows the child to get used to having his or her own room, which is seen as (18) _____. Americans traditionally have held independence and a closely related value, individualism, in high esteem. Parents try to instill (19) _____. American English expresses these value preferences: children should "cut the (umbilical) cord" and are encouraged not to be "tied to their mothers' apron (围裙) strings." (20) _____ children learn to "look out for number one" and to "stand on their own two feet."

Model Test 5

Directions: *In this part there are three short texts. For each text, you should first fill in the blank in the choices A, B, C (and D) with the best answer provided in the rectangle. Then, complete the text itself by filling in each of the blanks with the completed A, or B, or C (or D). Write your answer on the Answer Sheet.*

Text One

| apart   presented   range |

A. the (1) _____ of choice among them is limited

B. (2) _____ from minor adjustments

C. the clothing (3) _____ by our society

A status has been compared to ready-made clothes. Within certain limits the buyer can choose style and fabric. But an American is not free to choose the costume of a Chinese peasant or that of a Hindu prince. We must choose from among (4) _____. Furthermore, our choice is limited to a size that will fit, as well as by our pocketbook (钱包). Having made a choice within these limits we can have certain alterations made, but (5) _____, we tend to be limited to what the stores have on their racks. Statuses too come ready made, and (6) _____.

Text Two

| painful   distinguishing   inevitably |

A. but they are not its most (7) _____ features

B. the pain (8) _____ brought by such things

C. for commitment is in fact quite (9) _____

As a result, many people avoid the very attempts that are the source of true happiness. They fear (10) _____ as marriage, raising children, professional achievement, religious commitment, self-improvement.

Ask a bachelor why he resists marriage even though he finds dating to be less and less satisfying. If he is honest he will tell you that he is afraid of making a commitment, (11) _____. The single life is filled with fun, adventure, excitement. Marriage has such moments, (12) _____.

Text Three

| because | whatever | to | in |

A. (13) _____ it results in a declining market for manufactured goods

B. which is stable or (14) _____ decline

C. (15) _____ the consequences may be

D. that official attitudes (16) _____ population growth vary from country to country

One of the difficulties in carrying out a worldwide birth control program lies in the fact (17) _____ depending on the level of industrial development and the availability of food and raw materials. In a developing country where a vastly expanded population is pressing hard upon the limits of food, space and natural resources, it will be the first concern of government to place a limit on the birthrate, (18) _____ . In a highly industrialized society the problem may be more complex. A decreasing birthrate may lead to unemployment (19) _____ . When the pressure of population on housing declines, prices also decline and the building industry is weakened. Faced with considerations such as these, the government of a developed country may well prefer to see a slowly increasing population, rather than one (20) _____ .

Model Test 6

Directions: *In this part there are three short texts. For each text, you should first fill in the blank in the choices A, B, C (and D) with the best answer provided in the rectangle. Then, complete the text itself by filling in each of the blanks with the completed A, or B, or C (or D). Write your answer on the Answer Sheet.*

Text One

| greatly | too | very |

A. the number of births (1) _____ exceeds

B. has a (2) _____ marked effect on the available workforce

C. of those (3) _____ old to work

Although the size of the workforce depends a great deal on the size of the total population, there are several other influences which also affect it. The age distribution of the total population (4) _____ . If the population has a high proportion of very young people or (5) _____ , then the available workforce would be lower than if there were an evenly spread age distribution. If the population grows rapidly from natural increase, i.e. (6) _____ the number of deaths, then as the total population increases, the proportion in the workforce declines.

Text Two

| meet | define | resolve |

A. helping us (7) _____ and cope with our problems

B. to (8) _____ and understand our problems

C. helps us to (9) _____ our social needs

Social support cushions stress in a number of ways. First, friends, relatives, and co-workers may let us know that they value us. Our self-respect is strengthened when we feel accepted by others despite our faults and difficulties. Second, other people often provide us with informational support. They help us (10) _____ and find solutions to them. Third, we typically find social companionship supportive. Engaging in leisure-time activities with others (11) _____ while at the same time distracting us from our worries and troubles. Finally, other people may give us instrumental support—financial aid, material resources, and needed services—that reduces stress by (12) _____.

Text Three

| taking | talented | promoting | shifting |

A. and at where the population is (13) _____

B. where the debate about diversity is (14) _____ place

C. that the need for (15) _____, skilled Americans means

D. that expanding the pool means (16) _____ policies

It's very interesting to note (17) _____. It is taking place primarily in political circles. Here at the College Fund, we have a lot of contact with top corporate leaders; none of them is talking about getting rid of those instruments that produce diversity. In fact, they say that if their companies are to compete in the global village and in the global market place, diversity is an imperative. They also say (18) _____ we have to expand the pool of potential employees. And in looking at where birth rates are growing (19) _____, corporate America understands (20) _____ that help provide skills to more minorities, more women and more immigrants. Corporate leaders know that if that doesn't occur in our society, they will not have the engineers, the scientists, the lawyers, or the business managers they will need.

Model Test 7

Directions: *In this part there are three short texts. For each text, you should first fill in the blank in the choices A, B, C (and D) with the best answer provided in the rectangle. Then, complete the text itself by filling in each of the blanks with the completed A, or B, or C (or D). Write your answer on the Answer Sheet.*

Text One

| look | earning | opinion |

A. a closer (1) _____ at the survey indicates

B. those (2) _____ at least $150,000 per year

C. 23 percent had no (3) _____

Health experts have tried to get many restaurants to serve smaller portions. Now, apparently, some customers are calling for this too. A restaurant industry trade magazine reported last month that 57 percent of more than 4,000 people surveyed believed restaurants serve portions that are too large; (4) _____; 20 percent disagreed.

But (5) _____ that many Americans who can't afford fine dining still prefer large portions. Seventy percent of (6) _____ prefer smaller portions; but only 45 percent of those earning less than $25,000 want smaller.

Text Two

| transformed   shown   shocked |

A. when America will be (7) _____ from a gun culture to one

B. America has been (8) _____ by such incidents

C. Recent events in America; however; have (9) _____ that

(10) _____ the question of gun possession is now out of control and strong voices have called for immediate action to be taken. In seemingly peaceful schools students have guns into classrooms and opened fire upon their classmates. (11) _____ which seem to occur with greater frequency. The periodic deaths of innocent citizens and even foreign visitors from guns have forced legislators to pass laws to stop these senseless killings.

The day may not be far off (12) _____ which controls their use and possession.

Text Three

| a professional career |
| amateur performers |
| admiring fans |
| free of charge |

A. not only (13) _____, but professional artists as well

B. to make contact with their (14) _____

C. they rent out space to performers (15) _____

D. before beginning (16) _____

Some of the most popular attractions across America are the many free concerts offered to the public throughout the year. These involve (17) _____. The public parks of many cities across the country usually have bandstands and large lawns. As a service to citizens, (18) _____. Amateur groups, with nothing more than a desire to perform, offer their talents freely to the public. Semi-professional artists are pleased to get the chance to perform before the public to perfect their craft and nurture the hope of being discovered (19) _____. Famous professionals also give free concerts (20) _____. Often such concerts are sponsored by a large corporate organization and offered to the public free of charge as a cultural service and support for the arts.

Model Test 8

Directions: In this part there are three short texts. For each text, you should first fill in the blank in the choices A, B, C (and D) with the best answer provided in the rectangle. Then, complete the text itself by filling in each of the blanks with the completed A, or B, or C (or D). Write your answer on the Answer Sheet.

Text One

| go   match   raises |

A. biometrics (1) _____ difficult questions about privacy

B. you would see your insurance payments (2) _____ through the roof

C. to (3) _____ your health-insurance records with credit-card record

Not surprisingly, (4) _____ and the potential for abuse. Some worry that governments and industry will be tempted to use the technology to monitor individual behavior. "If someone used your fingerprints (5) _____ showing that you regularly bought lots of cigarettes and fatty foods," says one policy analyst, "(6) _____ ." In Toronto, critics of the welfare fingerprint plan complained that it would force people to submit to a procedure widely identified with criminals.

Text Two

| walls   correction   intimacy |

A. some kind of (7) _____ or serious business

B. (8) _____ are immediately torn down

C. creates an immediate (9) _____ between two people

In many traditional cultures the use of the family name is seen as a sign of respect. For Americans, however, it's the nickname that (10) _____ upon which to build a relationship. By speaking to another on a first name basis and using his nickname, (11) _____ and equality between two people is established.

At work bosses will refer to their employees by their nicknames. Should an employer use a worker's family name, you can be sure that (12) _____ will follow.

Text Three

| expected   come   well-paid   reducing |

A. to provide (13) _____ work for skilled workers

B. by (14) _____ the number of hours of each existing job

C. As would be (15) _____

D. Subsequent studies have (16) _____ up with similar results

Job sharing should not be confused with the term work sharing, which refers to increasing the number of jobs (17) _____, thus offering more positions to the growing number of unemployed people. Job sharing, by contrast, is not designed to address unemployment problems; its focus, rather, is (18) _____ and professionals who want more free time for other activities.

(19) ＿＿＿＿＿＿, women constitute the bulk of job sharers. A survey carded out in 1988 by Britain's Equal Opportunities Commission revealed that 78 percent of sharers were female, the majority of whom were between 20 and 40 years of age. (20) ＿＿＿＿＿＿. Many of these women were re-entering the job market after having had children, but they chose not to seek part-time work because it would have meant lower status. Job sharing also offered an acceptable shift back into full-time work after a long absence.

Model Test 9

Directions: *In this part there are three short texts. For each text, you should first fill in the blank in the choices A, B, C (and D) with the best answer provided in the rectangle. Then, complete the text itself by filling in each of the blanks with the completed A, or B, or C (or D). Write your answer on the Answer Sheet.*

Text One

| throw   ruin   inherited |

A. to (1) ＿＿＿＿ off large parts of it
B. to give too much (2) ＿＿＿＿ wealth to children
C. that would just (3) ＿＿＿＿ their lives

Nicola Horlick or "supermum," a famous British billionaire, owing to the fact that she has high-flying jobs and five kids—has spent her career making a reported £250m. She now seems determined (4) ＿＿＿＿. She already gives away about 25% of her income each year, she has just revealed, in a report on the state of charity in the city, that she will not be leaving most of the remainder to her children. "I think it is wrong (5) ＿＿＿＿." Horlick told the report's authors. "I will not be leaving all my wealth to my children because (6) ＿＿＿＿."

Text Two

| encouragement   rivalry   loyalty |

A. There is much (7) ＿＿＿＿ between supporters
B. shouting noisy (8) ＿＿＿＿ to their team
C. declare their (9) ＿＿＿＿ by wearing their team's colors

Sadly, not all the action always takes place on the ground. All too frequently, there is action in the stands, too. Football supporters, most of whom (10) ＿＿＿＿, in the form of shirts, are not known for their quiet behavior. They are often very noisy, (11) ＿＿＿＿ and singing deafening songs.

(12) ＿＿＿＿. Mostly, this is good-natured, but trouble can easily arise. Fans get angry if they feel that a referee has made a wrong decision, perhaps giving one of their team a red or yellow card unfairly, or perhaps failing to notice a foul (犯规) committed by a member of the other team.

Text Three

| a new era |
| special protection |
| in turn |
| profit most |

A. may have launched (13) _____ in economic history

B. so they'd (14) _____ from liberalization

C. which (15) _____ would improve human welfare

D. Asian, meanwhile, continues to plead for (16) _____

"The word 'protection' is no longer taboo (禁忌语)." This short sentence, uttered by French President Nicolas Sarkozy last month, (17) _____. Why? For decades, Western leaders have believed that lowering trade barriers and tariffs was a natural good. Doing so, they reasoned, would lead to greater economic efficiency and productivity, (18) _____. Championing free trade thus became a moral, not just an economic, cause.

These leaders, of course, weren't acting out of unselfishness. They knew their economies were the most competitive, (19) _____. And developing countries feared that their economies would be swamped by superior Western productivity. Today, however, the tables have turned—though few acknowledge it. The West continues to preach free trade, but practices it less and less. (20) _____ but practices more and more free trade.

Model Test 10

Directions: *In this part there are three short texts. For each text, you should first fill in the blank in the choices A, B, C (and D) with the best answer provided in the rectangle. Then, complete the text itself by filling in each of the blanks with the completed A, or B, or C (or D). Write your answer on the Answer Sheet.*

Text One

| in | than | for |

A. that he got his new home in exchange (1) _____ a red paper clip

B. the creative side rather (2) _____ the business side

C. Having announced his aim (the house) (3) _____ advance

Last weekend Kyle MacDonald in Montreal threw a party to celebrate the fact (4) _____. Starting a year ago, MacDonald bartered the clip for increasingly valuable stuff, including a camp stove and free rent in a Phoenix flat. (5) _____, MacDonald likely got a boost from techies eager to see the Internet pass this daring test of its networking power. "My whole motto (座右铭) was 'Start small, think big, and have fun'," says MacDonald, 26, "I really kept my effort on (6) _____."

Text Two

prose　　fingerprints　　intensity

A. I won't detect a polished piece of (7) _____

B. With a certain excitement and (8) _____

C. Writers have styles like (9) _____

"I promise." "I swear to you it'll never happen again." "I give you my word." "Honestly. Believe me." Sure, I trust. Why not? I teach English composition at a private college. (10) _____, I read my students' essays, hoping to find the person behind the pen. As each semester progresses, plagiarism (剽窃) appears. Not only is my intelligence insulted as one assumes (11) _____ from an otherwise-average writer, but I feel a sadness that a student has resorted to buying a paper from a peer. (12) _____ and after several assignments, I can match a student's work with his or her name even if it's missing from the upper left-hand corner.

Text Three

| cultural and linguistic integrity |
| bilingual speakers |
| native tongues |
| most of |

A. (13) _____ could use their own language

B. Whether (14) _____ these languages survive

C. browse the Internet using their (15) _____

D. many small languages could sustain their (16) _____

(17) _____ will probably depend on how strongly cultural groups wish to keep their identity alive through a native language. To do so will require an emphasis on bilingualism (mastery of two languages). (18) _____ in smaller spheres—at home, among friends, in community settings—and a global language at work, in dealings with government, and in commercial spheres. In this way, (19) _____ alongside global languages, rather than yield to the homogenizing (同化的) forces of globalization.

Ironically, the trend of technological innovation that has threatened minority languages could also help save them. For example, some experts predict that computer software translation tools will one day permit minority language speakers to (20) _____. Linguists are currently using computer—aided learning tools to teach a variety of threatened languages.

第三章　短文完成

第六节　答案及解析

Model Test 1

Text One

答案　1. like　2. evidently　3. at times of　4. B　5. A　6. C

详解

第1题考点是：动词词组 look like（看上去像）。第2题后的介词 to 表明，此处不缺介词，能用在这里的应该是副词 evidently。第3题放在名词词组前，符合介词词组的用法。

三个语言段填好后完整的语义和语法功能如下：A 的语法成分是：动词原形，在句子中可以作谓语或跟在不定式后作其他成分，意思是：看上去像个傻子。B 的语法成分是：状语，意思是：很明显在很大程度上。C 的语法成分是：名词加定语从句，但是缺必要成分，因此意思是不完整的，意思是：在遇到危险的时候，它将怎样。

这篇文章主要分析了人会怯场的原因。第4题之前是语法意义上的完整句，不缺动词和名词成分，所以正确答案应该是 B，作状语，完成后整句话的语义是：很明显，我们的自尊自信在很大程度上受到了威胁。第5题，不定式后应该用动词原形，完成后整句话的语义是：没有哪个正常人看上去像个傻子的。第6题补全后句子的语义是：我们大脑正是按照我们在身体遇到危险时会做出的反应来指导我们的身体的。在这个句子中，it would 之后省略了动词 react。

Text Two

答案　7. far　8. largely　9. selling　10. C　11. B　12. A

详解

第7题考点是：副词的修饰问题，too 之前不能用 largely 来修饰，可以修饰它的副词主要有 far，much，a little，a bit 等。第8题用在形容词之前，修饰形容词，应该是副词 largely 的用法。第9题用在名词之前，可以是及物动词。

三个语言段填好后完整的语义和语法功能如下：A 的语法成分是：主系表结构，意思是：它太快了。B 的语法成分是：so 引导的并列句，意思是：因此，销售报告在很大程度上是不准确的。C 的语法成分是：现在分词，意思是：销售任何东西，从计算机装置到如何准备所得税的服务。

这篇文章主要是讲电子零售业。根据第10题在句子中位置和作用，从语法上来看 B 和 C 都可以；再进一步根据语义判断，正确答案应该是 C，这句话是对网上零售业作的基本介绍。完成后句子的完整语义是：网络的功能之一就是提供一个拥有很多零售商的"电子商城"，可以销售任何东西，从计算机装置到如何准备所得税的服务；C 是现在分词作句子伴随状语的用法。第11题在句子中位置和作用应该和第10题相似，因此正确答案是 B。完成后句子的完整语义是：正如网上的其他事物一样，"电子商城"是很分散的，没有权威机构做交易记录，因此，销售报告在很大程度上是不准确的。第 12 题正确答案是 A，在这用到的是不定式的句式，it is too…to…（太……以至于不能……）；完成后句子的完整语义是：但是现在就对电子零售业下定论还为时过早。

Text Three

答案   13. less and less   14. as fast as   15. outscoring them   16. concentrate on
           17. A   18. D   19. B   20. C

详解

    从语法功能来看，第 13 题用在不及物动词 stumble 后，应该是状语的作用；就语义而言，stumble（蹒跚，结结巴巴地说话，踌躇）只能和 less and less 搭配。第 14 题考点是比较级的用法，根据语法规定，在涉及倍数比较的句型中，正确语序应该是：倍数+形容词、副词的比较结构+被比较的事物，因此正确答案应该是 as fast as。第 15 题之后已有介词 on，所以不可能填 concentrate on，所以正确答案是 outscoring them。第 16 题用在助动词之后，应该用动词原形，正确答案是 concentrate on。

    四个语言段填好后完整的语义和语法功能如下：A 的语法成分是：完整句，意思是：他结巴地越来越少。B 的语法成分是：who 引导的定语从句，意思是：阅读速度是其他孩子的三倍之快。C 的语法成分是：现在分词，意思是：在正确率、理解和词汇方面，超过了他们。D 的语法成分是：so 引导的并列句，意思是：因此，他可以把注意力集中在文章的意思上。

    这篇文章主要是介绍自动阅读者。第 17 题所在的句子是简单句，它之前之后都是句子的状语，整个句子缺的是主谓结构，因此正确答案是 A。完成后句子的完整语义是：经过练习，他停顿地越来越少，逐渐学会按照词组来阅读。根据语法判断，第 18 题可以是状语或者并列句；根据语义判断，正确答案是 D，在这尚未涉及与其他读者的比较问题，因此不能用 C。完成后句子的完整语义是：随着自动性的提高，他根本不用考虑词汇的意思，因此，他可以把注意力集中在文章的意思上。后面的两个题目，第 20 题更容易判断，它之前已经有了并列连词 and，而且前面也没有另外一个定语从句，所以在这不可能填 B，所以正确答案应该是 C，是 and 连接两个现在分词。完成后句子的完整语义是：在五年级的时候，自动阅读者的阅读速度会达到其他人的两倍，同时在正确率、理解和词汇方面，也超过了他们。第 19 题的正确答案是 B，作的是 automatic readers in the first grade 定语；完成后句子的完整语义是：西北大学的 Alan Rossman 发现在一年级的时候自动阅读者阅读速度是其他孩子的三倍之快，而且在阅读考试中取得的成绩是其他人的两倍之高。

Model Test 2

Text One

答案   1. scope   2. to   3. with   4. B   5. C   6. A

第三章　短文完成

详解

第1题，用在形容词的比较级后，介词前，应该是名词成分，正确答案是 scope；考点是固定搭配 have scope (for)（有施展……的余地；有发挥……的机会）。第2题后面用的是动词原形，所以不能用介词 with，因此正确答案应该是不定式 to。第3题是介词 with。

三个语言段填好后完整的语义和语法功能如下：A 的语法成分是：主谓结构，后面缺介词 for 的宾语，意思是：人口多为……提供了更多的余地。B 的语法成分是：不定式，在句子中可以充当谓语之外的任何成分，意思是：养活众多的人口。C 的语法成分是：被动语态，在句子中作谓语，意思是：人口少的时候可以获得。

这篇文章主要是讲人口过多的利与弊。第4题位于句首，后面是主谓结构，按照语法判断应该是状语，在这能作状语的只有 B 不定式。完成后句子的完整语义是：为了养活众多的人口，必须耕种贫瘠的土地，加大对肥沃土地的利用。第5题用于比较状语从句的连词 than 之后，后面没有任何其他成分，因此正确答案只能是 C。完成后句子的完整语义是：因此，每个人都产得少，这就意味着比人口少的时候获得的平均收入要少。第6题用在宾语从句 that 之后，后面有名词，因此应该用 A。完成后句子的完整语义是：其他经济学家认为人口多为一些像港口、公路和铁路这样的基础设施的专用和发展提供了更多的余地，而如果没有大的需求的话，这些设施是不太可能建成的。

Text Two

答案　7. conclusive　8. susceptible　9. likely　10. A　11. B　12. C

详解

先判断第8、9题中使用的固定搭配。第8题考点是固定搭配 be susceptible to，意思是：对……敏感，可被……；第9题考点是 be likely to do，意思是：可能做某事。第7题正确答案是 conclusive。

三个语言段填好后完整的语义和语法功能如下：A 的语法成分是：系表结构，后面缺介词 about 的宾语，意思是：对……并不确定。B 的语法成分是：系表结构，意思是：容易酗酒。C 的语法成分是：系表结构，后面缺 take up 的宾语，意思是：更容易开始干……

这篇文章主要是探讨可能导致儿童酗酒的原因。根据语法来看第10题前的主语 evidence 是抽象名词，应该跟单数的谓语动词，因此只能在 A 和 C 中选择；就语义和词汇使用的要求来看，be likely to do 和 take up 都是人发出的动作，因此不可能跟在 evidence 后，所以正确答案应该是 A。完成后句子的完整语义是：证据本身并不能确定地说明什么。做第11题时，首先需要判断谁是11题的动作发出者，即主语是谁，在这应该是 children 可数名词复数，所以正确答案应该是 B。完成后句子的完整语义是：研究发现亲生父母是酒鬼，而养父母不喝酒的孩子也容易酗酒。12题正确答案是 C，影响谓语动词单复数的主语的核心名词是 group，所以语法是正确的。完成后句子的完整语义是：这群孩子比亲生父母和养父母都不酗酒的孩子更容易酗酒。

· 271 ·

Text Three

答案 13. of the child   14. What we need
15. in the home   16. all the credit
17. B   18. D   19. C   20. A

详解

首先根据语法判断，13题位于名词词组之后，可以用介词词组作后置定语；然后根据语义和搭配，最合适的答案应该是 of the child。14题和16题应该结合起来判断，两题缺的都是名词成分，16题语义更明显，更容易判断，根据并列结构 not…nor（既不，也不），可以判断16题和 nor 后面的 all the blame（所有的批评）在结构上应该相似，在语义上应该相反，因此正确答案应该是 all the credit（所有的荣誉）。14题是句子的主语，正确答案是 What we need，主语从句作主语。15题正确答案是 in the home，作的是 men's place 的定语，而且语义也相符。

四个语言段填好后完整的语义和语法功能如下：A 的语法成分是：介词词组，意思是：对于儿童的健康成长。B 的语法成分是：主谓结构，意思是：我们所需要的则是。C 的语法成分是：不定式，意思是：分析男性在家里的地位。D 的语法成分是：谓语+宾语，意思是：既不应该接受所有的荣誉，也不应该承担所有的批评。

这篇文章的主要内容是关于如何重新评价男性在美国家庭中的地位和作用。根据语法判断17题所在的句子中缺少主语和谓语，符合这一要求的只有 B。完成后句子的完整语义是：我们所需要的则是认识到养育孩子需要两个地位平等的人的合作。18题所在的句子中缺少谓语，因此正确答案是 D。完成后句子的完整语义是：有迹象表明精神病学家、心理学家、社会工作者和家庭问题专家已经越来越清楚地意识到男性的作用，他们认为女性既不应该接受所有的荣誉，也不应该承担所有的批评。19题考点是动词词组 begin to do，所以正确答案是 C。完成后句子的完整语义是：相反，我们开始分析男性在家里的地位并确信他们在家中确实有位置。20题考点是常用搭配 be irrelevant to sth./sb.（与某事/某人无关）。完成后句子的完整语义是：他们的角色并非与儿童的健康成长无关。

Model Test 3

Text One

答案 1. rather   2. much   3. those   4. B   5. C   6. A

详解

第1题是考查副词的修饰问题，much 可以修饰形容词、副词的比较级，但不能修饰形容词、副词原形，因此正确答案是 rather。第2题缺的是名词或代词成分，由于 social interaction 是抽象名词，所以代词应该选择 much。第3题正确答案是 those，代词的名词所有格。

三个语言段填好后完整的语义和语法功能如下：A 的语法成分是：完整句，意思是：我们大多数人可以毫不费力地干这件事。B 的语法成分是：主谓结构，后面缺介词 of 的宾语，意思是：社会交往大多包括。C 的语法成分是：主从复合句，意思是：这就意味着我们要使我们的行动与他们的相符合。

这篇文章主要是介绍影响人的社会地位变化的诸多因素。第 4 题所在的句子中缺少主语和谓语，其后的动名词在句子中作宾语，因此正确答案是 B。完成后句子的完整语义是：社会交往大多包括辨别和选择合适的身份，以及让其他人依据和我们的关系来确认他们的地位。第 5 题后面是介词词组 of other people，据此可以判断正确答案是 C。完成后句子的完整语义是：这就意味着我们要基于不断进行评价和解释的思维过程来使我们的行动与其他人的相符合。第 6 题之前是 although 引导的状语从句，在这缺主句，所以 A 是正确答案。

Text Two

答案　7. only　8. completely　9. over　10. A　11. C　12. B

详解

7~9 这三道题有一定的难度，重在考查对副词的准确了解和掌握，做题时应该从语义和搭配入手，而不是做简单的语法判断。第 7 题正确答案是 only，想做的事情很简单，就是睡觉而已。第 8 题依据他前面的 clean out 和 all 这两个词汇提示，正确答案应该是 completely（彻底、全部）。第 9 题用 over（太，过于）来修饰 energized 的程度。

三个语言段填好后完整的语义和语法功能如下：A 的语法成分是：现在分词，意思是：只想睡觉。B 的语法成分是：谓语动词的过去时，意思是：彻底打扫她所有的衣橱。C 的语法成分是：现在分词，意思是：变得这样的过度活跃。

根据语法判断，第 10 题所缺的是状语；根据前面 lose all their energy and drive（丧失了全部的精力和活力）的语义判断，正确答案应该是 A。完成后句子的完整语义是：有些人好像丧失了他们全部的精力和活力，只想睡觉。11 题的语法功能和 10 题一样，在句子中作状语，此外 so...that（如此……以至于）是结果状语从句的连词，因此正确答案应该是 C。完成后句子的完整语义是：另外一些人的反应方式完全相反，他们变得过度活跃以至于无法找到足够消耗他们多余精力的活动。根据语法判断，第 12 题缺谓语，所以正确答案应该是 B。完成后句子的完整语义是：例如，一位女士说她已经彻底打扫了她所有的衣橱，而且准备去给她的邻居打扫。

Text Three

答案　13. cast off　　　　　　14. on a regular basis
　　　15. less than　　　　　　16. in family shelters
　　　17. B　　　　18. C　　　　19. A　　　　20. D

详解

13 题用在 have been 之后，应该是被动语态中的实义动词的过去分词，正确答案是

cast off（丢弃，摆脱）。14 题根据语法判断应该是句子中的状语，修饰谓语动词，根据语义判断，不需要地点状语，所以正确答案是 on a regular basis（经常地，定期地）。15 题用在 half of them 前，因此正确答案是 less than。16 题用在 stay 之后，in family shelters 是正确答案，表示待的地方。

四个语言段填好后完整的语义和语法功能如下：A 的语法成分是：定语从句，意思是：那些被家庭遗弃的人。B 的语法成分是：定语从句，意思是：他们中的 1/3 的人并不经常去学校。C 的语法成分是：that 引导的名词性从句，意思是：他们中定期去上学的人不足一半。D 的语法成分是：原因状语从句，意思是：因为他们不住在家里。

这篇文章主要是介绍在美国年轻人无家可归的原因。根据语法判断，第 17 题用在 about（大约）之后，不可能是 C 和 D；就语义判断，后面的信息应该有数字的信息，所以正确答案是 B。完成后句子的完整语义是：美国的一个教育部门根据各州的估计指出现在有 22 万无家可归的学龄儿童，他们中的大约 1/3 的人并不经常去学校。根据语法判断，18 题用在 and 后面，是并列成分，and 在这连接了两个并列的宾语从句，所以正确答案是 C。完成后句子的完整语义是：但是，国家流浪人口联合会估计无家可归的孩子的数量至少是这个数的两倍，而且他们中的定期去上学的人不足一半。19 题应该是对 "throwaway" youths 的补充解释，所以正确答案是 A。完成后句子的完整语义是：一部分特别难以统计流浪人口包括被家庭遗弃的青少年。20 题正确答案是 D，解释了为什么他们中的很多人没被算作孩子统计在内，这是因为他们没住在家里，而是流浪在街上靠自己生存。

Model Test 4

Text One

答案 1. reap   2. checks   3. walk   4. A   5. B   6. C

详解

第 1 题用在助动词 can 后，应该用动词原形，同时用在 big reward 前，应该是及物动词，因此正确答案是 reap（收割，收获）。第 2 题用在 no one 后面，应该用动词的第三人称单数的形式，所以正确答案是 checks，check up on 是固定词组，意思是：监督，督促。第 3 题正确答案是 walk，walk away 动词词组，意思是：走开，离开。

三个语言段填好后完整的语义和语法功能如下：A 的语法成分是：谓语+宾语，意思是：可以获得丰厚的回报。B 的语法成分是：主谓结构，缺少介词 on 后的宾语，意思是：没有人监督。C 的语法成分是：谓语+状语，意思是：可以离开，不仅不受惩罚。

这篇文章的主要内容是介绍计算机犯罪高发的原因。首先根据语法判断，第 4 题缺的是句子的谓语，而且其后没有 not only 的另一半 but also，因此 A 是正确答案。完成后句子的完整语义是：任何足够聪明可以为了自己的目的而改变这一信息的人都可以获得丰厚的回报。第 5 题用在连词 if 后，what 引导的宾语从句前，应该是主谓结构，正确答案是 B。完成后句子的完整语义是：如果没有人监督计算机在做什么，那么计算机犯罪很难被察觉。第 6 题正确答案是 C，not only...but also 这个并列结构，常常简化成 not only…but。完成后句子的完整语义是：但是，即使是犯罪被发现了，罪犯也可以离开，不仅不受惩罚，而且还能从他的前任雇主那拿到很好的推荐信。

Text Two

答案 7. available　　8. embarrassed　　9. astonishingly
10. C　　11. B　　12. A

详解

第 7、8 题都用在副词之后，应该是形容词，其中第 8 题是描写人的，所以正确答案是 embarrassed，形容人的感觉；第 7 题正确答案是 available，而且 readily available（现成的，可以轻松获得的）是常见的词汇搭配。第 9 题用在形容词 lazy 前，应该用副词 astonishingly。

三个语言段填好后完整的语义和语法功能如下：A 的语法成分是：定语，意思是：按一下按钮就可以轻松获得。B 的语法成分是：that 引导的名词性从句，意思是：人们很容易觉得尴尬。C 的语法成分是：完整句，意思是：人懒得出奇。

这篇文章主要分析了业余音乐家减少的原因。判断第 10 题缺的是整个一句话，因此正确答案是 C；而且它后面的例子就是具体阐述人到底有多懒，语义也相符。第 11 题用在 is 后，在句子中作表语，正确答案是 B，that 引导的表语从句。第 12 题用在名词词组 a famous, talented musician 之后，作后置定语，正确答案是 A。这也是 available 的典型用法。完成后句子的完整语义是：当只要按一下按钮就可以轻松听到著名的专业的音乐家的演奏，哪个业余提琴手，或者弹钢琴的还会想自己演奏来愉悦家人或朋友？

Text Three

答案 13. prevailing values　　14. the parents' culture
15. the process　　16. personal independence
17. B　　18. D　　19. A　　20. C

详解

方框内所有选项都是名词词组，因此完成 14～16 题主要靠语义来判断。13 题用在 these 之后，应该使用可数名词的复数形式，所以正确答案是 prevailing values。与 14 题前的 custom（风俗、习惯）和 value（价值观念）两个词有密切关系的词汇应该是 culture（文化），所以这道题的正确答案是 the parents' culture。15 题正确答案是 the process，考点是常用词组 in the process of（在……的过程中）。16 题正确答案是 personal independence。

四个语言段填好后完整的语义和语法功能如下：A 的语法成分是：名词词组，意思是：……这些主流的价值观给孩子们。B 的语法成分是：名词词组，意思是：父辈文化中的风俗习惯和价值观念。C 的语法成分是：介词词组，意思是：在他们社会化的过程中。D 的语法成分是：名词词组，意思是：培养个人独立性的第一步。

这篇文章主要是介绍文化传承。根据固定搭配 teach sb. sth.，17 题应该用名词，由于 17 题前已经有了 new generations of children，所以后面不可能再出现 children，所以不可能选 A；而且，这句话是解释文化传承是什么，所以在这教授给孩子的应该是文化，所以正确答案应该是 B。完成后句子的完整语义是：文化传承自人一出生便开始，是教授新一代父辈文化中的风俗习惯和价值观念的过程。根据语法判断，18 题用在介词 as 后，应该用名词；词组 be seen as 的意思是：被认为是……，那么 18 题的语义就可以从定语从句 which 所指代的事情来判断，which 在这应该代指 allows the child to get used to having his or her own room（使得孩子适应自己住一个房间），因此语义相符的选项应该是 D。完成后句子的完整语义是：这有助于保护父母的隐私并让孩子适应自己住一个房间，这被认为是培养个人独立性的第一步。19 题用在及物动词 instill（慢慢灌输）之后，应该是名词性质，正确答案是 A。完成后句子的完整语义是：父母努力将这些主流的价值观灌输给孩子们。20 题用在主谓结构前，应该是句子的状语，正确答案是 C。完成后句子的完整语义是：在社会化的过程中，孩子们学会先为自己着想，学会依靠自己。

Model Test 5

Text One

答案　1. range　　2. apart　　3. presented　　4. C　　5. B　　6. A

详解

第 1 题用在定冠词 the 后，介词 of 前，应该是名词性质，所以正确答案是 range。第 2 题正确答案是 apart，考查的是固定词组 apart from（除……以外）。第 3 题正确答案是 presented，过去分词作后置定语。

三个语言段填好后完整的语义和语法功能如下：A 的语法成分是：完整句，意思是：可以选择的范围是有限的。B 的语法成分是：介词词组，意思是：除了细微的调整外。C 的语法成分是：名词词组，意思是：由社会提供的衣服。

这篇文章的主要内容是讲我们能选择的社会地位是有限的。第 4 题用在介词 among 之后，应该是名词性质，因此正确答案是 C。完成后句子的完整语义是：我们必须从社会给我们提供的衣服中选择。第 5 题用在 but 连接的并列句中的主语之前，应该是在并列句中做状语，所以正确答案是 B。完成后句子的完整语义是：在给定的限制内做好选择后，我们可以做一些改变，但是除了这些微小的调整，我们还是受限于商店货架上所摆放的东西。第 6 题正确答案是 A，是 and 连接的并列句。完成后句子的完整语义是：同样地，我们的社会地位也是现成的，可以选择的范围是有限的。

Text Two

答案　7. distinguishing　　8. inevitably　　9. painful
　　　　10. B　　　　　　11. C　　　　　　12. A

详解

　　首先根据语法判断，第7题用在名词之前，应该用形容词；其次，根据语义判断，修饰 feature（特征），应该是 distinguishing（有区别的，不同的）。根据语法判断，第8题用在过去分词 brought 之前，应该用副词，所以正确答案是 inevitably。第9题正确答案是 painful（痛苦的），在句子中作表语，与主语 commitment（承诺，义务）相符。

　　三个语言段填好后完整的语义和语法功能如下：A 的语法成分是：but 连接的并列句，意思是：但是这些并非是它最与众不同的特征。B 的语法成分是：名词词组，意思是：这些事情不可避免地带来的痛苦。C 的语法成分是：for 连接的并列句，意思是：因为承诺事实上是比较痛苦的。

　　这篇文章主要讲很多青年人会逃避那些能给他们带来真正幸福的事情。因很多时候这些事情掺杂一定的痛苦。第10题用在及物动词 fear 之后，而且其后有具体的例子，所以正确答案应该是 B，此外 such…as（像……这种）是常用词组。完成后句子的完整语义是：他们害怕那些不可避免地会给他们带来痛苦的事情，例如：婚姻、养育子女、事业成功、宗教信仰以及自我完善。第11题和12题在语法功能上是一样的，因此应该从语义联系和逻辑关系上来判断。根据11题之前的 making a commitment（作出承诺）来判断，正确答案应该是 C。完成后句子的完整语义是：如果他够诚实的话，他会告诉你他害怕作出承诺，因为承诺事实上是比较痛苦的。第12题答案是 A，完成后句子的完整语义是：婚姻生活也有这种时候，但是这些并不是它最典型的特征。

Text Three

答案　13. because　　14. in　　15. whatever　　16. to
　　　17. D　　　　　18. C　　　19. A　　　　　20. B

详解

　　第13题用在完整句前，后面的句子不缺任何必要的语法成分，因此在这可填的是状语从句的连词，正确答案应该是 because。首先根据语法判断，第14题用在 or 之后，在句子中作并列表语，所以不可能用连词；其次，根据语义判断，14题语义应该与 stable（稳定的）相反，在这可以用介词词组 in decline，表示下降的状态。15题用在主谓结构之前，不可能用介词，因此正确答案是 whatever，在从句中作 be 的表语。16题正确答案是 to，attitude to/towards（对于……的观点态度）是常见的固定搭配。

　　四个语言段填好后完整的语义和语法功能如下：A 的语法成分是：原因状语从句，意思是：因为它将导致制成品需求市场萎缩。B 的语法成分是：定语从句，意思是：是稳定的或者是下降的。C 的语法成分是：让步状语从句，意思是：不论结果怎样。D 的语法成分是：that 引导的名词性从句，意思是：不同的国家对于人口增长的官方态度各不相同。

　　这篇文章主要内容是讲控制人口增长。根据17题前的名词 the fact，首先想到的是后面跟 that 引导的名词性从句，然后将 D 选项带回到原文中检验后可以发现语义也是相符的，完成后句子的完整语义是：目前在世界范围内进行人口控制的一个困难在于这么一个事实：由于各个国家工业发展的程度和食物及原材料的供应情况各不相同，因此各国对于人口增长的官方态度也各不相同。18题主要根据语义和逻辑来判断，这句话是在介绍developing country（发展中国家），句子的前半部分已经介绍了发展中国家的人口状况是vastly expanded，所以这不可能填B；而且也不可能和A构成因果关系，所以正确答案应该是C。完成后句子的完整语义是：在发展中国家，快速增长的人口给食物、土地和自然资源方面造成了很大的压力，所以控制出生率就成了政府最为关切的事情，不管会因此带来什么样的后果。19题的位置尽管既可以用定语从句，也可以用状语从句，但是B在语义上是不合适的，无法来修饰前面的unemployment（失业），因此正确答案是A。完成后句子的完整语义是：出生率下降会引发失业，因为它将导致制成品需求市场萎缩。第20题正确答案是B，作代词one的定语，定语从句里的stable or in decline与前面的increasing构成对比，符合词组rather than（而不是）所表达的逻辑关系。完成后句子的完整语义是：基于这样的考虑，发达国家的政府更愿意看到人口缓慢增长，而不是维持不动或者是下降。

Model Test 6

Text One

答案 1. greatly 2. very 3. too 4. B 5. C 6. A

详解

1~3题主要是考查常用副词的准确使用。最容易填的是第3题，正确答案是too，too...to（太……以至于不能）是固定的搭配。第1题正确答案是greatly，greatly经常用于exceed（超出），increase（增多），decrease（减少）这样的词汇前面，来形容幅度大。第2题，正确答案是very。

三个语言段填好后完整的语义和语法功能如下：A的语法成分是：主谓结构，句子缺少及物动词exceed的宾语，意思是：出生率极大地超过了。B的语法成分是：谓语＋宾语，意思是：对现有的劳动力有着非常显著的影响。C的语法成分是：介词词组，意思是：那些太老的，不能工作的。

这篇文章主要是讲影响劳动力规模的因素。第4题所在句子缺的是谓语，所以正确答案是B。完成后句子的完整语义是：总体人口的年龄分布对现有的劳动力有着非常显著的影响。第5题用在并列连词or后面，是or连接的并列成分，正确答案是C，of those too old to work与前面的of very young people形成了语义上的对比。完成后句子的完整语义是：如果人口中特别年轻的人或太老不能工作的人太多的话，可用的劳动力就会比人口年龄平均分布时要低。第6题正确答案是A，用在i.e.（也就是说）后面，是对前面the population grows rapidly from natural increase的解释。完成后句子的完整语义是：如果人口增长的速度远高于自然增长，也就是说出生率大大地超过了死亡率，那么随着人口总数的增长，劳动力的比例则呈下降趋势。

Text Two

答案 7. resolve 8. define 9. meet 10. B 11. C 12. A

详解

方框内的选项都是动词，因此 7~9 三道题主要靠语义和搭配做题。第 7 题是 and 连接的两个并列的动词，其宾语是 our problems，因此它的语义应该和 cope with（应对）相近或相同，因此正确答案是 resolve（解决）。同理可做第 8 题，第 8 题所缺词汇应该和 understand（理解）近义或同义，所以正确答案是 define（界定）。第 9 题答案是 meet，meet the need/demand（满足需要）是常用的词汇搭配。

三个语言段填好后完整的语义和语法功能如下：A 的语法成分是：现在分词或动名词，意思是：帮助我们解决或应对问题。B 的语法成分是：不定式，意思是：界定和理解我们的问题。C 的语法成分是：谓语+宾语，意思是：帮助我们满足我们的社会需求。

这篇文章主要讲社会支持如何帮我们减少压力。第 10 题用在 help us 后，因此只能选 B，完成后句子的完整语义是：他们能帮助我们界定和理解我们的问题，并找到解决问题的方法。根据语法判断，第 11 题所在的句子缺少的是谓语，所以正确答案是 C；完成后句子的完整语义是：和别人一起娱乐有助于满足我们的社交需求，同时可以让我们忘记自己的困扰和麻烦。第 12 题用在介词 by 后面，应该是名词性质，所以正确答案是 A，动名词的用法。完成后句子的完整语义是：最后，别人还可以给我们工具性的支持，即给我们提供经济支持、物质资源、所需的服务，这一切帮助我们解决或应对问题从而减少了压力。

Text Three

答案 13. shifting 14. taking 15. talented 16. promoting
17. B 18. C 19. A 20. D

详解

在 13~16 四个题目中，13 题最难选择，因此应该先从后面的题目入手。14 题正确答案是 taking，考点是动词词组 take place（发生）。15 题和 skilled（有技术的）并列，同时作 Americans 的定语，因此就形式而言，应该用过去分词；就语义而言，两者的语义应该是近似，所以正确答案是 talented（有天分的）。就 13 题而言，the population 是不可能发出 promote（促进，推广，宣传，提拔）的动作的，所以根据排除法，正确答案是 shifting。16 题正确答案则是 promoting。

四个语言段填好后完整的语义和语法功能如下：A 的语法成分是：and 引导的并列的介宾从句，意思是：在那里人口发生了迁移。B 的语法成分是：定语从句或地点状语从句，意思是：正在发生关于多样性的争论。C 的语法成分是：that 引导的名词性从句，句子缺少宾语，意思是：需要有天分的或有技术的美国人意味着。D 的语法成分是：that 引导的名词性从句，意思是：扩大规模就意味着推广政策。

这篇文章主要是讲多样性的好处。17题用在及物动词note之后，作宾语，就语法而言，合适的是B和D；就语义而言，正确答案是B，与其后的句子It is taking place primarily in political circles语义连贯。完成后句子的完整语义是：有趣的是看到在哪正发生着关于多样性的争论。就语法而言，18题用在及物动词say后，缺少的是宾语从句，由此判断C和D都可以；但是，18题还用在一个完整句前，且没有关联词语，这说明后面的句子省去了连词，能符合这种用法的是that的宾语从句，这说明18题本身是不完整，缺成分的，因此正确答案是D。完成后句子的完整语义是：需要有天分的或有技术的美国人意味着要扩大有潜力的雇员的规模。根据19题前的at where birth rates are growing，可以判断正确答案是A。20题的答案是D，that help provide skills to more minorities…作的是policies的定语从句。完成后句子的完整语义是：当注意到那些人口增长的地方以及人口迁移的地方，美国意识到扩大规模就意味着推广那些能向更多的少数民族和女性及移民提供技术的政策。

Model Test 7

Text One

答案　1. look　2. earning　3. opinion　4. C　5. A　6. B

详解

1~3题主要依靠语义和搭配做题。第1题正确答案是look，a close look at（认真研究）是常用搭配。第2题出现在 $150,000之前，正确答案应该是earning（赚钱）。第3题的答案是opinion（观点）。

三个语言段填好后完整的语义和语法功能如下：A的语法成分是：主谓结构，缺少及物动词indicate的宾语，意思是：对调查结果更为认真的研究表明。B的语法成分是：名词性质词组，意思是：那些年收入15万美元以上的人。C的语法成分是：完整句，意思是：23%的人没有意见。

这篇文章主要是探讨饭店给顾客提供的菜量的大小问题。根据第4题之前57 percent 和之后的 20 percent 判断，正确答案是C，是列举了参与调查的人不同的意见。完成后句子的完整语义是：根据一份餐饮业杂志上个月的报道，参与调查的4 000人中，有57%的人认为目前餐厅提供的菜量太大了，23%的人没有发表意见，20%的人持相反的意见。第5题出现在句首，that引导的名词性从句前，所以正确答案是A。完成后句子的完整语义是：对调查结果更为认真的研究表明很多买不起精美大餐的美国人仍然希望菜量大一点。第6题正确答案是B，与其后的 45 percent of those earning less than $25,000 构成并列结构。完成后句子的完整语义是：70%的年收入15万美元以上的人希望菜量小一点；但是只有45%的年收入25 000美元以下的人希望菜量小一点。

Text Two

答案　7. transformed　8. shocked　9. shown　10. C　11. B　12. A

详解

方框内的三个选项都是动词的过去分词的形式，因此做 7~9 题主要依靠词汇语义和搭配。其中，最容易判断的是第 9 题，能跟宾语从句的动词应该是 shown。其次是第 7 题，transform（改变）的常见搭配是：transform…into…（把……变成……）或者 transform…from…to…（把……从……变成……）。第 8 题正确答案是 shocked（震惊）。

三个语言段填好后完整的语义和语法功能如下：A 的语法成分是：时间状语从句或定语从句，但句子不完整，one 后面缺少定语；意思是：当美国从枪支文化转变成一个。B 的语法成分是：完整句，意思是：这些事件震惊了美国。C 的语法成分是：主谓结构，缺少宾语从句中的内容；意思是：然而，最近美国的一些事件表明。

这篇文章主要是讨论美国的枪支文化。第 10 题用在句首，后面跟有完整句，正确答案应该是 C。完成后句子的完整语义是：最近美国的一些事件表明枪支拥有的问题已经失去控制，人们强烈呼吁应立刻采取措施解决问题。第 11 题出现在句首，后面跟有定语从句，应该是主句中的主语和谓语，因此正确答案是 B。完成后句子的完整语义是：这些事件震惊了美国，而且这些事件似乎发生得日益频繁。第 12 题之前是句子的主句，后面是定语从句，符合这种用法的应该是 A。完成后句子的完整语义是：离美国社会从枪支文化转变成控制枪支拥有和使用的文化的这一天可能不会太远了。

Text Three

答案
13. amateur performers 14. admiring fans
15. free of charge 16. a professional career
17. A 18. C 19. D 20. B

详解

13~16 题主要应该根据语义和逻辑关系做题。13 题所在句子中的 not only…but…as well 是并列结构，13 题用在 not only 之后，应该与 but 后的 professional artists 形成对比，因此正确答案是 amateur performers，professional（专业的）和 amateur（业余的）是一对反义词。14 题所在句子中的 make contact with（和……接触，和……联系）的宾语应该是人而非事物，所以正确答案是 admiring fans。15 题用在完整句的后面，应该作的是状语，由此可知正确答案是 free of charge（免费地）。16 题用在 beginning 之后作宾语，正确答案是 a professional career。

四个语言段填好后完整的语义和语法功能如下：A 的语法成分是：并列的名词词组，意思是：不仅是业余表演者而且还有专业艺术家。B 的语法成分是：不定式，意思是：与他们的粉丝联系。C 的语法成分是：完整句，意思是：他们把场地免费出租给演奏者。D 的语法成分是：时间状语，意思是：在职业生涯开始前。

这篇文章主要介绍美国一些露天的免费音乐会。第 17 题用在及物动词 involve，应该用名词性成分，语法和语义都符合的应该是 A。完成后句子的完整语义是：这些音乐会不仅涉及了业余表演者而且还涉及了专业艺术家。18 题所在的句子缺少主语和谓语，因此正确答案是 C。完成后句子的完整语义是：作为给市民提供的服务，他们把场地免费出租给演奏者。根据语法分析,19题应该在句子中作状语,根据语义连贯分析,正确答案是D。完成后句子的完整语义是:一些半职业的艺术家们非常高兴能有在公众面前表演的机会来提高他们的技艺,而且有望在职业生涯开始前就被人发现。20题正确答案是B,在句子中做目的状语。完成后句子的完整语义是:为了和粉丝保持联系,知名的专业艺术家也会开免费的音乐会。

Model Test 8

Text One

答案 1. raises 2. go 3. match 4. A 5. C 6. B

详解

第1题用在抽象名词biometrics(生物测定学)之后,应该用第三人称单数的形式,所以正确答案是raises,而且,raise a question(提出问题)是常见的词汇搭配。第2题用在介词through之前,应该用不及物动词go;go through the roof是俚语,意思是:上涨到极大且通常出乎意料的程度。第3题正确答案是match,match…with…是固定搭配,意思是:使……与……相匹配/相符。

三个语言段填好后完整的语义和语法功能如下:A的语法成分是:完整句,意思是:生物测定学引起了关于隐私的一些棘手的问题。B的语法成分是:完整句,意思是:你会看到你的医疗保险费用飞速上涨。C的语法成分是:不定式,意思是:使你的医保记录和你的信用卡记录相符。

这篇文章主要是讲生物测定学引发的一些问题。根据语法判断第4题所在的句子缺少主语和谓语,根据and之后the potential for abuse(滥用的可能性)的语义判断,其前面并列的名词应该是privacy,所以正确答案应该是A。完成后句子的完整语义是:生物测定学引起了关于隐私和可能被滥用的一些棘手问题,这一点并不奇怪。第5题用在used your fingerprints之后,正确答案应该是C,use…to do…(用……做……)是常见的动词搭配。第6题跟在if从句后面,应该是引号内这句话的主句,因此正确答案是B。完成后句子的完整语义是:一位政策分析师说:"如果有人用你的指纹来将你的医保记录和你的经常购买大量香烟和高脂肪食品的信用卡记录联系起来,那么你将会看到你的医疗保险费用飞速上涨。"

Text Two

答案 7. correction 8. walls 9. intimacy 10. C 11. B 12. A

详解

方框内的选项都是名词,因此7~9题主要应该依靠词汇的语义和搭配来做题。第7题用在并列连词or之前,语义应该与or之后的serious business(严肃的事情)相近,因此正确答案是correction(纠正,处罚)。第8题用在复数的谓语动词前,应该是可数名词的复数形式,正确答案是walls,此外作torn down的宾语语义也是相符的。第9题正确答案是 intimacy（亲密，亲近）。

三个语言段填好后完整的语义和语法功能如下：A 的语法成分是：名词词组，意思是：某种处分或者严重的事情。B 的语法成分是：完整句，意思是：墙立刻就垮掉了。C 的语法成分是：谓语＋宾语，意思是：很快建立起人与人之间的亲密感。

这篇文章主要是讲在工作场合使用姓氏或昵称产生的不同的效果。第 10 题所在的句子是强调句型 It is...that 根据语法规定，第 10 题应该是 the nickname 发出的动作，缺的是谓语动词，因此正确答案是 C。完成后句子的完整语义是：但是，对于美国人来说，正是昵称很快建立起了人与人之间的亲密感，基于此关系也就建立起来。11 题是 and 连接的并列句，应该用完整句，正确答案是 B。完成后句子的完整语义是：通过称呼对方的名字或昵称，人与人之间就消除了隔阂，建立了平等的关系。第 12 题用在连词后谓语动词前，应该是从句的主语，正确答案是 A。完成后句子的完整语义是：一旦老板用员工的姓来称呼他，你就可以确定某种处分或者严重的事情就要来了。

Text Three

答案 13. well-paid   14. reducing   15. expected   16. come
      17. B   18. A   19. C   20. D

→ 详解

根据语法判断，13 题用在名词前，应该是形容词作定语；根据其后的名词 work 的语义判断正确答案是 well-paid（工资高的）。根据语法判断，14 题用在介词 by 后面，名词词组的前面，应该用动名词的形式，因此正确答案是 reducing。15 题用在助动词 be 后，应该是被动语态里的过去分词，正确答案是 expected。第 16 题正确答案是 come，come up with（想出，提出）是常用的动词词组。

四个语言段填好后完整的语义和语法功能如下：A 的语法成分是：不定式，意思是：为技术工人提供高薪的工作。B 的语法成分是：介词词组，意思是：通过减少每个已有工作的工作时间。C 的语法成分是：as 引导的定语从句，意思是：正如所预料的那样。D 的语法成分是：完整句，意思是：随后的研究得出了相似的结论。

这篇文章主要是介绍工作共享的概念。根据语法判断，17 题在 which 引导的定语从句作状语，根据语义判断，定语从句是在解释 work sharing 的含义，它不同于 job sharing，而且根据其后因此 thus 引导的结果状语可以看出 work sharing 可以给失业的人提供更多的岗位，因此中间的状语应该是方式状语，表示如何能够做到这一点，是通过减少每个已有工作的工作时间来实现的，因此 B 更合适。18 题在句子中作表语，根据语法要求，当 focus 作主语时，表语应该用不定式；此外，根据 and 之后的 professionals（专业人士）可以看出 and 之前的名词语义应该是相近的，skilled workers（技术工人）刚好相符，因此正确答案是 A。完成后句子的完整语义是：相反，工作共享的目的不是解决失业问题，而是为那些希望有更多自由时间做其他事情的技术工人和专业人士提供高薪的工作。19 题用于完整句前，而后面的句子没有连词，根据语法判断，此处应该用从句，因此正确答案是 C。完成后句子的完整语义是：正如所预料的那样，一大半工作分享者为女性。20 题缺的是独立的完整句，所以正确答案是 D。

Model Test 9

Text One

答案 1. throw   2. inherited   3. ruin   4. A   5. B   6. C

详解

根据语法判断，第1题用在不定式后，应该是动词原形；根据搭配判断，throw off（去掉，摆脱）是固定词组，所以正确答案是 throw。第2题用在名词前，应该是定语，正确答案是 inherited，过去分词作定语。第3题缺及物动词的原形，所以正确答案是 ruin。

三个语言段填好后完整的语义和语法功能如下：A 的语法成分是：不定式，意思是：把它的大部分都送掉了。B 的语法成分是：不定式，意思是：给了孩子太多继承来的财富。C 的语法成分是：完整句或定语从句，意思是：那会毁了他们的生活。

这篇文章主要内容是关于 Nicola Horlick，英国的亿万富翁对于自己遗产的态度和做法。第4题根据词组 be determined to do（下决心做某事），应该用不定式，根据它后面的句子 She already gives away about 25% of her income each year（她每年已经送掉了收入的25%）的语义，正确答案应该是 A。第5题还是不定式的典型用法，正确答案是 B。完成后句子的完整语义是：我认为让孩子继承过多的财富是不对的。第6题用在 because 之后，应该是完整句，因此正确答案是 C。完成后句子的完整语义是：我不会把我所有的财产都留给我的孩子们，因为那会毁了他们的生活。

Text Two

答案 7. rivalry   8. encouragement   9. loyalty   10. C   11. B   12. A

详解

7～9题主要依靠词汇语义和搭配做题。相比较而言，第8、第9题更容易判断。第8题用在 shouting 之后作宾语，而且是对 their team，因此正确答案应该是 encouragement（鼓励）。第9题用在 declare 之后作宾语，而且通过 wearing their team's colors 来表现，因此正确答案是 loyalty（忠诚）。第7题答案是 rivalry（竞争），与其后的 between 是常见的习惯搭配。

三个语言段填好后完整的语义和语法功能如下：A 的语法成分是：完整句，意思是：支持者之间有着不少竞争。B 的语法成分是：现在分词，意思是：冲着他们的球队大喊大叫，来鼓励他们。C 的语法成分是：谓语+宾语，意思是：通过穿着球队的颜色来表示他们对球队的忠诚。

这篇文章的主要内容是关于足球球迷之间的争执。第10题用在定语从句的关系代词 most of whom 后，应该是谓语的成分，因此正确答案是 C。完成后句子的完整语义是：球迷们通常穿着自己球队颜色的衬衣来表示他们对球队的忠诚，他们的表现可不能用安静来形容。第11题是 and 连接的并列状语，根据 and 后的 singing 可以判断，正确答案应该是B。完成后句子的完整语义是：他们通常非常吵闹，他们冲着自己的球队大喊大叫，来鼓励他们，还会唱着震耳欲聋的歌曲。第12题是独立的完整句，正确答案是A。

Text Three

答案 13. a new era　14. profit most　15. in turn　16. special protection
17. A　18. C　19. B　20. D

详解

首先可以判断方框内四个选项的语法成分，其中a new era 和 special protection 为名词词组，in turn 是介词词组，profit most 应该是谓语+宾语。根据语义和搭配关系，第13题正确答案是a new era，launch a new era 的意思是：开创新纪元。第14题用在助动词后，应该用动词，正确答案是profit most。第15题用在主语和助动词之间，应该是状语，所以正确答案是in turn（依次，轮流）。第16题用在介词后，应该是名词成分，正确答案是special protection（特殊保护）。

四个语言段填好后完整的语义和语法功能如下：A的语法成分是：谓语+宾语+状语，意思是：可能开创了经济史上的新纪元。B的语法成分是：so引导的并列句，意思是：因此他们会从自由贸易中获得最多的收益。C的语法成分是：which引导的定语从句，意思是：接下来将改善人民的福利。D的语法成分是：完整句，意思是：同时，亚洲继续祈求得到特殊的保护。

这篇文章主要内容是讲现在在西方国家保护主义已经不再是禁忌了。第17题所在句子中缺少谓语，所以正确答案是A。完成后句子的完整语义是：上个月法国总统萨科齐说的这句话很可能会开创了经济史上的新纪元。根据语法判断，第18题所在句子中缺的是从句；根据第18题前的抽象名词来看，正确答案是C。完成后句子的完整语义是：他们认为这么做可以提高经济效益和生产力，这将会改善人民的福利。第19题用在主句后，正确答案应该是B。完成后句子的完整语义是：他们知道自己国家的经济是最有竞争力的，因此他们会从自由贸易中获得最多的收益。第20题用在并列句前，应该是完整句，所以正确答案是D。完成后句子的完整语义是：亚洲继续祈求得到特殊的保护，但是在实践中却越来越多地进行着自由贸易。

Model Test 10

Text One

答案 1. for　2. than　3. in　4. A　5. C　6. B

详解

1～3题的考点都是固定词组。其中，第1题正确答案是for，介词词组in exchange for 意思是：交换；第2题正确答案是than，连词rather than 意思是：而不是，胜于；第3题正确答案是in，介词词组in advance 意思是：提前。

三个语言段填好后完整的语义和语法功能如下：A 的语法成分是：that 引导的名词性从句，意思是：他用一个红色的别针换来了他的新家。B 的语法成分是：名词词组，意思是：有创意的一面，而非商业的一面。C 的语法成分是：现在分词，意思是：提前宣布了他的目标。

这篇文章主要是关于加拿大的一个人通过网络来进行物物交换，最终换来他想要的房子的故事。第 4 题用在名词 the fact 后，正确答案应该是 A，that 引导的同位语从句。完成后句子的完整语义是：蒙特利尔的麦克唐纳先生开晚会庆祝他用一个红色的别针换来了他的新家。第 5 题用在句首主语之前，应该是状语，正确答案是 C。完成后句子的完整语义是：由于提前宣布了他的目标，麦克唐纳很可能从那些渴望知道网络能否通过这个大胆的能力测试的电脑达人那里获得支持。第 6 题用在介词 on 后，应该是名词，因此正确答案是 B。完成后句子的完整语义是：我真正关注的是有创意的一面，而非商业的一面。

Text Two

答案 7. prose 8. intensity 9. fingerprints 10. B 11. A 12. C

详解

第 7 题用在 a polished piece of 之后，应该是可数名词单数的形式，所以正确答案是 prose（散文，文章）。第 8 题用在 and 之后，应该和 and 之前的 excitement（激动）形式一致，即抽象名词，语义相近，因此正确答案是 intensity（紧张）。第 9 题正确答案是 fingerprints（指纹）。

三个语言段填好后完整的语义和语法功能如下：A 的语法成分是：完整句，意思是：我无法辨别一篇优秀的文章。B 的语法成分是：介词词组，意思是：带着些许激动和紧张。C 的语法成分是：完整句，意思是：作者的写作风格就像人的指纹一样。

这篇文章主要是讲一位大学英语写作老师对于学生抄袭行为的批评。第 10 题用在句首主语之前，应该是状语，正确答案是 B。完成后句子的完整语义是：带着些许激动和紧张，我读着学生的文章，希望能够发现藏在文章后面的那个人。就语法而言，第 11 题用在 assumes 之后，应该是省略了 that 的宾语从句；就语义而言，正确答案应该是 A。完成后句子的完整语义是：学生居然认为我辨认不出这篇优秀的文章出自一个原本很普通的作者，我觉得不仅我的智商遭到了侮辱，而且当我看到学生不得不从同龄人那里买文章时，我感到很悲哀。第 12 题用在 and 引导的并列句前，应该是完整句，正确答案是 C。完成后句子的完整语义是：作者的写作风格就像人的指纹一样，当我批过几次作业后，我就能将学生的作业和他们的名字联系起来，即使作业的左上角上没有名字。

Text Three

 13. bilingual speakers 14. most of

15. native tongues 16. cultural and linguistic integrity

第三章　短文完成

17. B　　　18. A　　　19. D　　　20. C

> 详　解

第13题作 use their own language 的主语，因此应该是指人，所以正确答案是 bilingual speakers（能说双语的人）。第14题用在名词词组 these languages 之前，应该是代词，正确答案是 most of。第15题用在 using 之后作宾语，而且可以用来浏览网页，所以正确答案应该是 native tongues（母语）。第16题作 sustain 的宾语，正确答案是 cultural and linguistic integrity（文化和语言的完整性）。

四个语言段填好后完整的语义和语法功能如下：A 的语法成分是：完整句，意思是：能说双语的人可以用他们自己的语言。B 的语法成分是：whether 引导的名词性从句，意思是：这些语言中的大多数能否保留下来。C 的语法成分是：动词原形+宾语+状语，意思是：用他们自己的语言浏览网页。D 的语法成分是：完整句，意思是：很多小语种能够保持它们文化和语言的完整性。

这篇文章主要是探讨在全球化的大背景下，应该如何保护一些小语种。第17题位于句首谓语动词之前，是句子的主语，在这正确答案应该是 B，whether 引导的主语从句。完成后句子的完整语义是：这些语言中的大多数能否保留下来很可能要取决于这些文化群体到底有多么希望通过他们的母语来保留他们的身份特征。根据语法，第18题应该是完整句；根据语义，A 更为合适。完成后句子的完整语义是：能说双语的人可以在一些小范围内——在家里、在朋友之间、在社区里使用他们自己的语言。根据语法，第19题应该是完整句；根据语义，D 更为合适。完成后句子的完整语义是：用这种方式，很多小语种能够保持它们文化和语言的完整性，同时可以和全球化语言并存，而不是屈服于全球化的同化大趋势。第20题正确答案是 C。完成后句子的完整语义是：例如，很多专家预计将来计算机翻译软件可以使说小语种的人用他们自己的语言浏览网页。